RETHINKING THE POLITICAL

McGill-Queen's Studies in the History of Ideas
Series Editor: Philip J. Cercone

RETHINKING THE POLITICAL

The Sacred, Aesthetic Politics, and the Collège de Sociologie

Simonetta Falasca-Zamponi

McGill-Queen's University Press
Montreal & Kingston • London • Ithaca

b 40443152

© McGill-Queen's University Press 2011
ISBN 978-0-7735-3900-6 (cloth)
ISBN 978-0-7735-3901-3 (paper)

Legal deposit fourth quarter 2011
Bibliothèque nationale du Québec

Printed in Canada on acid-free paper that is 100% ancient forest free
(100% post-consumer recycled), processed chlorine free

McGill-Queen's University Press acknowledges the support
of the Canada Council for the Arts for our publishing program.
We also acknowledge the financial support of the Government of
Canada through the Canada Book Fund for our publishing activities.

Library and Archives Canada Cataloguing in Publication

Falasca-Zamponi, Simonetta, 1957–
    Rethinking the political: the sacred, aesthetic politics, and the Collège
de Sociologie / Simonetta Falasca-Zamponi.

(McGill-Queen's studies in the history of ideas; 55)
Includes bibliographical references and index.
ISBN 978-0-7735-3900-6 (bound). – ISBN 978-0-7735-3901-3 (pbk.)

1. Collège de Sociologie – History. 2. Sociology – France – History –
20th century. I. Title. II. Series: McGill-Queen's studies in the history
of ideas; 55

HM477.F8F34 2011   301.0944   C2011-904853-1

This book was typeset by Interscript in 10/12 New Baskerville.

To Rich and Edoardo

Contents

List of Illustrations

Acknowledgments

OVER THE SEVERAL YEARS I WORKED ON THIS BOOK PROJECT, I have accumulated a long list of debts to several people and institutions. For financial assistance in the form of grants and awards, I would like to acknowledge the generosity of the European University Institute, as well as the American Philosophical Society, the National Endowment for the Humanities, the Center for German and European Studies at the University of California, Berkeley, and the Centre National de la Recherche Scientifique (CNRS). At the University of California, Santa Barbara, I was the recipient of several Faculty Career Development awards, Regents' Junior and Regents' Humanities Faculty fellowships, and Interdisciplinary Humanities Center awards, as well as grants from the Academic Senate and the Humanistic Social Science Research Program at the Institute for Social, Behavioral and Economic Research.

During my time as a Jean Monnet fellow at the European University Institute, I enjoyed the gracious hospitality of the Department of Political and Social Sciences and its staff. For their friendship and intellectual stimulation, I would like to thank in particular Christian Joppke, Gianfranco Poggi (and through him Tony Negri), Giovanna Procacci, Steven Lukes, Alessandro Pizzorno, Stefano Bartolini, Luisa Passerini, and Peter Wagner. In addition, the outstanding staff at the Institute's library facilitated my research work in ways too numerous to recount. During my research stay in Paris sponsored by the CNRS, I was hosted by the Institut des textes et manuscrits modernes, a research unit linked to the École normale supérieure. I wish to thank its director at the time, Jean-Louis Lebrave, and co-director Claire Bustarret. At the Bibliothèque nationale, Madame Annie Angremy helped me confirm my discovery of an unpublished lecture of Bataille at the Collège. Finally, during my several stays in Paris, I have relied on the friendship and hospitality of my dear friends Catherine Ouy and Livio Violante. They opened their doors to me and my family, and even when I was back in California, they assisted me with everything French, including the often maddening process of tracking copyright holders.

A large circle of friends and colleagues encouraged me and my endeavour during the good and bad times. I would like to acknowledge Jon Cruz, Roger Friedland, and Verta Taylor for their continuous support. I would also like to thank Lucia Re, Richard Wolin, Nitzan Lebovics, Claudio Fogu, Victoria Bonnell, and Martin Jay. Catherine Nesci was of crucial help with French translations and other French matters. I owe a special debt of gratitude to Didier Maleuvre who offered precious feedback on my first forays into French writing and did not hesitate to sustain my publishing efforts. I bow at his integrity and camaraderie. Carolyn Dean provided invaluable criticism and suggestions on an earlier draft of the book and maintained her faith in the project even in darker moments. Rich Kaplan attentively edited and commented on the several versions of the manuscripts. Dana Collins and Moira O'Neil helped tremendously with bibliographic research.

Special thanks to Pauline Roux for allowing me to reproduce a work of her late husband Gaston-Louis Roux, and to Julie Bataille for permitting me to reproduce a photograph of her father. I would also like to thank Julie Bataille for granting me permission to publish and translate Bataille's unpublished lecture, and Michel Surya for elegantly bringing that project to fruition.

At the press, Jonathan Crago shepherded the manuscript through the various stages of the publishing process. Although our opinions sometimes clashed, I appreciated his advice. I am also grateful to Peter Baehr and the anonymous reviewers solicited by the press for their attentive reading of my book. At home, Edoardo and Rich lived through my working schedule and witnessed my exhilarating moments and perpetual angst. I know I was not always my best; I thank them for their love and patience. In Italy, I found solace and replenished energies during summer stays with my mother and my sisters' families. Finally, I wish to acknowledge the memory of my father and two very dear friends: Bernhard Peters and Peppe Di Sabatino. I truly miss them.

In 2007, the indie pop/rock band *of Montreal* issued an album featuring the song "The Past is a Grotesque Animal." Kevin Barnes's emotional lyrics and gloomy lines included a little ode to Bataille: "I fell in love with the first cute girl that I met who could appreciate Georges Bataille/ Standing at a Swedish festival discussing the *Story of the Eye*." In a depressing tale of self-lacerations and despondency against a world of meaningless realities and absurd normalcy, Barnes took Bataille as a measuring stick for finding a soul mate, somebody worth talking to (although the girl still had to be "cute," I guess). Whether or not *of Montreal*'s fans share Barnes's appreciation for *Story of the Eye,* Bataille's iconic versatility as a damned hero, an austere librarian, a "pornographic" author, a mystic, poet, and essayist helped thrust him into the limelight of musical subcultures. A cult figure of underground circles in addition to being an exquisite writer for sophisticated readers, Bataille remains, however, largely unknown among sociologists. Ever heard of Georges Bataille? I ask graduate students. Their answer is inevitably negative. I hope my book will help close this gap without creating another trendy clique. I do not wish to mythologize Bataille; I simply want to illuminate the power of his existential quest, his profound intuition of sociology's unique and indispensable mandate to confront life's "burning" questions.

RETHINKING THE POLITICAL

Introduction

DURING AN EVOCATIVE CONVERSATION with the Italian philosopher Giorgio Agamben on the topic of Walter Benjamin, Pierre Klossowski reminisced about his 1930s Parisian encounters with the German critic and philosopher.[1] Among others, Klossowski recounted an episode in which Benjamin, "hands lifted in an admonishing gesture," expressed his consternation at the ideas being circulated among the groups frequented by Klossowski. "You work for fascism!" Benjamin decried[2] – a dramatic assertion that, according to Klossowski, warned against the risk of "playing the game of a pure and simple 'prefascist aestheticism.'"[3] Although Benjamin's vision of society, in Klossowski's interpretation, included a positive evaluation of affectivity and the "*free play of the passions*," in the reality of 1930s Europe the potential pitfalls of their attraction evidently worried Benjamin.[4] Torn by those fears, he concluded that in the face of fascism's ascent one could not but hold a firm stance against those who pursued "'the metaphysical and poetic upward valuation of the incommunicable.'"[5] In this regard, although sympathetic to and curious about them, Benjamin indicted the groups in which Klossowski

---

1 Klossowski had been the French translator of Benjamin's essay "The Work of Art in the Age of Mechanical Reproduction." The essay was first published in French as "L'œuvre d'art à l'époque de sa reproduction mécanisée" in the Frankfurt school's journal *Zeitschrift für Sozialforschung* 5 (1936). Only later was it printed in German. For the English version, see Walter Benjamin, *Illuminations*.

2 Agamben, "Bataille e il paradosso della sovranità," 115. A note on translations: when available, I refer to English translations of the works I cite. One notable exception are the writings of Mauss due to the scattered number of translations from his complete works.

3 Klossowski, "Between Marx and Fourier," 368, originally published as "Entre Marx et Fourier," iv. For other reminiscences of Benjamin by Klossowski, see "Lettre sur Walter Benjamin."

4 Klossowski, "Between Marx and Fourier," 368 (italicized in the original).

5 Ibid. (in quotation marks in the original).

participated. They included Contre Attaque, Acéphale, and the Collège
de sociologie, all headed by Klossowski's friend and fellow member
Georges Bataille.

As it turns out, Benjamin was not the only one wary of the potential
link between fascism and Bataille's political-cultural formations. Other
commentators and critics of the time raised concerns about Bataille's
presumed fascist affinities, especially in connection with the Collège de
sociologie's theorizing. To this day, scholars debate and take sides on the
issue of where to situate Bataille on the political spectrum.[6] Amid cries of
guilt or innocence, however, the matter at the heart of Benjamin's deep
unease has remained lamentably overshadowed. Lost in ideological
quibbles is the intractable but critical question underlying Benjamin's
alarm: How can we think the relationship between politics and aesthetics
in the age of mechanical reproduction? Or, more consequentially,
should aesthetics and politics be separated and compartmentalized in
the modern era? In his essay on the work of art, Benjamin made the case
that the relationship between politics and aesthetics exposed the diver-
gent impulses at the core of the modern age where the beauty of ma-
chines was beginning to compete with the sublimity of nature and where
political spectacle was replacing religious ritual. Because fascism constituted a product of these emerging contradictions, and in view of fascism's destructive scope and potential, Benjamin found it necessary to
ask: how does aesthetics play into the hands of fascism? Can affective
movements escape fascism's iron grip? And more importantly, one can
add, is a critique of modern instrumental reason inescapably linked to
reactionary outcomes?

Because the power of these interrogatives still resonates today, this
book contends that Benjamin's questions need to be newly taken up and
examined. When religious beliefs and cultural ideals hurl competing
claims against the legitimacy of the modern world order, and the tanta-
lizing attraction of emotional bonds and affectivity ebbs and flows to the
centre of our contemporary political arena, the relevance of Benjamin's
reflections on aesthetic politics is ever more significant. Thus, though it
might seem paradoxical, I suggest that despite or perhaps because of
Benjamin's apprehensive reactions to Bataille's endeavours, the Collège
de sociologie offers a unique prism through which to assess the thorny
relationship between politics and aesthetics in the modern age. Indeed,

---

6 See, among others, Wolin, *The Seduction of Unreason*. Bataille has become a larger-
than-life figure in twentieth-century thought and his importance goes beyond the question
of fascism examined in this book. Bataille's influence on Foucault and Derrida, in particular, makes his legacy especially significant.

by refracting in their multifaceted complexity the issues brought to the fore by Benjamin, the Collège exposes the limits and strictures of an aesthetic approach to politics and opens up space for a renewed reflection on the nature of "the political" and the question of democracy in a post-totalitarian era. For the dilemma ensues: Is it possible to reconcile affectivity with democracy, emotional unity with openness and tolerance, aesthetic concerns about expressive form with democratic decision-making? And what are the liabilities of such objectives? The Collège provides us with an unparalleled tool for addressing these questions since it took upon itself the task of exploring the nature of social bonds and the fate of communal yearnings during the critical years of fascism's expansion in Europe.

The Collège was founded in March 1937 in the dusty rooms of the café Grand Véfour at the Palais Royal in Paris; its birth was announced in July 1937 on the pages of the review *Acéphale*, a publication edited by Georges Bataille. It was not until November 1937, however, that a study group regularly gathered to pursue what its members defined as a deeper understanding of modern social existence.[7] Every other Saturday at 9:30 in the evening in the backroom of the bookstore Galeries du Livre, the Collège de sociologie, under the guidance of Georges Bataille and Roger Caillois (and less prominently Michel Leiris), held meetings in the form of lectures. Topics ranged from power to shamanism, from secret societies to festivals, from the army to Carnival.[8] These themes were all supposed to shed light on the Collège's newly acclaimed realm of "sacred sociology." The Collège's goal was to identify and interrogate living manifestations of the sacred's active presence, that is, all human activities that had a "communifying" value.[9]

One of several groups that sprouted in the 1930s, especially from the ranks of the literary avant-garde, the Collège distinguished itself from other "non-conformist" formations by its embrace of an unexpected favourite among politico-philosophical alternatives: Durkheimian sociology.[10] Although the Collège shared with other groups the prevalent hostility to idealist rationalism, it selected as its inspirational source a social science that had not only invoked the authority of causal laws from its inception

7 On the Collège, see the pioneering work of Denis Hollier in Hollier, *The College of Sociology*. The book was originally published in French in 1979 and re-edited in French in 1995 with updated material. See Hollier, *Le Collège de Sociologie*. On the general cultural and political climate of the time see Lindenberg, *Les Années souterraines*.

8 The Collège's meetings later moved to Tuesday evenings.

9 Hollier, *The College of Sociology*, 74.

10 On the "non-conformists," see Loubet del Bayle, *Les non-conformistes des années trente*.

but was also currently undergoing a serious crisis of confidence. By the 1930s, Durkheim's sociology had come to be perceived as and attacked for monopolizing French cultural life. Even though it had in actuality failed to attain a significant role in higher education and had been fading in terms of both the amount and creativity of its production, Durkheimian sociology was identified with the very essence of the disparaged university system along with the republican establishment and its moralism.[11]

Within this highly ideologized context, it was surprising that the Collège made recourse to Durkheim and elected sociology to play a key role as decipherer of human experience. The choice was due to the Collège's own intellectual interests as well as its selective, albeit innovative, interpretation of Durkheim. In its original manifesto, published with an introduction by Caillois a year after its foundation, the Collège had lamented the current lack of interest in what it considered "the richest human phenomena," those "primordial longings and conflicts of the individual condition transposed to the social dimension."[12] According to the Collège, the human sciences had been able to make tremendous progress in the study of those phenomena, yet their practitioners lacked the courage to apply the results to more contemporary societies. Because they had limited their analysis to "so-called primitive societies," scientists appeared at a loss when facing "the many problems posed by the interplay of instincts and 'myths'" in the modern world.[13] The Collège considered this situation unfortunate, charging that it created a divide between the drive to unearth the deepest elements of one's intimate experience and the desire to respond to "the urgent appeal from social facts."[14] Failure to combine individual psychological exploration with active involvement in communal issues would impede a holistic understanding of social phenomena, with negative consequences for any subsequent action one might undertake.

To bridge the divide, the Collège advocated locating "at the very heart of social existence" those processes that mobilized the sacred and revealed its presence both at the level of individual expression and on the more complex plane of social organizations.[15] The Durkheimians' ethnological research on primitive societies, and in particular Durkheim's last major work before his premature death in 1917, *The Elementary Forms of Religious Life*, provided an exemplary precedent and major stimulant

11 See Clark, *Prophets and Patrons*.
12 Hollier, *The College of Sociology*, 10.
13 Ibid.
14 Ibid.
15 Ibid., 11.

for the Collège's project. Just as Durkheim had uncovered the crucial role that mythical manifestations played in the creation and continuity of "primitive" communities, the Collège claimed, one could also study the "deep strata" of modern collective life, those irrational forces and virulent elements that lay the foundations of the social and made possible the actualization of the sacred in an era that had supposedly lost its magic.[16] "Sacred sociology," intended as the combined study of individual psychology and social institutions and whose aim was to uncover all human activities that promoted unity, would accomplish that goal. The Collège thus pronounced "sacred sociology" the real soul of the sociological discipline, the Collège's own reason for being.

Durkheim's work offered the Collège an ideal platform from which to launch its intellectual agenda. Like Durkheim, who was preoccupied with the lack of a common faith in the Republic's ideals, the Collège worried about the absence of collective passions among its contemporaries. The Collège, however, went beyond Durkheim's tenets and, as it revitalized French sociology, redrew its lines and distanced itself from the discipline.[17] Standing on the shoulders of Durkheim's interpretive analysis, the Collège enlarged sociology's epistemological scope beyond archaic societies by engaging contemporary reality. It exposed the absence of social diagnoses that effectively addressed the ills of the modern era and denounced scientific inaction in the face of lived experience. Finally, by calling on sociology to resolve an impending social crisis, the Collège encouraged it to reconfigure a different and more critical role for itself.

The Collège's willingness to engage the study of social structure through the optic of the sacred in present-day reality implied an active stance in the face of current historical events. In particular, fascism's growing threat in 1930s Europe motivated the Collège to initiate its exploration of those affective forces, instincts, and emotions that the Collège expected would enact the sacred in the modern era. At a time when authoritarian dictatorships seemed everywhere on the rise, fascism's ability to tap the sources of the sacred and ensure a sense of community led

16 Ibid., 10.

17 In his survey of French sociology, Claude Lévi-Strauss, who attended the Collège's lectures, thus interpreted the place of the Collège in French sociology: "During the years immediately preceding the Second World War, the 'Collège de Sociologie,' under the direction of Roger Caillois, became a meeting place for sociologists, on the one hand, and Surrealist painters and poets on the other. The experiment succeeded. This tight collaboration between sociology and all the tendencies or currents of thought that have as their object Man and the study of Man is one of the most characteristic traits of the French school." See his "La sociologie française," 517. On French sociology in the 1930s and the Collège de sociologie, also see Lourau, *Le gai savoir des sociologues.*

Bataille and his fellow Collegians to seek a response from sociology. It also spurred the Collège to raise critically urgent questions that few contemporaries were willing to address. Should one renounce reason? And was it possible to reconsider the role of emotions in socially meaningful behaviour while rejecting the fascist version of affective community?

These quandaries resonated with Benjamin's enigmatic reflections on aesthetic politics. As the Collège challenged conventions, defied prudence, and provocatively bypassed disciplinary rules and divisions, it addressed the fate of a world that seemed to be oscillating between an attraction for mythical experiences and a sober realization of the perils those experiences entailed. The Collège exposed the threats and risks of leaving the contradictions unresolved and, in the process, illuminated some of the problematics raised by Benjamin's discussion of aesthetic politics. The Collège also became a living example of the predicaments involved in tackling the dilemmas confronting contemporary societies. For, as we know, the Collège's analysis of the sacred attracted the ire of many who considered its theoretical dealings nothing less than an ambiguous flirtation with fascism. Questions then arise: Why did the Collège provoke such negative reactions? How can one reconcile these critical responses with the Collège's direct rebuke of fascism's version of the sacred? What was politically ambiguous about the Collège? Answers to these questions constitute the book's specific focus, as I explore the difficult terrain of politics' relationship to aesthetics.

The book's main argument is that the Collège's extreme belief in the power of the sacred and its conception of the social as a self-sustained organism unfettered by other spheres led inevitably to theoretical impasses that resulted in political ambiguity. For the Collège's magnification and privileging of the social implied more than the separation of the social from other spheres, in particular the aesthetic and the political. It also involved a narrow understanding, negative evaluation, and consequent rejection of both politics and aesthetics. The Collège saw politics as coinciding with current events and engagement in public affairs: politics belonged to the utilitarian and materialistic world of the profane and could not be relied on to build a community. As for aesthetics, the Collège identified it with art's illusion and superficiality and deemed it unfit for community construction. In the end, the sacred as a validation of the social became for the Collège a self-enclosed realm that should not be contaminated by the pettiness of politics and the deception of art and at whose centre stood instincts and myths. Rituals and symbols, which Benjamin had targeted as the ruses of modern authoritarian power, were isolated from a historical analysis of their political resurgence. Anthropology took over sociology. But the enforced separation of the aesthetic, political, and social spheres upheld by the Collège, I contend, hindered its ability to reflect on the risks of an aestheticization of the political that the recourse to myths and symbols entailed. It prevented the Collège from realizing and coming to terms with the profound political nature of its pursuit. It also threatened to result in exactly what the Collège denounced in fascism: the emptying out of meaningful experience in exchange for emotional gratification. One can surmise that this was Benjamin's fear as well.

While the issue of the College's political leanings certainly deserves attention, this book is not interested in providing an ideological reading of the Collège or in isolating the Collège's originality from the culture of its time. Rather, by examining some key historical and theoretical moments that highlight the Collège's conceptualization of the sacred, the book explores the limits and potential of the Collège's misrecognized political project. Through this analysis, the book also addresses long-standing questions about the relationship between politics and aesthetics in modernity. It thus situates the Collège within a larger intellectual context that felt uneasy about the relationship between politics and aesthetics; and it takes as the cause of such a common sentiment the failure to recognize the historicity of our modern understanding of aesthetics and of art's status as autonomous.

Since the misrecognition of aesthetics' political essence constitutes a central presupposition of the book, I will outline the general contours of aesthetics' historical genealogy as a discrete field.[18] In particular, I will review the historical-philosophical process that led to the proclamation of art's autonomy in the nineteenth century with the *l'art pour l'art* movement (art for art's sake) and the path that led art to be identified as a disinterested social realm detached from the passions and solidarity necessary to animate a social collectivity. Let me add that such history is not necessarily unilinear or uncontroversial and, indeed, presents multiple foci and perspectives. Yet, I believe that even a partial analysis will clarify

18 This genealogy is based on the presupposition that aesthetic ideas cannot be understood by examining them simply within a philosophical context. They need to be related to the larger cultural and social environment in which they develop and should be looked at as historical constructs. As several scholars have pointed out, art has not always been intended in the same way, and there is no stable or universal definition of art. In particular, aesthetics as a discipline emerged at a time when art came to comprise all the genres we now refer to as "fine arts," an appellation typical of modern Western societies. See Kristeller, "The Modern System of the Arts" in *Journal of the History of Ideas* 12: 496–527 and 13: 17–46 (1951–52), now in Kristeller, *Renaissance Thought and the Arts*; Woodmansee, *The Author, Art, and the Market*; Mattick Jr, ed., *Eighteenth-Century Aesthetics and the Reconstruction of Art*; Mortensen, *Art in the Social Order*; Peter and Christa Bürger, *The Institutions of Art*.

the logic of the Collège's ambivalent stance on art (and the ambivalence of other figures examined in this book as well). Along the way, the analysis will also bring to the fore the paradoxical destiny of a field of knowledge that, as it was taking shape and claiming an autonomous space for itself, became a site of political expression and contention.

As several scholars have argued, the concept of autonomous, disinterested art emerged as the result of a complex historical process originating in the eighteenth century. In the wake of Hobbes's philosophical approach, British moralists of the calibre of Addison, Shaftesbury, Hutcheson, Hume, and Alison set out to address the status of egoism and instrumentality in ethical questions. Lord Shaftesbury, in particular, developed a notion of disinterestedness, at first linked to moral issues, that later became the core concept of modern aesthetic theory and the key methodological principle in the newly emerging discipline of aesthetics.[19] Critical of "interest" in its meaning of "strategic" when applied to one's motives for action, Shaftesbury was also opposed to the idea of considering ethics in terms of an action's consequences, i.e., whether or not the action had positive effects on the common good. He thus argued that disinterestedness served to overcome what he considered the false choice between egoism and altruism; disinterestedness implied that moral life was fundamentally concerned with harmony and contemplation as opposed to action. Within this framework, virtuous "man" was like the art lover, and virtue was not about making the right decisions in view of reaching worthy ends; virtue, rather, stood for "no other than the love of order and beauty."[20]

At first preoccupied with moral issues, over time Shaftesbury turned his ethical concerns into an aesthetically informed theory that emphasized the importance of beauty and contemplation when defining a virtuous person. Thus, whereas he had originally discussed disinterest in opposition to interest in practical actions, Shaftesbury later employed disinterest to refer to the "virtuous man" as a spectator keen on contemplating the beauty of both manners and morals. Disinterestedness was contrary to action and also dismissive of the desire to possess or use a thing; it emphasized the perceiving act when contemplating an object rather than the object being contemplated. In this version, Shaftesbury's conception of disinterestedness shifted toward the perceptual and, in view of aesthetics' etymological meaning as "sense perception," made it

19 Stolnitz, "On the Origins of 'Aesthetic Disinterestedness.'"
20 Ibid., 133.

possible for the first time to think about a novel construct, that of "aesthetic disinterestedness."

This new, aesthetically oriented understanding of disinterestedness became a central axis of eighteenth-century British thought and moved other philosophers to plumb further the question of "aesthetic attitude" – the state of mind in which one is able to appreciate beauty. Now disinterestedness was connected with aesthetics rather than ethics, and emphasis was increasingly placed on the recipients' experience and their capacity to contemplate an object. As long as one remained a spectator, one's experience of an object would supposedly be disinterested because based solely on perception. Art historians or critics, for instance, were considered unable to have an aesthetic experience because they focused on specific aspects of the work they observed and did not develop a spontaneous "disinterested" appreciation.

According to Jerome Stolnitz, the new focus on disinterestedness and perceptual experience initiated by Shaftesbury in eighteenth-century Britain led to the gradual decline of the notion of beauty as an objective category. The perceptual experience of beauty was then emphasized rather than the qualities that made a thing beautiful. Since all objects of disinterested perception could provide sensate experience, aesthetics ascended to the position of a more general and encompassing theory that reached beyond art forms and genres and included literature and music, as well as nature and the sciences. Stolnitz comments: "[N]o object is admitted to or excluded from the realm of the aesthetic because of its inherent nature. It is the attitude of the percipient that is decisive."[21]

This new perspective on experience marked the birth of aesthetics as a distinctive realm.[22] It also allowed other value-categories to be included in the aesthetic. Sublimity, in particular, took into account one's sentiments of fear and horror in response to an experience of danger and promoted ugliness to an aesthetic status. Like beauty, ugliness inspired strong emotions and a sense of pleasure.[23] Finally, "good taste" was adopted as an evaluative tool, further demonstrating the influence of "disinterestedness" on the emergent aesthetic theory in Britain and continental Europe. The category of "good taste" was linked to the pleasure of the imagination and the lack of desire for possessions; as such, it was deeply rooted in the notion of disinterestedness.

---

21 Ibid., 142.

22 One could also say that the theory of aesthetic experience produced its own domain.

23 See in particular Burke, *A Philosophical Enquiry into the Origin of Our Ideas of the Sublime and Beautiful.*

In Germany, judgment of taste became central to Kant's influential re-definition of aesthetic essence and came to be identified by Kant with the human ability to share experiences in comparison to animals.[24] For Kant, disinterestedness in aesthetic judgment signified that taste, though sub-jective because based on feelings rather than concepts, was not arbitrary or private. It involved, at least in principle, the existence of what Kant called a *sensus communis*, or common sense, intended not in the ordinary meaning of simple but rather in the sense of shared. Aesthetic judgment for Kant required consensual understanding within a collectivity.[25]

As it turns out, Kant's view of the community that shared perceptual experience was quite selective and hierarchical since it alleged that only those with personal cultivation and freedom from immediate needs could pass aesthetic judgments. Nevertheless, the idea of *sensus communis* helped entrench the notion of disinterestedness in Kant's aesthetic theo-ry.[26] On the one hand, disinterestedness implied that the crucial factor in our experience of a beautiful object was not the object itself but the feelings of enjoyment it aroused in us. On the other, through reference to *sensus communis*, disinterestedness also implied that those feelings, be-ing in principle communicable and intersubjective, were not based on personal or sensual gratification and did not implicate a utilitarian di-mension. Kant's famous definition of art as "purposiveness without pur-pose" quintessentially summarized the peculiar role disinterestedness had come to play in his theory of aesthetic judgment.[27] That definition also helped solidify the identification of the aesthetic realm with non-instrumental ends.[28]

24 It is impossible in the context of this book to do justice to Kant's formulation of the Third Critique, let alone his overall theory of judgment. It should, however, be noted that Kant's goal in the *Critique of Judgment* was to examine the human faculty of judgment in order to determine whether judgment is organized by an a priori principle and also to es-tablish how it mediates between the faculty of understanding and reason.

25 As Mortensen points out, Kant even distinguished *sensus communis aestheticus* from *sensus communis logicus* in order to avoid confusing the former with the ordinary meaning of common sense. Mortensen, *Art in the Social Order*.

26 On Kant's *sensus communis* also see Summers, "Why Did Kant Call Taste a 'Common Sense'?"

27 Karl Philipp Moritz anticipated some of the elements that characterized Kant's aes-thetic theory. In particular, Moritz's 1785 essay for the *Berlinische Monatsschrifte* argued against the instrumental character of the work of art. See Woodmansee, "The Interests of Disinterestedness"; Abrams, "Art-as-Such"; Hess, *Reconstituting the Body Politic*.

28 One should also add that focus on the non-instrumental character of the aesthetic helped separate art from other human-made works between the seventeenth and eigh-teenth centuries. At this time, there developed "the basic notion that the five 'major arts' constitute an area all by themselves, clearly separated by common characteristics from the crafts, the sciences and other human activities." See Kristeller, *Renaissance Thought and the*

Did Kant's formulation of "purposiveness without purpose" advocate the isolation of art from the social world? This is the question of interest to us. For we have seen that the formation of aesthetics as a distinctive field, the specific domain of judgment of taste, took place in direct connection with the development of a theory of disinterestedness. Yet, as most interpreters of Kant would argue, there is no logical connection between Kant's claim that the judgment of an object's beauty occurs independently from the object's purpose (be it its original design or final use) and the assertion that art should be disconnected from social life. Indeed, according to Jonathan Hess, it would be a mistake to assume that disinterested taste implied art's retreat to the ivory tower and its isolation from the public realm.[29] The affirmation of art's autonomy and the idea that a work of art needed to be appreciated in its own terms were rather the result of the reception of Kant's aesthetic theory by his contemporaries.[30]

Furthermore, Hess argues that the paradigm shift that gave rise to the concept of autonomous disinterested art in the eighteenth century was a response to a political crisis in the public culture of the Enlightenment that led to promoting aesthetics as an alternative political agency. Although, as a normative category, this concept of art addressed specific problems in artistic practice that emerged after the expansion of the art market, it also spoke to distinctive anxieties at a particular historical moment when the modern institution of the public sphere was emerging.[31]

Arts, 165. This process contributed to the modern conception of art in the West as a distinct autonomous domain and the idea that art was to be evaluated according to internal criteria and as a manifestation of human activity. Also see Becq, "Creation, Aesthetics, Markets"; and Jay, *Songs of Experience.*

29 Hess, *Reconstituting the Body Politic.*

30 Wilcox, "The Beginnings of l'Art pour l'Art."

31 On the connection between art and the market at this time, see Woodmansee, *The Author, Art, and the Market.* Woodmansee argues that one needs to contextualize art's self-characterization as autonomous within an economic cultural history. A new literary and artistic culture in the late eighteenth century found in the opening of commercial markets a novel avenue for circulating works. Markets also provided cultural producers with means to achieve economic independence and gain freedom from the system of patronage. While in England such new markets had ensured authors and artists a receptive audience for their intellectual endeavours, the situation in Germany turned out to be less encouraging. First, the public for independent producers appeared quite limited; second, and more importantly, consumers seemed more inclined toward products with entertainment value and were uninterested in those of a more serious nature or that pursued edifying purposes. Facing the unfavourable economic circumstances of art's commercialization, and increasingly isolated, artists began to lament the public's inability to exercise good taste and posited as paramount the artist's genius along with the values of creation and expressive freedom against the constraints of use and pleasure. On this issue, see also Bourdieu, *The Rules of Art.*

Kant's notion of disinterested art provided an ideal space within which to envision a public forum away from concrete political or governmental action and where enlightened citizens could freely discuss political issues. Art was a self-proclaimed non-political space in which politics, however, worked as a motivational engine in a dialogue with the absolutist state and in order to widen participation in governmental decision-making.[32] Despite his elitist vision of community, in sum, Kant hinted at the presence of, or desire for, a public sphere.[33] His theory of aesthetic *sensus communis*, which posited the search for consensus as a natural characteristic of human beings, projected a model for politics and did not advocate art's isolation.[34]

At a time when the Enlightenment sought to create a supplemental realm in which to pursue its project of rationalizing politics, disinterested aesthetics stood as an alternative space for the nascent public sphere, a different way of becoming involved in public affairs. And it reflected a deep political innervation, a desire to exercise reason within a community steeped in consensus. Although seemingly founded on separation, Hess concludes, modern aesthetics originated in relation to politics: aesthetics and politics were mutually implicated.

Hess's interpretation provides a sharp rebuttal to the claim that Kant's theory of disinterestedness constituted the blueprint for the *l'art pour l'art* movement and its notion of art's autonomy popular in the 1800s.[35] The epitome of art's cry for independence, the *l'art pour l'art* movement was rather an extreme interpretation of the principles espoused by Kant and his predecessors. Wilcox calls it "a fantastically careless and incompetent misreading at that"[36] – a misreading, however, that had consequences. On the one hand, although a cultural construct and the result of a

---

32 Friedrich Schiller pushed this visionary side of Kant by focusing on aesthetic experience as the main vehicle to address the problems of political freedom and brotherhood. See *On the Aesthetic Education of Man in a Series of Letters*. On aesthetics and politics in Germany, see Chytry, *The Aesthetic State*.

33 On the notion of a literary public sphere and its political function, see Habermas, *The Structural Transformation of the Public Sphere*. Hess in part builds his argument on a critique of Habermas's view of the literary public sphere's relationship to politics.

34 See chapter 7 in Hess, *Reconstituting the Body Politic*.

35 The first to coin the phrase *l'art pour l'art* was Benjamin Constant in a journal entry of 1804 that summarized a discussion of Kant he had heard in Germany. However, Théophile Gautier is generally recognized as the one who in the preface to his 1835 historical novel, *Mademoiselle de Maupin*, introduced the principles of *l'art pour l'art*. On this history, see Wilcox, "The Beginnings of l'Art pour l'Art."

36 He continues, "The tremendous weight of his reputation, however, made some of his statements about art, as they were variously and superficially understood, the unquestioned dogma of *l'art pour l'art*." Wilcox, "The Beginnings of l'Art pour l'Art," 361.

specific historical moment, art's autonomous status came to be regarded as an accepted dogma, the unquestionable, universal truth about art's essence.[37] On the other hand, and a critical point for this book's discussion, the notion of autonomy heralded by the *l'art pour l'art* movement also obfuscated the original link between politics and the newly emergent field of aesthetics. Thus, the doctrine of *l'art pour l'art* not only managed to naturalize its own notion of art as autotelic and self-referential; it also stripped aesthetics of its political impulse and left us with an interpretive legacy that has been difficult to shake off.

Ignoring the modern relationship between politics and aesthetics, this book however argues, raises issues beyond an anachronistic understanding; it undermines our analytical abilities to interrogate and resolve the current crisis of the political (the disaffection with politics as usual). This is particularly the case because the historical coming into being of aesthetics, besides implicating politics, also carried political consequences. In the case of late eighteenth-century Germany, for example, Kant's attempt to reconstitute the body politic through art while insisting on art's non-political status ended up sustaining the political interests it was attempting to confront. By proclaiming its non-political status, art, to be sure, displaced politics and created an alternative space; yet it was unable to overcome concretely the strictures of the reigning absolutist politics and was rather subsumed by it.[38]

If, then, art's non-political ambitions carried unwanted political consequences, the question for us is: How did the Collège's sacred sociology fare as a self-proclaimed anti-aesthetic and anti-political response to 1930s fascism? What did the Collège risk by giving up aesthetics (at least in the version handed down by *l'art pour l'art*)? I contend that the Collège's attempt to conceive of the sacred as an alternative model of social intervention that shunned politics and aesthetics, while being fully entangled in them, led it to miscalculate or miss altogether the

37 Scholars such as Woodmansee and Mattick point to Foucault's notion of discontinuity as a useful concept for interpreting definitions of art over time. Within this context, the eighteenth-century definition of art appears as a shift from the idea held by the Greeks of art as the imitation of nature and as having a function.

38 Hess writes: "Ensuing from a frustrated attempt at a politicized Enlightenment, the doctrine of aesthetic autonomy transforms the public sphere's project to force the mechanistic state rationality of the absolutist body politic to overcome itself into a project in which the absolutist state and its reconstituted organic other prove to be compatible and capable of peaceful coexistence. The organic political body imagined by the concept of aesthetic autonomy simulates precisely the natural politics Enlightenment aspired to, but in doing so it supports the mechanical rationality of the absolutist state." *Reconstituting the Body Politic*, 241.

implications of its own political impulse. In particular, its closure to the historical nature of art's claim to autonomy and the inherited construction of art's meaning in modernity led the Collège to overlook that affectivity was the neglected side of aesthetics – a side that the art for art's sake movement had surgically removed from its self-definition as autonomous. By subscribing to the notion of art's independence as popularized by the art for art's sake movement, the Collège ignored the invented character of the modern category of art – its discontinuity with previous attempts to categorize what we now designate as artworks. In so doing, the Collège passed over the centrality of sense perception and the body in the making of modern aesthetic discourse. It also failed to accept the deeply aesthetic-political nature of its own attempt to access and establish a sacred community through the invocation of non-functional impulses, instincts, and emotions. Ultimately, I argue, the Collège underestimated the sensuous body's radical potential.

And yet, although an absent referent in the art for art's sake movement, the body played a critical and increasingly radical role in the eighteenth-century philosophical approach to aesthetics. Kant's formulation of disinterestedness, after all, developed on the basis of a new focus on sense perception that counteracted the emphasis on beautiful objects. No doubt Kant eventually eliminated the desiring body from his theory of taste and emphasized in contrast aesthetics' cognitive side.[39] Yet, be it glorified or assaulted, the body weaved in and out of the modern discourse on aesthetic experience and brought to the philosophical fore the crucial question of whether it was possible to reconcile emotional gratification with the ideal of a nobler life. The body as variously embedded in the aesthetic provided a springboard for achieving a higher, more beautiful, and more harmonious existence.

The connection between body and aesthetics, and the political nature of this relationship, was not missed by Benjamin, whose analysis of fascism identified two different and somewhat incongruous ways of approaching aesthetics' link to politics: one, as art proper in its historical incarnation of art for art's sake, and the other, as a discourse of the body.[40] Thus, for Benjamin, fascism's brutal subscription to the aesthetic

---

39 According to Hess, Kant's aesthetics was actually rooted in an understanding of the natural connection between body and mind. Ibid., 231. Also see Jay, *Songs of Experience*, chap. 4, "Returning to the Body through Aesthetic Experience: From Kant to Dewey."

40 See my *Fascist Spectacle*. Also see Susan Buck-Morss, "Aesthetics and Anaesthetics." Others might disagree with this line of interpretation. For a different take that tends to focus on Benjamin's opposition between the aestheticization of politics and the politicization of art, see Hess, *Reconstituting the Body Politic*.

model of self-referentiality (summarized in the motto *Fiat ars, pereat mundus*) showed its affinity with the *l'art pour l'art* movement. At the same time, fascism's ability to produce ritual values and solicit emotions from numbed bodies indicated the use of aesthetics in its Greek meaning of bodily sensations (*aisthesis*). In this latter instance, the aesthetic appeared fully implicated in the ruses of fascism's politics (although Benjamin did not see it as pernicious in principle). Even more consequentially, fascism's aesthetic politics depended on the subjects' response to the emotional solicitations of the Führer and not merely on the leader's artistic self-delusions. From this point of view, the bodily dimension of politics affected fascism's success and could not be discounted. One should add that it was this same particular ability of fascism that spurred the Collège's desire for alternative ways to forge communal bonds and enact the sacred. The Collège was all too aware of fascism's attraction. And yet, it missed considering such attraction a sign of aesthetics' potential or of aesthetics' link to politics.

The Collège was not unique in discounting the coming into being of aesthetics as a discrete discourse. On the contrary, its approach to art and politics confirmed a general orientation in French culture at the turn of the twentieth century and during the interwar period that struggled to come to terms with the rational Enlightenment tradition. Although this trend was not foreign to other national contexts, the French case is compelling because its secular faith continued to feed off anti-aesthetic sentiments. It thus promoted a desiccated, institutional vision of politics that countered the alternative model of the Revolution while surreptitiously longing for it. This is evident in Durkheim and his school, whose work greatly influenced the Collège and who are the subject of the first chapter. The trend can also be seen in Surrealism's struggle to re-envision experience in modern society, discussed in chapter 3. The Surrealists were caught between rejecting politics and transforming life, condemning aesthetics and identifying themselves as artists. In both cases, aesthetics was as ostracized as politics, and the two were seen as not only problematic but mutually incompatible.

Of course, as illustrated above, the negative view of aesthetics was founded on the modern notion of art as autonomous and detached from worldly affairs. In this guise, art had attracted the scorn of European intellectuals and cultural figures who, in the early twentieth century, attempted to redefine art's domain and value. In France, in particular, a new understanding of art inspired by anthropological reflections and the cultural movement of primitivism contributed to negative perceptions and a limited conceptualization of art's status and role in the modern West, a trend covered in chapter 2. This situation was made worse by the lack of development in France, as compared to Germany in particular (but also England), of a modern philosophical tradition in aesthetics.[41] While the perceptual dimension of human existence – a domain under which art was subsumed – had generally been neglected after Descartes in favour of the conceptual, beginning in the 1700s, a string of German thinkers from Baumgarten to Kant, Hegel, Schiller, and Nietzsche engaged with the realm of sensations.[42] Since art belonged to the sphere of the aesthetic, it was also conceived as connected to the senses and the body, the concrete level of the lifeworld.[43] In this guise, art found itself at the centre of philosophical elaborations.

The reincorporation of the material in philosophical discourse after the predominance of Cartesianism did not imply an overhauling of reason; it nevertheless envisaged a corollary logic that made possible knowledge of what otherwise seemed to escape rationality. Within this philosophical perspective, art, like all aesthetic discourse, indicated the importance of affect and experience. People's desires came to the fore as indicators of what a good life should provide, eventually inscribing the political in the aesthetic search for self-actualization. In an era dominated by economic individualism and new forms of subjectivity, the aesthetic, as Eagleton suggests, intervened "as a dream of reconciliation of individuals woven into intimate unity with no detriment to their specificity, of an abstract totality suffused with all the flesh-and-blood reality of the individual being."[44] The aesthetic, in sum, was not only fully enmeshed with the political; it also merged with a political project that, even though fundamentally ambivalent, contained a utopian moment. Within this context, whereas power could undoubtedly more effectively subjugate and coerce by penetrating bodies, as Foucault warns, it also emerged as vulnerable to attacks by some of the bodies' unleashed desires and impulses. For art and aesthetics contain an excess, an overflow of sentiments that sprout from material particularities and rebel against the strictures of order and functionality.

41 On the French approach, see Décultot, "Aesthetik/esthétique"; Tronchon, "Une science à ses débuts en France: l'esthétique"; Coleman, *The Aesthetic Thought of the French Enlightenment.*

42 Baumgarten was the first to introduce the term "aesthetics" using the Latin word *aesthetica* first in his 1735 dissertation and later in 1750 in a volume of the same title.

43 On the aesthetic in philosophy, see Eagleton, *The Ideology of the Aesthetic.* For the Marxist tradition, see Lunn, *Marxism and Modernism.*

44 Eagleton, *The Ideology of the Aesthetic,* 25.

Aesthetics' political and radical potential did not find a very receptive ear in early twentieth-century France despite the enormous cultural influence of Hegel and Nietzsche (and later Heidegger).[45] Politics and art instead came to be perceived as inadequate responses to the demands of the social. Alternatively, as in the case of the modern avant-garde, they were believed to be irreconcilable and mutually contradictory. The Collège and its leaders, Bataille and Caillois, were no exception to this anti-aesthetic posture. In his manifesto for the Collège, "The Sorcerer's Apprentice," Bataille indicted art, along with politics and science, for impeding "man" from fulfilling human destiny and pursuing "intense existence."[46] Whereas our diminished life hinders us from becoming whole persons, art, according to Bataille, precipitates our subservience by mystifying destiny and helping us escape it. Writers and artists create fictions that appear to counteract the servile nature of human society; yet, even when questioning the real world, they end up accepting its principles. What is worse, art becomes more deceptive when it joins politics because "men of action," political men who intend to transform the world, pursue only those goals that confirm "*that which exists.*"[47] They participate in struggles according to the rational principles dictated by science and end up missing the conflicting movement of destiny.

Bataille eventually saw in myth the decisive element that would ease the return to a "lost totality" and re-enact the sacred or facilitate its emergence.[48] Myth defied contingent reality and useful ends: it expressed and actualized sacred, communal yearnings. Myth, in sum, belonged to the realm of the sacred; art, with its illusions of fulfillment, was essentially profane, and Bataille and Caillois declared any partiality to art an impossible attraction. Thus impermeable to the radical vision of philosophy's aesthetic discourse, the Collège ignored and failed to reflect critically on the historical rootedness of its own presuppositions. It then found itself ill-equipped to assess the consequences of its own hypostatization of the sacred/social, especially when approaching the fascist phenomenon through the optic of the sacred. All in all, the Collège's neglect to link the body to aesthetics, its inadequate understanding of the mutual relationship connecting politics and aesthetics, its incapacity to question the accepted separation between the two in modernity, and its

45 See, among others, Roth, *Knowing and History.* On Alexandre Kojève, Hegel's interpreter in 1930s France, see Auffret, *Alexandre Kojève,* and Drury, *Alexandre Kojève.* On Nietzsche's influence in France see Haar, *Par delà du nihilisme,* and Pinto, *Les neveux de Zarathoustra.* On Heidegger, see Kleinberg, *Generation Existential.*

46 Hollier, *The College of Sociology,* 18.

47 Ibid., 17 (italicized in the original).

48 Ibid., 23.

ultimate rejection of both led it down a treacherous path. Entangled in conceptual and practical liabilities, the Collège became vulnerable to accusations of ambiguity. How could its pursuit of a sacred community avoid the entrapments of what Benjamin defined as fascism's aestheticized politics – the offering of illusory gratification via cults and rituals to counteract the perceived loss of communal spirit? This question haunted the Collège from its beginnings.[49]

In this book, I examine the Collège's supposed ambivalence and equivocal politics not in order to discount the validity of sacred sociology but to probe the Collège's potential for rethinking the political. Let me briefly identify what I mean by "the political" and its difference from "politics."

As any good dictionary would state, politics is about the art of governing; it is a specialized set of activities that deals with the functioning of the political system and the process of making decisions in the interest of the state and its citizens. Politics designates a particular domain separate from the other value spheres; it involves public administration, policymaking, and control of all affairs pertaining to government. This definition of politics, which is an invention of modernity, isolates a specific arena of social life from other activities – the economy, religion, aesthetics, the erotic, law, ethics. The pursuit of science and objectivity, both supposedly obtainable by delimiting a field of knowledge, reflected the process of differentiation of the "value spheres" in modernity, a process famously analyzed by Max Weber in his essay "Religious Rejections of the World."[50] Under these circumstances, and as the main subject of a new political "science," modern politics came to stand for all the functions described in the definition above; and it is with reference to those specific functions that we think of politics in our common usage today.

The political, in contrast, breaks free from the strictures of modernity's specialization and aims at overcoming narrow notions and definitions. It takes into account the historical juncture that made possible the separation of the spheres in the first place and interrogates the coming into being of different domains of life experience that have resulted from this separation. It also widens the range of knowledge that applies to politics; politics is seen in connection to the other spheres as well as in

49 To avoid any confusion, let me make it clear that I am not judging or faulting the Collège for not reflecting on the political nature of its work. I am simply providing an analysis of the factors that help explain the Collège's intellectual journey and the dilemmas it faced, as well as the elements that have given rise to the commentators' controversial assessments of Bataille's and the Collège's politics.

50 Weber, "Religious Rejections of the World and Their Directions."

terms of its cultural and symbolic dimensions. Following Claude Lefort, one can define the political as encompassing the ensemble of social structures, concepts, and principles that organizes a society.[51] The political is no longer a given positivity and no longer comprises law-governed institutions but is the process through which the ensemble of structures and ideas is instituted. This view of the political thus rejects the notion that society and politics be considered as two separate domains. Rather, society is constituted through its own self-understanding. From another perspective, Jean-Luc Nancy talks of the political as the place where we think about what it means to be in common, "the place where community as such is brought into play" while defining itself. The political is not "in any case, just the locus of power relations," he insists.[52] More consequentially, I would add, the notion of the political implies that we cannot evaluate the social as self-contained or in isolation.

This specific point is crucial for my discussion of the Collège (and Durkheim and Mauss) and in particular the argument in chapters 4 and 5. Here, after contextualizing the different elements and theoretical threads that contributed to the Collège's assessment of the sacred, I appraise the paradoxical nature of the Collège's emphasis on the social. I draw attention to the incongruity between the Collège's accepted compartmentalization of the value spheres in modernity – the separation it invokes of the social from the aesthetic and the political – and its notion of the sacred as encompassing a broad range of activities and practices. I also discuss how the sacred is imagined by the Collège as an alternative to traditional politics, yet in actuality becomes a displacement of politics rather than its dissolution. Ultimately, I insist on the double binding that occurs when the Collège rejects aesthetics' radical premises but is simultaneously unable to stop politics from hemorrhaging into the sacred. What are the results of these transfigurations of politics, then? Is it possible, as the Collège seemed to believe, to sidetrack and eventually sublate institutional politics?

This quandary hits at the heart of the Collège's ambiguity because it questions the Collège's allegiance to democratic values. For it goes without saying that the democratic ideal was the unwilling victim of the Collège's inquiry – the target of a common critique in the interwar years that questioned democracy's ability, both spiritually and politically, to overcome the widespread challenge of fascism. In 1930s France, the urge to rejuvenate the existing political order in the midst of an economic crisis emerged together with a cultural search for alternatives that

---

51 See in particular Lefort, *Essais sur le politique.*
52 Nancy, *The Inoperative Community*, xxxvii.

transcended the classic opposition of right and left. Eventually, the formation of a Popular Front led to a government presided over by the socialist
Léon Blum; however, demands for a transformed approach to politics
involved challenges to accepted norms and categories.[53] Democratic
principles could not escape this scrutiny since they were embodied by
those same parliamentary institutions accused of lacking vision and ideals.
The search for a "third way" that would avoid the perceived excesses of
socialism as well as the pettiness of bourgeois rule implied a re-evaluation
of dominant political notions and styles, including the meaning and
effectiveness of democracy.

In the case of the Collège, in particular, its acknowledgment of fascism's attraction entailed an indictment of democracy's weaknesses. How
could one resolve this dilemma? The Collège's answer, while exposing
fascism's abuses of the sacred, did not lead to salvaging democracy. Yet,
and this is the book's main conclusion and what I believe is the legacy of
the Collège, by embracing ambiguity the Collège avoided paying lip service to fascism or advocating an authoritarian turn. It instead provided
the impetus for reconfiguring the political and the issue of community
in the modern era. As I discuss in chapter 6, the Collège's courting dance
with equivocation brought to the fore the limits of a black and white view
of politics, one in which contradictions are eliminated and issues are
clear-cut. Through equivocation, the Collège demonstrated the compelling status of people's emotional search for shared identity, be it religious, national, or ethnic, and the urgency to address the role of affective
needs in the social arena. At the same time, the Collège initiated a critical debate on the difficulties and dilemmas inherent in the idea of unity
within heterogeneity – the impossibility of enacting community without
the risk of imposing exclusion and conformity.

The book thus highlights the prominence and importance of the
Collège's concerns and sociological elaborations and in the final chapter
links the Collège to the work of other intellectuals of the postwar generation, in particular Claude Lefort. In my view, Lefort has constructed a
political-philosophical model that offers the possibility of retaining the
potency of the Collège's original striving for community while addressing
the risks of totalizing tendencies inherent in the Collège's musings on the
sacred. Lefort's model does not shy away from the predicaments of equivocation. Instead, it specifically conjures and tackles ambiguity in order to
affirm the vitality of a renewed understanding of democracy. In a transformational approach to the notion of community, it invokes division as

53 On the Popular Front, see Jackson, *The Popular Front in France.* On the crisis of the
social, see Dean, *The Frail Social Body.*

the foundation for rethinking the political in a post-totalitarian era. Lefort, in sum, brings to fruition some of the Collège's most pressing questions on the nature of the social and its relationship to the political and offers an engaging framework within which to assess the cogency of the Collège's theorizing. To be sure, there are alternative ways to interpret the legacy of the Collège – ones that refrain from proposing institutional models of the political in the tradition followed by Lefort. Nancy is a case in point. These different interpretations, I would suggest, are not exclusive; they rather indicate the wealth and complexity of the Collège's intellectual endeavours, its currency in our present-day debate over the question of the political, and its ongoing significance for interrogating the relationship between politics and aesthetics in the modern era.

From this point of view, the book is as much the product of the Collège's interdisciplinary reach as it is an attempt to include other fields of knowledge, in particular sociology, among the disciplines that can benefit from the Collège's intellectual theorizing. In his foreword to the first English edition of the Collège's collected works, Denis Hollier observed that the Collège is absent from literature and sociology manuals despite its large presence in French thought. He cited the fact that the Collège's elaboration of theory defied classification because of its unorthodoxy.[54] It was declared unsociological for its lack of scientific rigour and foundations, and unliterary for its presumptive recourse to theoretical construction. The incommensurability of the Collège led to its marginalization. Although much has been written on Bataille and his fellow members since Hollier's pioneering publication, the Collège's visionary attempts at formulating a theory of the sacred have been underestimated by sociologists.[55] My book aims to amend this lack of attention while showcasing the Collège as a unique opportunity for the humanities and social sciences to find a common ground. If Bataille's critique of reason has influenced intellectuals such as Michel Foucault and Jacques Derrida

54 Hollier, *The College of Sociology*, viii.

55 The only English monograph specifically on the Collège, besides Hollier's volume, is by a humanist. See Richman, *Sacred Revolutions*. Richman interprets the Collège's reliance on Durkheim as a key moment in the development of a critical discourse in France that emerged out of an interest in anthropological thinking. Richman is interested in showing the radical potential of Durkheim's notion of collective effervescence at a time when fascism was also evoking the power of collective assemblies. Thus, as Richman puts it, her main contribution is "to reexamine group effervescence in relation to social upheavals," 5. My approach to the Collège takes a different direction. I examine the ambiguity that emerges out of the Collège's stance on the sacred in order, first, to reassess the modern relationship between politics and aesthetics and, second, to rethink the political and the question of democracy in a post-totalitarian era.

to challenge the language of subjectivity, it has also raised "the religious problem," as Foucault put it – the need to search for new paths after the death of god.[56] Through the optic of sociology, the Collège explored the sacred. In so doing, the book argues, it addressed the crucial philosophical question of how communities form out of diversity – a central issue for our time.[57]

56 See Paolo Caruso's conversation with Foucault in Caruso, ed., *Conversazioni con Claude Lévi-Strauss, Michel Foucault, Jacques Lacan*, 120.

57 For a discussion of the centrality of this issue in Bataille and its topical importance in contemporary philosophy, see the volume by Mitchell and Winfree, eds., *The Obsessions of Georges Bataille*.

Representing the Social:
Émile Durkheim and Marcel Mauss

BETWEEN NOVEMBER 1895 AND MAY 1896, Émile Durkheim gave a series of lectures on the "History of Socialism" at Bordeaux in which he introduced the doctrine of Saint-Simon and pronounced it the foundation of positivism.[1] Describing Saint-Simon's philosophy as "a great system," Durkheim acknowledged social science's (and his own) theoretical indebtedness to the French philosopher – "the first to conceive that between the formal generalities of metaphysical philosophy and the narrow specialization of the particular sciences, there was a place for a new enterprise."[2] Saint-Simon, not Comte, Durkheim claimed, ought to be considered the founder of positive philosophy. Durkheim particularly admired Saint-Simon's ability to combine philosophy with the analysis of social problems and his two-pronged approach to knowledge that posited ideas as the foundation of the social system.[3] In Durkheim's reading of Saint-Simon, "a social system is only the application of a system of ideas ... It is the idea, that is, knowledge, which ... is the moving power of progress ... For it is the positive source of all social life. A society is

1 The lectures, intended as the basis of a book on the same topic, have been translated into English with the title *Socialism and Saint-Simon*.

2 Ibid., 82 and 104. Durkheim then added about Saint-Simon, "Although he may have had precursors, never had it been so clearly asserted that man and society could not be directed in their conduct unless one began by making them objects of science," 105. See also Durkheim, "Sociology in France in the Nineteenth Century," in Durkheim, *On Morality and Society*. Here, referring to sociology, Durkheim wrote, "The honor of having first formulated it belongs to Saint-Simon," 6.

3 In *Socialism and Saint-Simon* Durkheim asserted that "one can easily perceive the bond that unites the philosophy and sociology of Saint-Simon; both have a social and practical goal," 91. On the relationship between sociology and philosophy in Durkheim, see Lukes, *Émile Durkheim*, 406–9. Célestin Bouglé, in his preface to Durkheim, *Sociology and Philosophy*, wrote that Durkheim's sociology "revives philosophy," xxxv.

above all a community of ideas."[4] Whether summoned by religion in those societies that still lacked a modern scientific system, or embedded in other forms of knowledge where scientific progress already presided, ideas constituted the source of social life. The ways in which we represent the world to ourselves in ever-changing historical determinations enable us to share a community. "What unites men into society," Durkheim affirmed, "is a common way of thinking, that is, of picturing things to themselves."[5]

For Durkheim, the key to understanding society resided in the mental processes that sustain common existence, and he emphasized in Saint-Simon what he himself was pursuing: the notion of society as an ensemble of ideas and collective beliefs, or "representations."[6] Beginning with *The Rules of Sociological Method* and his 1898 article "Individual and Collective Representations," continuing on to his assessment of sociology in France in 1900, and concluding with his later writings on the duality of human nature, Durkheim placed representation at the centre of his conception of society.[7] And he argued that representations should be treated as realities that, partially independent of their original substratum, formed a *sui generis* phenomenon suitable to the sociological analysis he was elaborating.

By positing the life of the mind as key to understanding the social, Durkheim rejected theories that interpreted mental activity as dependent on nature or as a function of the organism; even if cells constitute the material basis of ideas, knowing what happens at the cellular level would not inform us about the way individual representations work.[8] In contrast to organicist perspectives, Durkheim affirmed the originality of mental life and warned against trying to infer social laws from the realm of biology.[9] A more appropriate method was to establish analogies

4 *Sociology and Saint-Simon*, 90–1. Durkheim specifically cited Saint-Simon as saying that "[t]he similarity of positive moral ideas ... is the single bond which can unite men into society" (91).

5 Ibid., 92.

6 See Bouglé's preface to Durkheim, *Sociology and Philosophy*, xxxvii.

7 *Les Règles de la méthode sociologique* was first published in 1895; "Représentations individuelles et représentations collectives" in 1898; "La Sociologie en France au XIXe siècle" in 1900; and "Le Dualisme de la nature humaine et ses conditions sociales" in 1914.

8 According to Bouglé, for Durkheim "the existence of the memory is sufficient to establish that the life of representations cannot be inherent in neural matter; as it has its own way of being, so it exists by virtue of its own forces." See his preface in Durkheim, *Sociology and Philosophy*, xxxviii.

9 See "Value Judgments and Judgments of Reality," in *Sociology and Philosophy*, 91, where Durkheim wrote that society is the centre of a moral life and not a system of organs and functions.

between the laws of sociology and those of psychology for the precise reason that they both dealt with representations.[10] Durkheim's anti-organicist position and his interest in the psychological nature of ideas thus combined to support the *sui generis* reality of collective representations and led him to assert their prominence in a science of morals.

In Durkheim's vision, the function of society was to create the ideal.[11] A community based on a shared sense of the sacred, or indeed on any form of association, was properly understood as constituted by a spiritual nucleus that promoted the sentiment of the social. Representations played a crucial role in building such a sense of community. They were thus at the heart of social life and the core of the sociological enterprise.

From this early statement of the centrality of representations in society, Durkheim gradually built an epistemological system that posited sociology as the science of synthesis – a science that took into account the tension between the individual and the collective, the rational and the irrational, the mind and the body. For how could one explain the power of collective representations without understanding the dynamic relationship between group and individual, whole and parts, rational and irrational, spiritual and material, conscious and unconscious? These antinomies were not resolvable through the subsuming of one term by the other; collective representations did not ensue as an imposition of the group on the individual, nor was there a homology between whole and parts. Rather, Durkheim envisaged these relationships as a synthesis in which subjective particularities, which he considered relatively autonomous, become assimilated within a completely new and independent collective reality. The process is full of incongruities, Durkheim admitted, and cannot be grasped at the conscious level, but he believed it was sociology's task to account for and resolve the discrepancies that emerge from the synthetic reconciliation of seeming opposites.

It was this overture of Durkheimian sociology to the complexities and apparent contradictions of human existence that attracted the attention of intellectuals such as Bataille and Caillois through the work of Marcel Mauss. It was the openness of Durkheim's approach to the emotional side of human nature that appealed in surprising ways to a character such as Bataille. And it was the Durkheimians' emphasis on the communal spirit that made sociology the pivot of the Collège's experiment at collective theorizing. In what follows, and in order to contextualize the importance of the Durkheimian school for the Collège, I will analyse the

---

10 Durkheim, "Individual and Collective Representations," *Sociology and Philosophy*, 1–2.
11 Bouglé, *Bilan de la sociologie française contemporaine*, chapter "Sociologie et psychologie."

intellectual and epistemological terrain on which Durkheim built his
theory of the social, beginning with his theory that representation is central to society and moving to his definition of the sacred as ultimately
overlapping with the collective. I start with the importance of representations in Durkheim's explanatory model to show the cultural impetus at
the core of Durkheimian sociology – an impetus that particularly emerges in Durkheim's appeal to psychology and his attention to the dualism
of human nature. I then examine Durkheim's focus on the "primitives"
as an effort to demonstrate through empirical cases the successful resolution of the antagonism between the individual and the social. The
evaluation of the "primitives" allowed Durkheim to pose the question of
religion's origins and to postulate the identification between the social
and the sacred. But this analysis, I argue, also confronted him with theoretical impasses. In particular, Durkheim's pursuit of the social as distinct
from politics created a void in his explanatory model that could not account for modern incarnations of the sacred in the aftermath of the First
World War. It also resulted in a partial and inadequate understanding of
the "primitives"' social formations.

The second part of the chapter turns to Marcel Mauss and theorizes
the ambiguities inherent in Durkheimian social analysis vis-à-vis the conceptualization of politics. Mauss, I contend, exposed the rich potential of
Durkheim's cultural approach to sociology and at the same time brought
to the fore the problematic nature of the separation Durkheim implied
of the social from the other value spheres. I discuss sacrifice as the key
concept in Mauss's attempt to explain the sacred nature of community, a
concept that pointed to the violent foundations of society. I also show
the link between Mauss's emphasis on the power of group ideas and his
focus on the concept of "total man" and, later, of "total social fact."
Mauss's analysis of the gift as a total social fact in particular addressed the
importance of a comprehensive view of reality that could overcome disciplinary divisions and separations and also underlined the need to assess the multiple dimensions of a social phenomenon. Innovative and
unorthodox, Mauss's sociological approach was, however, caught in contradictions, and I conclude the chapter with an assessment of both the
limits and potential of Mauss's theoretical model.

The chapter's ultimate aim is to sketch the path that Durkheim and
Mauss followed in their elaboration of sociology and that, by charging
the social with an exceptional power and making of it a meta-category,
led the two to thwart some of the cultural impetus at the roots of
their sociological vision. This was indeed the identical path followed by
the Collège. Driven by the same desire as Durkheim to revitalize the

collective bond, Bataille and his fellow members theorized a social in excess by elevating community above all values.

SOCIETY AS REPRESENTATION: ÉMILE DURKHEIM

In "Individual and Collective Representations," Durkheim's objective was to counteract associationist and epiphenomenalist explanations that grounded representations in physiology. In order to make his case, Durkheim hypostatized the psychic nature of social phenomena. More specifically, by focusing on the possibility that a mental fact could be unconscious, he affirmed that "the limits of consciousness are not the limits of all psychic activity."[12] That we do not perceive a mental fact does not mean that it has no independent reality, exclusive of the physiological substratum on which it builds. Indeed, "representational life extends beyond our present consciousness" and develops relations and reactions that are not immediately caused by their material substratum.[13] When we are dealing with mental activity, either conscious or unconscious, we are faced with psychic life, mental representations that have their own force and way of being, i.e., a relative autonomy.[14] If, as Durkheim had previously affirmed in *The Rules of Sociological Method*, social facts are independent of and external to individual minds, and if, when considered at the individual level, "representational life is not inherent in the intrinsic nature of nervous matter" but "is something quite new," then, analogically, Durkheim argued, collective representations do not immediately derive from the individuals who espouse them.[15] Representations rather constitute social facts that impose themselves upon the individual; we are unable to grasp them consciously, even if they occur in our minds.

At the beginning of "Individual and Collective Representations" Durkheim had specified that sociology could not be reduced to the mere corollary of individual psychology, but, in contrast to Comte, he did not reject the whole psychological realm. On the contrary, his theoretical effort to found a science of morality came to rely on psychology when the latter was intended as going beyond mere introspection. Durkheim's general argument about the epistemological importance of considering society as

---

12 "Individual and Collective Representations," in Durkheim, *Sociology and Philosophy*, 22.

13 Ibid., 23.

14 This perspective has become the foundation of the school of Durkheimian cultural sociology in the 1990s. See in particular Jeffrey Alexander's voluminous work. Like Durkheim, Alexander has tried to resolve the contradiction of the social and the individual.

15 "Individual and Collective Representations," in Durkheim, *Sociology and Philosophy*, 24.

something different from the sum of its individuals was indeed predicated
on the analogy between society, on one side, and psychological life seen in
its relative autonomy from cerebral cells, on the other.[16] Sociology constituted a sort of "collective psychology" that studied the mental life of people in communities as opposed to single individuals.[17] In Durkheim's
sociological parlance, sociology dealt with the *sui generis* synthesis resulting from the union of representations encountering each other.[18]

The rehabilitation of psychology initiated by Durkheim allowed him to
define sociology's specific task and mandate; it did not, however, help
him completely disentangle the complexity of the relationship between
the two sciences.[19] While the dividing line between psychology and sociology was the evident separation between individual and social, the way in
which the two constituted neighbouring fields implied more than a similarity of laws. The question was intricate; in his last essay on the definitional status of sociology, "The Dualism of Human Nature and Its Social
Conditions," Durkheim was still struggling with it.[20] In that essay, published in 1914, Durkheim contended that sociology could not dispense
with the individual, who after all constitutes the basic element of human
groups. Sociology could, however, contribute to the understanding of human nature through an empirical approach that probed the peculiarities
of individuals and, more specifically, their constitutional duality. By the
latter, Durkheim meant individuals' perennial perception of the coexistence in their being of two heterogeneous elements: body and soul. In
this perception, Durkheim argued, the body is material and involves the
senses – it is profane; the soul, in contrast, is ethereal and has dignity – it
belongs to the world of the sacred. Also, our sensory element appears
egoistic for it responds only to our needs as individuals. In contrast, the
sphere of moral activity, which is connected to conceptual thought,

16 In the preface to the first edition of *The Rules of Sociological Method*, Durkheim supported idealism's tenet that "psychological phenomena cannot be immediately derived
from organic phenomena," xxxix.

17 Durkheim also wrote that in the same way that individual representational life is characterized by *spirituality*, collective representations exude *hyper-spirituality*. See "Individual
and Collective Representations," in *Sociology and Philosophy*, 34.

18 In "Individual and Collective Representations," note 1, Durkheim wrote that one
could call individual psychology simply "psychology": collective psychology could then be
called sociology. Bouglé affirms that for Durkheim "sociology implies a new psychology
which will have at its center the observation of the collective consciousness." *Bilan de la
sociologie*, 7.

19 For an engaging discussion of this issue, see Bruno Karsenti, *L'homme total*.

20 The essay is published in Wolff, *Émile Durkheim 1858–1917*.

pursues impersonal ends.[21] Durkheim concluded that *homo duplex* is the combination of extreme egoism and moral disinterestedness, carnal desires and spiritual aims. Although he saw the two tendencies as in conflict, he affirmed the importance of understanding their interpenetration.

Why was Durkheim so invested in resolving the puzzle of human dualism? How did the problem of human antonymic tendencies help him in his theoretical endeavours to define the realm of sociology? The answer, I believe, again points to the centrality of representations in Durkheim's sociological project. More specifically, the puzzle of human dualism allowed Durkheim to prove the fundamentally superior nature of the social by way of the mediating role of collective representations. For collective representations elevate humans to the highest spheres of the ideal and make them feel part of a larger and superior whole. Yet, they can do so only through the solicitation of the individual's material, bodily dimension. Thus, to the question how humans could contemporaneously inhabit two contradictory realms, Durkheim not surprisingly replied that the answer resided in religion, where this dualism is always present via the distinction between soul and body or, more pertinently, sacred and profane. He pointed to sacred things and argued that if they are "collective ideals that have fixed themselves on material objects," this is because a vital force is generated by the fusion of individual consciousnesses into a common one, and this force makes us feel the superiority of ideas and sentiments elaborated collectively.[22] Collective representations engender our sense of the sacred through their embodiment in material objects that symbolize them and make them vivid. By uniting individuals in feelings of awe, concrete embodiments of the sacred give them the feeling of communicating with each other. This means that the ideal and the material, or the sacred and the profane, combine to enact the community.[23] Or one could rephrase the argument by saying that collective representations, which manifest the social and therefore the

21 According to Durkheim, concepts are regularly shared by a community of people if for no other reason than that the language we use to communicate them is social and not somebody's invention or unique possession.

22 "The Dualism of Human Nature," in Wolff, *Émile Durkheim 1858–1917*, 335. The essay was a response to what Durkheim felt was a botched understanding of his argument in *The Elementary Forms*.

23 According to Bouglé, *Bilan de la sociologie*, 29, even Bergson, who is normally depicted as representing the antinomy of Durkheim's project, recognized the critical, though not central, role social life plays in the world of spirit and in the understanding of human intelligence. Some think that Bergsonian philosophy and Durkheim's sociology shared common elements, including the rejection of crass materialism. See Riley, "Durkheim Contra Bergson?"

sacred, are equivalent to communication through material symbols: representations symbolize the structure of society at the same time as they sanctify it.

With the discussion of human dualism, Durkheim reaffirmed his long-standing belief in religion's ability to resolve the antithesis between individual and group through the medium of representations. When beliefs and practices impose themselves on the collectivity, they manifest a power that does not derive from individual ideas but rather originates from some external source, an unknown force.[24] And he insisted, "If societies are organisms, they are distinguished from purely physical organisms in that they are essentially consciousnesses (*consciences*). They are nothing if not systems of representations."[25] Durkheim defined societies as "living consciousnesses, organisms of ideas." This definition allowed him to interpret the social as a "self" (*un moi*) that, like the individual, is produced by a coalescence of representations and is driven by affective forces. Once again aligning sociology with psychology, Durkheim stated that they were "both representations, emotions, impulses which are grouped and organized."[26] The life of society was of a "psychic order," Durkheim ultimately concluded, and the task of sociology was to study how collective representations formed and combined with each other to give shape to the social.

In her history of psychoanalysis in France, Elisabeth Roudinesco explains France's resistance to psychoanalysis in part by the success of psychological theories that remained attached to philosophical ideas founded on the primacy of consciousness as opposed to a "dynamic" unconscious.[27] Within this interpretive framework, one could say that Durkheim followed current French psychology in assigning consciousness a primary role, though Durkheimians related it to the group, not the individual. Durkheim's recourse to consciousness, however, complicated his attempt at overcoming duality; and he could resolve the theoretical conflict between individual and society only by resorting to a deindividualized social nucleus in the guise of the "primitives." Here lies

24 "Sociology in France in the Nineteenth Century," in Durkheim, *On Morality and Society*, 18.

25 Ibid., 13. See also Durkheim's letter to Mauss of 18 June 1894 in which he announced the possibility of teaching a course of psychology the following year. Durkheim, *Lettres à Marcel Mauss*, 34–6. The difficulty of translating the French *conscience* in English has been raised by several translators and interpreters of Durkheim. In general, though, translations have rendered *conscience* as consciousness and for the sake of consistency I have mostly followed the translators' choice.

26 "Sociology in France in the Nineteenth Century," in Durkheim, *On Morality and Society*, 14.

27 Roudinesco, *Jacques Lacan and Co.*, 223.

the crux of the matter; Durkheim took the "primitives" as a licence to avoid the complexities of the individual/social polarity – complexities that were much more at play in modern societies than in archaic ones. What, then, did the choice to focus on the "primitives" cost Durkheim's explanatory model?

Encountering the Primitives

In the 1901–02 issue of *L'Année sociologique*, a journal mainly devoted to book reviews and founded by Durkheim in 1896, Durkheim wrote a short essay on forms of classification that was intended as a further contribution to the study of representations.[28] The essay, which he co-authored with Mauss, demonstrated Durkheim's interest in examining the "primitives" in order to classify and explain general sociological phenomena, an interest already evident in *L'Année sociologique*'s focus.[29] Before writing *Primitive Classification*, Durkheim had also engaged with ethnographic material in essays on totemism and on the prohibition of incest.[30] However, only with *Primitive Classification* did Durkheim's parallel interests in the "primitives" and representation begin to combine and rise to occupy a critical place in his theoretical project on the social.

The essay started with a commentary on the developments of psychological research, which, according to Durkheim and Mauss, had made possible a more sophisticated understanding of representations.[31] The essay then continued by stating the importance of considering logical operations as complex phenomena that involved more than a given individual faculty. Durkheim and Mauss pledged to uncover the social origins of classificatory functions and claimed that such functions have a history and even a prehistory. If, in the beginning, humanity had lacked "the most indispensable conditions for the classificatory function,"[32] we

28 The first issue of the journal was, however, published in 1898. *L'Année sociologique* was a gathering point for young scholars working on sociological issues along the lines Durkheim was tracing. The journal included among its members Marcel Mauss, Henri Hubert, Robert Hertz, Célestin Bouglé, Maurice Halbwachs, André Durkheim, and several others. Most of the younger members died as soldiers in the First World War, including Durkheim's son André. On *L'Année sociologique*, see Philippe Besnard, *The Sociological Domain*.

29 Durkheim and Mauss, *Primitive Classification*. The essay was originally titled "De quelques formes primitives de classification: contribution à l'étude des représentations collectives," "On Some Primitive Forms of Classification: Contribution to the Study of Collective Representations."

30 See "La prohibition de l'inceste et ses origines," now in Durkheim, *Journal sociologique*, 315–52.

31 This theme reappears almost verbatim in other writings of Durkheim.

32 Mauss and Durkheim, *Primitive Classification*, 7.

would not be able to account for our contemporary classification schemes, they maintained, and they pointed to primary classifications as "the most rudimentary" and original.[33] In an evolutionist manner, although in principle free of evaluative judgments, Durkheim and Mauss affirmed that, from the methodological viewpoint, the study of "primitive" societies made possible an understanding of the progressive composition of a social phenomenon. Spurred by an interest in the condition of human nature, as well as its representations, they resorted to the "genetic" factor as a guiding element for selecting their research site. [34] The study of "primitives" would make it possible for them to retrace and reveal the origins in early social forms of the ideals produced by society.[35]

While I will examine later the substantive argument that Durkheim and Mauss developed to account for the modalities of primitive classification, we can begin to remark the curiously crucial role that ethnography played in the overall Durkheimian sociological project. For, as Victor Karady remarks, the Durkheimians' interest in archaic societies was paradoxical. If, on the one hand, their main concern was the crisis of modern societies, on the other hand, they spent an inordinate amount of time dealing with societies "without history" and studying the logic and functioning of "primitive" formations.[36] This orientation is even more disconcerting if we consider that, before founding *L'Année sociologique* in 1896, Durkheim had not been favourably inclined toward ethnological studies. Because he deemed comparative analysis central to the sociological enterprise, he preferred to entrust history with the task of supporting sociological research. French anthropology in its ethnographic orientation was roughly equivalent to a "simplistic" social philosophy, especially in the case of its main representative, Charles Letourneau.[37] It

33 Ibid., 9.

34 On this issue, see *The Rules of Sociological Method*, 138.

35 As Mauss and Durkheim wrote, "It was because men were grouped, and thought of themselves in the form of groups, that in their ideas they grouped other things ..." *Primitive Classification*, 82.

36 Karady, "Durkheim et les débuts de l'ethnologie universitaire" (1988), now in Hamilton, *Émile Durkheim*, 7: 139. In "Divisions et proportions des divisions de la sociologie" (1927), Mauss seemed to be aware of the issue as he noted that with regard to religion "we study, perhaps too much, the 'primitives' and not sufficiently the great religions, our religions." See *Œuvres*, 3: 200. See English translation in Mauss, *The Nature of Sociology*. For another angle on this question see Faublée, "L'École sociologique française et l'étude des religions dites 'primitives.'"

37 See "L'état actuel des études sociologiques en France" (1895), in Durkheim, *Textes*, 1: 73–108. Durkheim refers in particular to the Société d'anthropologie de Paris, founded by Paul Broca (on the Société, see chapter 2 of this book).

dealt with societies that, since they lacked objectified forms of customs and laws, were not amenable to objective comparisons. Sociology, in contrast, "must direct its research mainly towards the societies that one can study on the basis of truly historical documents; ethnographic information could only be used to corroborate, and in part illuminate, those documents."[38]

A few years later, Durkheim had evidently changed his opinion on the value of ethnography, partly due to his genetic understanding of social types. For Durkheim, complexity was the product of historical development and, because he assumed the identification of historical primacy with simplicity, he believed that in order to explain later developments one needed to examine basic types.[39] Since he shared with his era the belief that contemporary "primitive" societies constituted the most ancient societies, historically speaking, even if at the same time he fought unilinear evolutionism, Durkheim equated simplicity with the archaic.[40] By the end of the 1890s, he was ready to accept that the problems inherent in ethnological research were not as severe as he had previously deemed them.[41]

One should also add that Durkheim's interest in ethnology was not merely a function of methodological insights or theoretical postulates; it was also linked to his increasing focus on religion. We know that Durkheim's 1894–95 lecture course on religion marked an intellectual turn in his sociological perspective, which he vividly portrayed in a letter:

38 Ibid., 77–8. Durkheim criticized the use of disparate sources, especially travel tales, for studying primitive societies.

39 "Sociologie et sciences sociales," in Durkheim, *Textes*, 1: 143. According to Condominas, Mauss was responsible for Durkheim's change of mind on this question. See his "Marcel Mauss, père de l'ethnographie française."

40 For one contradictory statement, see Durkheim's preface to the second edition of *The Rules of Sociological Method*, where he writes that sociologists "refuse to explain the complex in terms of the simple," xxxix.

41 In a 1904 review of S.-R. Steinmetz' book *Die Bedeutung der Ethnologie für die Soziologie* (The Meaning of Ethnology for Sociology), Durkheim stated that ethnography helps us "understand our own evolution," especially because, contrary to history, it engages with still living people." See Durkheim, "Ethnographie et sociologie" (1904), in *Textes*, 1: 256. See also "Débats sur les rapports de l'ethnologie et la sociologie" (1907), in *Textes*, vol. 1 and *The Elementary Forms of Religious Life*, where Durkheim writes that "ethnography has often brought about the most fertile revolutions in the various branches of sociology," 6. *Les Formes élémentaires de la vie religieuse. Le système totémique en Australie* was first published in 1912. I will be using the 1998 edition. For the English edition, I will refer to *The Elementary Forms of Religious Life*, translated by Karen E. Fields. It should be added that some of the most notable Durkheimians were mainly and primarily concerned with ethnology. *L'Année sociologique* predominantly covered reviews of ethnological works and engaged in a debate over the interpretation of "primitive" societies and cultures.

"[I]t was not until 1895 that I achieved a clear view of the essential role played by religion in social life. It was in that year that, for the first time, I found the means of tackling the study of religion sociologically. This was a revelation to me. That course of 1895 marked a dividing line in the development of my thought ... entirely due to the studies of religious history which I had just undertaken, and notably to the reading of the works of Robertson Smith and his school."[42]

Robertson Smith's *Lectures on the Religion of the Semites* has been widely acknowledged as one of the most influential texts of its time,[43] and Mauss and Hubert, in charge of the *L'Année sociologique*'s section of religious sociology, also took it as an inspiration for their work on sacrifice.[44] One could, of course, argue that, considering his stated intention to build a science of morality and the tight link he saw between morality and religion, Durkheim's thinking revolved around religion before his encounter with Robertson Smith's work.[45] In this sense, Durkheim's uncoalesced concerns with "religious facts" ran parallel with, if they did not actually precede, his inclination toward ethnology. Yet, the catapulting of religion to first place in Durkheim's sociological system was due to two interconnected theses that the French thinker, inspired by Robertson Smith, embraced: first, religion is a social phenomenon;[46] second, and

42 Lettres au Directeur de la *Revue Néo-scholastique*, cited in Lukes, *Émile Durkheim*, 237. Lukes traces Durkheim's original thoughts on religion to 1886 and discusses the transformations these thoughts underwent following Robertson Smith's own understanding of religion's social nature. Robertson Smith was among the first to indicate the social nature of religion by focusing on ritual practices. Durkheim's theory of religion benefitted from reading Robertson Smith and Lukes writes about "the thinness and inconclusiveness of Durkheim's previous observations on religion." *Émile Durkheim*, 238.

43 The book was first published in 1889; a second edition followed in 1894.

44 See Hubert and Mauss, "Essai sur la nature et la fonction du sacrifice" (1899), in Marcel Mauss, *Œuvres*, vol. 1, English translation as *Sacrifice: Its Nature and Function*. In a December 1897 letter to Mauss, Durkheim volunteered to help him and Hubert write the first part of their essay on sacrifice, which he assumed would deal with Robertson Smith's theory. See Durkheim, *Lettres à Marcel Mauss*, 89–91. In the same letter Durkheim wrote that emphasizing the "sociological importance of the religious phenomenon is the culmination of all that I have done" (91).

45 See Durkheim's lectures on moral education delivered between 1889 and 1912, some of which appear in *Moral Education*. The book is based on the course Durkheim offered at the Sorbonne in 1902–03. According to Durkheim, religion and moral order "have been too inextricably bound together in history." *Moral Education*, 8.

46 As Lukes aptly put it, religion for Durkheim became "*the* primitive social phenomenon." See Lukes, *Émile Durkheim*, 240.

here is religion's link to the "primitives," religion contains in confused combination all the elements that are at the origins of collective life.[47]

Durkheim developed these theses in 1897–98 when, after discussing several definitions of religion, he proposed examining religious phenomena as "obligatory beliefs as well as the practices relative to the objects contained in these beliefs."[48] Durkheim claimed that religion originates in collective states, common emotions, and traditions, not in individual feelings, and he insisted on the material embodiments of the sacred.[49] As he hypostasized the correspondence between sacred and social, Durkheim was then confronted with the question of how collective representations develop and come to be embodied materially. A central element of his writings on religion, this issue became crucial to the argument advanced in *The Elementary Forms of Religious Life*. There, spurred by his faith in the genetic approach, Durkheim relied on ethnographic research on the "primitives" to explore the sacredness of the social and elucidate the meaning conveyed by religion's symbolic representations.[50] As it turns out, he also made the case that the social was tightly entwined with the sacred by highlighting the emotional side of human nature.

The Sacred, or the Political Absent

In the introduction to *The Elementary Forms of Religious Life*, Durkheim declared that all religions are comparable. They are all "species within the same genus" and all contain fundamental representations and ritual attitudes which, though taking different shapes, share with each other similar meanings and functions.[51] To begin with, all religions operate with the same classification of real and ideal things into two heterogeneous and mutually exclusive categories: the profane and the sacred. Furthermore, all religions have rituals that prescribe rules of conduct for

47 See Durkheim's preface to volume 2 of *L'Année sociologique* in *Journal sociologique*, 138: "Religion contains in itself, since the beginning, but in a confused state, all the elements that, in the process of dissociating and determining themselves and of combining with each other in multiple ways, have generated the diverse manifestations of collective life."

48 Durkheim, "De la définition des phénomènes religieux," in *Journal sociologique*, 158.

49 Lukes discusses what this definition of religion as more obligatory than other social phenomena achieved for Durkheim. See Lukes, *Émile Durkheim*, 241.

50 For a general discussion of Durkheim's study of religion, see Sumpf, "Durkheim et le problème de l'étude sociologique de la religion."

51 Durkheim, *The Elementary Forms of Religious Life* (*EF*), 4; *Les Formes élémentaires de la vie religieuse* (*FE*), 6.

the individual believer; prohibitions apply to profane things and serve to protect and isolate the world of the sacred. Finally, Durkheim emphasized that religious beliefs are shared by a collectivity; individuals feel connected to each other through their adherence to a common faith. The moral community thus formed constitutes a church whose necessary presence indicates religion's eminently collective character.[52]

Having postulated that all religions are comparable, Durkheim pledged to examine "the simplest and most primitive religion" that is known: totemism.[53] Through a discussion of central Australia's clans and by relying on several ethnographic accounts of the time, he explored the general sociological meaning of the religious realm. Whether he was correct in classifying totemism as a religion, or failed to assess the elementary status of the Australian strand of totemism, as some critics maintain, the value of his classic interpretation of totemic beliefs rested on a theory of religion's transfigured character; under Durkheim's pen, religion came to stand for the social while also constructing it.[54] In the first interpretive move in this direction, Durkheim focused on the totem. He concluded that, since every object that is marked with an image of the totem becomes sacred and since the material things from which the totem takes its name are also considered sacred, the members of the clan united under a specific totem are sacred too.[55] He argued that there must be an attribute they all share that helps them acquire a sacred character. There exists an anonymous, impersonal force, an energy that evokes the cult and exercises a strong authority over the participants in the cult. Durkheim adopted the Melanesian term *mana* to refer to such force and insisted on its impersonality, ubiquity, anonymity, and indefiniteness.[56]

After establishing this first point, Durkheim went on to ask: How did "primitive" societies come up with the idea of a force that penetrates people and things? He replied that since totemic representations are more important than the actual plant or animal that gives the clan its

52 According to this definition of religion, as Durkheim writes in *EF*, 44n68 (*FE*, 65–6n1), the group character of belief is more crucial than the issue of obligation. The latter comes automatically once one is part of a group.

53 Durkheim, *EF*, 21; *FE*, 31.

54 Durkheim here sketches a sophisticated approach to culture beginning in chapter 1 of book 2. On the sacred in Durkheim, see Isambert, "L'élaboration de la notion de sacré dans l'école durkheimienne."

55 As a methodological puzzle, it might be worth noting that in Australia the totemic images do not immediately appear as imitations, but instead consist of lines and geometric drawings.

56 Durkheim adopts Robert Codrington's definition of mana. See *EF*, 196–9; *FE*, 277–8.

name, the totem is first a symbol, an expression of something else. The totem stands for the totemic principle, for god; and since the totem is also the symbol of the clan and distinguishes clans from one another, the totem represents society, because god and society are ultimately one and the same.[57] "[T]he god of the clan, the totemic principle, can be none other than the clan itself, but the clan transfigured (*hypostasié*)."[58] Like god, society is superior to the individual who feels dependent on it; we submit to its rules even if they go against our instincts or desires, and we forget our interests and sacrifice ourselves for it. Society exercises moral power over us.

How does society acquire such power over its members or, in the specific case examined by Durkheim, over the "primitives"? Durkheim approached this question through recourse to the emotional side of human nature. As we sense a current of psychic energy investing our will and plying it accordingly, we act out of respect, he claimed. Such respect, however, is not based on reason or logical thinking. Rather, it emerges from an emotion that we feel and that moves us; it originates from the intensity of the mental state in which we find ourselves when receiving a certain suggestion or an order to act.[59] Since social pressure occurs through mental means (and is not material), we are led to believe that we depend on forces that exist outside us and we fail to see the connection of these forces to society. We thus create representations that transmute these social forces; in the case of the "primitives," mythical thinking is an act of transfiguration and misrecognizes the social by substituting mana for the moral authority of the collectivity.

Again upholding the central role of representations for building social ties, Durkheim emphasized that we become aware of the psychic energy elevating us and influencing our behaviour only when we are with others and feel the solicitation of the senses.[60] Religion empowers us when we perceive this sentiment directly, that is, when the social is truly lived as such, experienced in its full force and extent at assemblies and meetings, reunions and celebrations. Then, body and mind work in tandem to assert the sacredness of the social, and both body and mind are carried away by emotions. In a famous section of *The Elementary Forms,*

57 Lévi-Strauss disagrees with Durkheim's theory of symbolism as originating from society and instead sees it the other way around. See "La sociologie française."

58 Durkheim, *EF,* 208; *FE,* 295.

59 Moral authority, after all, depends on opinion, which Durkheim takes to be the social thing par excellence. "Opinion, eminently a social thing, is one source of authority," *EF,* 210; *FE,* 298.

60 Durkheim expressed the idea of the believer as a man "*qui peut davantage,*" that is, "who is capable of more," in *Textes,* 23 (italicized in the original).

for example, Durkheim describes the ceremony of corrobori – an occasion in which the uniformity and monotony of ordinary daily existence are replaced by an excitement that Durkheim ascribes to the physical contact in an assembly.[61] In this atmosphere, a sort of electricity circulates among the members of the clan and multiplies the palpable emotional intensity. An avalanche effect unfolds in which cries, noises, and screams grow to a point that Durkheim describes as "effervescence." It is during effervescence that the individuals give shape, content, and form to the several stimulations and suggestions that they have experienced in the hyper-excitement of the gathering. It is in the midst of this effervescence that the collective representation of religion emerges. More generally, it is within this ebullient climate that the religious idea is born.[62] As Durkheim had already argued in his article on individual and collective representations, ideas have power even if we are not conscious of them.[63] In the case of Australia, a strong and inescapable sense of society as the ultimate sacred ensues from the clan members' physical sensing of their own unity.[64]

To summarize the argument so far, Durkheim developed the theory that society needs to be evaluated as a community united by ideas – an ensemble of representations. For Durkheim, representations constituted social facts; thus, knowledge of psychological life was critical for formulating a science of morals. The epistemological challenge was how to reconcile sociology with psychology, or how to account for the duality of human nature – our simultaneous inhabiting of the material and spiritual worlds. Durkheim's solution was to identify religion and its binary differentiation of sacred and profane as the source of human duality. Within this context, Durkheim addressed the role of the body and mate-

---

61 Durkheim wrote that the "very act of congregating is an exceptionally powerful stimulant." *EF*, 217; *FE*, 308. One should add that the corrobori is accessible to women and the non-initiated, and Durkheim distinguishes it from a religious ceremony. See *EF*, 217n23; *FE*, 307n3.

62 "It is in these effervescent social milieux, and indeed from that very effervescence, that the religious idea seems to have been born," *EF*, 220; *FE*, 313. The notion of effervescence has been central to the current revival of Durkheimian studies. For a reflection on the notion's explanatory power see Ramp, "Effervescence, Differentiation and Representation in *The Elementary Forms*."

63 As Durkheim wrote, during festivals, clan members sense that superior, external forces are pulling them, and they imagine these forces to be in the guise of the totem that surrounds them at the celebratory events. They are not able to recognize that the sense of being transformed is provoked by the clan and that the forces they identify with the totem come from "feeling" the collectivity. What they see as powerful is religion through its totemic representations and material incarnations. *EF*, book 3, chapter 2.

64 See Friedland, "Drag Kings at the Totem Ball."

rial objects in the development of collective representations and described the power of symbols to enact the community.[65] *The Elementary Forms*, in particular, pointed to the mediating capacity of symbols to transfigure feelings; it also emphasized the critical role of ceremonies and cults for creating a sacred sense of togetherness. Research on the "primitives," more specifically on the people socially organized in clans, allowed Durkheim to argue that the transfiguration of the social occurred through religious beliefs and practices. When we are worshipping the gods, Durkheim argued, we are worshipping ourselves.[66] He thus affirmed the sacred nature of the social by drawing from archaic societies in which, according to his analysis, the effects of collective consciousness were pre-eminent and binding. He then elevated the primacy of the social to a general principle that encompassed all forms of social life, including the modern.

However, was Durkheim's model of the social as seamless as he made it appear in his narrative about the Australian clans? Was it effective when applied to contexts other than the "primitive" (Durkheim was the first to recognize that moments of collective effervescence are much rarer in modernity)?[67] These questions reveal the incongruities of Durkheim's model. First, Durkheim provided a very limited if non-existent discussion of the potential deficiencies of his model of the social. Second, he failed to account for the potential impact of factors other than, or in addition to, the unanimity of emotions postulated in the Australian example on the formation of collective consciousness. Conversely, he ignored the possibility that emotions can also be manipulated and do not always erupt spontaneously. In other words, I am arguing that Durkheim's interpretive model isolated the social from the political, as well as the "primitive" from the modern. He thus offered a sociological explanation of life in common that ultimately assigned the social a factotum status – an omnipotent role – and that expressed a partial or distorted vision of

65 On Durkheim and symbols, see Tarot, *De Durkheim à Mauss*, and Karsenti, *L'homme total.* Both Tarot and Karsenti hold that a theory of symbols remains underdeveloped in Durkheim, and Karsenti also argues that representations were more central than symbols to Durkheim's project.

66 According to Durkheim, we do not realize that the gods would not exist without the faithful who worship them. On this point, he differed from Robertson Smith. See Jones, "Robertson Smith, Durkheim and Sacrifice."

67 Durkheim refers to the French Revolution as one of the privileged social moments of sacred creations in modernity, the one in which no transfiguration takes place and where the process of society's sacralization is transparent. *EF*, 216; *FE*, 306. For illuminating comments on other aspects of *The Elementary Forms*, see Allen, Pickering, and Miller, *On Durkheim's* Elementary Forms of Religious Life.

historical processes, especially with regard to archaic societies.[68] In the particular case of the Australians, for instance, Durkheim considered the clan the social organization that defined the group but he ignored the clan's internal relations and power structure, focusing instead on how the clan evoked the numinous.[69] He seemed to assume that the "primitives" were immune to political dynamics, or that among them conflicts could be resolved via the meta-power of an emotionally charged collective consciousness. He thus saw effervescence as guaranteeing social cohesion in contrast to the model of social unity based on force and obedience. But he stopped short of evaluating the different outcomes that emotional unity can generate, and he took "community" as a supreme value no matter its form. The appeal of community led Durkheim to deflect political questions with the result that he failed to see the political implications of his own theorizing at the dawn of totalitarian movements and their offerings of communal bonding.

This is not to deny that Durkheim was an engaged and committed sociologist who was particularly interested in shaking the apathy that characterized people's political attitudes under the Third Republic.[70] According to Georges Davy, Durkheim believed that there was "no philosophy that does not end up having a *political and social application* and

68 An early example of missed opportunity emerges in "L'état, la morale et le militarisme," in *Textes*, 3: 160–3. In this analysis of the army and its fate in France after the 1870 defeat, Durkheim warned about the emergent cult of the army as "intangible and sacred," where by sacred he meant "not subject to the critique of reason." He then connected the notion of sacred to nationalism, which he distinguished from patriotism, but stopped short of generalizing the larger political dimensions of the sacred.

69 In writings such as "De la définition des phénomènes religieux," for example, Durkheim stated that the forms the sacred takes are the extension of public institutions. See "De la définition des phénomènes religieux," in *Journal sociologique*, 165. In an important section of his course on the origins of religious life, he argued that "society organized in clans ... is democratic; all the individuals in it are equal." See "Cours sur les origines de la vie religieuse" (1907), in *Textes*, 2: 98. Bouglé goes as far as to say that for Durkheim the clan is more a political than a domestic unit. Bouglé, *Bilan de la sociologie française contemporaine*, chapter "Ethnologie et sociologie," 44.

70 Durkheim's engagement in the Dreyfus affair is renowned. Lukes, however, writes that "both Georges Davy and Henri Durkheim agree that Durkheim's attitude to the *Affaire* was 'moral,' rather than 'narrowly political'; nor did he see it explicitly as a Jew." Lukes also argues that "it was his pedagogy lectures to future schoolteachers and his efforts to develop a national system of secular education ... that constituted his only direct contribution to the social regeneration he wished to bring about." *Émile Durkheim*, 333, 330–1. See Durkheim, "Individualism and the Intellectuals" in *Émile Durkheim, On Morality and Society* for a more engaged discussion of contemporary political and social issues. On Durkheim's specific relation to socialism, see Filloux, *Durkheim et le socialisme*. On Durkheim's relation to the cultural and political context of the Third Republic, see Surkis, *Sexing the Citizen*, and Joan Scott, *Only Paradoxes to Offer*.

inversely no politics without a philosophical foundation."[71] However, I hold that Durkheim's identification of politics with current events led him to a self-declared alienation from political analysis even though testimonials to his desire for a grander politics reveal that he was far from being a detached commentator.[72] Durkheim intended to shelter sociology from accusations of being unscientific and in his eyes this eventuality could be avoided only by giving up politics[73] – a sacrifice that was in turn contingent upon a limited understanding of politics as engagement in public affairs. Within this restricted meaning, it was inevitable that Durkheim would ignore the potential political ramifications of his theory of the social.[74] He thus missed the chance to inscribe the political within his sociological system and neglected the importance of the political in constituting the social, although such a relationship was implicit in his cultural approach to sociality.

What emerges from Durkheim's theory of society as sacred is then a cultural approach that rotates around affectivity, as is evident in the conclusions to *Primitive Classification*. Here Durkheim and Mauss argued that primitive classifications, not unlike scientific, are "systems of hierarchized notions" with "a purely speculative purpose."[75] Accordingly, knowledge is separated from both functions and interests. Although social relations model the classification of things and provide a schema through which classifications can be effected, the objective of primitive classification, Durkheim and Mauss claimed, was to connect ideas and unify knowledge, not to respond to practical concerns. Affective, as opposed to logical,

71 Cited in Lacroix, *Durkheim et le politique*, 35 (italicized in the original).

72 Maurice Holleaux remembers Durkheim saying that "politics had become in our days 'a thing so small and mediocre.' He always wanted it to be a big thing." Cited in Lukes, *Emile Durkheim*, 47. Anthony Giddens has persuasively argued that a link connects Durkheim's examination of the modern political system to his theory of moral authority. See Giddens, "Durkheim's Political Sociology." See also Barnes, "Durkheim's Contribution to the Reconstruction of Political Theory." For a critique of Giddens, see Hawkins, "Émile Durkheim on Democracy and Absolutism."

73 For some discussion of this issue, see Favre, "The Absence of Political Sociology in the Durkheimian Classification of the Social Sciences." On the fate of politics in early sociology, see Poggi, "The Place of Political Concerns in the Early Social Sciences."

74 In *Durkheim et le politique*, Lacroix claims that since for Durkheim the object of sociology was society incarnated in the state and endowed with a national culture, his sociological enterprise was fundamentally political in nature. Lacroix's examination of Durkheim's work particularly emphasizes the role of beliefs in power relations. Although Lacroix neglects the larger impact of rituals and practices in creating social unity, his call for redefining the political in Durkheim indicates the need to conceive of politics by moving beyond an analysis of the state and political power strictly defined. See also Richman, *Sacred Revolutions*.

75 Durkheim and Mauss, *Primitive Classification*, 81.

elements guide classifications; states of the collective spirit determine how things are grouped. Or, as Durkheim and Mauss wrote, "the same sentiments which are the basis of domestic, social, and other kinds of organization have been effective in this logical division of things also."[76] What individuals feel about things and how things affect them emotionally in a group determines the way in which they organize them; "it is this emotional value of notions which plays the preponderant part in the manner in which ideas are connected or separated. It is the dominant characteristic in classification."[77] In this sense, *Primitive Classification* affirmed the psychological impulse at the root of Durkheim's sociological project and displayed Durkheim's idea of the sacred/social as distant from the utilitarian and materialistic needs that dominate the realm of our "vulgar" existence – the profane.[78] For, indeed, as Durkheim and Mauss claimed in their critique of James Frazer's interpretation of totemism as "economic enterprise," there is no practical purpose to classification in terms of its origins: classification comes from the social, that is, the sacred. [79] One cannot explain human social behaviour on the basis of *homo economicus.*

Durkheim and Mauss recognized the importance of *homo symbolicus* for making sense of the social and affirmed the idea of the sacred as non-practical and linked to affectivity.[80] Rooted in analysis of the "primitives," their cultural understanding of sociality downplayed the prominence of

---

76 Ibid., 85.

77 Ibid., 86.

78 Durkheim, *EF,* 311; *FE,* 437.

79 On Durkheim's and Mauss's critique of Frazer, see Durkheim, "Sur le totémisme," in *Journal sociologique,* especially 319; Durkheim and Mauss's book review of Sir James Frazer's *Totemism and Exogamy*; and Durkheim's *Les formes élémentaires de la vie religieuse* for *L'Année sociologique* 12 (1909–12), now in *Journal sociologique,* 700–7. See also Mauss, "Notes sur le totémisme" (1905) and "Le totémisme et les origins de la religion selon Frazer" (1907), in *Œuvres,* 1: 162–4 and 180–3. According to Frazer, the Intichiuma ceremony of the Aruntas had the function of ensuring the means of subsistence for the tribe, as the different totemic groups engaged in work to increase each other's food resources through exchange. Groups expected the ritual, which relied on magic, to guarantee a positive outcome. The profit that the ritual was supposed to bring was not personal or direct but based on a principle of reciprocity. Frazer, however, interpreted the totemic group as an "industrial association." Although he maintained that the rituals' technique was borrowed from magic, not from economics, magic for Frazer was distant from religion and had a practical orientation – a position that Durkheim and Mauss rejected.

80 Durkheim subscribed to the "logic of feelings" argument. See his review of Théodule Ribot's *La logique des sentiments,* in which, citing Ribot, he wrote that "human groups form and are maintained by the community of beliefs, opinions, prejudices, and … it is this logic of feelings which is necessary to create and defend them." To this citation, Durkheim added, "The logic of feeling is this other logic that the scholar ignores and yet it has played and

interest in human action and offered a rich portrait of the emotional drives that motivate individuals to feel connected within a community. Having identified the central role of affect in creating the social, their genetic approach, nevertheless, left unanswered a whole set of questions about historical forms of institutionalization of the social, especially in modernity. For Durkheim, in particular, the social remained an overarching, all-powerful concept that seemed to operate above and independently of other spheres. Because Durkheim deemed community a supreme value, he then neglected to interrogate the different shapes that community can take and also left aside the question of how emotions can be reconciled with reason. Thus he failed to complement his brilliant intuition of community's affective roots and the power of representations with an adequate analysis of social structures and political relations within a specific social formation.

Mauss's notable interpretation of *The Gift* complicated Durkheim's approach to the sacred; in the process of affirming his own particular perspective on *homo symbolicus,* Mauss provided stronger support for Durkheim's thesis of the role of representations in constructing community. He also reintroduced the political into the Durkheimian vision of a social that was meant to be cleansed of all politics. Although he was unable to sustain fully his innovative theorizing and fell back into Durkheim's original aporias, Mauss's attempt to expand our understanding of social phenomena testifies to the power of the Durkheimians' interpretation of the social as well as to the limits of their analytical approach. For both Durkheim and Mauss, accounting for the emotional dynamics at the heart of sociality remained an unfinished work.

THE SOCIAL AS SYMBOLIC COMMUNICATION: MARCEL MAUSS

As his uncle's closest collaborator and the one who bore the responsibility of the Durkheimian school's legacy after Durkheim's death in 1917, Mauss pursued an intellectual itinerary that reflected Durkheim's scholarly preoccupations while also steering social interpretation in new directions.[81] Much more involved than Durkheim in ethnographic material and the history and development of religions, much less a grand

---

still plays a considerable role in life." See *L'Année sociologique* 9 (1904–05), now in *Journal sociologique,* 533.

81 Mauss was, however, less systematic than Durkheim. In an interview he declared, "[M]y theories are scattered and unsystematic, and there is nowhere that one can find them summarized." See Murray, "A 1934 Interview with Marcel Mauss," 165. On different aspects of Mauss's work, see James and Allen, *Marcel Mauss.* I am aware of the risks one incurs when referring to a "Durkheimian school" since this notion presumes a coherence of

theorist, Mauss formulated cultural notions with extraordinary impact on those who followed his teachings, including members of the Collège. And yet, although his "total" vision of social facts greatly enhanced Durkheim's intellectual bequest in the aftermath of World War I, he never renounced his uncle's sociological framework.[82] Amid a general revolt against Durkheim's sociology in France in the 1920s and 1930s, Mauss continued to promote and clarify Durkheim's thought and writings, and he kept alive the passion and excitement that had fuelled the Durkheimians' original interest in sociological understanding.[83]

Two articles on the definition of the sociological field written years apart demonstrate Mauss's faithfulness to Durkheim's trajectory. His 1901 entry "Sociologie," written in collaboration with Paul Fauconnet for the *Grande Encyclopédie*, followed Durkheim's main methodological and theoretical tenets and argued for the specificity of the sociological domain. "[S]ocial phenomena are the manifestations of the life of groups as groups," the article claimed.[84] And it continued by asserting that social phenomena do not mirror individual behaviour; they are embedded in institutions, including uses, customs, and superstitions as well as political and juridical organizations, and they should be considered as living and dynamic entities.

Mauss and Fauconnet sought to delineate a definitive space for the emerging science of sociology. To this end, they focused on sociology's relationship to psychology while disclaiming an individualized perspective, and they proposed that social life is fundamentally an "ensemble of representations" which constitute expressions of social groups and have society as their object.[85] Thus, collective representations contain psychic life of a different order from the one present in the individual because collective representations symbolize the structure, feeling, and modes of behaviour of a social group. As Durkheim had already warned, collective

---

programs and ideas not always confirmed in reality. For a discussion of this issue, see Besnard, "Présentation."

82 See Mauss's account in "L'œuvre de Mauss par lui même," 219; English translation, "An Intellectual Self-Portrait," in Besnard, *The Sociological Domain*.

83 Ibid.

84 Fauconnet and Mauss, "Sociologie" (1901), in Mauss, *Œuvres*, 3: 153. Mauss also affirmed that sociology deals with humans and not animals. See his discussion in "Rapports réels et pratiques de la psychologie et de la sociologie" (1930), in *Sociologie et anthropologie*, especially 285–6. See English translation, *Sociology and Psychology*. See also in *Œuvres*, 3: 297n1.

85 Fauconnet and Mauss, "Sociologie," *Œuvres*, 3: 160.

beliefs and feelings were not to be gauged by knowledge of individual psychology: the individual could by no means explain the social.

Years later, Mauss's 1927 article for *L'Année sociologique*'s new series revisited the main components of Durkheim's approach to sociology and reconfirmed the critical role representations played in the science of the social.[86] Mauss criticized the use of the term "physiology" in sociological studies, arguing that, on the one hand, the term evoked the metaphor of the social organism and, on the other, it failed to express in a clear manner what is "conscious, sentimental, ideal, voluntary, and arbitrary in the efforts and traditions of those collectivities of men that constitute societies."[87] Equally wary about the risk of substituting psychology for physiology, Mauss pointed to the limits of psychology: it eliminates the material side of social life, specifically the two important characteristics that distinguish a social fact – commonality and history. In spite of this critique, however, Mauss emphasized the importance of focusing on collective consciousness when exploring a social act. Indeed, he challenged as fictitious the division between acts and representations and argued that the two determine and presuppose each other.[88] Collective representations implied communication, a shared language, and a minimum repertoire of collective acts. Representations and behaviour were irreducible because "the concrete, complete fact is the whole: body and soul."[89]

In line with Durkheim's vision, representations stood at the centre of Mauss's analysis of the social, though in an original twist Mauss strongly emphasized their link to the material and concrete substratum of a group. As he declared in his 1924 communication to the Société de psychologie in Paris, the "group mind" cannot be separated from the soil, the physical. If we took only the content of consciousnesses as that which constitutes a collective representation, we would still be in the domain of interpsychology.[90] Mauss contended that sociologists should never consider people's ideas without focusing on the particular society within which those ideas emerge.

86 Mauss, "Divisions et proportions des divisions de la sociologie," in *Œuvres*, vol. 3; English translation in *The Nature of Sociology*.

87 Ibid., 209.

88 As Hollier writes, however, "Mauss only exceptionally (and often critically) employs the Durkheimian concept of collective consciousness. Yet, even if he hesitates to name it, all his discourse indicates a collective subject as the locus of consensus and guarantee of unity." See Hollier, "Malaise dans la sociologie," 58.

89 Mauss, "Divisions et proportions des divisions de la sociologie," in *Œuvres*, 3: 212.

90 Mauss, "Rapport réels et pratiques de la psychologie et de la sociologie," in *Sociologie et anthropologie*; English translation in *Sociology and Psychology*.

In "Introduction à l'analyse de quelques phénomènes religieux," published in 1908, Mauss, along with Henri Hubert, had already criticized the German current of *Völkerpsychologie*. According to this theory, the social is constituted by what is popular, common – a vague humanity conceived in the abstract.[91] Mauss and Hubert, in contrast, reclaimed a comprehensive approach to the social that entailed the critique of the split implicit in psychology between judgments properly called and value judgments, that is, between rational logic and the logic of feelings, affectivity.[92] The opposition between the two logics was misleading, and empirical studies had demonstrated that they indeed coexisted in the consciousnesses of individuals living in groups. Magic, for instance, is not immune to rationally based value judgments even if it is often believed to be dominated by capricious sentiments. Individual feelings can be "fooled" by chimeras, but collective sentiments are rooted in what is "sensible, visible, and tangible."[93] Since magic and religion deal with beings – real bodies – and rely on confirmation and proof – lived experience – they express and satisfy genuine, common needs that cannot be easily met with deception. Feelings in a group situation are coordinated and subject to rules, and even when contradictions exist – an inevitable occurrence – sentiments require explanation and are perceived by believers to be based on the empirical and the rational. Not by chance, Mauss and Hubert argued, religion and magic have developed into sciences, philosophies and techniques, laws and myths. Value judgments are fostered by experience and material reality. They are dominated by rules, which are in turn dictated by social forces and tradition. Judgments derive from social values behind which lie "sensations, collective needs, and movements of human groups."[94] Mauss and Hubert emphasized the critical importance of re-evaluating the logic of feelings when theorizing about the social. They argued that religious representations and rituals originate in sentiment or, as Mauss wrote in his 1923 discussion of Lévy-Bruhl, emotions are the engine of institutions and collective ideas.[95]

91 Hubert and Mauss, "Introduction à l'analyse de quelques phénomènes religieux" (1908), in Mauss, *Œuvres*, 1: 3–39. On Mauss and *Völkerpsychologie*, see Di Donato, "Marcel Mauss et la 'Völkerpsychologie.'"

92 Hubert and Mauss, "Introduction à l'analyse de quelques phénomènes religieux,", especially 26–7.

93 Ibid., 27.

94 Ibid., 31. See also Mauss's critique of Lucien Lévy-Bruhl in "Mentalité primitive et participation" (1923), in *Œuvres*, 2: 125–31; and "L'art et le mythe d'après M. Wundt" (1908), in *Œuvres*, 2: 195–227.

95 Mauss, "Mentalité primitive et participation," in *Œuvres*, vol. 2. According to Mauss, sociology's approach to value judgment positions it closer to phenomenology and the

Mauss's reliance on emotions and their concrete embeddedness allowed him to construct a theoretical apparatus that rejected functionalist interpretations. His budding conception of social phenomena as arbitrary, his discussion of the equivalence between words and actions, and his more general theory of symbolism provided an alternative model of social explanation that further emphasized Durkheim's culturalist approach and also stressed the critical importance of communities for assessing the sociological role of representations.[96] This is evident in Mauss's discussion of causality, whose origins he located in people's beliefs about the virtues of rites and words.[97] After explaining that in so-called primitive mentalities words and actions are not completely differentiated – words are actions and gestures and rituals are conceived as a language, that is, they are a form of communication for other people to see and understand – Mauss suggested that it is not only the magic of words but also the "creative power" of gestures that evoke the notion of efficacy.[98] He concluded that, since words and rituals are symbols, the origins of the notion of cause coincided with the origins of symbolism. For words and rituals – their rhythm, repetition, and unison – are believed to make things happen.[99] As societies create categories that "live and die with the people," symbols are a shared value, a common meaning for those groups who unanimously choose and adopt them, no matter how arbitrary their reference.[100] Mauss believed that one should not ask whether symbols are real or unreal in terms of the way they correspond to things. The question is rather how, even if in imaginary terms, symbols resonate with those humans who understand them and believe

phenomenological study of religion. See his comments on Max Scheler in "Phénoménologie et religion" (1925), in *Œuvres*, 1: 157–9. However, Karady in his introduction to Mauss's *Œuvres*, 1: xlix, claims that the Durkheimians grew isolated from new intellectual currents such as phenomenology.

96 On Mauss's conception of social phenomena as arbitrary, see, among others, "Les civilisations. Éléments et formes" (1929), in *Œuvres*, 2: 470. Mauss wrote, "*Every social phenomenon* has in fact an essential characteristic whether it is a symbol, a word, an instrument, an institution, whether it is even the language, or the best science, whether it is the best adapted instrument to the best and most different ends, whether it is the most rational possible, the most human, *it is still arbitrary*." See English translation in Mauss, *Techniques, Technology and Civilisation*.

97 Mauss, "Catégories collectives de pensée et de liberté" (1921), *Œuvres*, 2: 121–5.

98 Ibid. Also see "Introduction à l'analyse de quelques phénomènes religieux," in *Œuvres*, 1: 4, where Hubert and Mauss wrote that "the principle of all prayers is the recognized efficacy of the word." The topic of Mauss's unfinished thesis was prayer.

99 Mauss also connected sociology to psychology through the invocation of symbols. "Catégories collectives de pensée et liberté," in *Œuvres*, 2, especially 122.

100 Mauss, "Catégories collectives et catégories pures" (1934), in *Œuvres*, 2: 150.

in them.[101] As he wrote, "[T]here are no symbols unless there is communion, and the fact of communion creates a bond which might give the illusion of the real, but is in fact already the real."[102] General ways of thinking are not merely the work of humans: they are the work of humans who, because they are in communion with each other, create common representations. "Pure grammar, pure logic, pure art are ahead of us, not behind us," Mauss proclaimed. In fact, we create them.[103]

Mauss stressed the role of symbols as common signs, a way to communicate and be in communion with other people.[104] Via reference to language in particular, he argued that all signs, including a single word, presuppose a "mental process" through which we think of something, a symbol indeed.[105] This mental process could not be isolated from the audience to whom the signs are addressed; a sign has value only within a community of understanding.[106] Mauss's work on the obligatory expression of feelings, and in particular his analysis of oral funerary rituals, was meant to demonstrate that collective manifestations of sentiments are signs that reaffirm social links. One is obliged to scream, cry, or sing because the members of the group understand the screams' meaning. Not

---

101 On Durkheim and Mauss and their differences vis-à-vis the question of symbols, see Tarot, *De Durkheim à Mauss*, and Karsenti, *L'homme total*. For Tarot, Durkheim was always looking for something under the phenomenon while Mauss thought that everything was in the phenomenon. Accordingly, for Mauss the quintessential symbol was the gift while for Durkheim it was the totem, or for one a system and for the other an object.

102 Mauss, "Catégories collectives et catégories pures," in *Œuvres*, 2: 151. For Karsenti, *L'homme total*, Mauss's theory of symbolism relies on linguistics' relational logic. For Tarot, *De Durkheim à Mauss*, Karsenti's structuralist thesis is misleading, and he sees the philological concept of "translation" as more apt to describe Mauss's approach to symbols.

103 Mauss, "Catégories collectives et catégories pures," in *Œuvres*, 2: 152. Although Mauss postulated that sociology was part of anthropology, he insisted on focusing on concrete history. For him sociology dealt with humans, but with humans in concrete social determinations.

104 In his 1924 intervention at the Société de Psychologie on the question of the relationship between psychology and sociology, Mauss claimed that it was Durkheim and his school who best understood the notion of symbol as derived from religion and the law. See "Rapports réels et pratiques," in *Sociologie et anthropologie*. One also needs to note that Mauss excluded the differentiation between symbol and sign. See his debate with Jean Piaget and Henri Berr, "Débat sur les rapports entre la sociologie et la psychologie" (1931), in *Œuvres*, 3: 298–302.

105 See "Rapports réels et pratiques," in *Sociologie et anthropologie*, 260. Mauss credited psychological research on aphasia with contributing to building consensus around the issue of symbols.

106 In his 1925 discussion of Ogden and Richards' book *The Meaning of Meaning*, for example, he argued in accordance with the authors' analysis that signs have no sense outside their context, that is, outside their position within an ensemble of symbols. "Notes à l'essai sur les 'Divisions de la sociologie,'" note 6, in *Œuvres*, vol. 3.

simply a form of personal expression, crying is directed to others and therefore constitutes a symbolic form.[107] Sign and symbol, Mauss insisted, are the same thing.[108]

Mauss's argument about the social role of symbols was rooted in two main tenets. First, it presupposed that sentiments can be logical: sentiments and logic are tightly connected. Second, it affirmed that symbols do not merely represent social life: they produce it. Thus, there is no distinction between reality and representation. Symbols have a performative role, and Mauss was not worried about the circular dynamics that, within his model of sociological explanation, posited representations as both cause and effect.[109] Such circularity was real and inherent in the things themselves, and he deemed it vain to establish a logical or chronological primacy between societies, on the one hand, and ideas, on the other. This conviction had already emerged in 1908, when he and Hubert, in response to critics who suggested that they limit sociological research to traditional group practices, argued for the social nature of thought. "[T]here are ways of thinking in common as well as ways of acting in common," they claimed, and notions of soul, time, and the sacred are to be considered institutions that take form in specific societies and only in that form become present in individuals' minds.[110]

For Mauss and Hubert, the facts of social psychology and social morphology were inextricably intertwined, as was evident in the case of myths. They thus advocated dismantling the dividing line that separates ritual from myth and practices from ideas and criticized the approach

107 Mauss, "L'expression obligatoire des sentiments. (Rituels oraux funéraires australiens)" (1921), *Œuvres*, 3: 269–79.

108 Mauss, "Débat sur les rapports entre la sociologie et la psychologie" (1931), in *Œuvres*, 3: 298–302. Mauss, however, believed that the authority of symbols had gradually given way to the authority of reason.

109 According to Karsenti, *L'homme total*, Mauss's and Durkheim's ideas of representation differ on this point. For Mauss, representations "symbolize" the structure of the social group. Merleau-Ponty also stated that for Mauss the social fact, which he conceived not as "a massive reality" but as a "circuit of symbolic values, penetrates deeply the individual level. The regulations surrounding the individual, however, do not suppress the individual. One does not have to choose any longer between the individual and the collective." Merleau-Ponty added that Mauss "had the intuition of the social rather than a theory of it." Merleau-Ponty, "De Mauss à Claude Lévi-Strauss," 148–9. This thesis seems to be supported by some of Mauss's students. See, for example, Pierre Métais's testimonial according to which Mauss always advised, "No theory. You observe and describe." Cited in Fournier, "Si je devais réécrire la biographie de Marcel Mauss ... " 36. According to Berthoud, Merleau-Ponty best highlighted Mauss's difference from Durkheim. See Berthoud, "Pourquoi Marcel Mauss?" 15.

110 Mauss, "Introduction à l'analyse de quelques phénomènes religieux," in *Œuvres*, 1: 36.

that evaluated myths as deranged imagination or simplistic thought. According to them, myths has a practical value, possesses logic, and moves in parallel motion with rituals.[111] Thought and action work in unison and, as Mauss wrote in his study of prayer, myth has no reality unless it is attached to a particular usage through a cult – or alternatively, a ritual has no value without beliefs.[112] Ultimately, the most important issue for Mauss was myth's connection to belief and faith. A myth can only exist if people in a group feel the need to agree on the theme and content which constitute the myth.[113] Such need for consensus could only come from society: society imposes myth as the symbol through which it thinks itself. In other words, myth is a social fact, the normal manifestation of collective praxis: it is an institution around which believers gather and assemble.[114] Although Mauss did not specify ways in which consensus could be reached, the attention he paid to this issue in part corrected Durkheim's more simplistic tendency to crown the social as a spontaneous happening.

Mauss's argument about the relationship between thought and action, mythical beliefs and practices, faith and ritual are original features of his approach to the question of the social pioneered by Durkheim. Through what might be defined as a phenomenological perspective, Mauss conceived the social in terms of symbolic communication and identified the social with the sacred via a prior detour into religion.[115] His study of sacrifice, which moved from religious facts to social bonds, indicated the sacred nature of communities and the pivotal role of rituals within collectivities. Incidentally, the analysis of sacrifice also led Mauss in a direction that modified and amplified Durkheim's main tenet on the nature of the sacred. For Mauss, the notion of mana comprised the sacred rather than the other way around – a conclusion that raises some epistemological questions about the explanatory adequacy of the sacred/profane binary.[116] In addition, and critical for Mauss's own theoretical trajectory,

111 Ibid., 4.

112 See Mauss's unfinished thesis, "La prière" (1909), *Œuvres*, 1: 357–477. See English translation, *On Prayer*. Mauss claimed that, because it is a form of speech, praying at the same time reveals acting and thinking, belief and cult.

113 For Mauss, the myth is something the group agrees on by adhering to it, in part spontaneously and in part out of obligation. See "L'art et le mythe d'après M. Wundt," in *Œuvres*, vol. 2.

114 Mauss, "Introduction aux mythes" for the 1903 issue of *L'Année sociologique*, in *Œuvres*. 2: 269–72.

115 On Mauss's thought and its resonance with phenomenology, see Karsenti, *L'homme total*. According to Karsenti, Mauss combined explanation with understanding.

116 On the consequences of this difference on religious sociology, see Martelli, "Mana ou sacré?" See also Marcel Mauss, "L'œuvre de Marcel Mauss par lui-même," where Mauss

the study of sacrifice directed Mauss toward a theory of "total man" and, later, "total social fact" that radically questioned the traditional compartmentalization of science, thus opening up new horizons to sociological knowledge and breaking asunder the limits of Durkheim's more orthodox approach to social research.

Sacrifice: A Theoretical Turn

In 1899, Hubert and Mauss wrote an essay on the nature and function of sacrifice that, by defining sacrifice as the ultimate social act, argued for the overlapping identity of the sacred and social realms.[117] Their theory was based on Robertson Smith's innovative interpretation of the sacrificial ritual – an interpretation that, among other elements, introduced the idea of sacrifice as a communion where humans and gods share a meal.[118] Although Hubert and Mauss criticized Robertson Smith's theory at different levels, they held fast to his notion of communion and emphasized the performative role that the sacrificial ceremony plays by allowing the profane to enter into relation with the divine. For Hubert and Mauss, sacrifices established a communication between the profane and sacred worlds through the intermediary of a victim. However, only by being destroyed in the course of a ceremony did the victim acquire sacredness.[119] In this sense, they differed from Robertson Smith in their understanding of sacrifice as actively transformative. Whereas Robertson Smith theorized that the victim was endowed with a religious nature prior to the ceremony and came to sacrifice only in light of being sacred, for Hubert and Mauss the operation of sacrifice – the sacrificial act itself – conferred a sacred character on the victim. Against Robertson Smith, they argued that there was no common origin to sacrifice and that, while the objectives of sacrifices can vary greatly, the most important element and the common denominator of all sacrificial systems was their procedure.

By making rituals their central focus of analysis, Hubert and Mauss engaged the issue of the sacrificial moment's significance in the life of

---

said of the idea of mana that it "is probably more general than that of the sacred," 218. He then continued, "Durkheim tried to deduce it sociologically from the notion of the sacred. We were never sure that he was right and I still continue to speak of magic-religious foundations."

117 Mauss, "Essai sur la nature et la fonction du sacrifice," in *Œuvres*, 1: 193–307. See English translation, *Sacrifice: Its Nature and Function*.

118 Robertson Smith saw the origins of sacrifice in totemism, but his theory on this point has been rebutted by several scholars of religion as well as anthropologists. See his *Lectures*.

119 Mauss, "Essai sur la nature et la fonction du sacrifice," in *Œuvres*, 1: 302.

the group. After locating sacrifice within the general system of consecration – the process through which an object passes from the common to
the religious domain – they determined that sacrifice is differentiated
from other instances of consecration by its effects, which rebound beyond the specific object of consecration, that is, beyond the victim.[120] To
start with, the sacrificer is also affected and transformed during the ceremony.[121] In addition, and most significant for its theoretical implications, since a sacrifice always involves an intermediary between the
sacrificer and the divinity, the victim, with its death, provided the link
between the sacred and the group; the victim's destruction opened up
communication between the profane and the divine.[122] Thus, besides
sparing the sacrificer's death by substituting for him, the victim's immo-
lation granted the renewal of collective group existence. The victim took
on itself the sacred's destructive force whose intensity at times obliterated what came in contact with it; through personal renunciation, the victim then absorbed the violent consequences of the unchained religious
energies and rekindled social unity. The notion of sacrifice epitomized
and demonstrated the identity between sacred and social. The high degree of violence unleashed by sacrifices indeed testified to what was at
stake: the survival of the group. Such survival was inscribed within the
very logic of sacrifice. As the sacrificial ceremony unfolded, collective
forces, through their believing and acting in the ritual, developed a consciousness of their being and constituted and reconstituted themselves
as real, while sanctifying social norms.[123] What looked like religion was
socially embedded, Mauss and Hubert hinted; myths and rituals enacted

120 Ibid., 200. They also concluded that sacrificial ritual belongs to advanced forms of
religion.

121 Even the objects of sacrifice can undergo the same transformation. Ibid., 202.

122 Hubert and Mauss defined sacrifice as follows: "*Sacrifice is a religious act which, through
the consecration of a victim, modifies the condition of the moral person who accomplishes it or of those
objects with which that person is concerned,*" 205. Hubert and Mauss also directed attention to
the ambiguity of the sacred theorized by Robertson Smith: the sacred could be both pure
and impure and fostered both good and evil. Durkheim on his part insisted on the element
of destruction. See his 1898 letter to Mauss in Fournier and DeLangle, "Autour du
Sacrifice," 6–7. In general, however, Durkheim subscribed to Robertson Smith's theory of
the duality of the sacred, that is, of the sacred's pure and impure dimensions. Although this
distinction complicated his approach to the sacred/profane dichotomy, Durkheim did not
elaborate it in any specific way. Other Durkheimians, in particular Robert Hertz, worked
more closely on the topic of the sacred's ambiguity. For a discussion of some of the issues
related to this question, see Riley, "Renegade Durkheimians and the Transgressive Left
Sacred." As will be discussed in chapter 5, the Collège subscribed to the duality of the
sacred and particularly focused on theorizing the sacred horror.

123 Mauss, *Œuvres*, 1: 306.

a social logic.[124] One might add that in this view of the sacrificial ceremony violence also appeared to have a fundamental role in constituting the social, as the Collège would later maintain through reference to the same notion of sacrifice.

With their study of sacrifice, Hubert and Mauss established the link between sacred and social – a finding that was central to the theoretical and moral agenda of the Durkheimian school.[125] In addition, they also began to attend to another factor characteristic of French sociology's original approach to the social, that is, the mental and moral energies that enable a community to think of itself as such and to acquire social authority and force. According to Hubert and Mauss, beliefs and representations stood at the critical centre of the social and were a major driving power in the constitution of the collectivity. But why were beliefs so vital to the group's existence? In answering this critical question Mauss suggested engaging in the study of "the total man."[126] Only by grasping the total psycho-physiological complex of the person – the man of history – and only by tracing the relationship between mentality and organism could one fully understand beliefs and behaviour.[127] With an increasing interest in the "techniques of the body" and the "constrained" nature of instincts, Mauss advocated considering the complexity of human nature through "a man who lives in flesh and spirit at a specific point in time and space and in a specific society."[128] The "trinity" of body, individual consciousness, and collectivity needed to be taken into account in order to shed light on human existence and delineate the moral life of historical societies.[129]

124 Mauss, "Introduction à l'analyse de quelques faits religieux," *Œuvres*, 1: 17. According to Hubert and Mauss, this is why several social practices that derive from sacrifice and are a common feature of our world, including contracts and gifts, are not by any means religious. For a general discussion of the essay, see Colleyn, "Le sacrifice selon Hubert et Mauss."

125 On some theoretical differences between Durkheim and Mauss on the issue of sacrifice, see their exchange of letters prior to the completion of the essay, in Fournier and DeLangle, "Autour du Sacrifice."

126 Mauss, "Allocution à la Société de Psychologie" (1923), in *Œuvres*, 3: 280. See also "Rapports réels et pratiques," in *Sociologie et anthropologie*, 304.

127 For Mauss, the man of history was the average person living an average life whose faculties extended from the mind and spirit to the body. "Allocution à la Société de Psychologie."

128 Ibid., 281. For example, Mauss claimed that "civilized man" is not only duplex but divided and takes more and more distance from instincts and impulses in favour of reason and control.

129 As Karsenti recognizes, historians, and in particular Marc Bloch, criticized Durkheim's limited historical sense while they absolved Mauss of this sin. See Karsenti, *L'homme total*, 114–29.

Mauss's attempt at a sociological program, a total approach to understanding human interaction, aimed at establishing a "science of the concrete" that would remix all divisions while overcoming the dichotomy
between the general and the particular or the social and the individual.[130] Collective consciousness, that is, consciousnesses thinking together, was supposed to describe specific societies rather than society in
general (*la société*), and Mauss called for "a science of the body and soul
of societies." As he wrote, "In the same way that psychologically man
thinks, is directed, acts, feels at once with all his body, so this community
of bodies and minds that is a society, feels, acts, lives and wants to live
with all the bodies and all the minds of all these men. Society is their
whole, the whole of these wholes, it is this and nothing else."[131] Mauss
indicated some necessary measures for achieving a science of the concrete by stressing a vision of ensemble – the same vision that had led him
to argue for the valence of the concept of "total man." The notion of
"total social fact," which he elaborated in his famous 1925 essay *The Gift*,
provides another important stepping stone in the unfolding of his
thought and in his construction of a comprehensive "science of man."
Through the idea of total social fact, Mauss re-envisioned the role of sociological analysis; he also challenged Durkheim's careful attempt to
carve out the social from other domains.

The Gift *and Total Social Facts*

Mauss introduced the notion of total social phenomenon in the first
pages of *The Gift* and argued that in it "all kinds of institutions are given
expression at one and the same time – religious, juridical, and moral,
which relate to both politics and the family; likewise economic ones,
which suppose special forms of production and consumption, or rather,
of performing total services and of distribution."[132] The gift was one
such total phenomenon, and he described it as a form of exchange and
contract, a service that appears voluntary but is in reality obligatory and
subject to constraints. Although Mauss's analysis of the gift revolved
around specific archaic societies where the intermingling of "social facts"
occurred regularly, through the examination of archaic customs Mauss
aimed at establishing a general heuristic principle that would be valid
for all social interpretation. His discussion in *The Gift* thus refracted the

---

130 Mauss, "Divisions et proportions des divisions de la sociologie," in *Œuvres*, 3: 202.
131 Ibid., 203.
132 Mauss, *The Gift*.

centrality that, according to him, the total social phenomenon held within the study of the "concrete."

The key questions Mauss raised in *The Gift* were supposed to reveal the multifaceted nature of the institution of giving by addressing some critical issues. "*What rule of legality and self-interest, in societies of a backward or archaic type, compels the gift that has been received to be obligatorily reciprocated?*" But also, "*What power resides in the object given that causes its recipient to pay it back?*"[133] Mauss responded by first dismantling the theory of natural economy as a plausible interpretive key for the gift. Not only does the exchange of goods always happen between collectivities and not individuals, he contended, but what gets exchanged are more than economically useful things. Banquets, festivals, and women also become part of exchanges, and their presence indicates the existence of a more general contract binding all participants involved in the practice.[134] To explicate the phenomenon, Mauss introduced the notion of "total services" – an ensemble of seemingly voluntary forms of gifts that turn out to be compulsory. And he took the potlatch of the American Northwest as a quintessential example of a system of total services; the tribes who adopt it spend entire winters at a festival in which everything pertaining to the clan comes to be at stake – marriage, worship, power. In particular, since the potlatch is a total service of an agonistic type, Mauss argued, what we witness is the nobles' struggles to establish a hierarchy among themselves. Dominated by the principles of rivalry and hostility, infighting takes place during the potlatch through such surprising acts as the destruction of wealth and the obligation to reciprocate presents. Such irrational violence suggested to Mauss that an economy of exchange is not moved merely by rationality and interest.[135] Nor is the practice of "giving" an immediate, direct transaction. Rather, giving stands as a first movement in a chain of obligations: to give, to receive, and to reciprocate. This chain links the participating subjects in a relationship of mutual dependence and reinforces their social ties.

For Mauss, the case of the American potlatch was symptomatic of the total nature of the gift practice, and he argued that the critical elements for interpreting the exchange act in this case were both the economic

---

133 Ibid., 3 (italicized in the original).

134 In "Les origines de la notion de monnaie" (1914), Mauss had already claimed that money should be examined as a social fact and not as a material, physical thing. Mauss indicated the relevance of the notion of prestige inherent in the primitive money form, but also money's link to magical power. See *Œuvres*, 2: 106–15.

135 For an interpretation along these lines, see Karsenti, *L'homme total*, 374–5. Karsenti reminds us of Mauss's assertion that to give is to destroy. Karsenti also reaffirms the connection between gift and sacrifice.

notion of credit and the moral one of honour. For, as it turns out, the individual prestige of a chief is at stake in the destruction and consumption of goods. Since "[e]verything is based upon the principles of antagonism and rivalry," a real competition about who owns more wealth continuously operates in and underlies a potlatch.[136] Within this context, in the same way that the destructive character of the potlatch conveys the disinterested nature of the exchange transaction, the mere process of a never-ending reciprocation reveals the uneconomic side of exchange where, after one receives and becomes rich, one immediately loses everything, and more, in the return. Mauss concluded that, despite the interest attached to the things exchanged, what one really confronts with the potlatch system of gifts is the group participants' mutual dependence, both material and moral, and their feeling that "they are everything to one another."[137] It is, then, not surprising that the juridical and economic operations carried out during these potlatch ceremonies do not resemble forms with which the modern West is familiar. These operations, nevertheless, fulfill the same functions as our modern transactions and it would be a mistake to think that primitive societies practised only a barter regime. The gift entails the notion of credit, Mauss insisted, and a total system is enacted through giving, including religious, mythological, and aesthetic phenomena via rituals, tales, and dances. For this reason, the whole economy of exchange through gift-giving is more than a subject for economics; sociology has the potential of demonstrating the inadequacy of the figure of *homo oeconomicus* – a modern and not very felicitous construct.[138] Because it looks at total social facts and considers the whole, sociology is the most suitable science for pursuing the study of the concrete in order to understand from within people's lived experience.[139] For "we are speaking of men and groups of men, because it

---

136 Mauss, *The Gift*, 37.

137 Ibid., 33. Mauss reached this conclusion by linking the obligation to reciprocate to the Maori idea that a thing is endowed with a spirit (*hau*) that needs to go back to the owner. Accordingly, the thing one receives is active and has power because the gift always contains part of the owner's self. Gifts, despite their destructive premises, establish ties between souls; they sanctify bonds and show the interconnectedness of people's lives.

138 Ibid., 76.

139 On this point, see Dumont, "Une science en devenir." I am not going to evaluate *The Gift* essay beyond its influential connection to the Collège's project. However, it might be fair to mention that one of the main criticisms of Mauss's treatment of the gift is his focus on exchange when dealing with the economic aspect of the gift as a total social fact. Mauss is not interested in looking at the economy in terms of production. In this sense, Mauss ignores Marxism and its theories, despite being a socialist. See Terrail, "Entre l'ethnocentrisme et le marxisme." According to Hollier, in *The Gift* Mauss seems to study societies' representations of economic institutions rather than the institutions themselves and their functioning.

is they, it is society, it is the feelings of men, in their minds and in flesh and blood that at all times spring into action and that have acted everywhere."[140]

Mauss's notion of total social fact infused new life into a science that risked remaining aloof from the social context in which it was developing. Both substantively and methodologically, Mauss's approach attempted to "recompose the whole" after having divided it for practical purposes, and to overcome divisions between the particular and the general, the concrete and the abstract. Sociology was a science of relations, Mauss stated, a symbolic science that needed to surmount the classifications imposed by the individual sciences.[141] From this point of view, his discussion of the gift as total social fact was about much more than Mauss's interpreters and their reading of the phenomenon in terms of an economy of exchange would lead us to believe.[142] Among other accomplishments, the notion of total social fact in principle reincorporated the political into the social, as the gift-giving practice directed attention both to internal group dynamics, often based on a hierarchical system, and to the obligatory nature of collective participation.

Officially, though, and against his own innovative approach, Mauss refused to implicate politics in scientific (that is, sociological) endeavours. In a passage worth citing at length, he addressed the relationship between pure science and practical action: "One of the main advantages of a complete and concrete knowledge of societies and of types of societies, of every society and ours in particular, is that it allows foreseeing what an *applied sociology* or *politics* can be like. One needs to eliminate this from pure sociology with no hesitation ... *Politics* is not a part of *sociology*."[143] The indictment of politics for the sake of safeguarding sociology had

---

Once again, representations seem to be at the centre of the social, its engine. According to Hollier, the focus on exchange shows Mauss's indebtedness to linguistics as a model. See "Malaise dans la sociologie," 55–61.

140 Mauss, *The Gift*, 70.

141 Mauss, "Divisions et proportions des divisions de la sociologie," in *Œuvres*, 3: 204.

142 For a notable exception, see Mary Douglas, foreword to *The Gift*, x, where she claims that the book "is about politics and economics."

143 See his discussion in *L'Année sociologique*'s new series (1927), "Divisions et proportions des divisions de la sociologie," now in *Œuvres*, 3: 232 (italicized in the original). The whole chapter 4 ("Place de la sociologie appliquée ou politique") is indicative of Mauss's position on this question. In "L'œuvre de Mauss par lui-même," 220, Mauss also wrote, "In all this summary of my works I have said nothing about my written incursions in the domain of the normative ... Almost all of them are connected to a larger work on 'The Nation' (element of modern politics), which is almost complete. This work will not even be published in the collection of the Travaux de *L'Année sociologique*, so much I want to distinguish sociology as a pure science from an even absolutely disinterested theory."

been a long-standing practice for Durkheim who, although motivated to do research by the desire to apply its results to improving reality, also felt the need to disclaim any kind of association between theory and practice.[144] In the case of Mauss, there was no denying that sociological knowledge should eventually lead to a science of politics. Political problems, Mauss claimed, are social problems.[145]

Yet, Mauss maintained the separation between sociology and applied politics; furthermore, when it came to defining politics, he also differentiated archaic from modern societies. Thus, he argued that modern politics focuses on the state and that an important distinction separating archaic from modern societies is that in the former the state is not as set apart from the general social life as it is in the latter. He then proposed that in archaic societies the state is a fact of morals, mentality; it constitutes "the ensemble of general phenomena, which it in fact concretizes: cohesion, authority, tradition, education, etc."[146] Only among the "primitives," Mauss seemed to imply, is the art of politics (l'art politique) "but a supreme form of the art of living in common, morality."[147] Only among the "primitives" did it encompass the sphere of the moral and include all total facts. In other words, Mauss encouraged exploring the general link that held together different phenomena in a particular community (the total social facts), but only if that community belonged to archaic societies. For the others, he appeared to accept the existence of the divisions created by the modern differentiation of the value spheres, and he abstained from questioning the actual outcomes of such division. Mauss receded from his ambitious and creative theoretical project and realigned

---

Let me state here, as I did in the case of Durkheim, that I am examining the relationship of Mauss's theories to politics. I am not arguing that Mauss was politically disengaged. Indeed, he was very active in politics, especially in the co-operative movement, and was often distracted from his scholarly work by current issues. See Fournier, *Marcel Mauss*; English translation *Marcel Mauss: A Biography*. Several conflicts between Durkheim and Mauss arose in connection to Mauss's political commitments and their negative effects on his scholarly progress. See Durkheim, *Lettres à Marcel Mauss*.

144 See in particular *The Division of Labor*, preface to the first edition, where Durkheim stated, "We would esteem our research not worth the labour of a single hour if its interest were merely speculative. If we distinguish carefully between theoretical and practical problems it is not in order to neglect the latter category. On the contrary, it is in order to put ourselves in a position where we can better resolve them," xxvi.

145 Mauss, "Divisions et proportions des divisions de la sociologie," in *Œuvres*, 3: 238.

146 Mauss, "Fragment d'un plan de sociologie générale descriptive: classification et méthode d'observation des phénomènes généraux de la vie sociale dans les sociétés de type archaïque (Phénomènes généraux spécifiques de la vie intérieure de la société)" (1934), in *Œuvres*, 3: 310.

147 Ibid., 329. See also "Un Inédit de Marcel Mauss. Politique."

himself with sociological orthodoxy. His suggestive program of examining reality as total social fact came to an unexpected halt.

To summarize: Mauss's sociological itinerary followed the path of his uncle and teacher, Durkheim, and posited representations at the centre of the analysis of social life. Mauss, however, did not simply emulate Durkheim's teachings. He surpassed them by criticizing the distinction between acts and representations, on the one hand, and on the other by pressing for a science of the concrete that, historically grounded, would seriously engage the relationship between ideas as spurred by emotions and the experience of material reality. Thus, Mauss emphasized a phenomenological approach to the social intended as symbolic communication based on experience and he deepened our understanding of the ways in which thought and action interact. His discussion of sacrifice, in particular, allowed him to address the symbolic nature of sociality in relationship to the sacred and to demonstrate the active violent nature of the sacralizing process in producing collective sentiments and in ensuring the survival of the group. The analysis of sacrifice also indicated the need to consider social reality in its totality. Mauss reframed and reaffirmed the importance of sociology as the only science able to overcome artificial disciplinary divisions and argued that sociology confronted total social facts as the simultaneous presence and interconnectedness in one phenomenon of political, economic, religious, and other kinds of institutions. Although he was not able to avoid being caught in contradictions when applying his explanatory model, within his new vision archaic societies came to demonstrate the expansive role of the political in social co-existence.[148] In this sense, I would argue that despite a principled distance from politics in the name of science, Mauss's methodological pluralism, his notion of total social fact, and his undermining of rationality as the decisive explanatory factor for understanding social action all contributed to embed the political in a richer interpretive terrain. Following the distinction between politics and the political outlined in this book's introduction, I conclude that both Mauss's and Durkheim's culturalist models

148 At some point Mauss even extended his understanding of "l'art politique" beyond archaic societies. In his sociological discussion of Bolshevism, for example, as he critiqued historical materialism, Mauss claimed that giving primacy to specific social phenomena is always unwise. "Neither political things, nor moral things, nor economic things dominate in any society..." And more: "Politics, Morality, Economics are simply elements of the social art, the art of living in common." Political sense is ultimately the sense of the social, he insisted. See Mauss, "Fascisme et bolchevisme. Réflexions sur la violence," in *Écrits politiques*, 556, 557. See English translation, "A Sociological Assessment of Bolshevism (1924–5)," in Mike Gane, *The Radical Sociology of Durkheim and Mauss*. See also Busino, "Marcel Mauss, interprète d'un phénomène social total: le bolchevisme."

of social analysis actually implicated the political, even as they denied it – a cognitive dissonance that gave rise to ambiguity and unfulfilled potential and whose effects reverberated through the coeval culture.

In the decades following the rise of Durkheimian sociology, an ambivalent attitude toward politics and an inclination to criticize rationality through a return to the "primitives" re-emerged among the French avant-garde and at the Collège de sociologie. The Collège, in particular, focused on the need for affective communities and mythical thinking, and somewhat contradictorily affirmed the violent foundations of the social in an antipolitical attempt to counteract the fascists' emotional offerings. The Collège's incongruous attitude was founded on principles and epistemological confusions similar to those held by Durkheim and Mauss and was driven by the same desire to reinvigorate a disaggregating social body. Even more notable in terms of similarities, as we will see next, in the case of the Collège and of the avant-garde as well, negative quandaries about politics were faced through a simultaneous indictment of aesthetics, with the understanding that if science needed to dispense with politics, it also had to give up art.

2

Against Aesthetics:
The Anthropology of Objects

IN HIS INTRODUCTION TO *THE GIFT*, Mauss characterized the "total social phenomenon" as the expression of a multitude of institutions that included religion, jurisprudence, morality, and the economy.[1] Total phenomena were microcosms of social relations, complex wholes in which several aspects of social life intermingled and were put in motion, and Mauss advocated examining the potlatch as a totality that encapsulated the fleeting living moment in which society and its members become conscious of themselves and their interrelations. Rooted in an analysis of the "concrete," the study of "total facts" would make it possible to identify people's behaviour in the act of its making and in its wholeness and complex reality. It would also make possible the discovery of new truths about the social world.[2] Acknowledging sociology's shortcomings when subscribing to specialization and compartmentalization, Mauss affirmed that the analysis of concrete sociality would reveal the richness of human life. He thus emphasized the complex web of signification that lay behind what would appear as a self-explanatory act, the exchange. He also directed attention toward the aesthetic manifestations that accompany the performance of exchange obligations.[3] Dance, songs, drama, fabricated objects, ornaments, and food were part of "beauty rituals" that defied the rule of utility and morality; they promoted aesthetic emotions and sentimental values.[4]

Although Mauss acknowledged that in his analysis of exchange he had to omit and "pass over the aesthetic phenomena" he so eloquently evoked

1 Mauss, *The Gift*, 3.
2 See "Conclusion," *The Gift*, 80.
3 See "Programme," *The Gift* , 3.
4 Mauss specifically referred to Malinowski's description of the *kula* of the Trobriand and the "ritual of Beauty" in it. Ibid., 157n39.

in the conclusion to *The Gift*, aesthetics could not completely escape his sociologist's gaze, for it was part and parcel of the phenomena he defined as total.[5] Aesthetics represented one element among the panoply contained in the total social fact. And yet, as Mauss critically conceded in 1927 in *L'Année sociologique*'s new series, aesthetics remained undertheorized in the work of Durkheim's followers. Mauss particularly lamented the minimal space *L'Année sociologique* had devoted to aesthetics in Durkheim's original plan for the journal.[6] The decision was unjustified, especially if one considered the place occupied by aesthetics among the "primitives" and in "advanced" societies alike. Relegated to a section titled "Divers" (Miscellaneous), along with linguistics and technology, aesthetics did not enjoy the importance it deserved in the study of social life, despite the fact that artistic phenomena, especially in earlier civilizations, had flooded their banks and "overflowed their *boundary*."[7]

Mauss called "painful" the minimal attention that the new *L'Année sociologique* series devoted to aesthetics. He justified the decision to leave the journal's old plan intact in part by citing the deaths in the First World War of those Durkheimians most conversant with aesthetic matters. Expressing regret for this "involuntary" fault, he consoled himself and reassured the journal's readers that aesthetics held, alongside linguistics and technology, "an infinitely larger place in social systems, whether primitive or advanced, than the one we can give them here."[8] The domain of art was one of the largest in terms of its social ramifications, even though sociologists generally tended to focus on the more classical questions of morality, religion, and the economy.

One can almost feel Mauss's sense of impotence and frustration in his reflections on aesthetic matters. Even more striking and surprising, however, is the regret that emerges from Mauss's assessment of the negative turn he believed art had taken in the early 1900s. In a passage of "Divisions and Proportions of Divisions in Sociology," Mauss warned against being mystified by the fate of art in modern societies. If *l' art pour l' art* had implanted itself as a principle against art's more natural tendency to branch out and "color everything," in future civilizations this state of things would surely change.[9] Art would again extend its influence over those fields that

---

5 Ibid., 38. Mauss also stated that "these institutions have an important aesthetic aspect that we have deliberately omitted from this study." Ibid., 79.

6 The presentation appeared as "Divisions et proportions des divisions de la sociologie" in issue 2 of *L'Année sociologique*, now in Mauss, *Œuvres*, 3: 178–245.

7 Ibid., 193 (italicized in the original).

8 Ibid., 191.

9 Ibid., 194.

sociologists were naturally more inclined to explore and in which the aesthetic phenomenon, normally underestimated, was omnipresent.

Mauss journeyed far in his apology of aesthetics. He not only expressed regret about the Durkheimians' inability to illuminate art's value but he also demonstrated a strong belief in the sociological import of aesthetics. And he deplored the dominating role that the art for art's sake movement, with its isolationist stance, had been able to achieve. But what exactly did Mauss intend by aesthetics? And how did his idea fit within the Durkheimian sociological framework? This chapter begins by sketching Durkheim's and Mauss's perspectives on art. It highlights the differentiated notions of aesthetics they held for the "primitives," on one side, and the moderns, on the other. It then links Durkheim and Mauss to a larger cultural phenomenon in early twentieth-century France that, through reference to the "primitives," sought to reconsider the negative status of art in its modern form as autonomous. The chapter assesses how the return to the "primitives" via anthropology and museums led art to a transformational journey that undermined its own privileged status. It brings to the fore the parameters of the modern West's relationship to aesthetics and the inadequacies of a denigration of art as illusory and founded on beauty ideals. It also shows the contradictions that a negative evaluation of art entails when applied to traditional societies' cultural expressions. Finally, the chapter illuminates the anti-aesthetic trajectory of Georges Bataille, who, in the years prior to the foundation of the Collège, confronted the aesthetic realm and began to define his own critical approach to the study of the social. More generally, as chapter 1 introduced the problematic shadow cast on the political by a magnified notion of the social, this chapter focuses on aesthetics as another victim of this trend. It argues that the desire to reinstate communal bonds and rekindle the social implied that aesthetics, in its specious meaning as autonomous, could only be rejected. Indeed, aesthetics became the maligned culprit of social disengagement and elitism and was categorized as synonymous with selfishness and individualism. This trend particularly emerges in the magazine *Documents*, a vehicle for artists, ethnologists, and art historians edited by Bataille. It was at *Documents* that the anti-aesthetic movement initiated by ethnography came to fruition. And it was at *Documents* that dissident Surrealists reconceived art through a gradual but inexorable dismantling of its value.

SOCIOLOGY CONTRA ART

In his discussion of sociological domains for the new *L'Année sociologique*, Mauss addressed the issue of aesthetics' significance by pointing to the dominant presence of aesthetic elements among disparate but equally relevant social facts. He cited the beautiful imagery, rhythm, dance, music, and poetry in religion; etiquette, beauty of manners, and rituals in morality; and the sense of the beautiful in economics.[10] For Mauss, the notion of aesthetics had an expansive anthropological meaning that was not limited to the "noble" arts, though he surely opposed Wilhelm Wundt's "exaggerated" theory, which posited art at the origin of various social phenomena.[11] Mauss believed that art should be considered as a collective fact rather than an individual work of creation; he rejected the concept of genius held by the Romantics as well as the view that art is determined by individual psychology. To be sure, he did not discount the role of individual variations within the same era or style. He nevertheless emphasized the close link between the creation of an artwork and its enjoyment. Both moments were founded on a communicable sentiment, emotions, a shared social meaning. Art had both a social nature and a social effect that fluctuated historically;[12] production and reception mutually affected one another's unfolding.[13]

In his early observations on aesthetics, when he had not yet formulated his theory of the gift, Mauss saw connections among social institutions and condemned the artificial divisions that isolate phenomena, in particular artistic phenomena, by detaching them from their larger social context. On his way to conceptualizing "total social facts," Mauss warned of the risks of metaphysical analysis or of a "natural history" approach to social life. He also drew a complex picture of social reality where the value spheres, which Weber had deemed separate in modernity, still intermingled and would, in his opinion, continue to do so provided that artists ended their retreat into the ivory tower of aesthetic isolation. Mauss generally maintained an anthropological vision when discussing art matters and, not surprisingly, found the art for art's sake movement a quasi aberration. He thus remained critical of autonomous art, although, being more intellectually engaged with the archaic than with contemporary reality, he refrained from a direct analysis of *l'art pour l'art*'s historical origins and present status. Nor did he reflect on the different outcomes that the crossing of the spheres, including art, would entail

10 Ibid. On the Durkheimians and art, see Fournier, "Durkheim, *L'Année sociologique* et l'art." Fournier was inspired by Edward Tiryakian's article "L'École durkheimienne à la recherché de la société perdue: la sociologie naissante et son milieu culturel."

11 Mauss, "L'art et le mythe d'après M. Wundt," in *Œuvres*, 2: 195–227.

12 See "Les débuts de la poésie selon Gummere" (1903), in *L'Année sociologique* 6, now in ibid., 251–5.

13 In 1901, Mauss framed art within his vision of "social institutions" as a sedimented collective orientation. See Fauconnet and Mauss, "Sociologie," in Mauss, *Œuvres*, 3: 139–77.

within a secularized modern world. Mauss seemed generally unaware of contemporary attempts to challenge and overcome autonomous art's distance from social life and assumed that the predominance of art for art's sake was presently unassailable.

In general, and despite his good will, a limited theorization of aesthetic issues left Mauss, as well as other Durkheimians, in a weak position when it came to contributing original analyses of art in industrialized societies. First, as already mentioned, the Durkheimians accepted as a given art's autonomous status, and second, the little they wrote on aesthetic matters remained confined to the archaic. In an early issue of *L'Année sociologique*'s first cycle, Henri Hubert, who was the one Durkheimian most interested in aesthetic matters, exemplified this position; he stressed that the journal's focus on the prehistoric and ethnographic made it difficult to delimit art's domain in modernity precisely because aesthetics lacked autonomy in primitive societies.[14]

Given the limited space for art in Durkheim's sociological project, and his decidedly unsympathetic opinion about it, one should marvel at the giant leap Durkheim's students took away from their master's strict and austere outlook. In Durkheim's major works of the 1890s, art was both a sign of disconnected relations – anomie, lack of norms, and voided sociality – and a symptom of the egoistic pursuit of pleasure.[15] A goalless activity, it displayed no constructive role or character-building effect able to counteract the pathologies of extreme individualism. Art was deeply implicated in modernity's degenerating morality. Durkheim confined art to a treacherous zone of depravity and selfishness and never considered initiating a serious study of it. Several years after writing *The Division of Labor* and *Suicide*, he re-evaluated art's link to religion, the latter interpreted as the source of all collective life. Even then, his perspective on art had not altered substantially, although he shifted his focus from the ills of modern societies onto the sacred communities of the "primitives." *The Elementary Forms of Religious Life* examined symbolic life as autonomous (a point that marked Durkheim's radical redeployment of culture in non-functionalist terms) and at first favourably described the way religious reality was played out in the "primitives'" imaginary and then performed in ritual ceremonies. During festivals, Durkheim maintained, the strength of the social bond became transfigured into the symbolic

---

14 Hubert situated art within technology and, more importantly, within phenomena of representation, that is, collective thought. In Hubert's model, the individual artist constituted the expressive vector of collective representations. See Fournier, "Durkheim, *L'Année sociologique* et l'art."

15 See in particular *The Division of Labor in Society* and *Suicide: A Study in Sociology.*

and appeared disguised in the sacred objects of religious cults. Within this magical atmosphere, dances, songs, and movement contributed to reawakening the sense of the group and reconnected the individual to the collectivity by conveying excitement and agitation. Spontaneous and emotional, these aesthetic displays of goalless exuberance cemented collective representations and reinforced collective consciousness.[16] The dances and songs of primitive festivals were expressive means of recreation that helped confirm and amplify the sacred nature of society.

With *The Elementary Forms*, art seemed to have acquired a more positive status in Durkheim's moral framework, especially when measured against art's ability to partake in the sacred.[17] In reality, however, Durkheim continued to display a negative opinion about art's superficial nature, its distracting tendencies, and its lack of edifying features. While he appreciated art's role in fostering social sentiments, and prized both the purposelessness of artistic manifestations and their status as "useless expenditure," he still evaluated art works as "supplementary and superfluous works of luxury," a surplus of intellectual forces that should be usefully "employed."[18] Durkheim's perspective on art, in sum, appeared caught in the same dilemmas he confronted when examining the dualism of human nature and, in particular, the spiritual/material split. Fully embedded in the Cartesian tradition of privileging the mind over the body, Durkheim struggled to resolve the contradiction at the heart of his own endeavour: claiming a role for emotions in bringing forth what was ultimately a rational outcome – the superiority of the social.

Durkheim's ambivalent statements on art reflected the difficulties he was encountering in trying to reconcile the individual and the collective, rational and irrational. They also confirmed the limits of any attempt to make of the "primitives" a template for all historical social formations. For, in the end, Durkheim drew a discriminating line between modern and traditional societies when assessing the nature of aesthetic phenomena. He argued that aesthetic manifestations, when involved in a collective

16 Because they had no strategic purpose, Durkheim included dances and songs of primitive festivals within the aesthetic field.

17 "[Th]ere is a poetry inherent in all religion," Durkheim wrote, although he also suggested not exaggerating this factor. *EF*, 386; *FE*, 546.

18 Durkheim, *EF*, 385; *FE*, 545 (but the whole section 2 of chapter 4 in book 3 is worth reading in full). Durkheim stated: "Un surplus reste généralement disponible qui cherche à s'employer en œuvres supplémentaires, superflues et de luxe, c'est-à-dire en œuvres d'art." The term *employer* is reminiscent of Bataille's language in his theory of useless expenditure and unemployed negativity (but Fields's English translation renders *s'employer* as "to busy"). Durkheim's negative evaluation of both "useless" and "expenditure" is, however, the opposite of Bataille, who favoured these terms as implicit critiques of rational economy.

movement, communicated the social need for creation; when aesthetics referred to the individual artist's work, it instead became a materialization of egoism. In other words, in the case of primitive communities, collective representations granted the harmonious unfolding of emotional impulses. Once modern societies were at stake, *l'art pour l'art* showed the inanity of individualized forms of expression.

Did this conclusion imply that modern societies needed to retrieve the affective dimension they had lost in the process of their historical becoming? Durkheim was not theoretically well equipped to answer this question; neither, for that matter, was Mauss. In the more than thirty years that elapsed between Durkheim's first comments on art and Mauss's own reflections in the new edition of *L'Année sociologique*, the Durkheimian notion of aesthetics continued to lack sophistication. The same disdain for art's autonomy that surfaced in Durkheim's writings reappeared in Mauss's analysis, even as he was elaborating a more positive view of aesthetics' impact on social relations. Inspired by his concept of "total social fact," Mauss envisioned a larger role for aesthetics, now evaluated as a normal component of social life. In actual terms, Mauss's postulate of totality seemed to hold true only for archaic communities, and Mauss saw the contemporary world as characterized by the "unnatural" situation of art's autonomy.[19]

Considering the tradition in which Mauss's interest in the "primitives" developed and was embedded, one should not underestimate his effort to promote the sociological significance of aesthetics. Nevertheless, the most significant move in his sociological approach to the aesthetic sphere turned out to be his affirmation of the artistic nature of the "primitives'" symbolic expressions and production. At a time when Western art was constructing itself through a detour among the "primitives," and when anthropology sought its mission amid states' expansionist fantasies and colonial adventures, sociology's interest in art followed the ethnological route back to the "primitives." In a climate of nostalgia for the uninhibited emotional self, the "primitives" came to constitute a reference point, the premise for challenging the definitional scope of ethnological sciences but also for revolutionizing traditional understandings of the beautiful. The "primitives" served as a lightning rod for modern detractors of art at the same time that art became implicated in the

---

19 In his reflections on art in China, Mauss focused on the absence of *l'art pour l'art* in that country to reiterate the unnecessary division between aesthetics, religion, and science typical of modern societies. Aesthetic symbolism is not free-floating and is integrated in different art forms and rituals, he claimed. See "L'art et les cultes en Chine" (1913), in *Œuvres*, 2: 628–31.

reorganization of ethnography and the re-evaluation of anthropological studies. In a general critical assault against the superficiality of aesthetics, which had originally moved Durkheim to indict art and induced Mauss to lament art's restricted role in the present world, art suffered a major blow prior to being fetishized again on the cultural market.

ANTHROPLOGY AT THE MUSEUM

In the second half of the nineteenth century, French ethnology was at the centre of a definitional debate that embroiled the whole anthropological domain.[20] Was anthropology the study of human physical characteristics or did it also include ethnography – the study of diverse people's cultures? Was ethnography a subdivision of anthropology or a separate discipline? And should one reconcile the two? Paul Broca, founder in 1859 of the Société d'anthropologie and in 1876 of the École d'anthropologie, held that ethnography was the "descriptive study of people" and lacked the rigour necessary to build a human science.[21] Moreover, ethnography tended to slide toward the ideological terrain of social policy, as Paul Topinard, Broca's successor at the helm of the École d'anthropologie, observed. Physical anthropology, in contrast, sought to establish the scientific categorization of races on the basis of anatomical studies.[22] Influenced in part by its parent discipline natural history, anthropology claimed superiority over ethnography and proudly declared its trust in measurable facts and exact analytical procedures.[23] Not surprisingly, the Société d'ethnographie, founded in 1859 by a group of linguists headed by Léon de Rosny, posited itself at a theoretical and institutional distance from the anthropologists of the Broca school.

20 Until the late second empire, the terms "anthropology," "ethnology," and "ethnography" were used with shifting meaning. Ethnology was taken to mean "the joint study of the history and physical character of the races." See Williams, "Anthropological Institutions in Nineteenth-Century France," 333. The term "ethnology" lay dormant for decades until adopted by the Durkheimians in the 1920s. See also Dias, *Le Musée d'ethnographie du Trocadéro*, chapter 1. Dias contends that in the second half of the 1800s, anthropology was considered a general science that comprehended physical anthropology, linguistics, ethnography, ethnology, and archeology. Definitions of anthropology at the time were, however, confusing and often contradictory.

21 Ibid., 24. The École also comprised a Société d'anthropologie, a Laboratoire d'anthropologie, a museum, and a library. It was associated with the École de médecine and most of its members were doctors. See Conklin, "Civil Society, Science, and Empire in Late Republican France."

22 Dias, *Le Musée d'ethnographie du Trocadéro*, chapter 1.

23 For the influence on anthropology of its parent discipline, natural history, see Sturtevant, "Does Anthropology need Museums?"

Dedicated to the science of civilization, the Société d'ethnographie bashed biological materialism, pursued religious spiritualism, and shunned the "primitives" and "savages" in favour of people with a documented past.[24] The Société d'ethnographie held strong ideological and political concerns and lacked a solid scholarly orientation: wealthy patrons contributed to its activist character even as it failed to achieve scientifically driven results.

The two schools of anthropologists remained far apart for years and displayed their different positions in the journals they published, the teaching they offered, and the opposing research methodologies they applied. There was one point, however, that they shared: the appreciation of museums as laboratories for the construction of anthropological knowledge. In the theoretical framework described by Michel Foucault, techniques of order, observation, and classification, which were at the time being appropriated by museums, contributed to generating scientific information and understanding, with the exception that, in the case of museums, such processes took place not on the basis of bodies but of objects. Joining in the massive proliferation of museums throughout the West in the nineteenth century, small museological institutions began to sprout up in France. Both the École d'anthroplogie and the Société d'ethnographie counted on their own establishments for educational and research purposes.[25] Although mostly underfinanced and in disarray, museums became staples of the internally fractured anthropological science, and they served the diverse community of scholars that gathered

24 Dias, *Le Musée d'ethnographie du Trocadéro*, indicates that the Société d'ethnographie was interested in a science of civilization and therefore oriented its study toward the people of Asia and America rather than the "primitives" of Africa and Oceania. In terms of political alignment, the Société d'ethnographie was on the right, but it believed in monogenism and the equality of races. The physical anthropologists were on the left, but supported the polygenist theory of biological types. Internal disputes were not, however, uncommon at the Société d'anthropologie and contributed to weaken the anthropologists' scholarly stand in the early 1900s. Nevertheless, the Société d'ethnographie never had the prestige enjoyed by the École d'anthropologie and was marginalized for many years. See Stocking Jr., "Qu'est-ce qui est en jeu dans un nom?"

25 According to Dias, in *Le Musée d'ethnographie du Trocadéro*, between 1801 and 1880, two hundred and fifty-two museums were established in France. In Germany, the United States, and other countries, the anthropological passion for museums waned early as many scholars found the museums' rules to be too restrictive and not conducive to the cultural understanding of other people. The imperative of fieldwork came to the fore. See Jacknis, "Franz Boas and Exhibits." Williams explains the different situation in France by citing the backwardness of French anthropology, which was split between factions and lacked academic legitimacy until well into the 1920s. See "Anthropological Institutions in Nineteenth-Century France." See also Conklin, "Civil Society, Science, and Empire in Late Republican France" and Clark, *Prophets and Patrons*.

around them and the general public alike. At a historical juncture characterized by overseas expeditions, narcissistic nationalism, and the popular attraction of universal exhibitions, ethnographic museums in the 1850s were conceived as places to organize and eventually divulge knowledge to a wide audience. They promised to be sites that enhanced national stature through an exotic display of the country's conquering spirit and the education of its citizens concerning the nation's efforts. If some of the collections on which museums relied came from the old "cabinets de curiosités," they were now intended not only for scientists and experts as in the past, but for the "little people" as well. The pedagogical mission of the ethnographic museums combined with the emergent intention to conserve testimonials of indigenous people's life in the colonies before the inevitable transformation brought about by the conquering countries. With the revival of ethnographic studies at the dawn of the twentieth century, material culture and the objects constituting it became the heart of museum collections in France, the leading elements in the thematization of non-Europeans' history. Museums ushered in a new era for French ethnography and caused it to revisit its scientific status and redefine the scope of the anthropological domain, while also generating intractable questions about anthropology's relationship to the "objects" of its study. How museums' curators decided on an "ethnographic object" and how these objects were collected, selected, and presented became issues of crucial import.[26]

Objects as Knowledge

At their origins in the 1800s, museums were envisaged as vehicles of knowledge, and anthropological museums were designed to show the history and evolution of humans in their path to a "refined" civilization. As they became attached to the developing science of anthropology, museums contributed to orienting the latter toward the collection and classification of objects, an archival understanding of knowledge-building. When the Musée d'ethnographie du Trocadéro, the first full-scale, independent ethnographic museum in France, opened its doors to the public in 1882, its criteria for selecting and arranging objects reflected and reinforced the scientific direction that anthropology, as a field of study, was taking.[27] Function rather than form defined the place of the artifact in

26 On some of the problems related to ethnographic objects in museums, see Vitart-Fardoulis, "L'objet interrogé ou comment faire parler une collection d'ethnographie."

27 The Musée's immediate ancestor was the Musée ethnographique des missions scientifiques, which opened in January 1878.

the museum; the pedagogical relevance of the object depended on its being a testimonial of other peoples' way of life. The Musée d'ethnographie du Trocadéro featured over 10,000 pieces in its American collection and thousands more in the Asian, Oceanian, and European collections, all methodically ordered and labelled for the public's enlightenment. Moreover, it stuffed objects into cabinets that offered a vision of ensemble while annulling or diminishing the objects' individual and aesthetic dimensions.[28] Material specimens were shown within a reconstructed environment that detailed their use by the particular group that produced them, whether it was to procure food, build a shelter, or engage in commerce or defence. The objects were not valued for their appearance and features. In this sense, the ethnographic museum took its distance from the cabinet de curiosités, which had focused on the singularity and value of individual items. It also established its difference from the art museum, as it disconnected the object from its aesthetic dimensions and rejected the notion that objects speak for themselves.

To be sure, curators and other scholars in charge of the Musée d'ethnographie's pedagogical mission saw their task as different from that of an art or natural history museum; nor was antiquity, in and of itself, a fit category for establishing and defining the characteristics of an ethnographic object. Instead, the idea gradually emerged that the ethnographic specimen should be analysed from the point of view of its "practical and social utility," as Edmé-François Jomard, curator of the Bibliothèque Royale, had already stated in 1831.[29] Jomard had preceded his comment on the utility of the object with the consequential remark that "there is no question of beauty in these arts."[30] Ernest-Théodore Hamy, head of the Musée d'ethnographie du Trocadéro from 1880 to 1906, shared this orientation.[31] He deemed the ethnographic object to be a document that testified about people's existence, ways of living, and history. Objects could not be selected according to aesthetic criteria, Hamy claimed, al-

28 When he recounted his first visit to the Trocadéro, Picasso, for instance, expressed feelings of disgust caused by the bad smell and the clutter. See Paudrat, "From Africa," 141. In another instance, a polemic arose around the transfer of the American collection from the Louvre to the Trocadéro in 1887. The debate revolved around the relationship between ethnography and art and also around the idea that ethnography was in charge of representing the uses and customs of people, not their aesthetic achievements. Evaluated as an ethnographic object, even pre-Columbian culture was not deemed aesthetically valuable. See Williams, "Art and Artifact at the Trocadéro."

29 Ibid., 147.

30 Ibid.

31 Hamy also held the chair of anthropology at the Muséum national d'histoire naturelle beginning in 1892.

though he did not deny that they could be looked at aesthetically. In general, when it came to ethnography the questions whether its objects could ever be classified as art and whether "primitive" people demonstrated any artistic capability remained unanswered. Most scholars denied the possibility on the basis of a classical aesthetic ideal as exemplified by the Romans and Greeks in particular, and indeed the Renaissance.

Although attempts had been made since the eighteenth century to counteract classical aesthetics, the idea of evaluating "primitive" people's artifacts in artistic terms remained controversial at the end of the nineteenth century. An evolutionary schema still subtended the best efforts to evaluate the "primitives'" expressive potential, and artistic productions continued to be rated according to parameters based on a scale of technical competence or "progress."[32] Even when artistic sentiment was taken to be a universal faculty of humanity, as in Hamy's case, this position did not translate into an appreciation of the "primitives'" art on its own terms. For Hamy, the documentary value of the ethnographic object surpassed its potentially artistic content; objects needed to be classified in a system that assigned them a place in the evolutionary scale. Consequently, when it came to techniques of display, Hamy particularly favoured placing objects in reconstructed scenes of daily life.[33] Objects ought to be considered within an environment that contextualized their specific use; they acquired meaning only in relation to others in the same order. Materialistically and functionally evaluated, the objects collected in Africa, Asia, Oceania, and the Americas were supposed to tell a story that documented the progress of civilization. They were not expected to address the question of *Kultur*, in Norbert Elias's famous distinction.[34] When artistic talent was recognized in the "primitives," it remained confined to activities such as music and dance, and sometimes drawing. Invariably, objects were assessed for their "functions," be they

32 See Dias, *Le Musée d'ethnographie du Trocadéro*, chapter 3, and Williams, "Anthropological Institutions in Nineteenth-Century France," 124.

33 See Dias, *Le Musée d'ethnographie du Trocadéro*, 98.

34 As Dias writes, the emphasis on material objects implies that "the constitutive elements of culture can be materialized through objects, which means that cultural manifestations boil down ... to those one can observe in the material world." Ibid., 160. This focus was not true only of France. Edward Tylor's influential *Primitive Cultures* followed the same line. For some, however, such as Émile Soldi, the emphasis on materials made it possible to argue for the cultural importance of other societies' expressive creations since appeals to aesthetics in the case of the "primitives" were not considered legitimate. See Williams' discussion in "Art and Artifacts at the Trocadéro."

religious, cultic, or technical; they were not evaluated as individualized aesthetic expressions.[35]

It is no wonder that at the beginning of the twentieth century, when the "primitivist revolution" commenced, ethnography found itself in the position of a follower, rather than a precursor, of the taste for primitive art.[36] As Robert Goldwater observes, artists' taste for things primitive, which began to emerge in Paris in the early 1900s and later expanded into a popular cultural phenomenon and a collector's dream world, was not guided by museums of anthropology.[37] To be sure, the objects amassed in these museums' glass cases and halls may have helped prepare the taste for tribal art. We know, however, that in its embrace of the "primitives" the French avant-garde privileged the art from Africa and Oceania, not from the Americas, although the latter was more prominently featured at the Musée d'ethnographie.[38] Furthermore, the artists were mostly attracted by works in sculpture, whereas anthropologists had underplayed the value among the primitive people of this form of expression. In general, anthropologists did not equate aesthetics with the "primitives." They subscribed to a traditional conception of art not conducive to such a move.

Discovering "Primitive" Art

Traditional accounts assign to the fauve artist Maurice de Vlaminck the merit of valorizing African sculpture after noticing some statuettes from Dahomey and the Ivory Coast in a Paris bistro in 1905. Although the date, occurrence, and details of this event have been disputed in light of new documentation, de Vlaminck's recounting of that occasion is telling, revealing the role of museums in the avant-garde's reception of ethnographic objects.[39] In his memoirs, de Vlaminck reported that he was struck by something in the African statuettes that he had never before noticed during his frequent visits to the Musée d'ethnographie. There,

35 Jamin, "Objets trouvés des paradis perdus."

36 Following Rubin, "primitivism" is here intended as a Western phenomenon and indicates an interest in tribal art. It does not designate the art of "primitive peoples." See Rubin "Modernist Primitivism," 2.

37 Goldwater, *Primitivism in Modern Art.*

38 On the African collection at the Musée d'ethnographie, see Paudrat, "From Africa." The Surrealists were more attracted to Oceanian art. On the leader of the Surrealists, André Breton, and his interest in the "primitives," see Bonnet, "Á partir de ces 'mécaniques' à la fois naïves et véhémentes ... "

39 Rubin argues that the date was probably 1906 or 1907. See Rubin, "Modernist Primitivism." See also Paudrat's discussion in "From Africa."

as he plainly admitted, he had looked at artifacts as nothing more than "barbaric fetishes." Indeed, he continued, only after Picasso and Matisse saw some of the white African masks that André Derain had purchased from him did the Western passion and hunt for African art begin.[40]

Michel Leiris rightly observes that nothing had changed in the African artifacts kept at the Trocadéro since the time of de Vlaminck's and Derain's first visits.[41] Yet, those objects at some point turned in these artists' eyes from fetishes into signs of African art's grandeur. A chance encounter in a Paris bistro apparently provoked their change of mind. Then, in an escalation of the attraction for the "primitives," avant-garde artists discovered and found inspiration in the Africans' relationship to aesthetic matters, and in particular in the African approach to questions of volume and form. Unencumbered by the ethnographic legacy of disregard for primitive art, the avant-garde engaged with African material in ways that went well beyond the pedagogical and counter-aesthetic intent guiding the mission of anthropological museums. Within this trend of re-evaluation, in 1915 the author and art critic Carl Einstein published the first essay in Europe entirely dedicated to African aesthetics, its features, and strength.[42] Einstein reviewed and praised the Africans' distance from the theory of art as imitation of nature, typical of the West. Whereas, according to the established canon, artistic development was evaluated on the basis of skills and techniques that allowed for the perfect reproduction of the depicted subject, Einstein valorized those elements in African art disdained by the standard-bearers of aesthetic taste. Indeed, it was because African art did not conform to natural proportions and was deeply anti-idealistic that it attracted the anti-intellectual and anti-analytical orientation of avant-garde painters.[43] With Cubism, in particular, African sculpture's characteristic overcoming of natural reality met the avant-garde's sensibility for conceptual forms.[44] If, as Leiris

40 See Goldwater, *Primitivism in Modern Art*, 86–7.

41 Leiris, "The Discovery of African Art in the West."

42 See his "Negerplastik ('La sculpture nègre')." According to Paudrat, Einstein had come into contact with African art at the Museum für Völkerkunde in Berlin between 1904 and 1907. See "From Africa," 151.

43 In 1920, in the review *Action,* Juan Gris referred to African art in opposition to Greek art and defined it as anti-idealistic: "African sculpture is a striking proof of the possibility of creating an *anti-idealistic* art." Cited by Leiris in "The Discovery of African Art in the West," 26 (italicized in the original).

44 According to Einstein, African art was tightly connected to religion. He believed that the artwork was both independent of and more powerful than the individual artist who executed it. Furthermore, African art's conception of space excluded the role of the spectator: there were no effects to pursue, and volume was expressed in terms of structural composition and not mass. See his "Negerplastik."

remarked, Cubism rejected imitation in favour of breaking up real life connections among objects, African sculpture offered models of essentiality, plastic autonomy, and a powerful rhythmic quality. These features appealed to Picasso and other Cubists at a time when their own work was oriented toward assaulting perception in favour of a more analytical style.

Whether the avant-gardists considered the African samples they collected to be art remains unclear.[45] Nevertheless, their fascination with Africa gradually allowed primitivism to gain legitimacy in the complex circuit of the Parisian art world. In 1913, an exhibit at the Galerie Levesques displayed African sculpture for the first time, and labelled it as such. A volume of reproductions, *Sculptures nègres*, was published in April 1917 edited by the collector and art dealer Paul Guillaume.[46] Then, in 1919, the exhibition of African and Oceanian art, held at the Galerie Devambez in Paris between 10 and 31 May, became a pole of attraction for a multitude of visitors.[47] From that moment, the primitivist fad grew into a popular phenomenon. It extended to other cultural forms and culminated in 1925 in the jazz show of the Revue nègre at the Théâtre des Champs Elysées featuring the "African" dance of Josephine Baker.

The Musée d'ethnographie had made it possible for avant-garde painters and writers, concerned with finding new solutions to the constraints of naturalism, to view the rich panorama of ethnic cultures.[48] Whether tribal art directly influenced modernist movements, in particular Synthetic Cubism, or more likely displayed an affinity with them, the artists' attraction for the expressive manner in which aesthetics was realized in some ethnographic objects made possible the phenomenon of primitivism. One has, however, to note that the avant-gardists who espoused primitive art were not interested in ethnological information about the people who inspired them or in the cultural significance of the ethnographic objects they admired. They were instead enthused by the expressive potential of these products as an enticement for rethinking accepted

45 Rubin states that the African masks purchased and owned by avant-garde artists, including the first Fang mask famously purchased by de Vlaminck and considered the first icon of the primitivist fad, were of mediocre artistic quality. See "Modernist Primitivism," 13.

46 See Paudrat, "From Africa," 152.

47 Of course, "African art" is in itself a problematic category that assumes the unity of vastly differentiated ethnic cultures. See Laude, *La peinture française (1905–1914) et l'art nègre* and Blachère, *Le modèle nègre* for a discussion of the more common, but not less problematic, category "art nègre," which was generally used to indicate primitive art and included Africa and Oceania. After the Cubists, primitive art mostly referred to the art of Africa and Oceania. See Rubin, "Modernist Primitivism," 7.

48 According to Goldwater, *Primitivism in Modern Art*, this was also the case in other countries. Paudrat cites the example of the Italian painter Carlo Carrà who, after visiting the Musée in 1899, was struck by its mediocrity and insignificance. See "From Africa," 137.

notions of visual imagery and traditional figurations of space. In this sense, the avant-garde continued a tradition of relationships with the "primitives" in France that was based on little knowledge of the populations embraced as "primitive."[49] Picasso's legendary (though of doubtful authenticity) statement "Art nègre? Connais pas" ("Negro art? I don't know it.") indicates the artists' interest in tribal works' technical solutions beyond the provenance of their creators. The same formula, "art nègre," which became a substitute for primitivism and covered Oceanian art in addition to African, reveals the idiosyncratic nature of the primitivist orientation.

The artists' ignorance of ethnological knowledge paralleled the anthropologists' obliviousness to the aesthetic dimension of the artifacts they studied. Despite the success of "art nègre" at the beginning of the century, artistic considerations remained absent from anthropological works. To be fair, in the second half of the 1800s the German scholar Leo Frobenius published several works that directly engaged the aesthetic culture of Africa.[50] Léopold Senghor, one of the founders of the "Négritude" movement in the 1930s, praises Frobenius for providing him, Aimé Césaire, and Léon Damas with the vision and idea of negritude, as well as the revelation of Africa's artistic and emotional soul.[51] Frobenius's reflections, however, did not find fertile ground in a European context that was still skeptical about the "bizarre" nature of the "primitives'" material production. Not surprisingly, the Durkheimians showed little appreciation for Frobenius's work. Durkheim never reviewed him in *L'Année sociologique*, and Mauss found Frobenius a "questionable," though popular, representative of the German ethnological school of cultural history.[52] In general, the avant-garde's primitivist orientation had minimal impact on scholars of "primitive" people. The artists' attraction for African sculpture, but also the popular acclamation of African dance, as well as the emerging interest in pre-Columbian America and Oceania, did not reverberate in anthropology. The Musée d'ethnographie, for one, under the aegis of the new director, René Verneau, who succeeded Hamy in 1907, continued its documentary approach even as it began to suffer an institutional crisis. Similarly, in the case of artists, their passion for tribal objects did not convert into a desire to know the "primitives" better. As for the

49 Montaigne's essay "On Cannibals" is cited by many as the initiator of a move to valorize the "primitives" in order to criticize the developmental path of Western societies.

50 See among others, *Der Ursprung der afrikanischen Kulturen*, 1898; and *Die Masken und Geheimbünde Afrikas*, 1898.

51 Senghor, foreword to *Leo Frobenius 1873–1973*. Négritude was a francophone cultural and political movement.

52 See Mauss, "Les civilisations: éléments et formes" (1929), in *Œuvres*, 2: 467.

anthropologists, they retained their conception of culture and of their craft more generally, unaffected by art's allure and primitivism's fever.[53]

With regard to the Durkheimians, their unhappiness with the impressionistic style of French ethnography led them to a positivistic accentuation of rigorous facts and first-hand research as means for generating knowledge of the "primitives."[54] It is, then, understandable why Mauss supported the idea of ethnographic museums, and why art remained an elusive field in his theorizing.[55] In 1913, in a report he compiled on the status of ethnography in France, Mauss lamented the critically stagnating situation of ethnographic studies and advocated museums in addition to teaching programs and fieldwork as a remedy.[56] In his efforts to promote the recognition of anthropology as an academic field, Mauss, through his reference to museums, upheld the value of material culture: objects, if scientifically obtained and classified, advanced anthropological knowledge. His opinion was shared by the anthropologist Paul Rivet with whom Mauss, along with Lucien Lévy-Bruhl, founded the Institut d'ethnologie in 1925 with the intention of providing an institutional certification for anthropological work.[57]

Affiliated with the Université de Paris, the Institut's vision was to establish anthropology as the synthetic study of the multiple aspects of the

53 One should, however, note the exception of Lucien Lévy-Bruhl who published his influential work on the "primitives" in the 1910s and 1920s. Lévy-Bruhl emphasized the mythical dimension at the core of primitive mentality and directed attention to the role of dream in the representation of reality. In a sense, Lévy-Bruhl's approach was closer to the tradition begun with Montaigne in the sixteenth century that embraced the "primitives" and their good qualities as indirect critiques of civilization. This tradition was taken up in the early 1900s by literary primitivism, a current quite different from artistic primitivism. See Blachère, *Le modèle nègre*, on Guillaume Apollinaire, Blaise Cendrars, and Tristan Tzara. According to Blachère, Lévy-Bruhl was responsible for some evolutionist understanding of the "primitives" despite his admiration for them. His book on primitive mentality reinforced the intellectuals' complacent belief in the devaluation of reason by non-Westerners and was used to support critiques of Cartesian reason.

54 As Conklin remarks in "Civil Society, Science, and Empire in Late Republican France," 262n19, the Durkheimians were in a complex situation. They did not encourage the founding of anthropology as an independent field and instead believed that the study of other cultures was sociology's domain.

55 However, the reborn *L'Année,* published as *Annales sociologiques* in 1934, included among its separately published five series one with the heading "Social Morphology, Technology, Esthetics" under the direction of Halbwachs. See Clark, *Prophets and Patrons,* 214n19.

56 Mauss, "L'ethnographie en France et à l'étranger," in *Œuvres,* 3: 395–435.

57 Paul Rivet was one of the anthropologists at the Muséum national d'histoire naturelle and had worked as an assistant to Verneau. He had spent five years in Ecuador between 1901 and 1906 on a scientific expedition and was a reputed Americanist.

human being, from the physical to the cultural. The same vision under-
lay the ideal ethnographic museum Mauss and Rivet had begun to plan
in those years; the vision involved uniting physical anthropology and ethnography under the common and newly rediscovered umbrella discipline of "ethnology." When Rivet became director of the Musée
d'ethnographie in 1928, he seized the opportunity to fulfill Mauss's and
his own hopes.[58] He rescued the museum from the state of disarray in
which it had been languishing for decades and radically transformed it
into a site for developing a comprehensive, synthetic "science of man."
Having undergone several innovations and major restructuring, the reconfigured Musée d'ethnographie came to be housed in the reconstructed and refurbished Trocadéro Palace, now Palais de Chaillot. Ambitiously
renamed Musée de l'Homme, it opened its doors to the public in 1938.[59]

Conceived as a teaching tool for the Institut d'ethnologie, the Musée
d'ethnographie, under Rivet's direction and well before its restructuring, generated among other initiatives a plan that encouraged travellers
and nationals living in the colonies to collect objects and donate them to
the museum.[60] Devised as an economical way to increase the museum's
collections, the plan included the distribution of a manual that was supposed to ensure the scientific status of the material being gathered. This
manual, conceived by the ethnologist Marcel Griaule and compiled by
Michel Leiris, then a collaborator of the Musée, specifically advised not
selecting pieces on the basis of their exceptional or beautiful characteristics or under the solicitation of subjective taste. Driven by scientific aspirations, the Musée was looking for everyday tools and specimens that
represented the typical daily existence of the populations who produced
them, not objects that would qualify for the primitive art market then in
full bloom. In other words, specimens were supposed to constitute testimonials.[61] The intent behind this orientation was to establish the Musée
as an institution of popular education and a first-rate research centre. As

58 In 1928 Rivet inherited from Verneau the chair of anthroplogy at the Muséum national d'histoire naturelle. Traditionally, that position also involved taking up the director-
ship of the Musée.

59 At the time, the idea of a Museum of Man was intended to counteract racist ideolo-
gies and show the equality of humanity. Jamin claims that, as a socialist, Rivet pushed an
ideological agenda in anthropology. See "Objets trouvés des paradis perdus."

60 The Musée was modestly subsidized by the Ministry of Colonies. Representatives
from the ministry and from the colonies made up half of its advisory council. See Conklin,
"Civil Society, Science, and Empire in Late Republican France," 271.

61 Compiled in 1931 on the occasion of the *mission* Dakar-Djibouti, the thirty-page
manual "Instructions sommaires pour les collecteurs d'objets ethnographiques" is kept at
the Archives du Musée de l'Homme. See Jamin, "Objets trouvés des paradis perdus" for a
critique of the manual's vision of ethnographic objects. Jamin also indicates that the manual

it turns out, however, the museum's pedagogical mission was conceived over art's dead body, reflecting the troubled relation French anthropology had long maintained with aesthetics.[62] Even though anthropologists recognized the artistic potential of all people, they took objects as illustrative of collective representations; they did not consider them in subjective, individualized terms. Function was privileged over form and testimonials over artistic expression. As Leiris asserted in a short note for the *Nouvelle Revue Française*, the objects, photographs, and observations collected and displayed at the museum were documents: the curators' challenge was to confront them as a living reality and not dead matter.[63]

The new Musée de l'Homme came to epitomize the cultural and social contradictions France was experiencing at the turn of the twentieth century, including the problem of art's social role and the issue of colonial expansion. Those participating in the reconstruction of the Musée, however, showed little awareness of the contradictions raised by aesthetic questions and imperialistic links.[64] The goal of building the discipline of anthropology on a scientific foundation overshadowed any other concern. Since museums lacked funds for acquisitions, the colonies became the only chance for the methodical study of "primitive" societies in their "pure" state before the West spoiled them.

This fantasy of scientific neutrality led Rivet and Georges-Henri Rivière, his collaborator at the Musée from 1928 to 1937, to rely on and tap the colonies as a source for materials and knowledge.[65] At the same time, the fantasy directed Rivet and Rivière to adopt the traditional counter-aesthetic orientation that had guided much of French anthropology up

---

was financed through a boxing match by Al Brown on the occasion of the gala for the ethnographic-linguistic expedition to Dakar-Djibouti.

62 The "Instructions" however included categories such as "Esthétique" and "Monuments de la vie sociale."

63 The risk of considering objects as dead was a complex question but, according to Leiris, techniques of presentation would resolve the dilemma. See Leiris, "Du Musée d'ethnographie au Musée de l'Homme."

64 See Jamin, "Objets trouvés des paradis perdus." Anthropologists, including both Mauss and Rivet, also rhetorically relied on references to the colonies and nationalistic motifs to obtain the attention and favours of various ministries. In this way, they were hoping to enhance ethnographic museums and expand the legitimization of ethnological studies. Anthropologists never challenged or put into question the idea of "empire." See Conklin, "Civil Society, Science, and Empire in Late Republican France."

65 Rivière described himself as a man "without any scientific qualifications" at the time Rivet asked him to be his assistant. See Rivière, "My Experience at the Musée d'Ethnologie," 17. Rivière had musical aspirations, but in 1928 had arranged a successful exhibit of pre-Columbian art at the Musée des arts décoratifs with the ethnologist Alfred Métraux, a close friend of Bataille.

to that point as they reorganized the museum's collections. Within this context, Rivet's affirmation is not surprising: "Buying ethnographic objects on the art market is a solution as expensive as it is unscientific."[66] Objects were to be collected in loco, through ethnographic missions such as the research launched at Dakar-Djibouti in 1931. Artifacts had to be contextualized and were supposed to testify to the life of average people; rare artificats represented only limited and privileged groups.[67] Rivet recommended avoiding the current practice of seeking the precious object, the unique specimen that stood out – a practice encouraged by the primitivist fad. He favoured instead the average utensil, the "humble" tool, the unrefined pot. He also argued that ethnography needed to study wholes. To this end, he suggested adopting the comparative method advocated by Mauss.[68]

The ethnographers did not want to eliminate aesthetics from their realm of study but, as Rivière specified in his project for the renovation of the Trocadéro, they did not wish to turn ethnography into a subsection of art institutions either. Although very close to the avant-garde, Rivière joined Rivet, as well as other collaborators at the museum, including Leiris, in downplaying aesthetics' role in the emergent practice of ethnographic field research. Ethnography's main goal was to develop a comprehensive knowledge of "primitive" and archaic civilizations.[69] Museums were supposed to display and popularize such knowledge

66 Cited in Conklin, "Civil Society, Science, and Empire in Late Republican France," 284. Rivière also stated that "in primitive societies, the aesthetic sentiment far from accumulating in specialized objects circulates in institutions, occupations, beliefs." Cited in Jamin, "Aux origines du Musée de l'Homme," 58.

67 "Now, what is especially important to know are all the aspects, or at least the average aspect, of a civilization and not the exceptional aspect that caters to the privileged classes." See Rivet, "L'étude des civilisations matérielles," 133. Rivet's social commitment in part explains his "ideological" inclinations. Jacques Soustelle, who held deep socialist beliefs and who replaced Rivière as an assistant to Rivet in 1937, will particularly insist on the museum's mission as a popularizer of knowledge in a democratic way: the museum did not need to focus on artistic works but rather on everyday tools with which average French people could identify. See Conklin, "Civil Society, Science, and Empire in Late Republican France," 278–9. On the ideological mission of French ethnology, see Jamin, "De l'humaine condition de 'Minotaure.' "

68 Rivet actually introduced what he defined as a cartographic method based on distribution cards. See "L'étude des civilisations matérielles," 131.

69 Rivière, "Le Musée d'ethnographie du Trocadéro," 58. Rivière was also training as an ethnologist. In one unpublished document he recounted, "I realize I was then Mauss's favorite student. We talked for nights walking through Paris ... He linked his encyclopedic knowledge of Oceania with his childhood memories at Épinal. He wished that everything of interest to him find an echo at the Museum." See Leroux-Dhuys, "Georges Henri Rivière, un homme dans le siècle," 23.

through objects, specimens, and documents taken as materializations of phenomena, representations of wholes. In this sense, the ethnographers' intent to valorize the "primitives" led them to intentionally avoid any aesthetic evaluation. Aesthetics was negatively cast and any reference to it could only spoil the authentic and genuine nature of archaic cultures.

Despite the apparently clear-cut nature of the museum curators' approach, ambiguities continued to confound the relationship between aesthetics and ethnography in France well into the 1930s. First, the Musée did not exclude art specimens from its search for ethnographic objects. Furthermore, as the *mission* Dakar-Djibouti demonstrated, many of the specimens collected for the Musée were gathered on the basis of their aesthetic appeal: the ethnographers singled them out for their artistic merits following their own personal taste.[70] The *mission Dakar-Djibouti* indeed magnifies and exposes the problematic path French ethnology had taken and continued to follow even after its reorganization in the second half of the 1920s.

Posited as a scientific endeavour, the ethnographic and linguistic Dakar-Djibouti expedition, which took place in North Africa during 1931–1933, was organized by the Institut d'ethnographie and the Muséum national d'histoire naturelle under the sponsorship of the Musée d'ethnographie. Marcel Griaule, then an assistant at the Laboratoire d'ethnologie at the Université de Paris, was charged with its direction.[71] The first of its kind, the expedition pursued its objectives under the rigorous control of research and teaching institutions. Led by ethnographers who, in contrast to past practices, had also undergone an ethnological apprenticeship, one of the expedition's primary goals was to supply material for the Musée's African collection.[72] The expedition also aspired to create an archive of diverse civilizations. Once in the field, however, the mission ended up focusing mainly on the spectacular dimensions of the traditional societies it examined, that is, their ritualistic

70 On the occasion of the 1984 exhibit on African Masterpieces from the Musée de l'Homme, at the Center for African Art in New York, Susan Vogel wrote that "it is now accepted that among the thousands of ethnographic specimens in the Musée de l'Homme are many works of art." Vogel also remarked, "The deeper we searched in the Musée de l'Homme's files, the more often we encountered a subversive love of beautiful objects, a search for aesthetically pleasing works by members of the anthropological expeditions." See her introduction to Vogel and N'Diaye, *African Masterpieces from the Musée de l'Homme*, 11.

71 Griaule had already been on a mission in Abyssinia. For an account in English of Griaule's innovative ethnographic approach, see Clifford, "Power and Dialogue in Ethnography" in Clifford, *The Predicament of Culture*.

72 The expedition's researchers included Michel Leiris, the ethnomusicologist André Schaeffner, and as the only woman member Deborah Lifszyc. See Michel Leiris's account of the expedition in *L'Afrique fantôme*.

and cultural activities. Furthermore, because of the materialistic episte-
mology to which the mission subscribed – the notion, that is, of the object as document – the ethnographers' work centred around the
gathering of specimens, believing that all phenomena found expression
in an artifact.[73] Culture was grossly reduced to material manifestations
and positivistically evaluated on the basis of the specimens that supposedly represented and embodied it. It followed that not only was an aesthetic object asked to stand for a whole culture; objects of various natures
were also considered equivalent in terms of both their evidential worth
and exhibit potential. As Jean Jamin writes, "a Dogon lock had the same
testimonial value as a mask or a statue."[74] The Musée displayed its ethnological collections following the same assumption; jars and pots were
crammed together next to intricately carved masks.

Jamin, one of the most eloquent critics of the limitations vexing
French ethnography in the first half of the twentieth century (in particular its voyeuristic tendencies and links to colonialism), contemplates the
possibility of considering the Musée's undifferentiated approach to objects within the Surrealist perspective of subversion.[75] Following this
logic, the juxtaposition of a painting with an object of daily life serves to
demystify the auratic character of artworks in museological institutions
and to dispel the image of art and museums as cultural treasures. But is
the Surrealists' penchant for deauraticization applicable to other cultures, Jamin skeptically wonders? Or is their anti-aestheticism reductive
and even insulting when extended to traditional societies, since it denies
them any artistic capacities and/or individual creativity? For Jamin, what
one risks with an interpretive move along the lines of Surrealism is the
production of a mechanistic, functional image of "other" cultures – an
image that eschews formal, syntactical analysis and remains at the descriptive level. The structure of an object, however, is not necessarily a
function of the use for which the object is devised, Jamin argues.[76] By
evoking the dilemma of use and function as opposed to form and

73 Reports on the expedition also display several problematic areas concerning both
the researchers' relationship to the indigenous population and their method of appropriation of the objects they considered worth sending back to the museum. In terms of subject-
matter, half of the objects brought back from the mission were ritualistic or related to
recreation. See Jamin, "Objets trouvés des paradis perdus" and "Aux origines du Musée de
l'Homme."

74 Jamin, "Objets trouvés des paradis perdus," 92.

75 In relation to voyeurism, Jamin talks about "objects *to see*" (objets à voir), ibid., 77.
The mission was also interested in the "other" of visibility, that is, secrecy: esoteric knowledge and secret language in the case of the Dogon.

76 Jamin, "Aux origines du Musée de l'Homme."

structure, but also the metonymical mistake of taking the part for the whole on the basis of its being "representative," Jamin reveals and denounces the epistemological consequences of French ethnography's unresolved relationship to the aesthetic issue. He also lays out the opposed tendencies that sustained such a relationship and that, on the one hand, negated the presence in primitive cultures of any aesthetic value or, alternatively, defined anything in those cultures as artistic, while rejecting the notion of uniqueness.[77] The *mission* Dakar-Djibouti can be taken as exemplifying the contradictory tendency at the heart of French ethnography. In 1933, issue 2 of the lavish art magazine *Minotaure* was entirely devoted to the "booty" pillaged by this expedition and featured articles by Rivet and Rivière and Griaule.[78]

The theory of an affinity between ethnography and Surrealism is, in the end, not only inadequate, according to Jamin, but also inaccurate, especially if one takes into account colonialism, embraced by ethnography and condemned by Surrealism. Jamin is particularly critical of what he considers James Clifford's romanticized notion of "ethnographic surrealism," a construct according to which juxtapositions and incongruities are central to the ways researchers approach their objects and in which ethnography is interpreted as following the model of collage.[79] Jamin admits that Clifford's expression specifically refers to the work that emerged from *Documents*, a journal that, as its subtitle indicates, covered "doctrines, archéologie, beaux-arts, ethnographie" and whose collaborators included Leiris, Rivet, Rivière, Griaule, and eminent art critics and historians.[80] And indeed, Rivière reminisced in 1968 that in the

77 Jamin here sees a connection between ethnographic practice and the teachings of the French school of sociology, which was keen on issues of social cohesion and integration. Ibid.

78 "Booty" is how Rivet and Rivière referred to what was collected during the expedition. See "Mission ethnographique et linguistique Dakar-Djibouti," 5. More than 3,000 objects were collected during the expedition. *Minotaure* was at first edited by dissident Surrealists. Among its topics, it listed Ethnographie et Mythologie. In 1938 Griaule published the book *Masques Dogons* entirely dedicated to the analysis of Dogon masks encountered during the expedition.

79 See Clifford, "On Ethnographic Surrealism," in *The Predicament of Culture*. By referring to ethnographic surrealism, Clifford was interested in undoing categories that often blind us and force us to work with highly laden concepts, hampering the potential of cultural analysis. In the revised edition of *The Predicament of Culture*, Clifford specifies that by "Surrealist" he meant a general attitude, "a pervasive ... modern sensibility," and not a specific historical phenomenon limited to France (118n1). Conley supports Clifford's orientation in her study "Modernist Primitivism in 1933."

80 The full title of the journal for the first three issue was *Documents: Doctrines, Archéologie, Beaux-Arts, Ethnographie*. Later issues substituted "Variétés" for "Doctrines." The title was then *Documents: Archéologie, Beaux-Arts, Ethnographie, Variétés*.

1 The Dakar-Djibouti Expedition. Cover page of
Minotaure 2 (1933), special issue on the *mission*
Dakar-Djibouti. Drawing by Gaston-Louis Roux,
who participated in the expedition as the official
painter

illustrations of *Documents* "could be seen side by side a Zapotec urn and a scene from the Folies Bergères" in the collage style evoked by Clifford.[81] Jamin, however, finds the notion of ethnographic surrealism objectionable because it obliterates the implications for ethnography of this anti-aestheticism. It also assigns little importance to the fact that most of *Documents'* contributors were dissident Surrealists, and among the ethnographers there was no notable surrealist inclination.

Jamin's critique of Clifford rightly alerts us to the risks of romanticizing the relationship between art and ethnography. Yet Jamin fails to see that Clifford's reference to *Documents* raises the issue of the role that ethnography played in the negative redefinition of art being conjured up by French intellectuals at the time. Even though some of *Documents'* contributors had come to ethnography by way of a detour through art, it was in fact through the ethnographic "encounter," that is, by tackling ethnography, that art was reframed and contradictorily rebuked in

81 Rivière, "My Experience at the Musée d'Ethnologie," 17.

Documents.[82] By overcoming art and its supposed inauthenticity, *Documents* then imagined a solution to the impending social crisis and to what many believed was the deadly desiccation of human essence in modernity.

Because of its engagement with art and ethnography, and because Bataille was *Documents*' general secretary and one of its founders, I will next discuss *Documents* as illuminating the fate of aesthetics in 1930s France. [83] In particular, *Documents* shows how the derogation of aesthetics became a self-definitional move for those, including Bataille, who were becoming politically or socially committed in an economically and politically ravaged Europe. Although politics and art were later again joined under a similarly negative evaluation, especially at the Collège de sociologie, in *Documents* aesthetics was deemed even guiltier than politics of precipitating the collapse of social bonds. After *Documents* ceased publication, ambiguities surrounding the modern critique of aesthetics remained a staple of the 1930s. These ambiguities became painfully evident in the Surrealists' botched attempt to engage actively in the political arena, as we will see in the next chapter.

DOCUMENTS

De-aestheticizing the Ethnographic Object

Documents was founded in 1929 with the financial support of Georges Wildenstein, an art merchant and publisher of *La Gazette des Beaux-Arts*. After producing fifteen issues, it ceased publication in 1930, apparently because its anti-conformist orientation did not please its financer.[84] Wildenstein expected the journal to be an art magazine and to be more lucrative. Over time, however, it became increasingly clear that *Documents* was taking an unusual direction in terms of its editorial choices. Georges

82 Rivière states: "Such was the encounter between two realms: that of science ... and the aesthetic." Ibid., 17. In *Documents* 7 (1930), Leiris described his trajectory as going from art to ethnography. See "L'œil de l'ethnographe," 405–14.

83 Bataille was the mastermind behind *Documents*. In his recollections Rivière states that Bataille was the "editor-in-chief." See Rivière, "My Experience at the Musée d'Ethnologie," 17.

84 As mentioned earlier, my reading of *Documents* focuses on the journal's anti-aesthetic direction as it developed in concomitance with the rediscovery of the "primitives." I pay less attention to the other original aspects of the review, such as its juxtapositions of "art" with popular culture or its innovative use of photography. I acknowledge that *Documents* became for Bataille a forum from which to counter the Surrealists' project, but I do not specifically examine Bataille's writings for *Documents* from the angle of his critique of the Surrealists. I speak more directly of Bataille's relationship to the Surrealists in chapter 3. On *Documents*, see Ades and Baker, *Undercover Surrealism*.

Bataille, according to Leiris, was principally responsible for turning the publication into an original cultural experiment, a Janus-faced review that reflected Bataille's personality. Thus, from one side, the journal looked at the "high spheres of culture"; from the other, it surveyed a "savage zone where one ventures with no maps or passports of any sort."[85]

The journal's inaugural issue revealed the incongruous and unconventional approaches the publication was ready to take toward artistic, archeological, and ethnographic topics. The first three articles dealt with scholarly subjects in the respective fields of Sumerian art, Siberian and Chinese art, and plastic arts. Yet, Dr Georges Couteneau, author of "Sumerian Art: Conventions of the Statuary," announced that the journal's plan was to have a broader public engage in artistic forms normally appreciated only by a few experts.[86] Couteneau continued with a plea not to dismiss Sumerian art because of its exaggerated forms: Western canons should not affect our aesthetic evaluations. Along similar lines, Paul Pelliot's article on Siberian and Chinese art stressed the importance of closely examining the relationship of influence among artistic styles, especially when one style, in this case Siberian, is not well studied.[87] For Pelliot, one needed to overcome old aesthetic prejudices and preferences in order to develop more accurate analyses of styles and timelines. This meant exploring the uncommon within the field of "legitimate" art, including, as Josef Strzygowski argued in his own contribution to the debate, monuments that, as in the case of nomad art, have not been conserved.[88] One ought to take a distance from the higher styles of stone architecture and explore the less precious art of wood or brick constructions. Strzygowski proclaimed the need for an objective science that would overcome the aesthete's point of view in order to research the essence of things as well as their evolution.[89]

85 Leiris, "De Bataille l'impossible à l'impossible 'Documents,'" 688. Leiris specifically situated the public disclosure of Bataille's intentions for *Documents* in issue 4 of the magazine.

86 "L'art sumérien: les conventions de la statuaire," 1–8. Couteneau worked at the Louvre and was on the editorial board of *Documents*.

87 "Quelques réflexions sur l'art sibérien et l'art chinois, à propos de bronzes de la collection David-Weill" 9–21. A renowned sinologist, Pelliot was also on the editorial board of *Documents*.

88 "'Recherches sur les arts plastiques' et 'Histoire de l'art,'" 22–6. Josef Strzygowski was a professor at the University of Vienna and a member of the editorial board of *Documents*. Beginning with issue 5, *Documents* stopped listing members on its editorial board.

89 Strzygowski argued for examining original monuments according to a global grid that would take into account the relation between things within a totality. He also stated, "We draw a neat distinction between objective research and the research of the aesthete." Ibid., 26.

An unconventional approach to art emerged in *Documents* from its inception and set the tone for the future. The journal intended to foster an alternative notion of aesthetics and at the same time develop a scientific procedure for studying heterogeneous artifacts. "The most irritating works of art, the ones not yet ranked, and some heteroclite and so far neglected productions, will be the object of as rigorous and scientific studies as those of the archeologists," a publicity text for *Documents* read.[90] To be sure, the journal's title itself signalled the incongruous approach its contributors were embracing: the word "documents" strongly echoed ethnography's counter-aesthetic position as well as its methodology of relying on objects as testimonials.[91] If science and rigour characterized ethnography via its link to documents, then, the journal's title seemed to suggest, the same could be expected from art if one treated its expressions as documents. Following this logic, the anti-aestheticism sported by French ethnology became *de rigueur* at *Documents*; and the journal sided with ethnology's museological perspective. In their turn, Rivet and Rivière, who were both on the journal's editorial board, found in *Documents* the perfect forum in which to express their opposition to examining ethnographic objects in artistic terms. Other ethnologists also participated in the journal. Although their ethnological credentials varied, Marcel Griaule, André Schaeffner, and Michel Leiris, all of whom left for the *mission* Dakar-Djibouti a few months after *Documents* disbanded, wrote regularly for the review.

Unsurprisingly, in view of the developmental trajectory of French ethnology in the 1920s, most of the "ethnographic" contributions to *Documents* confronted the contentious issue of ethnography's relation to aesthetics. Equally unremarkable, the ethnologists' articles emphasized the testimonial character of material objects while negatively assessing art's status. Thus, Rivet's and Rivière's publications for issues 1 and 3 of *Documents* unequivocally supported a documentarian approach to ethnography that downplayed the centrality of artistic concerns. In "L'étude des civilisations matérielles; ethnographie, archéologie, préhistoire," Rivet, after grouping ethnography together with archeology and prehistory in "the one and same science" that studied material civilizations, encouraged them not to seek the beautiful, unique, or artistic pieces at

---

90 Cited in Leiris, "De Bataille l'impossible à l'impossible 'Documents,'" in *Critique*, 689.

91 In his introduction to the 1991 reprint of *Documents*, "La valeur d'usage de l'impossible," Hollier hypothesizes as one meaning of "document" something lacking value and originality, a meaning that comes close to the Surrealist idea of the ready-made. *Documents*, viii.

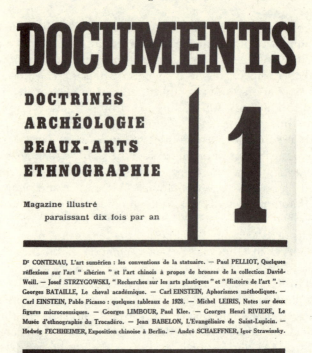

DOCUMENTS

DOCTRINES
ARCHÉOLOGIE
BEAUX-ARTS
ETHNOGRAPHIE

1

Magazine illustré
paraissant dix fois par an

Dʳ CONTENAU, L'art sumérien : les conventions de la statuaire. — Paul PELLIOT, Quelques réflexions sur l'art " sibérien " et l'art chinois à propos de bronzes de la collection David-Weill. — Josef STRZYGOWSKI, " Recherches sur les arts plastiques " et " Histoire de l'art ". — Georges BATAILLE, Le cheval académique. — Carl EINSTEIN, Aphorismes méthodiques. — Carl EINSTEIN, Pablo Picasso : quelques tableaux de 1928. — Michel LEIRIS, Notes sur deux figures microcosmiques. — Georges LIMBOUR, Paul Klee. — Georges Henri RIVIERE, Le Musée d'ethnographie du Trocadéro. — Jean BABELON, L'Evangéliaire de Saint-Lupicin. — Hedwig FECHHEIMER, Exposition chinoise à Berlin. — André SCHAEFFNER, Igor Strawinsky.

PARIS. - 39, rue La Boétie.   Prix : 15 fr.

2 Cover page of the first issue of *Documents*, April 1929

the expense of those that were useful and prosaic.[92] When considering what constitutes a civilization, one should not neglect any element, no matter how insignificant it might seem; and he insisted that ethnography, archeology, and prehistory avoid researching a particular civilization's precious side. In its turn, Rivière's "Le Musée d'ethnographie du Trocadéro" expressed the fear that the current art fad for appreciating the art of the "primitives" would undermine the Musée d'ethnographie's mission and essence. Becoming an art museum was not a wise option for the Musée, Rivière argued: the adoption of aesthetic criteria for selecting artifacts hampered ethnography's power to portray the daily reality of a civilization. In order to safeguard ethnological knowledge, one needed to ostracize art. Art museums were indeed fit only for higher cultures, he concluded.[93]

92 Rivet, "L'étude des civilisations matérielles," 130.
93 See Rivière, "Le Musée d'ethnographie du Trocadéro." When announcing the *mission* Dakar-Djibouti in *Documents*, Rivière cited, among the many objectives of the mission,

As a music expert, André Schaeffner also found himself struggling against classic aesthetic standards when confronted with non-Western traditions.[94] His main "ethnographic" piece for *Documents* discussed musical instruments and their role as objects/documents in a museological institution.[95] Schaeffner challenged all methods that, when classifying musical instruments, ruled out unorthodox or primitive ways to produce sounds, including the practice of beating on the ground. In his perspective, ethnography's strength lay in the fact that it was not supposed to look for the artistically exceptional. It aimed at expanding both our knowledge of human artistic experience in general and our understanding of unfamiliar people and customs in particular.[96] Within this framework, no music can be deemed unfit. And he added that a museum of ethnography was more suited than other specialized and exclusive institutions, such as conservatories and art museums, to account for those invariable elements that characterize all musical civilizations. In addition, an ethnographic museum would take into account that art is not isolated from other social ends such as magic, religion, and war. Borrowing from a political vocabulary, one could say that for Schaeffner ethnography was more democratic than art in its intent to deal with the everyday and the normal. Ethnography considered the multiple uses of objects without fixating on artistic purity and in so doing it expanded our appreciation of musical traditions. One needed to open up the horizon of artistic sensibility and overcome the limitations of aesthetic orthodoxy. Within this context, Schaeffner's attempt to gain legitimacy for the "primitives'" musical expressions implied differentiating the latter from high art. It appeared to him that only by separating the two could one ensure fair treatment for indigenous cultures.

Along the same lines, Griaule countered Western aesthetics by uncovering the alternative rules Abyssinian painting applied to religious portraits. He indicated the importance of knowing about a pot's social use

---

the development of "natural and social sciences." He did not mention art. See his introduction to Leiris, "L'œil de l'ethnographe," 406.

94 Schaeffner's inaugural piece for *Documents* was on Stravinsky (his role at the journal was as music critic). See "Igor Strawinsky, musicien vivant." But even when he commented on the musicological tradition of the West, Schaeffner selected topics that challenged normalized and accepted notions of music appreciation and implied a re-evaluation of misunderstood works. In one of his articles he wrote that "*music* is richer than *Music* and no less susceptible to greatness." See "Les 'Lew Leslie's Black Birds' au Moulin Rouge," 223.

95 Schaeffner, "Des instruments de musique dans un musée d'ethnographie."

96 Schaeffner recommended displaying the musical instruments of a civilization in a separate glass case and not with other objects of that same civilization, even though for comparative purposes the instruments would still share the same room or space. Ibid.

in addition to its artistic value.[97] Griaule did not deny that ethnography was interested in both the ugly and the beautiful. For him, however, ethnography was not after rarity and uniqueness and did not exclude the possibility that there is aesthetic value in something serially fabricated. Indeed, ethnography tended to "mistrust the beautiful, which is most often a rare, that is, a monstrous manifestation of a civilization."[98] According to Griaule, ethnography ultimately needed to undo Western taste in its twentieth-century bourgeois incarnation. In this sense, ethnography ought to shift attention from form to meaning, from container to content, from aesthetic exclusivism to multiple dimensionality.[99] Griaule did not follow Rivière in denying artistic autonomy to the "primitives" in order to honour them. On the contrary, he dismantled the category of pure art so that he could support the value of indigenous cultures. Like the other ethnologists, he indicated the inadequacy of classic aesthetic notions. His anti-aestheticism, though, contradictorily came to cohabit with the search for alternative aesthetic forms.

In the case of Michel Leiris, his critique of the aesthetic field most often unfolded while writing about topics that would be conventionally defined as artistic, even though he interspersed articles on Pablo Picasso and Alberto Giacometti with original ethnographic interpretations of various subjects.[100] No matter the disciplinary angle, though, Leiris never failed to unleash his discriminating judgment against art and its dominating status. Thus, his contribution to the inaugural issue of *Documents* discussed two images from manuscripts of the fourteenth and fifteenth centuries that represented microcosmic figures in their relationship to the universe.[101] After describing how the two figures expressed a symbolic reality that attempted to map out man's role within the macrocosm, Leiris made his substantive point: the need for revisiting the modern tendency to attribute aesthetic meaning where only symbolic significance might be at play. Taking the example of Leonardo's famous drawing of the man inscribed in a circle, which closely resembled the two figures he was examining, Leiris challenged the official view of Leonardo's

---

97 See Griaule, "Légende illustrée de la Reine de Saba" and "Poterie."

98 Griaule, "Un coup de fusil," 46.

99 From the point of view of ethnographic theory, Griaule emphasized the use value of an object against its exchange value. See Hollier's comments in "La valeur d'usage de l'impossible."

100 Together with Bataille and Einstein, Leiris was the most prolific writer at *Documents*. He wrote articles on Joan Miró, Hans Arp, Kalifala Sidibé, Antoine Caron, Pablo Picasso, and Alberto Giacometti, among others. On Einstein's collaboration with *Documents*, see Joyce, *Carl Einstein in* Documents.

101 Leiris, "Notes sur deux figures microcosmiques des XIVᵉ et XVᵉ siècles."

naked man as the graphic figuration of an aesthetic canon concerning the proportions of the human body. He defiantly suggested looking instead at the mystic pentagram of Cornelius Agrippa as inspiration, and he more pointedly indicated the need to end art's dominant role when explaining and understanding material culture.

The monopolizing potential of the aesthetic was a recurring target of Leiris's thematic analyses whether he wrote about paintings or more mundane topics. Thus, his short definitional entry on "Civilisation," for the regularly featured "Dictionnaire" ("Dictionary") section of *Documents*, derided our attachment to a culture that rejects what is savage while hiding its own "ferocity" under the mantle of the "civilized."[102] In so doing, not only do we forfeit our instincts; we also ignore the ritualistic meaning of the "primitives'" practices and forms of expressions, and we ultimately tame the "savagery" of their statues and masks by turning them into "Art," "that horrible word with a capital letter, which one should only write with a pen full of spider webs."[103] For art is atrophied, Leiris disparagingly stated, and Grand Art only signals a distance from our emotions and expressivity and, more generally, human nature. Art, in sum, does not have any organic relationship to us, Leiris insisted in another article, and aesthetic ideals, conventions, and hierarchies are obstacles to our own deepening humanity.[104]

Several of Leiris's contributions for *Documents* lashed out at art's inadequacies and extreme platitude.[105] To him, art appeared "estranged" from our humanness, and he came to advocate the aesthetic of the disagreeable as an alternative approach to beauty.[106] Leiris also counterpoised classic aesthetics, with its focus on the values and hierarchies of the "white man," to ethnography's ability to speak of the totality of people;[107] ethnography provided the counter altar to Western aesthetics' exclusivism. Although in the pages of *Documents* Leiris did not advocate a scientific path to ethnographic research, he recommended to

102 Leiris, "Civilisation."

103 Ibid., 222. For this reason, Leiris denied Black Americans such high designation as they were headed well beyond the deadly notion of art.

104 "L'homme et son intérieur." See also "Toiles récentes de Picasso," where Leiris made an exception for Picasso's work, and "Le 'caput mortuum' ou la femme de l'alchimiste," where Leiris stated that in order to reconnect with our human nature, or nature more generally, we need to overcome the duality of soul and body, spirit and matter, 465.

105 See in particular his articles on Picasso and Giacometti, especially "Toiles récentes de Picasso," and "Alberto Giacometti."

106 "L'homme et son intérieur." Hollier draws attention to the way the topic of fetishism is featured in *Documents* and sees it interpreted in a reverse mode from Marx's original assessment. See "La valeur d'usage de l'impossible."

107 Leiris, "L'œil de l'ethnographe."

his fellow artists and writers that they travel as ethnographers in order to recover their human essence. Disdainful of the European evaluation of indigenous cultures as inferior and aware of the racism underpinning such judgments, Leiris privileged the exotic mental voyage into primitive spaces in search of a poetry that would survive the deadly spirit of bourgeois Europe.[108] As he operated at the crossroad between ethnography and the avant-garde, he subscribed to the ethnographers' distrust of art even though, unlike the ethnographers, he espoused an almost existentialist rejection of the artist's bourgeois principles. Leiris's voice in the pages of *Documents* was more attuned to the malaise of the modern white world, despite the fact that he later became one of the strongest critics of ethnographic authority.[109] In his anti-aestheticism, he was also much more critical of art as a historical notion than were the ethnographers, since the latter preferred to draw disciplinary distinctions between the artistic and ethnographic fields rather than formulate critiques of the category art.

Leiris's position was more aligned with Carl Einstein's, the pioneer critic of African sculpture, who in his essays for *Documents* attacked aesthetic orthodoxy, and in particular the Renaissance identification of art with nature, and assaulted the idea of art as having to follow the rules of proportion and perspective.[110] Against the reliance of "scientific fetishism" on physical laws and human reason, Einstein invoked the arbitrary, the free, and the hallucinatory, and he found in Picasso's work an art that overcomes conventional reality and mechanical representations at the same time that it dispenses with metaphors and allegories. Whether he praised the engravings of Hercules Seghers for their ability to destroy the optimistic unity of nature or denounced references to the nightingale as the worst recourse to allegory and ornament, Einstein's critique of traditional aesthetics was relentless.[111] And he condemned all artistic approaches that privileged representation.[112]

In the end, whatever the disciplinary perspective or analytical stand, art was at the centre of a flagellating operation at *Documents*, and it seems that the attempts at desacralizing it and turning it into a document did not necessarily redeem its devilish status. Art became another of the

---

108 See (under "Revue des publications") Leiris, "Jean Brunhes, *Races*," 6.
109 See Clifford, "On Ethnographic Authority," in *The Predicament of Culture*.
110 See in particular, Einstein, "Pablo Picasso. Quelques tableaux de 1928" and "Aphorismes méthodiques."
111 Einstein, "Gravures d'Hercules Seghers" and "Rossignol."
112 Einstein, "L'exposition de l'art abstrait à Zurich."

white man's mystical obsessions. But it was Bataille in particular who pushed *Documents*' agenda to the point of exploding art at its seams. It was Bataille who through a more thorough aesthetic critique superseded art by promoting its (ugly) other.

A Counter Aesthetic: Georges Bataille

Bataille's distinctive contribution to *Documents* emerges as an all-out attack against aestheticism through a two-sided intervention that, on the one hand, criticized architectural forms, idealism, and the tectonic and, on the other, promoted an interest in the repulsive and the heterogeneous.[113] Bataille had already displayed his intent to assault decency and beauty in writings prior to *Documents*. In particular, his first book *W.C.*, which was presumably written in 1926 but never published, was "violently opposed to all dignity." Bataille destroyed it shortly after its completion[114] Together with the equally disturbing 1927 essay "L'Anus solaire," the book had motivated Bataille's friend Dr Camille Dausse to suggest starting psychoanalytic treatment, advice that Bataille followed with good results in spite of an ongoing proclivity for "intellectual violence."[115] Although Bataille's first article for *Documents*, "Le cheval académique," had none of the obscene content of *W.C.* or the undignified rhetoric of "The Solar Anus" (to the contrary, it adopted the neutral tone and learned oratory of the expert), it nonetheless pursued the same objective violently anticipated by *W.C.* and "The Solar Anus": the dismantling of idealist categories, albeit through an analysis of representations. More

113 See "Architecture," where Bataille writes, "In effect, only the ideal being of society, the one that orders and forbids with authority, is expressed in the properly called architectural compositions," 117. Architecture constituted for Bataille the expression of society's being, and he identified it with authority.

Several of Bataille's writings for *Documents* are translated into English, in Bataille, *Visions of Excess*. When available, I will rely on the English translations.

114 See "Notice autobiographique" (written in 1958), in Bataille, *Œuvres Complètes* (hereafter cited as *OC*), 7: 460. We know from Leiris that the story concerned a young, rich, and beautiful English lady by the name of Dirty who was involved in several scenes of orgies. According to Leiris, who was among the few who read the manuscript, the first chapter of *W.C.* became the first chapter of Bataille's political novel *Le bleu du ciel* (*Blue of Noon*). See Leiris, "De Bataille l'impossible à l'impossible *Documents*."

115 See Bataille, "Notice autobiographique," *OC*, 7: 460. For "L'Anus solaire," see Bataille, *OC*, vol. I; English translation "The Solar Anus," in Bataille, *Visions of Excess*. Camille Dausse was friend to many Surrealist poets and artists. Walter Benjamin also cites him as a friend in a letter to Gretel Adorno of 12 October 1939. See Scholem and Adorno, *The Correspondence of Walter Benjamin*.

specifically, the article discussed the differences in the design of horses that appeared in the original coins issued by the ancient Greeks and in those that, imitating the Greeks, were made by the Gauls.[116]

With the goal of demonstrating that different styles often correspond to opposite forms of social organization, Bataille compared the Greek coins' idealist inspiration to the suggestive style adopted by the Gauls. He then drew general conclusions about the two peoples' civilizations. The Greeks' perfect and aesthetically harmonious portrayal of horses expressed the orderly character of their social system, their idealization of spirit and perfection, and their rejection of ugliness. The Gauls' approximate and fantastic sketching, in contrast, despite being inspired by the Greeks, transformed the classic horse into a frenetic monster that communicated the sense of instability, disorganization, and violence at the basis of the Gauls' social existence. The Gauls' deformed horse, Bataille argued, expressed and promoted "aggressive ugliness, transports linked to the view of blood or to horror, excessive screaming – in other words, what has no meaning, no usefulness," and therefore escapes the enticements of order and authority.[117] The Gauls avoided calculation and vowed faith in impermanence; for Bataille, however, their imperfect horse design was not an indication of technical deficiency. The Gauls purposefully challenged "scientific arrogance" and geometric rules through the pursuit of deformed images. The Gauls' representations pushed forth the dark, inordinate side of humanity along with its frightening and at the same time burlesque dimensions. In so doing, Bataille contended that the Gauls did not merely counteract the organizing principles guiding the Greeks: they also more generally attacked and refuted order's pre-eminent role.

In Bataille's hands (or words), the academic horse, which he described as "one of the most accomplished expressions of the *idea*," became a means to delve into the heart of horror. Bataille adopted a formal critique of canons of beauty, canons that, identified with idealism and spiritualism, also rested on orderly principles and geometric certainty.[118] Within this interpretive context, Bataille was not surprised that the Greeks, who most desired to see noble ideas guide the course of things, manifested their aspirations through the depiction of the horse's body. As he wrote, "the ugly or comic bodies of the spider or hippopotamus would not have reflected

116 At the time, Bataille was employed at the Cabinet des Médailles at the Bibliothèque nationale, and had already published scholarly articles on numismatics in *Aréthuse*, a specialized review of art and archeology. See *oc*, vol. 1.

117 Bataille, "Le cheval académique," 30.

118 Ibid., 28.

such elevation of the spirit."[119] The horse was the academic animal par excellence and perfectly embodied the Greeks' desire for elevation. The Gauls' plastic displacement of the horse's noble status, in contrast, showed the Gauls' "monstrous mentality." In addition, the deformed horse demonstrated the artificiality of idealistic pursuits of perfection.

With "Le cheval académique" Bataille began to sketch a critical approach to aesthetics that, by opposing matter and the formless (*informe*) to reason and harmony, challenged major Western philosophical conceptions.[120] To be sure, Bataille was wary about this opposition; for him, materialism could never enter a hierarchical discourse without the risk of becoming another form of idealism.[121] In other words, the beast could never cross over to beauty, nor could the monstrous transform into its other. The notion of "useless expenditure" that Bataille later developed began to emerge here as the battle cry in a fight against the category of art and its tricks.[122] In contrast to most of *Documents'* contributors, Bataille never addressed conventionally defined art topics in the journal (except for a lip-service homage to Picasso and primitive art); yet almost all his writings for *Documents*, beginning with "Le cheval académique" and "Architecture," combined a critique of elevation with an assault against ideal beauty.[123] *Documents* became for Bataille the forum from

119 Ibid., 29.
120 See the short dictionary entry "Informe," *Documents*, 382. In it Bataille assaulted the need claimed by philosophers for everything to have a form. Other *Documents'* contributors hinted at this issue. See Leiris "Crachat" (section 2: L'eau à la bouche), ibid., 381–2. On the notion of "informe," see Bois and Krauss, *Formless: A User's Guide*. See also Didi-Huberman, *La ressemblance informe*.
121 See Bataille, "Matérialisme," 170, and "Le bas matérialisme et la gnose," 1–8, English translations as "Materialism" and "Base Materialism and Gnosticism," in Bataille, *Visions of Excess*.
122 In contrast to Einstein, Bataille was not willing to entrust any redeeming feature to art, although he acknowledged that contemporary paintings opened the way to bestial monstrosity and undermined the belief in humans' perfection. See "Architecture," 117.
123 On Picasso, see Bataille, "Soleil pourri" and English translation "Rotten Sun," in *Visions of Excess*; on primitivist art see "L' art primitif" (this was a book review of M.G.H. Luquet's *Art primitif*). See also "Joan Miró: peintures récentes." In 1930, issue 3 of *Documents* was entirely dedicated to Picasso. Bataille's "Soleil pourri" stands out for its detached tone, a tone which was quite at odds with the other contributors' high praise for Picasso. (Mauss also contributed a very short note on Picasso for this issue where he claimed that the so called primitive art is nothing less than art pure and simple. See "M. Marcel Mauss ... ," 177). Bataille centred his discussion on the sun's ambiguous status both as a concept of elevation, when cherished by poets, and as a vision of ugliness that results from actually staring at the sun (something we do not usually do). For Bataille, the maximum of elevation corresponded to a sudden, violent fall. Academic painting only showed the elevation, while Picasso's work displayed interest in the rupture of elevation.

which to launch an evaluative analysis of aesthetics and its guilty role qua representative of order and authority. And it was by setting up this prosecutorial trial against aesthetics that Bataille formulated an original discussion about the coexistence in nature of beauty and ugliness, formal and formless, normal and monstrous, high and low, ideal and material.

Bataille did not propose to reverse or reshuffle hierarchical order's constitutive elements; such a move would mean following the Surrealists' mistaken assumptions. He instead envisioned the dismantling of hierarchical principles through a critique that, while contrasting human nature to the general natural realm, directed attention toward ugliness, the formless, and the monstrous.[124] Thus, in "Figure humaine," which Leiris cited as the essay that finally revealed Bataille's intentions for *Documents*, Bataille questioned the notion of a normalized human nature presided over by rationality.[125] Through a gallery of nineteenth-century photographs that depicted families, couples, and individuals in impossibly unnatural poses (including wearing corsets and cushions as was the fashion at the time), Bataille made the case that the "improbable" aspect of these figures revealed the regular existence in humans of the monstrous dimension. The normal, Bataille suggested, implies its own sublation; it relies on the presence of the unmeasurable and does not exclude hideousness. This is evident when we examine flowers which are supposed to embody the naturalized meanings of beauty and love. In reality, Bataille argued as a counterpoint to such an idealized image, stench and putrefaction surround plants' withering and decay. Flowers rot like corpses, and "*love smells like death*" (*l'amour a l'odeur de la mort*).[126] Moreover, if plants and flowers sprout following an elevating movement from low to high, they also grow underground with roots that, reaching far below, are nourished by putrefaction. The horrid has the power to generate, Bataille continued, and what appears ideal, noble, and sacred is firmly rooted in the ground, in dirt. This axiom is confirmed in the case of human anatomy where the big toe, situated in the lowest part of the body, is believed to be dirty because it sticks to the mud; and yet, Bataille

124 See, for example, Bataille, "Métamorphose" (part 3: Animaux sauvages), 333–4.

125 Bataille, "Figure humaine," 194–201. Leiris, in "De Bataille l'impossible à l'impossible 'Documents,'" describes Bataille's intent as "against the reassuring idea of human nature," 690. For an interpretation of "Figure humaine," see Didi-Huberman, *La ressemblance informe*.

126 "Le langage des fleurs," 163 (italicized in the original). See English translation, "The Language of Flowers" in Bataille, *Visions of Excess*, 13. One has to note, however, that Bataille accepted the identification of flowers with love. Bataille also wrote that flowers "seem *to conform to what must be*, in other words they represent, as flowers, the human *ideal*" (12).

ironically pointed out, the big toe ensures the human body's erection, its striving for heaven and the high spheres.[127] Bataille derided those who pursued the ideal while damning the material, unaware of the fictitious nature of their discriminating categories. At the same time, Bataille was not promoting a reverse hierarchical system: the horrid could never be assimilated.[128]

If Bataille attacked the notion that form determines beauty, he also condemned the idealization of beauty, which, as in the case of flowers and toes, "assign[s] moral meaning to natural phenomena" by negatively connoting what is low. For him, in contrast, the deformed – what supposedly deviates from nature and its orderly plan – promotes the theorization of a counter aesthetic attraction for the ugly.[129] The ambiguity between low and high, or material and ideal, that emerged from Bataille's discussion of the big toe and flowers thus continued to take an unusual turn in Bataille's work at *Documents*, as he raised the question of seduction's link to the ugly, the base, and the monstrous. "[E]xtreme seductiveness is probably at the boundary of horror," he wrote for the short "Dictionary" entry "Œil" (Eye).[130] And in "Les écarts de la nature," he focused on the curiosity that for centuries and in different circumstances surrounded such "unnatural phenomena" as Siamese twins.[131] From communicating terror in the sixteenth century to engaging voyeuristic crowds at fairs in the 1800s, these "monsters" have continuously attracted our attention. And he reflectively concluded that, because of their

127 See "Le gros orteil"; English translation "The Big Toe," in Bataille, *Visions of Excess*.

128 Hollier writes about Bataille's base materialism (also called heterology): "Heterology is not a product of the aestheticization of the repugnant. Disgust here is not a modality of aesthetic experience but a fundamental existential dimension." See *The College of Sociology*, xix. For Bataille's early elaborations of heterology, see "La valeur d'usage de Sade (Lettre ouverte à mes camarades actuels)," in *OC*, vol. 2; English translation "The Use Value of D.A.F. de Sade (An Open Letter to My Current Comrades)," in *Visions of Excess*. Carolyn Dean discusses this writing as Bataille's response to Breton and the Surrealists, who had rehabilitated the figure of de Sade against prevalent critical assessments. For Bataille, such rehabilitation was another example of the Surrealists' tendency to elevate and thus to transfigure reality, or one could say, in the specific case of de Sade, de-realize his marginality, thus depriving him of his status as "tragic man." See Dean, *The Self and Its Pleasures*.

129 "Le langage des fleurs," 164; English translation "The Language of Flowers" in Bataille, *Visions of Excess*, 13. Also see "Informe" and "Le 'Jeu lugubre'"; English translation "Formless" and "The 'Lugubrious Game,'" in Bataille, *Visions of Excess*. With reference to Bataille, Didi-Huberman talks of a reversing iconography that puts into question the notion of resemblance. See "Comment déchire-t-on la ressemblance?", 103.

130 See "Œil" (part 2: Friandise cannibale), 216; English translation "Eye," in Bataille, *Visions of Excess*, 17.

131 "Les écarts de la nature"; English translation "The Deviations of Nature," in Bataille, *Visions of Excess*.

incongruity, for which nature is solely responsible even if monsters are considered an accident, Siamese twins leave us troubled but also seduce us. The fact that monsters are irreducible to a common measure (which Bataille saw as a magnification or amplification of individual personal incongruities) awakens the human spirit to the highest degree. It also once again exposes the reality of a beauty of order and an order of beauty that desolately overlaps with the platitudes of our lives.

Bataille's operation of dismantling accepted aesthetic categories was radical and inflexible at *Documents* and resulted in a final essay in which Bataille unleashed critical scorn for museums, art, and aesthetics. He ultimately raised the troubling question: can art ever attain the horrific, that which reveals our existence?[132] Or better: Can modern art, so highly praised by the avant-garde and *Documents'* collaborators, ever cease to escape horror when "one goes to the art dealer as to a pharmacist looking for well-presented remedies against some dubious diseases"?[133] Art is a palliative, a distraction, Bataille declared, falling short of sounding art's death knell. Unlike the Surrealists who, by opposing *l'art pour l'art*, pursued the rehabilitation of art's revolutionary potential, Bataille did not express any triumphalistic desire to redeem art and sublate it into life. Although he maintained an interest in the sensual aspects of the world, his analysis privileged animate and inanimate beings, or the organic and inorganic, much more than artifacts. The photographs that accompanied some of his writings for *Documents* ("Le gros orteil" and "Le langage des fleurs," for example) testify to this inclination, as Bataille challenged art's reliance on nature from within by directly confronting the natural realm. In so doing, Bataille questioned the identification of beauty with perfection and the ideal, all of which art was supposed to inherit from nature, and he challenged people to deny the natural perfection of a big toe or the anti-idealist obscenity of a flower's part.

In an original move, Bataille contested the "natural" through the microscope of science (here intended both metaphorically and in the material sense of magnified images). He zoomed in on the invisible nature that eludes our eyes, either because we cannot see it (the pistil) or because we avoid looking at it (the hairy big toe). Photography thus became Bataille's preferred medium for critiquing visuality. He relied on the scientific pose of dispassionate neutrality, which photography equipped him with, to question science's pretense to transparency and exhaustibility and to denounce science's fleshless constitution, inadequate relation

132 Bataille, "L'esprit moderne et le jeu des transpositions."
133 Ibid. 490 (*On entre chez le marchand de tableaux comme chez un pharmacien, en quête de remèdes bien présentés pour des maladies avouables*).

 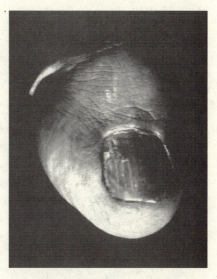

3 *Campanula Vidalii.* Photograph by Karl Blossfeldt that accompanied Bataille's article "Le langage des fleurs" (The Language of Flowers) in *Documents* 3, June 1929. © 2010 Karl Blossfeldt Archiv / Ann u. Jürgen Wilde, Köln/Artists Rights Society (ARS), NY

4 The Big Toe. A photograph by Jacques-André Boiffard that accompanied Bataille's article "Le gros orteil" (The Big Toe) in *Documents* 6, November 1929. CNAC / MNAM / Dist. Réunion des Musées Nationaux / Art Resource, NY

to the material world, and disincarnated idealism.[134] Bataille no doubt trusted photography's ability to reproduce reality, that is, to "document" it independently of any semantic potential. He thus evidenced the difficult position he was holding as a critic of order and reason who revolted against science by adopting its means – the "naturalness of seeing." In the end, however, what emerges from Bataille's critical interventions at *Documents* is his absolute rejection of visuality when dealing with the art realm.[135] Even the desire Bataille alluded to in "Le langage des fleurs" – a desire rooted not in ideal beauty but rather in the deadly, putrefying end-limit of the flower – was not stirred by images, and certainly not those that, selected by Bataille, reproduced flowers in all their fixed and formal rigidity. Desire rather emanated from an awareness of the flower's doomed disfiguration, its deadly smell. Art, as far as Bataille was concerned, could be flushed down the drain along with illusions of beauty,

134 See Damisch, "Du mot à l'aspect. Paraphrase." On photography in *Documents*, see Krauss, *The Originality of the Avant-Garde*.

135 See Jay, *Downcast Eyes*.

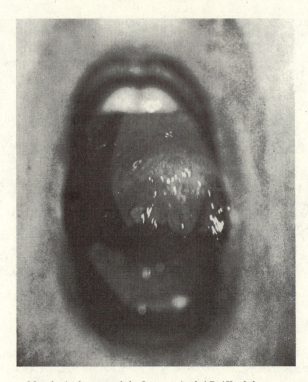

5 Mouth. A photograph by Jacques-André Boiffard that accompanied Bataille's article "Bouche" (Mouth) in *Documents,*
5 November 1930

propriety, and moral ideals. Art transpired trouble, and Bataille discouraged any attempt at befriending it.

By the time *Documents* ceased publication, Bataille had radically dismantled aesthetics, both as a category of artistic evaluation and as a potential critical tool for challenging Cartesian reason or the modern ethics
of production. At a time when the avant-garde and cultural critics close
to Marxist theory (the Frankfurt school in particular) were painstakingly
exploring ways in which the work of art could achieve an emancipatory
potential and escape its appropriation by the cultural establishment,
Bataille struck down art. Although he shared with Horkheimer and
Adorno a concern about the "administered world" of the post-Enlighten-
ment era – the fear of an enslaved existence under the auspices of a ra-
tionalized technocratic system – an existential bent and a search for the
wholeness of the person separated Bataille from the critical theorists'

vision of "integral humanity." Any partiality to art constituted an impossible attraction for Bataille. He therefore developed a meta-political denunciation of art's deceptive role that, as it turns out, placed him very close to his future co-leader at the Collège, Roger Caillois. For both, aesthetics was at the centre of a modern crisis that, by loosening bonds and promoting individualism, had extinguished the flame of the sacred. For both, the critique of aesthetics constituted the necessary step for remedying the lamented depletion of the social. Not surprisingly, after the closing down of *Documents*, Bataille completely shut off any question of aesthetics and focused instead on politics.[136] From late 1931 to early 1934, he participated in the Marxist review *La Critique sociale* and in late 1936 founded the political group Contre-Attaque, shortly thereafter moving away from mainstream political engagement while actively participating in Acéphale and the Collège de sociologie.

In those turbulent years, however, the Surrealist avant-garde movement, which Bataille had opposed in his aesthetic theories, found itself confronting similarly inextricable dilemmas on the relationship between politics and art. The next chapter will examine Surrealism within the framework of that dilemma and as both counterpart and breeding ground for Bataille's and Caillois's own attempts to deal with politics and aesthetics prior to embarking on the experimental Collège de sociologie.

---

136 Two more issues of *Documents* were printed in 1933 and 1934 by Pierre d'Espezel (see Maubon, "'Documents': una esperienza eretica," 49).

3

The Avant-Garde Meets Politics

IN A SEMINAL ESSAY ON SURREALISM written in 1929, Walter Benjamin first exposed the experiential, lived-in basis of a movement that many commentators of the time obstinately catalogued as artistic. Citing the Surrealists' acknowledged precursor, Arthur Rimbaud, and his handwritten reflections on a passage from "Saison en enfer," Benjamin unveiled the Surrealists' problematic relationship to their literary proclivities. "There's no such thing," Rimbaud had declared referring to his own poetic verses "on the silk of the seas and the arctic flowers."[1] In the same way, Benjamin suggested, the Surrealists' critical reflections about their craft revealed desecrating intents; the Surrealists pushed the limits of the poetic through a delicate movement that denied poetry as a specialized field while simultaneously expanding its reach into living experience. Only superficially could the movement be defined solely in relationship to art. In reality, it was "the most integral, conclusive, absolute of movements," and it promised to overcome the artificial division between art and life.[2] Thus, the Surrealists' motto fittingly proclaimed, "Poetry must be made by all, not by one."[3]

According to Benjamin, the Surrealists' revolutionary act was to shatter the sacred through a materialist anthropology of profane illuminations.[4] What Peter Bürger has defined as the main aim of the historical avant-garde – the sublation of art into life – was identified by Benjamin some forty years earlier as the original core of the Surrealists' experiment.[5]

---

1 Benjamin, "Surrealism," 178, in *Reflections*.
2 Ibid.
3 The Surrealists borrowed the motto from their favourite poet, Lautréamont. See Nadeau, *The History of Surrealism*, 50.
4 For Benjamin's reading of Surrealism along these lines, see Cohen, *Profane Illumination*.
5 Bürger, *Theory of the Avant-Garde*.

The Surrealists, not unlike other intellectuals of the time, were highly skeptical of the isolationist, exclusionary, and individualist nature of art as an institution and, in particular, of the orientation of the art for art's sake movement. Art's lack of social engagement especially attracted their ire and became the motivational force behind the Surrealists' critical attack on beauty, negatively defined as an empty concept. But whereas others, including Durkheim and Mauss, saw scarcely any possibility for art to play a constructive role in building a morally sound society, a strong cohesive whole, the Surrealists envisioned a revolutionary future for art via the reversal of art's autonomous status. They believed that once art ceased to be an isolated sphere and became a state of mind as well as a way of being and a practical behaviour, it would be able "to penetrate reality," inform it, and transform it.[6]

The Surrealists purposefully criticized the modern world, which they deemed dominated by "bourgeois" rationality, and advocated an open defiance of the order of things. After the enormous catastrophe of the First World War, they observed, nothing could, or should, remain the same.[7] Repulsed by the political and economic rationales that had led to the war and its human carnage, the Surrealists contested the bourgeois principles at the basis of Western civilization. They indicted modern "man" and his inability to prevail over the monster society he had created. They also denounced the blindness of politics and the inanity of poetry. In this context, although at times contradictorily, they put in motion a radical project that reconceptualized the individual's human potential and envisioned a new model of existence. In the process, they reinvented the relationship between politics and art with the goal of simultaneously transforming the world and changing life.[8]

It was Surrealism's unorthodox way of rethinking art's role in terms of an existential project that attracted Caillois to the movement in the early 1930s. And it was a shared unconventional view of politics that later produced the unfathomable alliance of the leader of the Surrealists, André Breton, with Georges Bataille in the short-lived movement of Contre-Attaque. This chapter examines the Surrealists as a group that

6 See Nadeau, *The History of Surrealism*, foreword, 35.

7 When they founded Futurism in 1909, well ahead of the first major conflict of the twentieth century, the Futurists also imagined a program of social transformations. They, however, lacked the sense of moral urgency that spearheaded the Surrealists onto the main stage of the 1920s cultural scene.

8 See "Discours d'André Breton au congrès des écrivains pour la défense de la culture" (1935), in Nadeau, *Histoire du Surréalisme*. The original French edition of Nadeau's book differs in parts from the English version. For an English translation of the "Discours," see Breton, *Manifestoes of Surrealism*.

encapsulated and confronted the dilemmas of art's function in an original way. More specifically, it details the contradictory impulses the Surrealists experienced when they sought an art that mattered socially while rejecting the idea of art as subordinate to practical ends. The chapter discusses how Surrealism at first conceived its revolutionary position outside the boundaries of art and distanced itself from the aesthetic realm through invocations of science. The chapter then proceeds to portray the ways in which the Surrealists' positions shifted in the face of historical events. I consider the trajectory that led the Surrealists from an anti-aesthetic perspective to one that accepted conventional art canons, and I indicate how the Surrealists' confrontation with political events pushed them to rethink their relationship to art. I conclude that the unresolved dilemmas posed by the politics/art duo and the retrieval of art's traditional definition ultimately defeated the Surrealists' original attempt to incorporate art into life.

This survey of Surrealism and its approximation to "the political" then leads into an examination of the way Caillois and Bataille confronted Surrealism's legacy and core dilemmas.[9] I will sketch out Caillois's and Bataille's separate intellectual paths before they joined in 1935, when Contre-Attaque was founded, and will illustrate how Bataille and Caillois began to combine their critique of art with a concern for the social via an interest in affective movements. Ultimately, I argue that the combination of political concerns with original intellectual explorations directed Bataille to investigate fascism. Fascism's novelty, as well as its success, suggested to Bataille the need to reinscribe affectivity in the analysis of social forms – a task later taken up by the Collège.

THE SURREALIST REVOLUTION

In his classic history of Surrealism Nadeau persuasively argues that the group born in 1922 from a break with Dada did not think of itself as an artistic school or a literary faction, nor did it conceive its role in terms of harbinger of a new aesthetic movement.[10] The Surrealists, rather, aimed

9 According to Michel Surya, this question was particularly important to Bataille. See his *Georges Bataille, la mort à l'œuvre*, translated into English as *Georges Bataille: An Intellectual Biography* (from which I will cite).

10 For a discussion of how the word "Surrealism" was chosen, see "Manifeste du Surréalisme," in Breton, *Manifestes du Surréalisme*, 38–9; *Manifestoes of Surrealism*, 24–5. See also the definition of Surrealism in "Manifesto of Surrealism" (1924), now in *Manifestoes of Surrealism*, 26: "Psychic automatism in its pure state, by which one proposes to express – verbally, by means of the written word, or in any other manner – the actual functioning of thought. Dictated by thought, in the absence of any control exercised by reason, exempt

at pursuing knowledge through the exploration of the imaginary, dreams, the marvellous – the hidden side of reason and logic. In the first *Manifesto of Surrealism* (1924), Breton called for an expanded and deepened comprehension of the mental world whose doubtless richness was being obfuscated by an almost exclusive attention to useful experience. Dream and reality could eventually be reconciled in a sort of absolute reality, or "surreality."[11] Breton applauded Freud's discovery of the unconscious, which lent hope to the expectation that "imagination is perhaps on the point of reasserting itself, of reclaiming its rights."[12] By opening the way to the exploration of psychic activities, until then ignored, Freud's work on dreams allowed the Surrealists to assert the complementarity of sleeping and waking, the continuity (well captured by Breton's later idea of "communicating vessels") between a state of conscious perception – wakefulness – and dreams.[13] The unconscious shed light on the free essence of thought.[14]

The Surrealists aimed at recovering something existent, but unidentified, that inhabited the individual mind. Free-floating poetic expression – "spoken thought"– became their means to retrieve the unknown and transform ordinary phenomena through their rebirth as poetic objects. According to the Surrealists, this metamorphosis would occur through an unconscious process based on the illuminating power of the images created by poetic evocations. If poetry, since Baudelaire, had served as a tool of metaphysical knowledge and had helped in the search for the self, now, with the Surrealists and after Apollinaire, poetry would overcome the limits of the human condition in order to create new scientific information and a new reality.[15] Sense perception would be revitalized and retrained to escape the risks of deadly passivity and to produce a novel dynamic relation between subject and object. Unfettered by the dictates of reason, the supposedly infinite possibilities contained in the

---

from any aesthetic or moral concern." For the original French version see, *Manifestes du Surréalisme*, 40

11 Breton wrote, "I believe in the future resolution of these two states, dream and reality, which are seemingly so contradictory, into a kind of absolute reality, a *surreality*, if one may so speak." See *Manifestoes of Surrealism*, 14; *Manifestes du Surréalisme*, 27.

12 See Breton, *Manifestoes of Surrealism*, 10; *Manifestes du Surréalisme*, 23.

13 Although the Surrealists admired Freud, Freud had little sympathy for their work. See the revealing correspondence between Freud and Breton in *Les vases communicants*, appendix, 200–7, translated into English as *Communicating Vessels*.

14 Ibid. In the Surrealists' journal *La Révolution surréaliste* (issue 1 of 1 December 1924), Pierre Reverdy wrote that dream is not "the contrary of thought … it is merely a freer, more abandoned form of thought. Dreams and thought are the two sides of the same material." Cited in Nadeau, *The History of Surrealism*, 93n16.

15 On these issues, see Balakian's discussion in *Surrealism*, foreword.

human mind promised to enact a richer sensory world and to prepare the groundwork for a deeper, more satisfying, and meaningful life.

The Surrealists did not plan to create poetry. They believed, however, that if poetry could imagine "arctic flowers," in the same way the exploration of the human mind could lead to realities until then imagined only as poetic inventions. Poetry revealed the means to conceive of and enact a new way of living through enhanced sense perception. Thus, although the Surrealists did not intend to found a literary or artistic school, they deemed writing in the mode of automatism the main technique to attain the poetic. Language, and more precisely unbound language, represented the chief form of surreal expression.[16] At a time when Ferdinand de Saussure was elaborating a theory of language as a semantic field whose meaning was socially constituted and depended on relationships in a system of signs, the Surrealists seemed to assign an almost absolute power to creative language.[17] Language was unconstrained by conventions and social rules and had a performative power.[18] Language, as Benjamin put it, "takes precedence," even as it discards syntax and logic.[19] And yet, it is apparent that for the Surrealists language could not serve a literary style or constitute the basis for an artistic revolution.[20] The Surrealists understood language and poetry within their overall scientific project of pursuing the production of previously non-existent realities. Although they rejected conventional science's obvious limitations and replaced scientific logic with intuition and automatic psychism, their approach to surreality was rigorous and systematic.

16 This was Breton's position in the "Manifesto." See Breton, *Manifestoes of Surrealism*, 33; *Manifestes du Surréalisme*, 48, where he talked of language as "unrestricted" or "sans reserve."

17 Balakian, however, argues that the Surrealists anticipated structuralism. See Balakian, *André Breton*.

18 See "Legitimate Defense" (1926), in Nadeau, *The History of Surrealism*. Also see Breton, "Les mots sans rides," first published in *Littérature*, nouvelle série 7 (December 1922), then in *Les pas perdus*; English translation "Words without Wrinkles" in *The Lost Steps*: "We were beginning to distrust words; we were suddenly noticing that they had to be treated other than as the little auxiliaries they had always been taken" (100).

19 Benjamin, "Surrealism," 179 where he also cited Breton: "Quietly. I want to pass where no one yet has passed, quietly! – After you, dearest language." The Surrealists' language produced energy and was in "a state of effervescence," Breton later wrote. Cited in Balakian, *Surrealism*, 113.

20 Breton was critical of the Futurists' "words at liberty." In 1936 he wrote that "one must be the most naïve of men to grant any attention to the futurist theory of 'words at liberty,' based on the childish belief in the real and independent existence of words." See his "Legitimate Defense," in Nadeau, *The History of Surrealism*, 249.

The Bureau of Surrealist Research, which they founded in 1924, epito-mized the scientific character of the Surrealists' endeavour; at the same time, it displayed Surrealism's deconstructive assault on traditional conceptions of art. The bureau worked as a laboratory where all were welcome to contribute experiences that engaged with the surreal. Experiments were conceived to help build an archive of unconscious ac-tivities and anyone with tales of amazing coincidences, curious dreams, or purely instinctual ideas was invited to visit the bureau. The official journal of the movement, *La Révolution surréaliste,* featured the style and appearance typical of scientific publications, and while words were the main tool of the Surrealists' craft, literature, because of its fictitious na-ture, was banned from the journal.[21] "We have nothing to do with litera-ture," the Surrealists proclaimed in 1925.[22] Science was supposed to counteract art. Not surprisingly, the first *Manifesto of Surrealism* defined surrealist practitioners as "simple receptacles," "recording instruments."[23] Nothing could be further from the idea of genius and closer to a neutral understanding of science than an *"appareil enregistreur"* pouring out auto-matic writing.[24]

The Surrealists resorted to science in order to dispense with the ills of literature – a path not unlike the one taken by turn-of-the-century soci-ologists and anthropologists with regard to art. And although the Surrealists' radical pursuit of the mind's liberation was founded on and required poetry, the latter was newly conceived as a technical tool. Only in this guise could poetry be embraced. Only in this transfiguration could the Surrealists trust poetry to attain what they wished for: the trans-formation of human experience in all its aspects, from the personal to the political. In this sense, the Surrealists' negative assessment of art led to the revolutionary outcome of foregrounding art's sublation into life.

21 The first issue of the journal was published in 1924 and publication continued until 1929.

22 "Declaration of January 27, 1925," in Nadeau, *The History of Surrealism,* 240. The "Declaration" also asserted, "*Surrealism* is not a new means or expression, or an easier one, nor even a metaphysic of poetry. It is a means of total liberation of the mind." The first Surrealist Manifesto also attacked basic realism and its ultimate literary expression, the novel, as baneful banality. Hollier illustrates the 1930s rejection of the distinction between politics and literature by engaged writers in *Absent without Leave.* See in particular the chap-ter "A Farewell to Art."

23 "But we who have made no effort whatsoever to filter, who in our works have made ourselves into simple receptacles of so many echoes, modest *recording instruments* ..." See Breton, *Manifestoes of Surrealism,* 28; *Manifestes du Surréalisme,* 42.

24 In 1919, Breton and Philippe Soupault composed their first experiments in auto-matic writing, *Les champs magnétiques.*

That was the novelty Benjamin recognized in the movement: rather than suppressing art, Surrealism's experimental penchant re-envisioned it as an inclusionary practice melded into the fabric of everyday life.

The Surrealists overcame the strictures of conventional aesthetic definitions and situated themselves in an uncharted realm outside established rules and classifications. And yet, they soon found themselves plagued with questions that tested the movement's original orientation and forced them to revisit the entire issue of art's status. An urgent matter arose just one year after the publication of the *Manifesto*: a military conflict that Surrealism felt at loss to resolve.

The Politics of Engagement

In *The Hollow Years*, Eugen Weber described the post-World War I situation in France as a time in which patriotism came to be considered an absolute evil. The idea of pacifism, a word invented at the end of the 1890s, began to take root on French soil after the Great War's massacres confronted the nation with questions about the legitimacy and implications of appealing to the fatherland. During the world conflict France had suffered the highest losses of any of the belligerent countries, besides countless wounded and disabled: one out of every five men mobilized, or about 1,400,000 soldiers, died.[25] With keen awareness of this dreadful reality, the generation that survived the war adamantly vowed to oppose any future armed intervention: the pain and loss inflicted by combat had been too overwhelming and were felt as ultimately senseless.

France's confrontation with Morocco in 1925 offered the pacifists a concrete stage for affirming their stance. The idea of unconditional patriotism seemingly buried with the dead of the Great War was being resurrected by the colonial conflict in Morocco; intellectuals, among other supporters, hailed the armed intervention.[26] As representatives of the First World War generation, the Surrealists instead filled the pacifists' ranks. Several had been on active duty at the front, and their dismissal of the traditional values of family, patriotism, and religion was partly the result of their war experience. On 2 July 1925 the *groupe surréaliste* signed an appeal to intellectual workers that invited them to "dishonour" the

25 Weber, *The Hollow Years*, chapter 1.

26 The intellectuals who hailed the war signed the manifesto "Les intellectuels aux côtés de la patrie." Weber did not consider the case of the Moroccan war in his discussion of France's "extreme pacifism." Eventually in 1933 the Surrealists attacked pacifism as a betrayal of class warfare. See Shattuck, *The Innocent Eye*, 16.

war as intrinsically negative, especially in its colonial manifestation.[27] Shortly thereafter, a tract entitled "La Révolution d'abord et toujours!" declared the fatherland "the most bestial concept" and harshly denounced European civilization.[28] In a self-critical move, the tract also affirmed that the revolution could be conceived only in its social, and not merely ideal, form. Revolution was not an abstraction; it needed to be directed at concrete social relations.

The French colonial conflict constituted a defining moment in the history of Surrealism and marked the beginning of a new, more political direction for the group. Over the following ten years, the Surrealists tried to come to terms with the difficulties they faced reconciling the movement's will to change the world with its desire to transform life. A seesaw of positions ensued that Breton later acknowledged and summarized in his 1934 essay "What is Surrealism?" There, he distinguished two phases in the historical evolution of the movement: one that he defined as intuitive and the other as based on reason. The first was founded on the belief in the omnipotence of thought and its ability to achieve emancipation autonomously.[29] It was linked to the idea of the primacy of the mind over matter – an idealist disposition that Breton now deemed unhelpful (*fâcheux*). The second phase in Surrealism's history, which Breton saw as tightly connected to the Moroccan war and the published tract "La Révolution d'abord et toujours!" resulted from the Surrealists' awareness of the limits of their own movement. The war had confronted the Surrealists with the need to bridge the gap between idealism and praxis, and eventually drove them to recognize the primacy of matter over thought in a process that landed them with Marx via a detour through Hegel. Surrealist activity at that point, Breton admitted, evolved in a more practical direction not limited to automatic texts or poetic production. The whole question of knowledge came to be reformulated in light of a materialist perspective. Accordingly, the Surrealists concluded that a social revolution was required before, or at least in tandem with, a revolution of the mind.

In this new phase, the Surrealists at first stressed their subscription to the idea of revolution as formulated by the Communist International and the French Communist Party. In the tract published by the communist

27 See tract "Appel aux Travailleurs intellectuels," in *Tracts surréalistes et déclarations collectives*, I: 51–3.

28 Ibid., 54.

29 *Qu'est-ce que le surréalisme?* now in Breton, *Œuvres complètes*, 2: 231; English translation in *What is Surrealism?*, where Breton wrote about "a purely *intuitive* epoch and a *reasoning* epoch," 116.

newspaper *L'Humanité* on 8 November 1925, they disclaimed any
Surrealist theory of revolution and argued that revolution meant the passage of power from the bourgeoisie to the proletariat.[30] Although the
tract affirmed the validity of Surrealism's experiment, it argued that the
revolution was economic and social in character and could not be determined by the mind – a radical shift, indeed. Not surprisingly, in 1927 the
Surrealists joined the French Communist Party.

The cohabitation of Surrealism with communism, however, was not a
linear affair. Polemics, schisms, and attacks punctuated the association
between the two and spurred the Surrealists to initiate a long and painful
self-examination at whose centre stood the issue of art's relationship to
politics. The Surrealists asked: should they abandon their peculiarities in
order to facilitate the revolutionary process? And could and should they
produce in the service of the revolution? According to Breton, the answer that emerged from the movement initially revealed two alternative
tendencies: one, which Breton positioned as ideologically on the right,
consisted of those who wanted to remain at the speculative level. Breton
was particularly wary of this position since it entailed the risk of making
of Surrealism a mere artistic and literary phenomenon, something he
had always rejected. The other tendency, more ideologically on the left,
was accused by Breton of overemphasizing the Surrealists' practical engagement and of sacrificing the movement's core to political militancy.
Breton found both tendencies inadequate. He believed that, in the spirit
of their origins, the Surrealists should proclaim neither politics nor art.
Their revolutionary agenda should instead accommodate both the desire to assault intellectual hierarchies and the intent to develop a method for assessing the relationship between conscious and unconscious.[31]
Internally divided, the Surrealists were seemingly stuck in an intellectual
quagmire and could not vanquish art's spectre.

The 1930 *Second Manifesto of Surrealism* reflected the difficulties faced by
the movement and Breton's attempts to find yet another solution to the
Surrealists' predicament. Frequently citing Hegel, but also Engels, Breton
reaffirmed Surrealism's adherence to historical materialism and rejection
of the Communists' orthodox revolutionary demands. Breton adamantly
opposed the idea of a proletarian culture and advocated the application of
dialectical methods to domains other than the social, specifically citing art,
love, dreams, madness, and religion.[32] He sought a philosophy according

30 "We never believed in a 'surrealist revolution.'" See "Les Intellectuels et la Révolution"now in Pierre, *Tracts*, 1: 64.
31 See Breton, *What is Surrealism?*
32 See Breton, *Manifestoes of Surrealism*, 140; *Manifestes du Surréalisme*, 171.

to which "surreality will reside in reality itself and will be neither superior nor exterior to it." [33] The Surrealists would abrogate idealism in favour of materialism without, however, renouncing the interests that had driven them to explore the domain of thought in the first place. Breton deemed "weak" those Surrealists who were content with the artistic results of their automatic writings and criticized them for avoiding a rigorous scientific exploration of the flow of unconscious images. Nevertheless, he still clung to the idea of Surrealism as a non-artistic movement.[34] Cowardice might have pushed some Surrealists to find shelter in literature and art as an "alibi."[35] Art, however, was not the essence of Surrealism; it constituted a deviation from and a diminution of Surrealism's original nature.

The second manifesto, Nadeau argues, was taken by Breton as a "reminder of *principles*" and an occasion to purge the movement of its undesired members.[36] Breton's analysis indeed spared few in its attempt to rein in the different factions. Breton was trying to avoid being trapped into having to choose between art and politics, and he made it clear that Surrealism worked autonomously and did not belong to either. In July 1930, however, the Surrealists named their new official publication *Le Surréalisme au service de la Révolution* (Surrealism at the service of the revolution) and declared their allegiance to the communist Third International.[37] In 1932, one of the key figures of the movement, Louis Aragon, disavowed Surrealism in favour of the Communist Party. (Only a few years earlier he had declared, "The Russian Revolution? Forgive me for shrugging my shoulders.")[38] Then, in 1934, at a time of considerable turmoil in France, a more militant phase in the history of the movement began. On 6 February of that year, an apparent attempted coup d'état by right-wing paramilitary organizations in the aftermath of riots in Paris resulted in the fall of the government led by the Radical Party.[39]

33 Breton, *What is Surrealism?* 126; *Qu'est-ce que le surréalisme?* in *Œuvres complètes*, 2: 244. According to Breton, the container coincided with the content.

34 Breton, *Manifestoes of Surrealism*, 157–8; *Manifestes du Surréalisme*, 189–90.

35 Breton, *Manifestoes of Surrealism*, 163; *Manifestes du Surréalisme*, 195. Breton specifically wrote of a "literary" alibi.

36 Nadeau, *The History of Surrealism*, 164 (italicized in the original).

37 In the tract "Aux Intellectuels révolutionnaires," written by Louis Aragon and Georges Sadoul, the Surrealists denounced Trotsky in favour of the Third International, although Breton had showed great admiration for Trotsky and later became very close to him. See *Tracts*, 1: 186–8.

38 On this declaration, see the exchange between Aragon and Jean Bernier, editor of the leftist review *Clarté*, in Nadeau, *The History of Surrealism*, 100–1.

39 For a brief description of the circumstances that led to these events, see Nadeau, *The History of Surrealism*. Shattuck downplays the danger of the coup d'état in *The Innocent Eye*. Also see Jackson, *The Popular Front in France*.

The left, worried about an impending fascist menace, reacted strongly. Counter-demonstrations began immediately, followed by a general strike on 12 February that helped cement the antifascist alliance of communists and non-communists and eventually led to the creation of a Popular Front against the extreme right.[40]

The Surrealists immediately took an active role in the new political movement, and on 10 February they published a tract inviting all workers to unite against fascism.[41] A few months later, on 18 April, they reiterated the importance of unity of action with an inquiry into the topic of political collaboration.[42] Fully engaged with the political events of the time, the Surrealists once again faced a definitional crisis, especially when forced to respond to the Communists' invitation to produce propaganda. In yet another showdown with the party, they reformulated their political positions and, against all odds, vindicated their status as artists; they questioned the power of politics and reaffirmed the value of art. [43]

The Power of Art

The Surrealists' confrontation with Communist orthodoxy saw its denouement at the Congress of Writers for the Defense of Culture organized by the French Communist Party in June of 1935.[44] The Congress took place in the wake of a Franco-Soviet treaty that stipulated mutual assistance between France and the Soviet Union in case of war. The Surrealists found the treaty highly questionable. What would be the effect of such an alliance on social relations in France? What tricks would the French bourgeois government play on the working class? Ultimately, would such an alliance intensify France's imperialistic pursuits? Even more worrisome for the Surrealists was the prospect of a reactionary cultural movement unchained by the Communists' subscription to the idea

40 According to Weber, *The Hollow Years*, 140, the date of 6 February marked the end of anti-parliamentarism among the French Left.

41 See "Appel à la Lutte," where the Surrealists invited workers to a "Unity of Action," in *Tracts*, 1: 262–4.

42 "Enquête sur l'Unité d'Action," *Tracts*, 1: 265–7.

43 On the Surrealists' relationship with the French Communist Party (PCF), see Thirion, *Révolutionnaires sans révolutions*. Also see Lewis, *The Politics of Surrealism*. The relationship between Surrealism and the PCF lasted from 1927 to 1935. For Nadeau, the Surrealists' adherence to the party was only formal. See *The History of Surrealism*, especially 135.

44 On that occasion, Breton was denied the right to speak and the text of his presentation could be delivered by Paul Éluard only after the Surrealist Paul Crevel committed suicide on the premises. On the Congress, see among others Shattuck, *The Innocent Eye*, and in particular "Having Congress: The Shame of the Thirties," 3–31.

of fatherland. This concept was anathema to the Surrealists; they were thus alarmed by the dismissal of the proletarian cause in the name of national unity that was being carried out in the pages of *L'Humanité*.[45] They also objected to the bourgeois government's attempt to pitch French against German proletarians via the surreptitious suggestion that French culture needed to be defended against a German assault.[46]

The Surrealists' response to the French-Soviet pact forced the movement to rethink the relationship of art and literature to politics. After eluding the topic for many years, Breton finally tackled it head on, and this time he showed no wavering or hesitation. In his 1934 "What is Surrealism?" Breton had already hinted that, judging from the definition he had formulated in the 1924 *Manifesto*, Surrealism might have seemed detached from any aesthetic (or moral) concern. In reality, he claimed, it was more precise to say that Surrealism was disengaged from a "conscious" aesthetic preoccupation.[47] A year later, in his speech to the Congress of Writers, Breton distinguished between a "manifest" and a "latent" content in the work of art and declared that "independently of what its 'manifest content' can consist of, the work of art lives in so far as it incessantly recreates emotions."[48] He warned against privileging content over form and insisted that the poet's exploration of human problems contained in itself the seeds for potential social change and for the

45 The paper wrote, "If the proletarians, to cite Marx, 'don't have a fatherland,' they however have at this moment ... something to defend: it is France's cultural patrimony." Cited in Nadeau, *Histoire du Surréalisme*, 418.

46 One of the legendary events in the history of Surrealism occurred during the Saint-Pol-Roux banquet of 1925, when the Surrealists caused a roar with cries of "Long Live Germany!" On this episode, see Nadeau, *Histoire du Surréalisme*. Also see the Surrealists' "Hommage à Saint-Pol-Roux," in *Tracts*, 1: 41–9.

47 In the manifesto, Breton had declared his wish for an automatic thought which would not only be subtracted to the control of reason "but also disengaged from '*all aesthetic or moral preoccupations.*'" In retrospect, Breton admitted, one "should at least have said *conscious* aesthetic or moral preoccupations" (italicized in the original). See *What is Surrealism?* 116; *Œuvres complètes*, 232.

48 See Breton, *Manifestoes of Surrealism*, 238 and Nadeau, *Histoire du Surréalisme*, 420. Claude Cahun had already been anticipating these arguments in a report that she was supposed to prepare for the literary section of the AEAR (Association des Écrivains et Artistes Révolutionnaires) between 1933 and 1934. Cahun had deemed poetry a need of human nature that could not therefore disappear in a future society. She had argued against the existence of rules for "revolutionary" poetry and had stated the importance of the poet's sensibility. Like Breton, Cahun had borrowed the categories of "latent" and "manifest" content from Tristan Tzara's essay "Essai sur la situation de la poésie" and she hailed the indirect way in which poetry can have propagandistic effects. Nadeau, *Histoire du Surréalisme*, 388–95.

reorganization of the economic structure. Indeed, that is where the power of art resided, and no slogan or scripted declaration could surpass it. The emancipation of the spirit could not be subordinated to political ends. Breton concluded: "'Transform the world,' Marx said; 'change life,' Rimbaud said. These two watchwords are one for us."[49]

Breton affirmed what the Surrealists had been convinced of all along. Art is not the privileged means to achieve the flowering of the mind or an end in itself or an instrument of politics; art has an independent life. Yet now Breton placed less emphasis on the scientific rigour of the Surrealist method and openly declared that the Surrealists were "artists." Just a few months earlier, on the occasion of a Surrealist exhibit in Prague in April 1935, he had articulated this position more eloquently. At that time, the Czech communist press, following conventional canons, described Breton and Éluard as "the two greatest poets of contemporary France" and two important contributors to the development of Marxist aesthetics in the footsteps of Engels.[50] According to local press releases, Surrealist poetic activity worked toward the cause of the proletarian revolution and against the capitalist system: through poetry and unity, revolutionary "artists" would defeat fascism.[51] In an interview with the journal *Haló noviny*, Breton and Éluard accepted the classification of Surrealism as an art form. They spoke in their role as artists and poets and affirmed the importance of "authentic" art for revolutionary social action. Breton, in particular, described Surrealism as a mode of knowledge based on dialectical materialism that aimed at resolving the antinomies between action and dream, logical and natural necessity, objectivity and subjectivity. This mode of knowledge would then produce artistic and political manifestations – "Surrealist works" that were supposed to express Surrealist ideas. Breton conceded that Surrealist poems and paintings were different from other poetic and plastic productions. Nevertheless, he clearly addressed Surrealism as an artistic-literary avant-garde, a characterization that disavowed the movement's original intentions.[52]

The Surrealists were now adopting conventional rules to define themselves and their work, and one could argue that the schizophrenic

49 Breton, *Manifestoes of Surrealism*, 241 and Nadeau, *Histoire du Surréalisme*, 422.

50 "Bulletin international du Surréalisme," in Nadeau, *Histoire du Surréalisme*, 407, 403.

51 Ibid., 407. Breton's intervention in Prague focused on the relationship between artistic and political avant-garde. See his speech of 1 April, "Political Position of Today's Art" (1935), in Breton, *Manifestoes of Surrealism*, 212–33 and "Position politique de l'art d'aujourd'hui," in *Position politique du surréalisme*, now in Breton, *Œuvres complètes*, 2: 416–40.

52 See Nadeau, *Histoire du Surréalisme*, 409, interview to *Haló noviny* in Prague of 9 April 1935. Asked about Soviet art in the interview, Breton defined it as an imitation art that reflected the new world rather than inventing it.

relationship they established with the Communist Party triggered their confrontation with the issue of self-identity. Their rapprochement with dialectical materialism pressured them to specify the concrete ways in which they could contribute to a proletarian revolution. In addition, the Communist Party's impatience with the Surrealists' peculiarities forced the latter to respond in terms that were mutually understandable. The Communists wanted to enlist the Surrealists as artists and writers, without the extra burden of surrealist "theatrics." After a long period of resistance to the party's demands, the Surrealists accepted the Communists' framing of the question concerning artistic engagement and eventually addressed the inadequacies of an art of propaganda while upholding art's autonomy.[53] Most consequentially, they took the stance of speaking as artists. Not surprisingly, at the Congress of Writers they also proposed "the right to pursue, both in literature and in art, the search for new means of expression; the right of the artist and writer to continue to study the human problem in all its forms."[54] Ironically, once they acknowledged their role as artists, the Surrealists ceased to identify with the Communist Party. In the face of restrictions to intellectual freedom advocated by the party, the Surrealists' break with the Communists was inevitable. The revolutionary spirit itself was at stake.

After more than a decade of intellectual quarrels over their movement's essence, the Surrealists' confrontation with art came to a halt. Surrealism renounced its original anti-aesthetic impulse and reluctantly resolved to uphold art and its right to autonomy. At the same time, the Surrealists became wary of the negative consequences a politicized art would inflict on the creative process. Politics and art, in the traditional terms they had come to identify them with, seemed irreconcilable. In the attempt to be socially active, for a short while the Surrealists tried an alternative route. Since they had always thought that poetic subjectivity draws from a collective emotional source, they reconceived the terms of their political engagement. In 1935, free from an excruciatingly fragile relationship with the Communist Party, they co-founded with Georges Bataille the Union for Struggle of Revolutionary Intellectuals under the name Contre-Attaque. Inspired by the ex-Surrealist Roger Caillois and led by Bataille, this new movement focused on the issue of "affective

53 See for example Breton's interview to *Indice* (Revue socialiste de culture, Tenerife), in *Position politique du surréalisme*, now in *Œuvres complètes*, where Breton declared, "Artistic imagination must remain free ... The work of art, lest ceasing to be such, must be untied from all sorts of practical ends" (2: 446).

54 See the August 1935 manifesto that announced the break from the Communist Party: "On the Time when the Surrealists were Right" ("Du temps que les Surréalistes avaient raison"), in *Manifestoes of Surrealism*, 244 and *Tracts*, 274–81.

movements" in an attempt to reimagine collective bonds. Politics was then recast in new categories of interpretation where emotions took central stage.

Contre-Attaque confirmed the Surrealists' uneasiness at combining political changes with cultural transformations. When confronted with historical events, the Surrealists entered the fray by renouncing either politics or art, or both. They ultimately felt unable to reconcile the movement's seemingly contradictory aspirations; their desire to overcome and dissolve divisions only seemed to confirm the reality of existing separations. Bataille and Caillois had come to Contre-Attaque following different trajectories from the Surrealists, as well as from each other, but fuelled by an analogous quest for unconventional means to intervene in the social. And like the Surrealists, they struggled at coming to terms with their own activism while distancing themselves from traditional notions of art and politics. The path Caillois and Bataille took before landing at Contre-Attaque illuminates the way in which their journey, like the Surrealists', intuitively posited an expansive understanding of "the political" only to disavow it shortly thereafter. What they shared with Surrealism helped them define their own intellectual engagement later pursued at the Collège de sociologie.

PRELUDES TO CONTRE-ATTAQUE

Art on Trial: Roger Caillois

Roger Caillois joined the Surrealist movement in 1932 at the age of nineteen while still a student preparing to enter the prestigious École Normale Supérieure.[55] After replying to an evening newspaper inquiry about the literary taste of those youth wishing to attend the Grandes Écoles, Caillois decided to send a copy of his response to Breton, whose *Manifesto of Surrealism* he had cited among his preferences. Breton invited Caillois for a visit, and the young student eventually became a regular at Surrealist meetings, a "fanatic" member, as he later recalled.[56]

---

55 Caillois was also at the time participating in the group Le Grand Jeu led by his friend Roger Gilbert-Lecomte. For a general biography of Caillois, see Felgine, *Roger Caillois, biographie.*

56 See Caillois, "Entretien avec Hector Bianciotti and Jean-Paul Enthoven" of 28 November 1978, in Lambert, *Les Cahiers de Chronos,* 147. Caillois also stated that he had been "as if recruited by André Breton." See also Caillois, "Intervention surréaliste (Divergences et connivences)," in *Cases d'un échiquier.*

Surrealism's main attractions for Caillois were its ferocious critique of aesthetic genres and its destructive unmaking of literature. Accordingly, in "Spécifications de la poésie," his first publication for the review *Surréalisme au service de la Révolution* in May 1933, Caillois lamented the lack of critical evaluation in poetry – an absence that for him seriously compromised poetry's status. Instead of expressing "severe thought" (*pensée sévère*), he claimed, poetry ended up being an exercise in rambling by anyone who felt a literary inclination.[57] Caillois advised reorganizing poetry through both a critique of empirical imagination based on superficial resemblances or correspondences and the break-up of the opposition between the poetic and the real. Caillois considered the image to be a key component of both science and the concrete. Poetry should not be seen as autonomous, he argued. The elusive belief in freedom of the mind needed to give way to understanding the "*necessity of the mind*" (*nécessité d'esprit*) in order to expand the limits of the real.[58] In another Surrealist publication in which he made recourse to the Freudian concept of "determination" or "overdetermination" ("*détermination*" or "*surdétermination*"), Caillois insisted that work of systematization, not an aesthetic approach, could make poetry valuable.[59] Lyrical imagination in a wakeful state ought to be approached with the "scientific rigour" that Freud had demonstrated in his work on dreams. In both cases, the affective systematization of representations was at stake.

At the time of his involvement in Surrealist circles, Caillois was deeply committed to the project of a scientific understanding of lived experience – what he would later define as the "logic of the imaginary."[60] This phenomenology aimed at exploring the affective, lyrical side of the imagination while avoiding turning lyricism into an autonomous domain or a literary poetic genre. Caillois pursued the logic of the imaginary to overcome the dichotomous opposition of rational and irrational, abstract and concrete and eventually moved away from automatic

57 "Spécification de la poésie," in Caillois, *Approches de l'imaginaire*, 15.

58 Ibid., 18 (italicized in the original).

59 See "Systématisation et determination," published in 1934 in *Intervention Surréaliste*, now in Caillois, *Approches de l'imaginaire*, 19–24. Also see Caillois, *La nécéssité d'esprit*, translated into English as *The Necessity of the Mind*. The book was written between 1932 and 1934 but remained unpublished at the time. See Hollier's afterword to the English edition for an illuminating interpretation of the book. Hollier sees the book as an "autobiographical essay" (155).

60 See Caillois, "The Logic of Imagination (Avatars of the Octopus)." The original French title was "La logique de l'imaginaire."

writing.[61] Although his negative position vis-à-vis art had initially aligned him with the Surrealists, Caillois's own exploration into the field of the logical led him to think of Surrealism's automatic writing as both wrong and superficial.[62] Automatic writing showed Surrealism's complacency with the literary, Caillois later contended. "I had imagined that Surrealism was the end of literature, but in trying it out, I realized that it was an avatar of literature," cliché, indeed, he affirmed.[63] Surrealism was ultimately unable to "reveal the veritable functioning of thought, which is the opposite of automatism."[64] Therefore, with a call for "automatic thinking," Caillois proceeded to undermine the legitimacy of the literary project pursued by Breton. He relied on rigour in his study of the mechanisms of "overdetermination" in lyrical thought and the development of affective themes in individual consciousness.[65] On this basis, he dismissed literature's central role in accessing "*affective imagination.*"[66] The scientific method was meant to cancel out an aesthetic approach; in 1935, when he left the Surrealists, Caillois launched a stark attack against them as well as against literature.

Taken aback by what he considered Surrealism's lack of seriousness in investigating irrationality, Caillois published a group of writings that, as he later reminisced, intended nothing less than liquidating art altogether.[67] *Procès intellectuel de l'art* opened with a letter to Breton accusing

61 At this time, Caillois resorted to the new term "ideogram" to pursue his task. According to the dictionary definition, the term designated "signs presenting images of ideas or of things," but Caillois warned about the need to add a modifier to the definition: "mental" or "emotive." Caillois, *The Necessity of the Mind*, 8–9.

62 See his "Témoignage" (1973), in Lambert, *Les Cahiers de Chronos*. For the English translation see "Testimony (Paul Éluard)," in Caillois, *The Edge of Surrealism.*

63 Caillois, "Testimony," *The Edge of Surrealism*, 63.

64 See "Entretien avec Hector Bianciotti and Jean-Paul Enthoven," in Lambert, *Les Cahiers de Chronos*, 147.

65 One should note that the subtitle of *The Necessity of the Mind* is *An analytic study of the mechanisms of overdetermination in automatic and lyrical thinking and of the development of affective themes in the individual consciousness.*

66 See Caillois, *The Necessity of the Mind*, Preliminary Definition, 1 (italicized in the original). Also see "Spécification de la poésie" and "Systématisation et determination," in *Approches de l'imaginaire.*

67 Caillois denounced the Surrealists' lack of seriousness and defined what they engaged in as "simple social games." See "Argument," in *Approches de l'imaginaire*, 12. For Caillois' reminiscences, see Roger Caillois, "Notes pour un itinéraire de Roger Caillois," 166, where Caillois wrote, "I was looking for, I was hoping for a veritable liquidation of art, which to me appeared timid and flat, even odious, hypocritical alibi and shameful concession, not worth the attention of a mind anxious to go to the bottom of things. I thought art needed to be submitted to a harsh inquiry in order to discover behind the aesthetic façade the most severe drives (*les plus graves impulsions*) it served to dissimulate. I believed in the

Surrealism's leader of being "definitely on the side of intuition, poetry, and art – and of their privileges."[68] Caillois, in contrast, called for "no less than substituting for all artistic activity an objective study of the different manifestations equally considered, from delirium to masterpieces, where the mysterious power of the imagination revealed itself."[69] *Procès intellectuel de l'art* condemned "pure art," as well as pure poetry and pure painting, and against them posited those "impure" elements still present in art that, by eschewing formalism and abstractedness, revealed the workings of empirical imagination.[70] Although he conceded that by discarding purity art might be able to help understand imagination, Caillois indicted art for its uselessness, superficiality, inability to deepen our knowledge of the mind, and a tendency to adulation. He thought of art as uncertain and deceptive, dangerously facile and seductive.[71] Since he identified the novel with art's ultimate failure, Caillois ended *Procès intellectuel de l'art* wishing the "irreparable" crisis of literature. If there was nothing to expect from beauty to begin with, the degeneration of literary styles, under the auspices of the novel, turned art into a real threat and pushed to the limits aesthetics' ability to dissimulate our deepest impulses, forces, and instincts. Caillois opposed art to the power of the imagination, madness, violence, or what is unusual and dark. Wishing to psychoanalyze nature in order to uncover its deep secrets, he dismissed art and its theatrics as only able to graze the surface of things.[72]

Caillois's disagreement with the Surrealists was intellectually motivated and rooted in an original understanding of the aesthetic field. Since Caillois took the critique of art seriously, he expected the same rigour from those who only a couple of years earlier had attracted his supreme respect.[73] For Caillois, the task could be nothing short of eliminating art and showing its impure character and lack of essence, in addition to its inferior status vis-à-vis science. Art was unable to produce ideas and

---

virtue of madness and violence, of the unusual and gratuitous, in an all irresistible drive, an all blind force and nocturnal instinct, ferocious, implacable."

68 See "Letter to André Breton," in Caillois, *The Edge of Surrealism*, 84, and "Procès intellectuel de l'art," in *Approches de l'imaginaire*, 36.

69 "Notes pour un itinéraire de Roger Caillois," in *Roger Caillois*, 165–6.

70 By "empirical imagination," Caillois intended the "ability to make use of the concrete for mostly passionate ends but where the part played by a stretched intellectuality was nonetheless not negligible." See "Notice sur l'impureté dans l'art," in "Procès intellectuel de l'art," in *Approches de l'imaginaire*, 47 (italicized in the original).

71 See his "Découverte de l'art," first published in the *Nouvelle Revue Française* of January 1970, now in Lambert, *Les Cahiers de Chronos*.

72 Caillois, "Notes pour un itinéraire de Roger Caillois."

73 In "Intervention surréaliste," in *Cases d'un échiquier*, 214, Caillois stated, "I was taking distance from Surrealism in order to take further distance from literature."

enhance the mind's pursuit of knowledge;[74] science, in contrast, could penetrate the working of the imagination through a rigorous method that also took art as its domain of application.[75] In sum, for Caillois science ultimately commanded art, and he damned any temptation toward art's charms as deadly. Much more radical than the Surrealists, at a time when the latter were struggling to reconcile art with politics, Caillois's critique of art was total.

Although his negative evaluation of aesthetics was different from Bataille's iconoclastic attitude in *Documents*, Caillois shared with Bataille a contempt for art. However, in those same years in which Caillois was coming intellectually of age, Bataille put aside aesthetic concerns and began to engage with political questions. His activities and writing after the closing down of *Documents* reveal the process that in the mid-1930s led Bataille to initiate a long-lasting, albeit tempestuous, collaboration with Caillois.

A Politics of the Impossible: Georges Bataille

The dominant cultural and intellectual influence in the 1920s, especially among young people, was Surrealism.[76] Although a close friend of many Surrealists and active in Surrealist circles, Bataille stood among the few who never gave their allegiance to the indisputable leader of the Surrealist movement, André Breton.[77] In 1926, Bataille had published anonymously a transcription of thirteenth-century poems from old French in the review *La Révolution surréaliste*. The principle of these poems, "Fratrasies," was "to have absolutely no meaning," Bataille later wrote.[78] In time, however, Bataille became increasingly critical of the

---

74 See Caillois, "Notice sur l'impureté de l'art," in "Procès intellectuel de l'art," in *Approches de l'imaginaire*, 49n1.

75 Caillois stated, "But we are not giving up applying the scientific method to the art domain." Ibid., 53.

76 According to Marcel Duchamp, Breton "incarnated the most beautiful dreams of youth." Cited in Surya, *Georges Bataille*, 515n22. Also see Thirion, *Révolutionnaires sans révolution*.

77 Bataille was however fascinated by Breton. Surya argues that at the beginning of his encounter with the Surrealists Bataille might have considered joining them. See Surya, *Georges Bataille*, 79. See also Bataille, "Le Surréalisme au jour le jour," in *OC*, 8: 177, where he wrote with reference to Breton, "I was so tired of my boring life with neither glory nor means, so envious of the more real life of these renowned writers." Also see Bataille, *OC*, 7, notes, 615: "The influence of Surrealism on me has been very important, but I was never part of the group, with whom my relationships have often been hostile."

78 *OC*, 8: 176. "Fratrasies" were first published in *La Révolution surréaliste*, March 1926.

Surrealist movement, as attested by his writings for *Documents*.[79] Breton in turn made Bataille one of the main targets of his criticism in the 1930 *Second Manifesto of Surrealism*, where he also ferociously attacked dissident Surrealists. Bataille had clearly struck a (negative) chord with Breton, in spite of having no substantial written record upon which to ground his "fame" of being scorched by Surrealism's leader over several pages of *The Second Manifesto*.[80] The fact that most of the dissident Surrealists had joined *Documents*, at whose helm Breton clearly recognized Bataille, reinforced the negative opinion Breton had apparently held of Bataille since their first encounter.[81]

Materialism emerged from the *Manifesto* as the most relevant issue of contention between Breton and Bataille. Breton accused Bataille of anti-dialectical materialism and of a clichéd critique of idealism, and he rejected Bataille's assault on spirit while deriding his obsession with horror. Bataille, on his part, missed no opportunity to dismantle what he maintained were the false presuppositions of Surrealism's artistic revolt.[82] Bataille's critique of idealism, along with his focus on the materialistic interpretation of low matter, the heterogeneous, and the repulsive aggressively demoted Surrealism's stance while denouncing its principles. In an article for the avant-garde review *Bifur*, which was supposed to appear in 1931 but remained unpublished until 1968, Bataille specifically laid out his negative analysis of idealistic orientation. The title of the essay unquestionably implicated the Surrealists: "The 'Old Mole' and the Prefix *Sur* in the Words *Surhomme* and *Surrealist*."[83] Prefaced by a little-known citation from Marx, "In history as in nature, decay is the laboratory of life," the article indicted idealism through a critique of authoritarianism and

---

79 In the years prior to *Documents*, Bataille had published very little except the pamphlet *Notre-Dame de Rheims* and the short novel *Histoire de l'œil* (*Story of the Eye*) as well as a few scholarly articles for the art and archeology review *Aréthuse*.

80 In the 1962 edition of the Manifesto, in *Manifestes du Surréalisme*, Breton's critique of Bataille filled six pages (214–20). On this issue see Surya, *Georges Bataille*, 128.

81 On the relationship between Breton and Bataille, see Surya, *Georges Bataille*, especially the chapter "Excrement philosopher." Also see "Le Surréalisme au jour le jour," in *OC*, vol. 8, where Bataille mentioned that, according to Leiris, Breton thought of him as an "obsessed," (*obsédé*), 177.

82 According to Surya, Bataille indeed "conceived *Documents* as a war machine (*machine de guerre*) against Surrealism," 118. Bataille never cited Breton in *Documents*. Several collaborators of *Documents* were ex-Surrealists, among them Georges Limbour, Robert Desnos, Michel Leiris, and Georges Ribemont-Dessaignes.

83 The article "La 'vieille taupe' et le préfixe *sur* dans les mots *surhomme* et *surréaliste*" was first published in *Tel Quel* no. 34 (Summer 1968). See English translation in Bataille, *Visions of Excess. Bifur* ceased publication in late 1930. On *Bifur*, see Lawton-Lévy, *Du colportage à l'édition. Bifur et les Éditions du Carrefour*.

imperialism in politics, revealing the way in which aesthetic and political issues were intrinsically imbricated in Bataille's theoretical vision. Bataille identified Surrealism with a form of bourgeois revolt whose subversion rested on the unfortunate establishment of new values against old. In particular, Bataille interpreted the Surrealists' appeal to and reliance on the Spirit, seen as an authority above the contingent world, as the sign of the Surrealists' inevitable failure to bypass their bourgeois condition (and conditioning). Bourgeois revolutionaries' "guilt feelings" toward the working class led them to the "representation of revolution as a redemptive light rising *above* the world, *above* classes, the overflowing of spiritual elevation."[84] For Bataille, Surrealism constituted a reincarnation of revolutionary spiritualism; it thus sided with the eagle, which politically symbolized imperialism and authoritarian power.

Bataille counterpoised to the eagle the old mole that Marx had linked with the proletarians in the *Communist Manifesto*, and he pitched the heavens against the bowels of the earth. Bataille recognized that the urge to elevation characterizes human morality; even Friedrich Nietzsche, whose anti-conformism ended up being another form of Icarian adventure with no connection to the below, the human masses, could not escape. By evoking images of decomposition and repugnance, Bataille denounced the reactionary "Icarian complex" of bourgeois revolutionaries, whose high aim brings about their downfall, as Icarus was thrown down by the melting power of the sun. For Bataille, the substitution of new values for old only confirmed the reigning power of idealism, even after the death of God had been proclaimed. By adding the prefix "sur" to "realism," the Surrealists exemplified this orientation toward high ideals, even as they introduced (and adulterated) values traditionally considered low (the unconscious and sexuality, among others). Their field of activism remained literary, Bataille continued, and they disregarded the "vulgar interests" of the collectivity. In the same way, their use of the poetic condemned the Surrealists to idealistic elevation.[85] In the end, Bataille pointed out that there could be no better proof of Surrealism's idealistic subversion than Breton's conclusion in *The Second Surrealist Manifesto*, where he invoked the power of "the *idea* against the bestiality of all beings and all things."[86] Surrealism's Icarian propensity was not

---

84 Bataille, "The 'Old Mole,'" in *Visions of Excess*, 34 (italicized in the original).

85 For another evaluation of Surrealism as idealistic, see the exchange between Aragon and Jean Bernier, editor of the leftist review *Clarté*, in Nadeau, *The History of Surrealism*, 100–1. Bernier called Aragon "an *idealist* ... against all pragmatism." See "Documents surrealists," in Nadeau, *Histoire du surréalisme*, 205.

86 Bataille, "'The Old Mole,'" in *Visions of Excess*, 43.

sympathetic to human agitation, the base materialism of the masses, Bataille insisted.[87]

With his allegiance to filth and the heterogeneous, and in contrast to the Surrealists, Bataille described the materialistic roots of human nature as growing in decomposing soil. He also began to sketch his own political interpretation of a community at a distance from the authoritarian power of the idea – a headless community he later brought to life in the group Acéphale.[88] In this sense, whereas *Documents* had opposed the formless to beauty and promoted the "naturalization" of ugliness, the horrible, and the monstrous, "The 'Old Mole'" converted aesthetic motifs into tools for rethinking politics. Bataille's most intense period of political activity began at this time; he collaborated with the review *La Critique sociale* and participated in the group Le Cercle communiste démocratique, both headed by the Russian dissident communist Boris Souvarine.[89]

The late 1920s and early 1930s saw a major outpouring of writings by Bataille, most driven by political reflections. In these often unpublished essays, Bataille presented several of the themes and concepts that characterize his œuvre as a whole; he also reflected the zeitgeist of a time sandwiched between the ghost of a past, gruesome war and the spectre of a future world conflict. Confronted by fascist and communist dictatorships and disillusioned about the possibility of working-class revolution, Bataille embarked on an original social and cultural analysis. At its centre stood the idea of "unproductive" expenditure, one of Bataille's most important interpretive concepts.

In "The 'Old Mole'" and some of the articles he had written for *Documents*, Bataille had already exalted base materialism and putrefaction as sources of new energy. If the flower grows in height, it is only because of its roots deep in the verminous ground below. Similarly, in human relationships, he contended, the working class as the abject – the wretched of the earth – provides the sole source of existence through a

87 Bataille's pointed critique of Surrealism in "The 'Old Mole'" hurled back accusations of inadequate materialism at Breton. One might argue that through his long-standing confrontation with both Surrealism and Breton, Bataille defined his own vision of an endless fall, the only countermeasure to the continuous elevation of new value systems. In a posteriori evaluations of Breton, and curiously echoing Caillois, Bataille also mentioned Breton's "lack of rigor" (*manque de rigueur*) as a problem. See "Le Surréalisme au jour le jour," *OC*, 8: 173.

88 Bataille wrote about "the *loss of the head*" in the essay. See *Visions of Excess*, 43 (italicized in the original).

89 For Souvarine's controversial opinion of Bataille, see his "Prologue" to the reissued volume of *La Critique sociale*. See also Piel, "Quand un vieil homme trempe sa plume dans le fiel," for an outraged response to Souvarine's accusations (especially of fascism) against Bataille.

movement of expenditure that overcomes the bourgeois imposition of material utility and conservation and also demonstrates the value of destruction.[90] Building on these early analyses, Bataille continued to posit expenditure and loss as not only intrinsic to economic institutions but also as necessary elements of human pleasure.

In his 1933 "La notion de dépense," which was a blistering analysis of bourgeois principles, Bataille argued against the notion of usefulness as exclusively related to the acquisition and conservation of goods and the reproduction and conservation of human lives.[91] If one followed this principle, he reasoned, the most valuable part of existence would consist of "productive social activity" and pleasure would constitute only a subsidiary element. Bataille, in contrast, challenged individuals to reflect on the value in their lives of acts that do not follow the logic of conservation. Do not acts of waste respond to, and aren't they an expression of, some need? Wouldn't it be fair to suggest that human society has an "interest" in loss? In truth, Bataille admitted, we deny such possibility on the basis of conceptions that are totally at odds with our actual life practices – practices that often include the satisfaction of "disarmingly savage needs."[92] Bataille observed that human activities include consumption, not merely production and conservation. And he distinguished between consumption to the end of producing and conserving life and consumption for unproductive ends. Bataille called the latter *dépense*, "expenditure," where loss comes to be opposed to conservation and is unconditional.

By arguing that production and acquisition are a function of expenditure and stand subordinate to the end of destruction, Bataille turned standard notions of the economic process upside down; he defined the power of the wealthy as the power to lose.[93] Accumulation was a function of waste and, as the institution of the potlatch studied by Mauss showed, nobility, honour, and rank derived from loss, the ability, that is, to waste wealth and possessions. In modern bourgeois societies, Bataille argued, the market economy has so altered the physiognomy of the exchange relationship that stability has replaced the risky venture embodied by the

---

90 For Bataille's discussion of the proletariat and negativity, see also his article with Raymond Queneau, "La critique des fondements de la dialectique hégélienne," first published in *La Critique sociale* in 1932, now in *OC*, vol. 1 (English translation "The Critique of the Foundations of the Hegelian Dialectic," in Bataille, *Visions of Excess*).

91 See *OC*, vol. I (English translation "The Notion of Expenditure," in Bataille, *Visions of Excess*).

92 Bataille, *Visions of Excess*, 117 and *OC*, 1: 303, 304.

93 "[W]ealth appears as an acquisition to the extent that power is acquired by a rich man, but it is entirely directed toward loss in the sense that this power is characterized as the power to lose." Bataille, *Visions of Excess*, 122 and *OC*, 1: 311.

gift. The wealthy classes refuse to engage in expenditure, even though they have received "with wealth the obligation of functional expenditure."[94] In contrast, they consume in private. In a reinterpretation of Hegel, Bataille argued that within this context only the popular classes can maintain the principle of loss via a struggle that threatens the existence of their masters. The rich, despite hiding behind the ideology of equality, build their status through an agonistic act of separation from the workers that relegates the proletarians to the ranks of the abject: one cannot be superior without an inferior counterpart holding on to "human nature." The proletarians then epitomize and display those "irrational" impulses that the wealthy strive to suppress. Class struggle becomes the actualization of those irrational impulses; it constitutes the workers' mode of expenditure and guarantees the eventual loss of the bourgeois class.

Inspired by Mauss's study of the gift, Bataille deemed free expenditure not only necessary but unavoidable. If the bourgeoisie, motivated by stingy calculations, have led to the atrophy of human agitation, then class struggle, he suggested, would bring loss back into human existence.[95] Although still clinging to the Marxist idea of the inevitability of revolution, Bataille introduced "affective" elements, in particular horror and pleasure (or the pleasure of horror), as constitutive of human societies. He combined traditional critiques of politics with a sui generis approach to the political that particularly emerged from his discussion of art's link to pleasure and the principle of loss.

Bataille cited sacrificial cults, competitive games, and art production as examples of unproductive expenditure. He then distinguished real from symbolic expenditure within art.[96] Pointing to literature and theatre as symbolic representations of tragic loss, Bataille defined poetry as synonymous with expenditure when "applied to the least degraded and least intellectualized forms of the expression of a state of loss," and even more with "creation by means of loss."[97] He thus compared poetry to sacrifice, that is, the production of sacred things.[98] In poetry loss coincides with the destruction of the practical order through particular

---

94 Bataille, *Visions of Excess*, 124 and *OC*, 1: 313.

95 Bataille had already introduced the notion of loss as excretion in "La valeur d'usage de D.A.F. de Sade" ("The Use Value of D.A.F. Sade"), now in *OC*, vol. 2. Also see "L'œil pinéal" ("The Pineal Eye"), *OC*, vol. 2. See English translations in *Visions of Excess*.

96 This reference to the symbolic probably reflected Mauss's emphasis on this dimension of sociability within the total social fact.

97 Bataille, *Visions of Excess*, 120 and *OC*, 1: 307.

98 "In the etymological sense of the word, sacrifice is nothing other than the production of *sacred* things," Bataille declared. Bataille, *Visions of Excess*, 119 and *OC*, 1: 306 (italicized in the original). At this time sacrifice emerged as a topic of interest for Bataille.

image associations.[99] Although a few years later he would condemn and liquidate art altogether in his main writing for the Collège, "The Sorcerer's Apprentice," at this time Bataille was still weighing Mauss's attempt to come to terms with the symbolic and construct a theory of solidarity.[100] Within this provisional plan, art could not be renounced.

As several commentators have remarked, Bataille was highly critical of the contemporary liberal society represented by Western democracies. According to him, they relied heavily on the authority of the state and ignored individual affective drives. Bataille was generally skeptical of the role of the state even in the case of the Soviet Union, where communism was reduced to a "party of official mercenaries" and perilously approximated the fascist model. An unorthodox Marxist, Bataille considered the autonomous force of anguish based on the hatred for the state the only element able to play a liberating role for the proletariat.[101] The three so-called revolutions of the twentieth century, Bolshevism, fascism, and Nazism, had exposed the shortcomings of a conservative understanding of the state's role. For Bataille, now disillusioned with the communist experiment, fascism raised even more troubling questions about the relationship between affective forces and politics. How to understand fascism's success, or more generally fascism, became Bataille's major preoccupation.

Fascism and Heterogeneity

In November 1933, Bataille's key article in *La Critique sociale*, "The Psychological Structure of Fascism," addressed the issue directly.[102] Fascism, indeed, constituted for Bataille the litmus test for assessing the deficiencies of current communist and democratic governments as well as for sketching alternative ways to reawaken affective forces and induce subversion in established democracies. Bataille's previous opposition to the state as the ultimate expression of imperative forms of authority remained strong in his analysis of fascism, though less so in "The Psychological Structure" than in "Fascism in France," an unpublished writing of the same period.[103] An original element, however, appeared in both writings:

---

99 Bataille, *oc*, 1: 631n11.

100 As Mary Douglas argues in her foreword to Mauss, *The Gift*, "Refusing requital puts the act of giving outside any mutual ties ... A gift that does nothing to enhance solidarity is a contradiction," vii.

101 See Bataille, "Le problème de l'état," *oc*, vol. 1.

102 See Bataille, "La structure psychologique du fascisme," in *oc*, vol. 1, and the English translation in *Visions of Excess*.

103 Bataille, "Le fascisme en France," in *oc*, vol. 2.

6 Georges Bataille, circa 1933. Photo collection Julie Bataille

Bataille's urge to understand fascism's essence through a specific focus on the god-like figure of the leader and on the affective relations linking the followers to the duce. Bataille relied on the psychoanalytical findings of Freud to decipher such relations and dismissed as inconclusive any economic explanation of the fascist phenomenon. His preface to "The Psychological Structure" could not be clearer: Marxism had failed to account for the formation of political or religious society; it did not realize that it was at the level of the superstructure that an elucidation of fascism resided. Strictly economic interpretations would not suffice; they were the starting point of the analysis rather than its ending.

Bataille thus proceeded to describe the mechanisms that make possible the surge of fascism in societies based on production and commensurability. He began by defining these societies as homogeneous; he then emphasized the bourgeois tendency to reduce human nature to an interchangeable entity (as in the cash nexus described by Marx).[104] Social

104 According to Bataille, because they are excluded from profit, the proletarians are able to maintain their irreducible human nature (at least outside of working relations).

homogeneity is a fragile condition, he argued, and any contradiction in the system of production might cause an internal dissociation that not even the state is able to prevent. Those who stop supporting homogeneous society then join other non-homogeneous elements who lead a non-commensurable existence. Fascism constituted one case in point and needed to be understood within this theoretical framework.

Heterogeneity and its workings became a main topic of concern for Bataille, although he did not provide a precise definition of the term.[105] He suggested that the heterogeneous world is made up in part of the sacred and that heterogeneous things provoke reactions similar to those incited by sacred things. Moving between psychoanalysis and French sociology, Bataille relied on Durkheim's assessment of religion and described the heterogeneous as containing a dangerous force (mana) which requires it to be separated from homogeneous things through a prohibition (taboo). Bataille included all unproductive expenditure in the heterogeneous realm and highlighted the affective reactions that heterogeneous elements elicit from people: heterogeneous reality presented itself as a shock; it provoked both attraction and repulsion. Bataille concluded that fascism, or better Mussolini and Hitler as fascist leaders, belonged to heterogeneity. They emanated force and broke the rhythm of homogeneous life; at the same time, an affective link united them to their followers.

Bataille focused his interpretation of fascism on the issue of its attraction – what he saw as the emotional waves connecting leader and led. "[T]he unity of fascism is located in its actual psychological structure and not in the economic conditions that serve as its base."[106] Fascism combined religious appeal with military force resulting in a form of political sovereignty that exercised total oppression.[107] For Bataille, this reality indicated the urgent need to develop a system of knowledge about affective social reactions, those movements of attraction and repulsion whose enormous power and consequentiality fascism had so clearly demonstrated. He

105 Bataille compared the exclusion of heterogeneous elements from homogeneous consciousness to the censorship of unconscious elements by the "I" in psychoanalysis. He invoked the need to build knowledge of the "*nonexplainable difference*" ("*différence non explicable*"). See Bataille, *Visions of Excess*, 141 and *OC*, 1: 345 (italicized in the original).

106 Bataille, *Visions of Excess*, 157 and *OC*, 1: 367.

107 In the heterogeneous, Bataille distinguished between elevated, superior forms and miserable, inferior forms. Although he did not assign values to these terms and took them as historical categories, for him fascism belonged to the former because it appealed to noble sentiments in the traditional sense. Bataille, however, specified that fascism rejected the impure forms of the heterogeneous. In this way it rejoined homogeneous society, which always oppresses inferior elements.

believed that such knowledge could become a weapon for the subversive formations needed in view of both communism's failure to fulfill its mandate and its fascist turn through reliance on personality cults.[108] Bataille still held that communism and fascism were opposites since the former, in its original impetus, was driven by truly subversive impulses.[109] He nonetheless judged that further knowledge of affective movements was necessary considering the lack of scientific progress in this area.

The historical turn of events in the months immediately following the publication of "The Psychological Structure" left Bataille no time for delving deeper into the study of attraction and repulsion – dynamics that he saw as crucial for understanding the fascist phenomenon. The upheavals of February 1934, and the general strike that ensued, made the need to act even more imperative.[110] Bataille participated in the demonstration of 12 February where a range of political groups converged in protest against fascism. The day before the strike, he ruminated about whether a violent or a peaceful event would make the protest successful but seemed convinced that the rally would not stop fascism from expanding.[111] The day after the strike, on 13 February, Austrian workers were killed during a socialist insurrection, and the Austrian chancellor, Engelbert Dollfuss, imposed authoritarian rule. Bataille wrote about this event, "From all sides … the fascist grip is tightening up."[112]

During the first half of the 1930s, Bataille remained highly pessimistic about the current political and human situation, as his major writing of the time, the novel *Le Bleu du ciel* (*Blue of Noon*) also testifies. He had, after all, made the case that the current understanding of the fascist phenomenon was insufficient at best, if not distorted and inadequate, and he ultimately warned that "social agitation cannot be dissociated from man's profound agitation."[113] The obstinacy of continuing to analyse fascism in

108 "Le fascisme en France," *oc*, vol. 2, emphasized this point, showing Bataille's profound disillusionment with the Soviet experiment.

109 On the relationship between fascism and communism for Bataille, see "Le fascisme en France," *oc*, vol. 2. Also see "Essai de définition du fascisme," *oc*, vol. 2, where Bataille insisted that "it is out of the question to speak of fascism when referring to the communists," 216.

110 At this time, Bataille signed the tract "Peuple Travailleur, Alerte!" for the Cercle communiste démocratique. The tract exhorted workers to form a unique front and participate in the strike. See Bataille, *L'Apprenti Sorcier*, 108. We might recall that at this time the Surrealists also invoked active unity with their tract "Appel à la Lutte."

111 See Bataille, "En attendant la grève générale," *oc*, vol. 2.

112 "De toutes parts … se resserre l'étreinte fasciste." See "En attendant la grève générale," *oc*, 2: 262.

113 Bataille, "L' échec du Front Populaire," in "En attendant la grève générale," *oc*, 2: 265.

relation to the economic structure could not but reduce the possibility of finding a solution to the inexorable fascist takeover of Europe.[114] Only a year earlier, in 1933, Hitler had ascended to power in Germany and appeared to be expanding his range of territorial ambitions. Bataille sombrely wrote: "30 January 1933 is certainly one of the most sinister dates of our epoch."[115] Continuing to promote militant activism, he founded Contre-Attaque.

CONTRE-ATTAQUE

According to witnesses, Caillois and Bataille first met at Jacques Lacan's apartment in 1934.[116] At the time, Caillois was elaborating his theory of imagination as well as honing his critique of Surrealism's approach to poetry; Bataille had published, besides his articles for *Documents*, the important essays on expenditure and fascism for *La Critique sociale*. Both Caillois and Bataille were intrigued by psychoanalysis and excited by the possibility of expanding its application to realms outside the individual unconscious.[117] Both were convinced of the importance of affective life and its resonance at the social and scientific levels. When discussing his relationship with Bataille, Caillois has talked about "intellectual osmosis" – an osmosis that might help explain why Bataille was attracted to a project that Caillois began elaborating in 1935.[118]

The idea for Contre-Attaque had been conceived by Caillois sometime during the first half of 1935. Bataille wrote a letter to Caillois on 4 August of that year that mentioned "the project you have implanted in my head" and asked whether Caillois was still interested in pursuing it. The present political situation required urgent action, Bataille added.[119] Two months later, on 16 October, Caillois sent a letter to the editor of the *Nouvelle Revue Française*, Jean Paulhan, mentioning a text he was submitting and

114 In the same way, Bataille believed that the revolutionary impulse of the working class came from emotional values – anguish – and not economic advantages. See "Le problème de l'état," *OC*, vol. 1. Also see Bataille's review of André Malraux, *La condition humaine*, in *OC*, vol. 1.

115 Bataille, "En attendant la grève générale" (1934), in *OC*, 2: 262.

116 In his interview with Gilles Lapouge, Caillois cited an incorrect date, 1936; we know that Bataille and he were already corresponding in 1935. See Lapouge, "Entretien avec Roger Caillois"; English translation, "Interview with Gilles Lapouge, June 1970," in Caillois, *The Edge of Surrealism*.

117 See "Notes pour un itinéraire de Roger Caillois," 166, where Caillois wrote, "[P]sychoanalysis appeared to me as a prodigious revelation."

118 See Caillois, *L'Homme et le sacré*, Avant-propos (no pagination), and *Man and the Sacred*, introduction, 15.

119 Bataille, *Lettres à Roger Caillois*, 41.

wondering whether its political nature might be suitable for the journal.[120] In a subsequent letter of 30 October, he specifically referred to the text as the manifesto for the Union d'intellectuels révolutionnaires, which would be issued a few days later and signed by Bataille and Breton, among others, but not Caillois. In his epistolary exchange with Paulhan, Caillois gave some of his reasons for not participating in the Union, citing in particular what he deemed were deviations from his own original idea.[121] Caillois did not envisage the group as some kind of political party with a specific program. He was interested in probing "delicate ideological questions."[122] His correspondence with Bataille shows that Caillois resisted all attempts to persuade him to join the nascent movement or sign the manifesto that was eventually issued. That Breton favoured and welcomed Caillois's association with the group did not seem to make a difference either. Caillois remained unmovable.

We know very little about Caillois's political ideas at the time. Although the Surrealists had entered the most political phase of their history in the 1930s when Caillois joined them, in his memoirs and reminiscences Caillois never cites the Surrealists' political engagement as a source of either interest or disagreement. An examination of the Surrealists' declarations, however, reveals that in 1933, when Breton, Crevel, Éluard, and Thirion wrote a tract criticizing the Communist Party's position against the war, Caillois signed it. The tract, "La Mobilisation contre la Guerre n'est pas la Paix," criticized an "abstract" opposition to military intervention that ended up supporting the reconciliation of class antagonism, opposing civil war, and defending imperialism.[123] In 1934, Caillois also signed the "Appel à la Lutte" of 10 February which invited all workers to unite against the fascist menace. Although he did not sign the

120 Cahiers Jean Paulhan 6, *Corréspondance Jean Paulhan-Roger Caillois*, 29.

121 Ibid., 30. Caillois has been recognized as the originator of Contre-Attaque only recently. Bataille claimed paternity of the same organization. See Bataille, *Lettres à Roger Caillois*, 42n2. See also "Notice autobiographique," *oc*, 7: 461, where Bataille wrote, "In 1935, Bataille personally took the initiative to found a small political group which, with the name of Contre-Attaque ... " However, in a 9 February 1937 document, "Constitution du 'journal intérieur,'" Bataille wrote, "In July 1935, Roger Caillois and Georges Bataille together envisioned to found an association of revolutionary intellectuals." See *L'Apprenti Sorcier*, 337. Breton also claimed paternity. See Bataille, *Lettres à Roger Caillois*, 46n3. Short, who was among the first to study Contre-Attaque, did not seem to have knowledge of Caillois's role in the project. See Short, "The Politics of Surrealism, 1920–1936." Also see Short, "Sur 'Contre-Attaque.'"

122 Cahiers Jean Paulhan 6, *Correspondance Jean Paulhan-Roger Caillois*, 30.

123 See *Tracts*, 1: 240–45. The tract was in response to the Amsterdam-Pleyel movement against the war. For the signatories of the tract, there was nothing more fallacious under the capitalist regime than contrasting war to peace.

"Enquête sur l'Unité d'Action" of 18 April, he supported the defence of Trotsky in a tract of 24 April ("La Planète sans visa") that criticized the French Communist Party's official position on the Russian revolutionary. Previously, in 1932, Caillois had also signed a collective declaration against colonialism with the title "Murderous Humanitarianism."[124]

At the end of 1934, when Caillois definitely broke with the Surrealists, he stopped signing their political manifestos. He did so even though, in his letter to Breton of 18 December 1934, which recognized the impossibility of continuing his collaboration with the group, he affirmed his willingness to support Surrealism on those ventures where they were in agreement, including politics.[125] In fact, his idea-project of Contre-Attaque reveals that Caillois was preoccupied with the current political situation – a situation that seemed to be dominated, if not concretely at least emotionally, by the fascists. As Caillois wrote to Paulhan, he needed to determine the "affective particulars" (*données affectives*) of the different political movements operating in the 1930s.[126] He was interested in developing knowledge and understanding of the era's political landscape, although he did not intend to found a political party. Practical engagement, it seems, was not on Caillois's horizon, and this *prise de position* might have created the distance between him and Bataille that eventually led Caillois to refuse to join Contre-Attaque. At least, this is implied in his note to Paulhan: the militant character that Contre-Attaque had assumed under Bataille's and Breton's leadership did not please Caillois.

In the several post-1930s interviews, books, and articles published by Caillois, he never discussed the issue of Contre-Attaque, and because his connection to Contre-Attaque has only recently been established, none of his interviewers specifically questioned him on the subject. Nor have newly found documents on Contre-Attaque shed much light on Caillois's influence on the group. If anything, they have complicated matters further because they indicate that already in January 1935 Bataille was discussing the creation of a group and journal with people who later joined Contre-Attaque.[127] By then, he had met Caillois, but we begin to see a mention of Caillois's "project" as a response to the contemporary political situation only much later in the year in the correspondence between Bataille-Caillois and Caillois-Paulhan. The history of Caillois's relationship to

124 Ibid., 262–4, 265–7, 268–9; and 2: 441–4.

125 "Lettre à André Breton" of 27 December 1934, in *Procès intellectuel de l'art*, in Caillois, *Approches de l'imaginaire*.

126 Cahiers Jean Paulhan 6, *Correspondance Jean Paulhan-Roger Caillois*, 29.

127 See letter of Bataille to Leiris of 20 January 1935, in Bataille, *L'Apprenti Sorcier*, 119–24.

Contre-Attaque thus remains in many ways obscure. What we do know is that Caillois had transposed his interest in human affectivity to the analysis of political movements; he thought it necessary to examine the dynamics of lyrical factors in social relationships. *La nécéssité d'esprit* had laid claims to a logic of the imaginary and the need for and possibility of a science that penetrated the irrational side of concepts, that is, their affective dimension. Contre-Attaque, or the idea of it, mediated Caillois's lyrical interest in the social, at least in a preliminary way, and there are points of convergence between the manifesto Contre-Attaque published and ideas Caillois developed in those same years. It is difficult, however, in view of their osmotic relationship, to decipher what Caillois and Bataille took from each other during their exchange on the Contre-Attaque project.[128]

Be that as it may, Bataille replaced Caillois as leader of Contre-Attaque. The latter feared that the whole approach had become too militant; Bataille, in contrast, believed that it was necessary to set aside the search for knowledge and become actively engaged. On 7 October 1935, Bataille's efforts to constitute the Union de lutte des intellectuels révolutionnaires finally led to the publication of the tract "Contre-Attaque."[129] It was signed by Breton and Éluard, among others, marking the unlikely, albeit temporary, collaboration between two of the most important protagonists of twentieth-century French intellectual life: Bataille and Breton. With fourteen points and divided into two parts ("Resolutions" and "Union's positions on some essential points"), the manifesto began by laying out one of the major lines of contact between the Surrealists and Bataille's associates: their fundamental critique of patriotic beliefs and traditional politics. The manifesto declared its opposition to the notions of fatherland and nation and stated its intention to eliminate capitalist authority while affirming the desire to take action and stop "discussing."[130] More originally, the manifesto proposed rethinking the traditional political tactics of revolutionary movements in the face of a changed target; it was now time to fight democratic regimes and not autocracies. The cases of Germany and Austria had recently demonstrated the inadequacy of the revolutionary movement's approach.

128 Annamaria Laserra tries to untangle some of the knots of the story in "Bataille e Caillois: osmosi e dissenso."

129 The exact title was "'Contre-Attaque': Union de lutte des intellectuels révolutionnaires," now in Bataille, *OC*, vol. 1. The Union opposed the communist-based association of artists and writers (AEAR). Breton published the tract in his *Position politique du surréalisme* a month later. See also *Tracts*, 1: 281–4.

130 A critique of parliament and discussion was not unusual at this time.

CONTRE-ATTAQUE

LA PATRIE ET LA FAMILLE [1]

Dimanche 5 janvier 1936, à 21 heures, au Grenier des Augustins, 7, rue des Grands-Augustins (métro Saint-Michel).

CONTRE L'ABANDON DE LA POSITION RÉVOLUTIONNAIRE

Réunion de protestation

Un homme qui admet la patrie, un homme qui lutte pour la famille, c'est un homme qui trahit. Ce qu'il trahit, c'est ce qui est pour nous la raison de vivre et de lutter.

La patrie se dresse entre l'homme et les richesses du sol. Elle exige que les produits de la sueur humaine soient transformés en canons. Elle fait d'un être humain un traître à son semblable.

La famille est le fondement de la contrainte sociale. L'absence de toute fraternité entre le père et l'enfant a servi de modèle à tous les rapports sociaux basés sur l'autorité et le mépris des patrons pour leurs semblables.

PÈRE, PATRIE, PATRON, telle est la trilogie qui sert de base à la vieille société patriarcale et aujourd'hui, à la chiennerie fasciste.

Les hommes perdus d'angoisse, abandonnés à une misère et à une extermination dont ils ne peuvent pas comprendre les causes, se soulèveront un jour excédés. Ils achèveront alors de ruiner la vieille trilogie patriarcale : ils fonderont la société *fraternelle* des compagnons de travail, la société de la puissance et de la solidarité humaine.

PRENDRONT LA PAROLE DIMANCHE 5 JANVIER :
Georges BATAILLE, André BRETON, Maurice HEINE, Benjamin PÉRET.

---

(1) Il va de soi que *famille* et *patrie* restent solidaires de *religion*, sujet beaucoup plus vaste qu'on n'imagine et sur lequel nous nous exprimerons dans une réunion ultérieure.

7 A copy of the flyer announcing Contre-Attaque. Georges Bataille, *Œuvres complètes*, vol. 1. © Éditions Gallimard

The signatories of the manifesto were aware of their movement's potential for violence and indeed embraced it as the only way to constitute a popular government, "*an inflexible dictatorship of armed people.*"[131] Contre-Attaque, however, was not advocating disorganized, irrational violence. On the contrary, it invoked the creation of forces that were "disciplined, fanatical, capable of exercising come the day a merciless authority," while also maintaining moral exaltation as a necessary element for achieving freedom.[132] The Union did not abjure Marxism; but on point eight it noticeably underscored that historical transformations had brought about new social structures which needed to be studied and understood for any revolutionary action to be successful. A "science of forms of authority" was essential.[133] In addition, as Bataille had anticipated in his writings for *La Critique sociale*, it was necessary to borrow fascism's political weapons, that is, its ability to satisfy fundamental human aspirations toward affective exaltation and to do so without falling into the local conservatism of nationalist causes and ideals. The manifesto addressed itself to "men, all over the earth."

Contre-Attaque was interested in achieving power and did not shy away from affirming its will to fight.[134] Along with these objectives, however, and with the intention of circulating new ideas about revolutionary action, it planned a series of intellectually oriented pamphlets under the title *Cahiers de Contre-Attaque*. The *Cahiers* were designed to explore the issues of power, sexuality, and moral renewal and to discuss the question of authority in relation to how to build a social bond, a human community. The first and only issue that saw the light of day in May 1936 tackled the topic of family life in light of pursuing a moral revolution that would transform slaves into masters and eliminate servitude.[135]

131 Bataille, *oc*, 1: 380.

132 Ibid. This language was very close to Caillois', as will become clearer in the next chapter.

133 Ibid., 381.

134 On Contre-Attaque's will to fight see for example Bataille's letter of 22 October 1935 to René Michaud, in *L'Apprenti Sorcier*, 154: "What we essentially envisage is evidently action – action that is urgently needed after the leaderships of the old parties have refused it. In our opinion, in the current circumstances, action needs to take the most engaging and most violent direction."

135 For the whole text of the Cahiers see *Tracts*, 1: 284–90. Their common interest in the master/slave relationship shows the similarity between Bataille and Breton who were both influenced by Hegel. According to Marguerite Bonnet, Breton had done his own reading of the German philosopher and did not attend Alexandre Kojève's famous seminar on Hegel. See her introduction to Breton, *Œuvres complètes*, 2: xvii. On Hegel's influence on Bataille via Kojève, see Derrida, "From Restricted to General Economy." Also see Larmore, "Bataille's Heterology," and Queneau, "Premières confrontations avec Hegel." In

The pamphlet critiqued socialism's failure to take down democratic regimes and highlighted the victorious power of fascism's tactics. It advocated the transformation of the Popular Front into a Popular Front of
Combat in charge of expressing the need to renew political forces. It
emphasized people's emotional life as a means to achieve power and
launch a counterattack. Ultimately, the *Cahiers* reaffirmed the group's
intention to defeat fascism with its own weapons while maintaining a
firm anti-capitalist stance.

The *Cahiers*, along with other initiatives such as the establishment of a
political commission, indicated the group's goal of advancing knowledge
of aspects of political revolution that had been neglected by traditional
scholarship. Bataille had enunciated this goal in "The Psychological
Structure" a couple of years earlier and it would become the core issue at
the Collège. Overall, however, a feverish need to act characterized
Contre-Attaque. The frantic tone of the articles Bataille wrote for the
Cahiers, as well as his correspondence and the tracts issued by Contre-
Attaque, communicate this sense of frenzy. The question for Bataille remained the one he had posed in the April 1935 tract that called for the
formation of the future Contre-Attaque: "What to do? In the face of fascism, in view of communism's inadequacy?"[136] At the time, Bataille was
unsure about ways to enact a new approach. He believed that one needed to situate oneself at the same level as fascism, "that is, the mythological
level," as he had written in a letter to Pierre Kaan dated 14 February
1934, but he remained unsure about how to achieve that goal.[137] By the
fall of 1935, Bataille displayed no doubts about openly affirming subversive values. One of the first flyers announcing the meeting of Contre-
Attaque of 5 January 1936 attacked "[t]he fatherland and the family."
Another, "Sous le feu des canons français ... et alliés," dared to avow
a preference for Hitler's "anti-diplomatic brutality" in contrast to the

---

a couple of letters to Kojève at the time of Contre-Attaque, Bataille implicated Hegel. In
November 1935, in particular, he indicated that he was interested in showing "how it is
possible to move from the level of the *Communist Manifesto* to that of *The Philosophy of Mind*."
See Bataille, *Choix de lettres*, 120.

136 Bataille, *L'Apprenti Sorcier*, 124 (with Jean Dautry and Pierre Kaan). We do not know
why the April attempt at constituting a group failed, or which of Caillois' ideas inspired
Bataille. We also do not know what happened between April and August of that year, when
Bataille wrote to Caillois about wanting to pursue his project. Nevertheless, the advance of
fascism was doubtlessly prompting Bataille's engagement and, one could also add, that of
several intellectuals at the time. See among other groups the case of the Front commun
contre le fascisme, founded in 1933 by Gaston Bergery, a member of the Radical Party.

137 Ibid., 112.

logorrhea of diplomats and politicians.[138] The daily order of Contre-Attaque's political commission for 8 December 1935 was "Affective exaltation and political movements."[139]

These unconventional and, for many, provocative *prises de position* were part of a larger interpretive framework that linked patriotism to authority and proclaimed the need for a "fraternal society"; under the banner of anti-fascism a human community would counter nationalistic attempts to undermine people's power. Enraged and disappointed by the Franco-Soviet pact, which clearly relegated an anti-capitalist proletarian revolution to a second plane, the members of Contre-Attaque attacked France along with bolshevism and imperialism. For Bataille, in particular, the lack of a critical analysis of democracy's ability to face and defeat fascism was very troublesome. Even more disturbing was the socialists' anachronistic belief in revolution within the context of bourgeois society's changed conditions. For Bataille, politics after fascism would never be the same. Revolution needed to be rethought.

His piece for the *Cahiers*, "Vers la révolution réelle," was a précis of the ideas he had elaborated on the changed political landscape during the Contre-Attaque period. Bataille observed that classical liberal revolutions had always occurred under autocratic regimes and could not be replicated when the regime in question was a democratic one. The disparities between the two systems required differentiated approaches. In the case of autocratic regimes, the desire to end the king's domination united people in a struggle against a common target: revolutions aimed at the fall of royal power, the cutting off of the head. Bataille contended that without a sovereign exercising personal power the concentration of popular anger necessary to engender a revolt could not be achieved. "[T]he crowned head plays its role of unifying insurgent crowds," he wrote.[140] Within this interpretive framework, the proletariat played a fundamental role in liberal insurrections. Outside these stated conditions, Bataille however insisted, there is no historically known chance of reversing power. Because democratic rule lacks a form of centralized power and responsibilities can easily be shifted during governmental crises, democracies, unlike autocratic regimes, fail to engender a unified opposition. "What

138 See Bataille, *oc*, 1: 398. Some changes were then made to the tract, such as the addition of "sans être dupes" (without being deceived). See *Tracts*, 1: 297–8. On the tract and the Surrealists' problematic reactions to it, see Dubief, "Témoignage sur Contre-Attaque" and Short, "The Politics of Surrealism."

139 See Bataille, *L'Apprenti Sorcier*, 174.

140 Bataille, *oc*, 1: 415.

becomes intolerable in the case of autocracy is authority. In democracy, it is the absence of authority," Bataille ruminated.[141]

The consequences of this reality worried Bataille; to ignore the structural differences between democracies and autocracies could be lethal for the left. According to him, when democracies undergo a crisis, two internal political currents emerge, one on the left and one on the right. The movement on the left is immediately weakened by the lack of authoritarian institutions to be dismantled; its negative force has the opposite effect of facilitating the emergence of a movement from the right, as epitomized in the fascist case. This dreadful outcome required reconsidering the whole approach to revolution. In particular, democracy could not be fought as an authority to be "decomposed," but had to be looked at as a formation that lacked authority and against which only an imperative violence would prevail. One needed to use fascism's means because fascism was the only movement to issue from a crisis of democratic regimes.[142]

Bataille's need to determine the factors that would ensure a successful revolution led to his interest in fascism. He focused on what he considered fascism's novelty: organic movements that, turned into organized forces, were able to reinstate authority within a decomposing democracy. Such movements did not appeal to class interests but instead elicited strong emotions that led to violence and the pursuit of power. For Bataille, the ultimate lesson to be learned from the Italian and German cases was that their form of political struggle had been effective. This form of political struggle, therefore, needed to be adopted in order to achieve opposite goals. Bataille envisaged the formation of a French revolutionary movement that, with its rigorously organized force, would oppose war, assume a universalist conscience against nationalist interests, and advocate the end of economic exploitation.[143] This movement would not be satisfied by mere symbolic measures of the kind fascism was providing: economic transformation was a sine qua non.[144]

---

141 Ibid., 417.

142 "We must stop to believe that the innovative means of our adversaries are necessarily bad means. We must, in contrast, use them back against our adversaries." Ibid., 422. The fascists had already copied from the Bolsheviks, according to Bataille.

143 Of course, a movement based on the aspirations of a mass rather than a specific political formation (such as the proletariat) carries the risk of eventually taking a reactionary direction. Bataille, however, judged such possibility highly unlikely in 1930s France, due to several historical factors that differentiated France from Germany and Italy.

144 Bataille claimed that "the analysis of the processes that characterize the superstructure do not imply misrecognizing the economic realities that *condition* these processes." Bataille, *oc*, 1: 417, note (italicized in the original).

The Popular Front appeared to Bataille to contain within itself the seed of the organic movement he envisioned; it had been born out of the crowd's excitement of 12 February 1934, was not a party movement, and lacked a permanent status. The Popular Front's weakness, however, was that its leadership engaged in conventional electoral politics rather than basing itself on the "tumultuous reality" of the crowd – a sign of anachronism, of being blind to the current reality.[145] Bataille pointed to the importance of "direct and violent drives," the emotions and rage that exhale in the street where life erupts in opposition to the individual's isolation.[146] That is where the force of the people is truly expressed. "[S]trength results less from strategy than from collective exaltation," Bataille maintained, and it developed out of the masses' passions rather than political formulas.[147] Crowds were at the basis of Bataille's new vision of politics.[148] Within that vision, the crowds' anguish created the impetus for a revolt against the powers that condemned the masses to impotence.[149]

Through the Contre-Attaque experience, Bataille developed a unique understanding of political relations that, although generated from an analysis of fascism's novelty, was intended to make possible larger radical changes. The definition and scope of the political field needed to be questioned in terms of alternative approaches that addressed existential concerns through reference to the heterogeneous. This goal allowed Bataille to overcome his scorn for politics, suppress his distrust of Breton, and join the Surrealists at Contre-Attaque. There, he shared with the Surrealists a common platform that challenged conventional political beliefs and redefined militancy.

Eventually, Contre-Attaque succumbed to an internal controversy that marked the split between the Surrealists and Bataille's friends. Contre-Attaque's peculiar approach to politics, with its accent on emotions and crowds, supposedly led one of the group's members, Jean Dautry, to coin the term "surfascisme."[150] Intended as "a surpassing of fascism," or "going

145 Ibid., 427.

146 "Popular Front in the Street," in *Visions of Excess*, 161 and *OC*, 1: 403. This was another article Bataille wrote for the *Cahiers de Contre-Attaque*.

147 Bataille, "Popular Front in the Street," in *Visions of Excess*, 167 and *OC*, 1: 411.

148 In 1937 Bataille founded a Society of Collective Psychology, whose objective was to "study the role, in social facts, of psychological factors, more particularly unconscious ones." See Bataille, *OC*, 2: 444. Pierre Janet was the president of the society and Bataille its vice-president.

149 See also "Notes additionnelles sur la guerre," in *OC*, vol. 1. In the flyer "La patrie et la famille" that announced Contre-Attaque, Bataille also posited anguish against the trilogy of fatherland, father, master (393).

150 See Dubief, "Témoignage sur Contre-Attaque." Dautry was an ex-collaborator of *La Critique sociale* and *Masses*. See Galletti's short summary of his life in Bataille, *L'Apprenti*

beyond it by making use of it," the expression apparently became a source of contention for the Surrealists and a prelude to their departure from Contre-Attaque.[151] Probably taken aback by the combination of the prefix "*sur*" with fascism, the Surrealists used the term to accuse Contre-Attaque of surfascist tendencies, or "extreme fascism."[152] Whether the Surrealists believed that Contre-Attaque had gone too far with its critique of democracy is not clear. As a matter of fact, Breton's interventions at Contre-Attaque's preliminary meetings of December 1935 indicated the opposite; he showed his total support for the group's program and ideas. Breton stressed the importance of the superstructure, anguish, and crowd psychology. He referred to Freud and his study of collective psychology, as well as to Robertson Smith, both of whom Bataille had cited in "The Psychological Structure." He discussed church and army – Freud's examples of the construction of "artificial" crowds through affective identification – and conceded that extreme affectivity in a crowd could lead to the inevitable lowering of the intellectual level.[153] Breton, in sum, fully subscribed to Contre-Attaque's agenda, whether or not it differed from the positions he had previously held.[154] The fact that he and Bataille had been able to overcome their strong antagonism by collaborating at Contre-Attaque demonstrates that they both recognized in Contre-Attaque the

---

Sorcier, 110. Dautry had also redacted Contre-Attaque's tract "Sous le feu des canons français ... et alliés" of March 1936, in *Tracts*, 1: 297–8. The tract contained a reference to Hitler that the Surrealists found inappropriate. Dautry eventually became general secretary of Contre-Attaque after Bataille resigned on 2 April 1936. See Bataille, *L'Apprenti Sorcier*, 279.

151 In reality, Bataille had set up a Comité contre l'union sacrée (Committee against the sacred union) without consulting the Surrealists. On the differences between the Surrealists and Bataille's friends, see Dubief, "Témoignage sur Contre-Attaque," Surya, *Georges Bataille*, and Short, "Sur 'Contre-Attaque.'"

152 On 24 March 1936, a text signed by Breton and others stated, "The Surrealist members of the group Contre-Attaque report with satisfaction the dissolution of the so called group, within which had emerged some tendencies called 'superfascist' whose purely fascist character has become more and more evident." See Breton, *oc*, vol. 2, Trois interventions d'André Breton à Contre-Attaque, Inédits I, Notes et variantes, 1665. Pierre Andler has claimed the paternity of the neologism "*surfascisme*." See Bataille, *L'Apprenti Sorcier*, 11n1. Andler indeed used the term in a document of 17 April 1936 in which he summarized Contre-Attaque's idea of using fascism in order to overcome it. He wrote, "In the same way that fascism is in the end nothing more than a surmarxism, Marxism on its feet, similarly the force that will reduce fascism cannot but be a *surfascisme*." Bataille, *L'Apprenti Sorcier*, 296.

153 Breton, *oc*, vol. 2, Inédits I 1931–1935, Trois interventions d'André Breton à Contre-Attaque, 585–611. Church and army will become the focus of the Collège's analysis of community.

154 See Bonnet's comments in Breton, *oc*, 2: 1657–8.

only avenue for resolving the antinomies of the present historical situation. That the Surrealists ultimately launched their accusation of fascism against the other Contre-Attaque members is puzzling.[155]

The negative aura of fascism eventually followed Bataille to the Collège where, closer to co-founder Caillois's desire, he put aside politics in order to focus on the sociology of the sacred. Learning from Contre-Attaque's failings and deficiencies, and with its mandate as a non-political activist organization, the Collège countered Contre-Attaque's militancy by pursuing scientific knowledge of the elements required to conceptualize and enact new social bonds. What Contre-Attaque with its *Cahiers* had initiated as a side activity became central at the Collège: the systematic study of how to build a universal community that would rest on stronger social ties.[156] Riding the wave of Contre-Attaque and its disappointing ending, Bataille re-evaluated old themes and concerns in the new unorthodox research group. By implicating affective movements, as well as heterogeneity and the overcoming of fascism, he maintained the old focus even as he changed targets. The secret society Acéphale, founded by Bataille in 1936, anticipated the Collège's stance of seeking to reignite social emotions while abandoning politics (and liquidating art).

155 In this sense, Henri Pastoureau's a posteriori declaration that the Surrealists coined the term "surfascisme" makes matters even more confusing, or certainly less straightforward in terms of interpretation. See letter of Pastoureau to Galletti, cited by Galletti in Bataille, *L'Apprenti Sorcier*, 297n3. "The word *superfascist* has been invented by us Surrealists. It can both designate a surmounted fascism (positive) and an exacerbated fascism (negative) ... In any case, nobody thought of any relationship whatsoever with Italian or German fascism." Pastoureau was the one who redacted the Surrealists' text accusing Contre-Attaque of fascism. The text, "La rupture avec Contre-Attaque," was published in *L'Œuvre* on 24 May 1936. Adding even more confusion to the enigma, in a previous letter of 28 January 1981 (Lettre à J.P.), Pastoureau wrote, "I was the one who redacted the text on the exhortation of Breton ... In my mind, the term '*surfasciste*' did not mean to be insulting but only to be polemical. Indeed I wrote '*called "surfasciste"*' – it is now that I underline 'called': called by Dautry, as Dubief has reminded us. I in fact did no longer remember who invented the word." *Tracts*, 2: 446 (italicized in the original).

156 See Bataille, *L'Apprenti Sorcier*, "Programme," 281–2 (and notes 282–4).

4

From Contre-Attaque to the Collège: A Headless Interlude

DURING THE EARLY 1930S Caillois had pursued a general phenomenology of the imagination as part of his plan to expand the scientific knowledge of human experience. According to him, a newly founded science of the imaginary would systematically and coherently reveal the underlying poetic structure of a seemingly rational empirical reality. A strict methodological approach to poetry would put an end to the traditional opposition between the mysterious, non-utilitarian, and marvellous, on the one hand, and the secular, utilitarian, prosaic, on the other. Caillois's search for lyrical objectivity thus covered a vast array of phenomena that, despite their apparent heterogeneity, could be examined as an organic and interdependent totality. Caillois ultimately sought to identify, in its ever changing forms, the function of the mind that synthetically presided over the diverse elements constituting the whole.

After departing from Surrealism, Caillois directed his attention to myth as a privileged manifestation of imaginary life. Consequently, he addressed the issue of representation, so central to Durkheim's sociological project, and brought his approach more in line with Mauss's conceptualization of the total social fact. As Caillois pointedly wrote in the introduction to *Le Mythe et l'homme*, myth best illustrated "the collusion of the most secret and virulent individual psychic drives with the most imperative and troubling pressures of social existence."[1] Wanting to steer further away from the Surrealists' instinctual understanding of lyricism, Caillois analyzed mythical images as means to increase knowledge and incite action.[2] He expanded Durkheim's analysis of collective representation and constructed an anti-utilitarian theory of myths that, by weaving

---

1 See Caillois, "Avertissement," *Le Mythe et l'homme*, 13.

2 Caillois invited readers not to be surprised when in the course of the book they would see him abandon his observational posture. Ibid.

in biology and psychology, vindicated myth's primacy in the explanation and understanding of human phenomena.

This chapter begins by discussing Caillois's increasing interest in myth as an important component of his, as well as Bataille's, theoretical understanding of affective movements. It delineates Caillois's original approach to mythological thinking and sketches out his reading of the lyrical roots of collective representations as elaborated in his theory of the imaginary. It also directs attention to the distinction Caillois drew between art, negatively evaluated as individualized and desacralized, and myths seen as affectively based and socially integrating. The chapter then retraces the intellectual path that led Bataille, in the wake of the critical experience at Contre-Attaque, to direct his energy toward founding a secret society and homonymous journal called Acéphale. By focusing on Acéphale, the chapter assesses the existential turn that in the late 1930s pushed Bataille to displace the political through its transfiguration into the sacred, here conceived in terms of strong communal bonds. The chapter also illustrates Bataille's growing inclination toward science as a legitimate means for assembling knowledge about the sacred. More generally, the chapter shows that Bataille's struggle to define Acéphale as apolitical in the midst of European fascism foreshadowed the future predicaments the Collège faced in its struggle to confront the modern crisis of the social – the lack of meaningful community. The discussion of Acéphale thus illuminates at its embryonic stage the Collège's evaluation of the role of affect in social life.

THEORIZING MYTH

Caillois built the scaffolding for his intellectual pursuit into the realm of myth in the collection *Le Mythe et l'homme*, where excursions in comparative biology set the scene for his original analysis of cultural representations. Within this model, representations revealed the encrusted social valence of beliefs and practices normally relegated to the emotional and psychological sphere, and made possible the decoding of their original (and disguised) meanings. Eventually, Caillois's interest in representations moved to the analysis of the religious realm generally conceived as the sacred. He thus met the challenge posed by the Durkheimians when discussing affective logic in connection to rationality and the social.[3]

---

3 See especially Hubert and Mauss, "Introduction à l'analyse de quelques phénomènes religieux," in Mauss, *Œuvres*, vol. 1. Whereas psychologists saw only a division between rational and sentimental logic, for Hubert and Mauss, "when one studies these two logics in the conscience of individuals living in groups, one finds them naturally and intimately linked." Ibid., 27.

Indeed, a direct link to Durkheim eventually paved the way for the creation of the Collège de sociologie, as Caillois later acknowledged in a letter to Jean Paulhan written in parodist Latin: "Secundatus qui genuit Durkheimium qui genuit Collegium Sociologicum."[4]

In his painstaking attempt to affirm the specificity of the social, Durkheim had placed collective representations at the heart of communal existence. Not surprisingly, in a 1936 introduction to the discipline of sociology, Armand Cuvillier proclaimed that a sociological spiritualism pervaded Durkheim's work to the point that collective representations had come to explain everything for him.[5] Durkheim, to be sure, never renounced the objectivism of his original definition of social fact as formulated in *The Rules of Sociological Method*. He nevertheless placed increasing emphasis on those elements in the life of societies that addressed the soul of the "organism" rather than, or in addition to, its functions. Specifically, religion, as the most original social phenomenon, exemplified the active character of collectively held beliefs and practices; it indicated the centrality of images and symbols in their role as mediators in the process of society's self-awareness and becoming.[6] Conceived at the intellectually puzzling crossroads of the relationship between the individual and the collective, the rational and the affective, representations allowed Durkheim to overcome the dichotomies that vexed his project of developing a sociological science. Thus, Durkheim elaborated a notion of social facts as not merely inert objects but sentimental, emotional "things": in their social form, sentiments expressed, with a rigorous logic, the thinking of the group as it penetrated individual consciousness. For Durkheim, even if collective representations had a seemingly psychological foundation, their social imprimatur excluded any individual influence and made them independent of one person's determinations.[7] Only society generated

4 Literally, "Secondat who generated Durkheim who generated the College of Sociology." An admirer of Louis de Secondat, baron de Montesquieu, Caillois claimed that Montesquieu was not merely a precursor of Durkheim but directly influenced him. See Cahiers Jean Paulhan 6, *Correspondance Jean Paulhan-Roger Caillois*, 71, letter of early 1938. In his 1936 *Introduction à la sociologie*, 10, Cuvillier discussed Montesquieu's influence on Durkheim's idea that social phenomena follow laws. Durkheim's Latin thesis was on Montesquieu. It was translated into French (along with another essay on Rousseau) by Cuvillier with the title "Montesquieu et Rousseau précurseurs de la sociologie."

5 Cuvillier, *Introduction à la sociologie*, 67.

6 See Karsenti's discussion in *L'homme total*. On the role of the symbolic in Durkheim's work, also see Tarot, *De Durkheim à Mauss*.

7 Karsenti, *L'homme total*, 62, writes on this issue, "On the one hand, there is a sovereign collective conscience, though disembodied. On the other hand, there is a multiplicity of individual consciences whose socialization can only be conceived negatively, that is as the obedience to an authority that remains external at the same time that it is internalized."

collective representations; being supra-individual, representations in turn made possible the constitution of society. In the case of religious representation, the essence of social action found expression at the individual level in the sentiment of being acted upon but without knowing by whom.[8]

Following Durkheim's lead, Caillois's *Le Mythe et l'homme* focused on myths as an eminent manifestation of imaginative life – one that best caught the collusion of individual and social demands. To Durkheim's concerns about dualism, however, Caillois added the desire to construct a systematic classification of imaginary life and its forms of expression, which he conceived as interdependent and organically blended in a totality.[9] Methodologically, Caillois was closer to Mauss and his idea of total social fact; he opposed compartmentalization and specialization. Thus, Caillois's famous piece on "The Praying Mantis" took the biological realm as an entry into the explanation and understanding of mythology.[10] While he did not deny that accounts of myths based on an external point of view – their conditioning by natural phenomena (moon's phases, eclipses, etc.) – had generated powerful explanations, he argued that such accounts missed the crucial role of myth's internal drives. Wishing to challenge functional interpretations, Caillois explored the kinds of emotional needs myths fulfill. "Why do myths have such an effect on sensitivity?" Caillois asked in "The Function of Myth."[11] How do outer demands interact with inner necessity in producing a myth? In other words, how do social, historical, and natural determinations (the outer components of myths) combine with myth's own logic?

As *La Nécéssité d'esprit* had made clear, Caillois subscribed to Freud's concept of overdetermination, which emphasized multiple causes and the lack of univocal meaning when explaining a phenomenon and dream work in particular.[12] Caillois especially rejected linking mythology to the instinct for self-preservation and any other theory that assumed utilitarian

8 See Durkheim, *EF*, 211; *FE*, 299: "[M]an is well aware that he is acted upon but not by whom."

9 Caillois wrote, "[T]he method that foregrounded these investigations intended to inscribe them into a *total* system." See *Le Mythe et l'homme*, 14 (italicized in the original).

10 One version of "La mante religieuse" was first published in 1934 in the Surrealist journal *Minotaure*. For the text of that version in English, see "The Praying Mantis," in Caillois, *The Edge of Surrealism*. For another version see Caillois, *The Necessity of the Mind*, chapter 5, "The Objectivity of Ideograms."

11 "The Function of Myth," in Caillois, *The Edge of Surrealism*, 116. "Fonction du mythe," now in *Le Mythe et l'homme*, was first published as "Le mythe et l'homme" in *Recherches philosophiques* no. 5 (1935–1936), 252–63.

12 In "The Function of Myth," Caillois defined overdetermination as "a knot of psychological processes, all coinciding in a way that can be neither fortuitous, occasional, nor personal." See *The Edge of Surrealism*, 122. Caillois was, however, very critical of psychoanalysis'

ends. In this sense, he denounced rationalism as unable to resolve the
critical question of myth's essential function. Caillois believed that myths
have an internal logic, a structure that directly reflects imagination. He
was also convinced that myths constitute sites for emotional investment,
albeit not at the level of individual psychology: myths generate affective
movements. The essay on the praying mantis, whose subtitle is "From
Biology to Psychoanalysis," sought to investigate how affective themes develop in individual consciousness by considering which biological facts
resonate in the human psyche.[13] Caillois wished to establish the "correspondence" between animal behaviour and human mythology and to decipher "how a representation could have a separate and, as it were, secret
effect upon each individual in the absence of any symbolic dimension,
whose meaning was chiefly defined by its social usage and whose emotional efficacy stemmed from its role in the collectivity."[14] Thus, Caillois
examined the praying mantis as an exemplary phenomenon that, by virtue of certain external characteristics (name, form, and habits), success-
fully provoked people's affective reaction.

Originally conceived as an ideogram, "The Praying Mantis" became
the first substantive chapter in *Le Mythe et l'homme*; it displayed Caillois's
search for the lyrical objectivity that, separately and almost secretly, acted
upon each individual's emotions and made myths possible. In the case of
the mantis, Caillois claimed, the insect's own characteristics and mythical
production inspired imagination without the official intermediary of collective representation.[15] In particular, the female mantis's pattern of de-
vouring her mate after the sexual act elicited human sexual fantasies. It
also suggested that castration anxieties could derive from the male's fear
of being consumed by the *femme fatale* in a nightmarish re-enactment of
the mantises' behaviour during nuptials.[16] For Caillois, the example of
the praying mantis proved that humans possess imaginations which, like

---

results with reference to the explanation of myths, even though, as he wrote, "one should
not cite the failures of its faithful in order to refute the doctrine." Ibid., 116.

13 Caillois stated, "Comparative biology should supply very valuable correlations as well,
given that representation in certain cases replaces instinct, and that the actual behavior of
an animal species can illuminate the psychological virtualities of man." Ibid., 122. In "The
Praying Mantis" he had specified, "I am not claiming that men, after having carefully observed mantises, were deeply affected by their habits. I am merely stating that as both these
insects and mankind are part of one and the same nature, I do not exclude the possibility of
invoking the insects to explain, if need be, people's behavior in certain situations" (69n1).

14 Ibid., 69–70.

15 Caillois, "The Objectivity of Ideograms," in *The Necessity of the Mind.*

16 Caillois prefaced his thesis with a long list of ancient and modern myths about the
mantis and homophagy. Among them, he also included images of the mantis as a machine.

phantasms, evoke the behaviour of other species (fear of being devoured by the woman is coupled with the decapitation of the male mantis during intercourse). Myths arise from our anxieties and fears and, in the manner of Baudelairian "correspondences," find resonance in reality, in this case the actual behaviour patterns of the mantis.[17] The insect, however, does not cause our mythologizing process. In other words, what we think about the mantis or other species in the animal world is surely based on actual facts: the fundamentally biological connection between sexuality and nourishment. Yet, the representation we create of reality possesses a lyrical nature that sprouts from our own imagination.

With "The Praying Mantis," Caillois formulated a model of lyrical objectivity for the kind of science of the imaginary he was pursuing. Relying on comparative biology, he argued that humans and insects possess a common nature and that the same biological law governs them and determines their convergence. In the case of humans, however, laws do not condition action but rather representations: whereas the insect acts, Caillois wrote, humans mythologize.[18] For Caillois, therefore, the mantis as an objective ideogram both inspired and embodied man's castration anxieties; it "materially realized in the external world the most tendentious virtualities of affectivity."[19] Additionally, the case of the mantis led Caillois to place the origins of mythologizing in those processes of the imagination that precede social intervention.[20] According to him, biology acted on culture, and even the content of myths was in part determined by our interest in anything suggestive of our own body: something in our psyche is solicited by the biological reality and turns on human affectivity.[21] In this sense, one could argue that Caillois understood representations more along the lines of Mauss's conceptualization of the total social fact than within the socially determined model of Durkheim. Caillois

17 Caillois appreciated Baudelaire. A quote from the poet introduced his article "Pour une orthodoxie militante: les tâches immédiates de la pensée moderne," first published in *Inquisitions* 1 (June 1936), translated as "For a Militant Orthodoxy: The Immediate Tasks of Modern Thought," in *The Edge of Surrealism*. Other articles of Caillois also prominently reflected Baudelaire's influence. Caillois had co-founded *Inquisitions* with fellow ex-Surrealists Louis Aragon, Jean Monnerot, and Tristan Tzara in June 1936. The journal, which ceased publication after the first issue, expressly stated its interest in human phenomenology.

18 "*Here a conduct, there a mythology,*" Caillois wrote in "La mante religieuse," in *Le Mythe et l'homme*, 70 (italicized in the original).

19 Ibid., 72. For an illuminating discussion of this essay see Hollier, "Mimesis and Castration 1937."

20 Caillois talked about a "biological conditioning of the imagination." *Le Mythe et l'homme*, 83.

21 Ibid., 81.

insisted on the affective origins of mythical imagination rather than on the social determinants of time and space categories emphasized by Durkheim. No doubt, Caillois was aware of the collective character of mythical imagination. In "The Function of Myth" he raised the important issue of the tight connection between myth and rituals: "Ritual realizes the myth and allows people to experience it," he wrote.[22] Festivals later became Caillois's point of reference as the one place where mythical time is celebrated and people become conscious of their social link.[23] Yet, the primary goal of "The Praying Mantis" was to elaborate a theory that, while it stressed the affective side of human sociality – the expressive component of mythical activity – also emphasized, contrary to a rationalist logic, the non-utilitarian function of myths. Caillois was interested in illuminating human psychological virtualities. Reference to comparative biology allowed him to pursue exactly that route.

The use of comparative biology was demonstrated in another well-known essay of Caillois's Surrealist years, "Mimetism and Legendary Psychastenia," first published in 1935.[24] Here, following the interpretive vein of "The Praying Mantis" where he had criticized functional explanations of the female mantis's behaviour during copulation, Caillois attacked and dismantled interpretations that defined mimicry as a mere device for self-preservation and self-defence. More specifically, on the basis of a comparative biological analysis that considered animals and humankind as part of the same nature, Caillois, in an anti-Darwinian mode, examined mimicry as a pathological attempt on the part of the animal organism to immerse itself in the environment. He found the equivalent of this phenomenon at the human level in the personality disorder defined by Pierre Janet as psychastenia. After presenting several occurrences of mimicry among insects, including the infamous mantis, Caillois determined that defence mechanisms and the preservation of existence were not the main causes of mimetic behaviour. In some cases, perfect assimilation to the environment created an even worse situation for the creatures involved and accelerated their death.[25] Caillois concluded

---

22 Caillois, *The Edge of Surrealism*, 119.

23 Caillois wrote several book reviews on mythology. See for example his comments on A.H. Krappe, *La genèse des mythes*, a book he criticized. The review was published in the May 1938 issue of *Nouvelle Revue Française*, now in Lambert, *Les Cahiers de Chronos*. In a letter to Jean Paulhan of 27 March 1938, Caillois stated the importance of the note he wrote on Krappe because it demonstrated his own, opposite, approach to mythology. See *Correspondance Jean Paulhan-Roger Caillois*, 74.

24 Caillois, "Mimétisme et psychasténie légendaire," in *Minotaure* 7 (1935). See English translation as "Mimicry and Legendary Psychastenia," in *The Edge of Surrealism*.

25 See the case of the Phyllidae, "Mimicry and Legendary Psychastenia," 97.

that a more plausible answer to the scientific enigma produced by animals' imitating tendency was that mimicry was a luxury, even a "dangerous luxury," and did not serve any utilitarian purpose.[26] Mimicry's ultimate goal was to "*become assimilated into the environment*" as instinct followed a "veritable *lure of space*," a desire to disappear and get lost in the surroundings.[27] In other words, mimicry was a disorder of space perception; in humans, it caused the loss of the distinction between organism and environment and resulted in the undermining of one's sense of personality – the dissolution of the subject. This was evident in the disorder of schizophrenia: here, the represented space, as opposed to the perceived space, confused the schizophrenics' consciousness of their position in the world, thwarting their ability to distinguish the real from the imaginary.[28]

Although Caillois was aware that the rarefaction of the self was only "a disturbance," the phenomenon of psychastenia proved to him the inadequacy and limitations of a rational utilitarian logic that eschewed the imaginary, "the obscure realm of unconscious determinations."[29] Mimicry and psychastenia revealed that, along with an instinct of self-preservation, there is an attractive "*instinct d'abandon*," a drive toward reduced existence, a diminished energy: "*the inertia of the élan vital.*"[30] The organism assimilates into its environment as a form of self-obliteration, a return to the inorganic. The process, in sum, had no goal or use. For this reason Caillois defined it as a "luxury," a term that Bataille, in a different vein and with different presuppositions, was at the time associating with "useless expenditure" and waste. For Bataille, expenditure was involved in the production of the sacred, the phenomenon that both he and Caillois were about to explore at the Collège de sociologie. In the "Mimicry" essay, however, Caillois, far from theorizing the sacred, was still fully occupied with demonstrating the common root of biological mimicry and psychastenia. As he wrote in the essay's conclusion, citing Pythagoras, "*nature is everywhere the same.*"[31] At the same time, *Le Mythe et l'homme* also contained a last substantive piece, "Paris, mythe moderne,"

26 Ibid.
27 Ibid., 98, 99 (italicized in the original).
28 Claudine Frank directs attention to Lacan's *Le stade du miroir* where he cited Caillois. Lacan praised Caillois for using the term "*legendary psychastenia* to classify morphological mimicry as an obsession with space in its derealizing effect." See Caillois, *The Edge of Surrealism*, 90,
29 Ibid., 102.
30 Ibid. (italicized in the original). Caillois's critique of Bergson emerges here. See also "The Function of Myth" for a similar critique.
31 Ibid. (italicized in the original).

which, while still addressing the issue of myth's non-utilitarian function, began to raise a question that would shortly become central to the Collège's project: What happened to myths in the modern world?

Myth versus Art, or Sacred and Profane

In the essays written in the first half of the 1930s, Caillois's theory of mythical representation had plunged into the depths of human affectivity only to re-emerge from it by denying any instinctual or self-preservation basis to myth. In "Paris, a Modern Myth," in contrast, Caillois engaged with the issue of nineteenth-century urban mythology in order to take apart the aesthetic understanding of myths. Echoing his past negative evaluation of literature as obsolete individualized fiction, Caillois argued that myths were not ornaments. He then proceeded to dismantle the claim that since myths are part of the imaginary, literature, as art's narrative form, might be the place where new myths can be generated. He deemed this project impossible, unless, that is, literature gave up the pursuit of the beautiful and renounced aesthetics. For Caillois, art responded to, and elicited, individualized reactions expressed in terms of taste and choice. Nothing, he claimed, could be further from myth, which "was a *collective* property by definition; it justified, sustained, and inspired the existence and activity of a community, people, professional body or secret society."[32] According to Caillois, the contention about literature's mythical status boiled down to one main issue: the opposition between the individual and the collective, or the profane and the sacred. As he declared at the second International Congress of Aesthetics and Art Science held in Paris in 1937, "[T]he difference between myth and art coincides with one of the most absolute oppositions one could conceive of: that between the sacred and the profane."[33]

In his speech at the Congress, Caillois presented a stark contrast between myths and art; while myths are sacred, socially based, and integrating, art is an individual operation that rejects emotions and constitutes itself as a separate sphere. The false identification of myths and art thus needed to be dispelled. Even if the two were sometimes found together, as was the case in Greek tragedy and fantastic literature, the nature of myth was not of the same order as the aesthetic. The latter included the enjoyment of beauty and the notions of masterpiece and perfection. Furthermore, the work of art was only "inspired" by

---

32 Caillois, "Paris, a Modern Myth," in *The Edge of Surrealism*, 176; "Paris, mythe moderne," in *Le Mythe et l'homme*, 154 (italicized in the original).

33 Caillois, "Le mythe et l'art: nature de leur opposition," 280.

collective representations, whereas myths expressed the variable sentiments of the group and were not individually enjoyed. Myths manifested the authority of the collective, emanated from society, and were
enacted through rituals and ceremonies that reaffirmed the centrality
of the social and its rules. Desacralized and individualized, art, in contrast, circulated values that testified to the dissolution of its sacred character. Unable to inspire collective emotions, art's new values were a sign
of social decomposition.

Drawing from his ongoing negative evaluation of art, in the second
half of the 1930s Caillois reinstated a strongly Durkheimian perspective
in his analysis of representation. As he redefined his approach to the
imaginary via a new attack on aesthetics, he identified social influence as
the main trait of myths. Then further elaborating Durkheim's notion of
moral constraint, Caillois ultimately argued that, in order to exist, a myth
must exercise authority on the group and be "capable of inciting people
to action" (*provoquer à l'acte*).[34] While literature, to be sure, could be influenced by society, it did not constrain, let alone inspire, agency. He
concluded, in a reversal of terms, that when myth loses its power of constraint it becomes literature and meets its worst fate.[35]

Caillois sought to institute a necessary distance between myth and literature in order to avoid confusing the category of the superfluous,
which he identified with the aesthetic realm, with the non-utilitarian,
which he had adopted in his own theory of myths. Paradoxically, his examination of the modern myth of Paris relied on literary works to build
a strong case against art, while at the same time reaffirming myths' distinctive features. Caillois cited Charles Baudelaire and Honoré de Balzac
as examples of writers who had been able to exercise power on the collective imagination. By moving away from a literature of evasion and
from art for art's sake, Balzac and Baudelaire had actually participated in
the production of myth. Indeed, they had succeeded in evoking an epic
myth of Paris so powerful that its accuracy was not in doubt. Their representation of the big city enhanced collective imagination and, even more
crucially for Caillois, inspired a vision of the modern hero as aggressive
and enterprising. "[N]either the Romantic hero, nor the *modern* hero is
content with the lives that society would have him lead. But the first

34 Caillois, "Paris, a Modern Myth," in *The Edge of Surrealism*, 187; "Paris, mythe moderne," in *Le Mythe et l'homme*, 173.

35 Caillois's condemnation of art in his Surrealist years, as already discussed in chapter 3, continued to characterize his evaluation of individualized narrative forms throughout
the 1930s.

withdraws from society, while the second opts for its conquest,"[36] Caillois wrote. Balzac's and Baudelaire's heroes did not withdraw into their individual selves and avoid conflict; rather, they confronted life and acted on it. In so doing, Caillois claimed, these authors opened the way for a literature that gave up its search for the beautiful, rejected evasion, and encouraged engagement.

The activist stance Caillois had displayed in the introduction to *Le Mythe et l'homme* re-emerged in "Paris, a Modern Myth." Here, besides affirming the existence of myths in the modern era, Caillois stressed literature's potential when it gave up aesthetics. He emphasized myth's power as a collective phenomenon and concluded that myth was "*imperative and exemplary*"; it constituted "a collective, exalted, and rousing representation of society."[37]

Caillois's incursion into the sociological field as it had been mapped out by Durkheim resulted in an analysis of collective representations as mediators between the social and the individual. As he drifted away from a general phenomenology of the imagination and focused on myths, Caillois added to his original pursuit of knowledge an "imperative" desire to devise the laws that guided social action; his goal was to exercise a decisive impact on reality. Caillois did not envisage any conflict between science and engagement, disinterest and interest. Indeed, he thought the opposite was true; one needed to move "from conceptualization to execution."[38] Although he had rejected the politics of Contre-Attaque only a couple of years earlier, his mounting concern with both the decomposition of social ties and the apparently impoverished condition of mythical imagination led him to approach the social and its problematic status in an era of political turmoil. His interest in myths was not an aesthetic whim; rather it constituted a fundamental inquiry into the affective drives that compose the psychological life of individuals and order their experience. As he made clear in the concluding essay to *Le Mythe et l'homme*, the knowledge he was advocating could not but appeal to human sensibility and exert an attraction over it.[39] This knowledge, which he defined as "orthodoxy," differed from ordinary scientific knowledge

---

36 Caillois, "Paris, a Modern Myth," in *The Edge of Surrealism*, 185; "Paris, mythe moderne," in *Le Mythe et l'homme*, 169 (italicized in the original).

37 Caillois, "Paris, a Modern Myth," in *The Edge of Surrealism*, 188; "Paris, mythe moderne," in *Le Mythe et l'homme*, 173 (italicized in the original).

38 Caillois, *Le Mythe et l'homme*, "Avertissement," 14.

39 The conclusion, subtitled "Pour une activité unitaire de l'esprit," had been previously published in a slightly variant version as "Pour une orthodoxie militante: les tâches immédiates de la pensée moderne," in *Inquisitions* (1936).

because, all results being equal, orthodoxy influenced people's emotions and affectivity. It spoke to them, involving and addressing the fate of the totality of being and not just rationality.[40] Caillois had grown defiantly combative by 1937 and appeared ready to fight, although not quite in demonstration-filled streets. In fact, he remained outside politics strictly speaking; the intellectual circle of the Collège de sociologie became the next stage for his bellicose and "emotional" sense of activism, the place where his idea of a sentimentally bound sacred community evolved.

But could politics really be escaped? And how did Bataille come to embrace this new project/group of the Collège? How did he resolve to abandon the political militancy of Contre-Attaque in order to opt for activist, sociologically driven research? We can find an initial answer to these questions in the existential community of Acéphale.

AN EXISTENTIAL COMMUNITY: ACÉPHALE

With the end of Contre-Attaque in 1936, Bataille, who had been at the group's helm for its short duration, renounced the call for direct political confrontation that had characterized the movement. He also gave up the faith he had previously expressed in emotionally charged crowds protesting in the streets. A programmatic document drafted before the official closure of Contre-Attaque on 4 April 1936, and distributed to some Contre-Attaque members, indicated Bataille's shift of emphasis from militancy to the question of values, from the notion of human group to the concept of human totality, from the focus on collectivity to seeking new ideals of togetherness.[41] The first point of the "Program" explicitly stated the need "[t]o form a community that creates values, values that create cohesion."[42] The document proceeded to lay stress on "being" (*l'être*) and its personal accomplishment within a universe specifically

40 See "Pour une activité unitaire de l'esprit," in *Le Mythe et l'homme*, 186n1. See also the editorial discussion of Caillois's "Pour une orthodoxie militante," in *Inquisitions*, 66–68, where Caillois stated, "I call *Orthodoxy* a knowledge that engages affectivity at the same time as intelligence, a knowledge conscious of the fact that it constitutes a doctrine and can determine action ... Orthodoxy is aggressive knowledge." Ibid., 66 (italicized in the original).

41 See "Programme," in Bataille, *L'Apprenti Sorcier*, 281–4 (also in Bataille, *OC*, vol. 2). In April 1936, Bataille was at Tossa del Mar visiting André Masson. According to Michel Surya, and judging from their correspondence, Masson had anticipated the direction taken by Bataille after Contre-Attaque. See Surya, *Georges Bataille*, chapter "From Contre-Attaque to Acéphale: André Masson."

42 See Bataille, *L'Apprenti Sorcier*, 281.

defined as "acephalic."[43] It advocated the end of particularistic communities, be they national, socialist or linked to a church, in favour of a universal community. It recognized, in a Durkheimian mode, the organic character of society and invoked the renewal of the world. It shunned happiness as an end in itself and affirmed the Nietzschean emphasis on violence and the will to power. The document illustrated Bataille's retreat from politics, yet also proved that his withdrawal did not convert into inaction. On the contrary, Bataille maintained that one should not be afraid to fight with the goal of destroying the existing world.

The April 1936 text brought to the fore issues that became central to the project Bataille initiated on the ruins of Contre-Attaque – a project that took shape in the public form of a journal and in the more esoteric incarnation of a secret society, both named Acéphale.[44] Bataille was moving toward a more meditative direction in his work and sought to explore the existential human condition without renouncing the will to act. In his inaugural article for *Acéphale*, "The Sacred Conspiracy," published in the journal's first issue in June 1936, Bataille admitted that the journal intended to launch nothing short of a violent conflict.[45] "What we are starting is a war," Bataille proclaimed – a war against a "civilized" world dominated by profit and work, the value of reason, and the exclusion of ecstasy.[46] In place of such a world, and in the spirit of the Nietzschean death of God, Bataille advocated the end of authority. In blunter terms, he called for the cutting off of the head.[47] The symbol of *Acéphale*, designed by the artist André Masson at Bataille's request, was indeed a headless man, graphically signifying that human life must cease

43 Ibid., 282, point 5 of the "Programme." The idea of a "headless" community had already emerged in Bataille's essay "The 'Old Mole.'"

44 For Marina Galletti, the "Programme" proves the link between Contre-Attaque and the new group of Acéphale that this document was supposedly initiating. See Bataille, *L'Apprenti Sorcier*, 283n1.

45 See Bataille, *Visions of Excess*, and "La conjuration sacrée," in Bataille, *OC*, vol. 1. I will not use italics when referring to the secret society or when referring to both the society and the journal. The journal's editors were Georges Bataille, Pierre Klossowski, and Georges Ambrosino.

46 See Bataille, "The Sacred Conspiracy," in *Visions of Excess*, 179.

47 According to Bataille, the theme of the death of God was first introduced at a meeting of Contre-Attaque in July 1935. See "Constitution du 'journal intérieur,'" in *L'Apprenti Sorcier*, 337. *Cahiers de Contre-Attaque* was indeed supposed to publish an issue on Nietzsche (338). Bataille traced his decisive reading of Nietzsche to 1923. See "Notice autobiographique," in *OC*, 7: 459 where Bataille wrote, "Decisive reading of Nietzsche in 1923," and "I came to know Nietzsche's work in 1923; it gave me the impression that I had nothing else to say" (615). See also "Notes" for *La Souveraineté*, probably written in 1958, in *OC*, 8: 640.

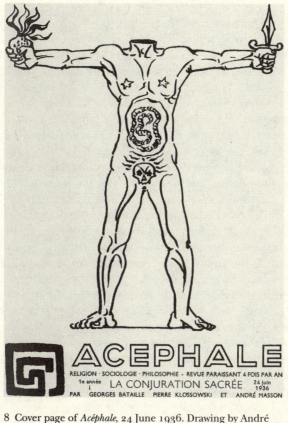

8 Cover page of *Acéphale*, 24 June 1936. Drawing by André Masson. © Artists Rights Society (ARS), New York/ADAGP, Paris

acting as master of the universe.[48] Existence should find its grandeur through the freedom to escape one's head, Bataille claimed, as well as through the refusal of boredom and the pursuit of fascination and ecstasy. In this sense, the war launched by *Acéphale* implied the re-envisioning of the human condition and a declared distance from everyday politics, now considered in negative terms. A definitive break from Contre-Attaque's militant spirit marked Bataille's novel experience at *Acéphale*

48 See Bataille, "Constitution du 'journal intérieur,'" in *L'Apprenti Sorcier*, 339. On the origins of Bataille's discovery of the acephalic figure, see Camus's introduction to the reissue of *Acéphale*, iii.

and guided his evolving critical analysis of both politics' shortcomings and his own past involvement in the fray.[49]

There is no doubt that Bataille considered his previous engagement in politics a weakness, proof of his inability to perceive politics' destructive role. As he wrote in a letter to the philosopher Pierre Kaan on 4 November 1936, politics was a "plague" – even as it absorbed our affective interest – and one needed to detach oneself from it in order to eventually precipitate its demise.[50] For Bataille, political agitation in its violent form often appeared as the only way to counteract the order of a pacified, fragmented existence, which was badly in need of an energetic shake-up. Nevertheless, Bataille considered such agitation a vain exercise, and he was skeptical about the aptitude of politics for responding to peoples' profound aspirations. Even worse, Bataille held that politics had deprived human existence of its awareness of the fundamentally violent nature of the external world.[51] Politics was bypassing violence and promoting its annihilation. Thus, whereas Christianity had already prohibited violence and turned it from a natural phenomenon into original sin, socialism went further by planning to found a stable social order rid of what it viewed as irrational violence. Alternatively, political movements that resorted to violence only enslaved it without recognizing its constitutive role. Politics, Bataille concluded, showed itself to be fundamentally deceptive, a smokescreen hiding the more essential question of existence. According to Bataille, however, one should not hide from violence; "[v]iolence has to be looked at directly and hopelessly."[52] Nor should violence be limited or subdued. Violence is essential to human existence; it is an integral part of our experience of the world.

In light of politics' inability to recognize the value of violence, Bataille developed a ruthless and absolute critique; any close encounter with political matters had to be avoided as one would avoid pestilence. Bataille's flirtation with politics appeared definitely over, and he even recast the experience of Contre-Attaque as an effort whose original "apolitical" intentions had been sacrificed to the illusion that action could obtain

49 On Bataille and his politics during the 1930s, see Besnier, "Georges Bataille in the 1930s."

50 Bataille, *L'Apprenti Sorcier*, 314–5.

51 Bataille was aware of the vagueness of his expressions. As he wrote on 7 February 1937, "Such considerations are at such a distance from normal thinking that I find it hard to communicate in understandable terms what I wish to undo here." See "Ce que j'ai à dire ..." *L'Apprenti Sorcier*, 327 (De telles considérations sont si loin de la réflexion habituelle qu'il est difficile de communiquer une représentation sensible de ce qui est ainsi annulé).

52 Ibid., 332 (La violence doit être regardée sans espoir en face).

results.[53] Contre-Attaque had become political in spite of its premises, Bataille seemed to be arguing, but the time had come to redress the situation. In the document "Constitution du 'journal intérieur,'" dated 9 February 1937, which, according to Marina Galletti, marks the beginning of the secret society, Bataille repeatedly emphasized the apolitical spirit of Acéphale's members, their choice to fall back into intimacy, the inner life.[54] Joining the group Acéphale meant taking leave of the past.[55] It meant abandoning political action in order to be part of a moral community, an "order" infused by religious spirit, an affective mystical movement. Without renouncing active life, Acéphale rejected prosaic engagement and appealed to limitless ends. It exalted experience and pursued the totality of being. Acéphale invoked myths and emotional values and expressed new exigencies and novel aspirations.[56] It also indicated that religion would now have to replace politics.[57]

The shift to religion, in conjunction with an apolitical stance, appeared in plain view in *Acéphale*'s inaugural article "The Sacred Conspiracy." It featured in capital letters the sentence "We are ferociously religious." One of the article's epigraphs sported Kierkegaard's phrase: "What looks like politics, and imagines itself to be political, will one day unmask itself as a religious movement."[58] And lest one forget, *Acéphale*'s subtitle included *Religion*, next to *Sociology, Philosophy*. Religion was a motivating and prominent element in the journal. And it was not conceived as a

---

53 See Bataille, "Constitution du 'journal intérieur,'" *L'Apprenti Sorcier*, 337."

54 The initiation into the secret society was premised on the refusal of politics. Dubief, one of Acéphale's members, makes it clear in the act of faith in the society he wrote: "Practically, I declare to repudiate, by definitively adhering to Acéphale, all essential and vital political action ..." See Dubief, "Principes," in *L'Apprenti Sorcier*, 347. Dubief also had the harshest words for politics: "All political enterprises at this point only make me vomit" (346).

55 See Bataille, "Ce que nous avons entrepris il y a peu de mois ..." a document of spring 1937, *L'Apprenti Sorcier*, 367.

56 "Constitution du 'journal intérieur'" however indicated two texts both by Bataille that anticipated Acéphale's state of mind: "The notion of Expenditure" and "Sacrifices," both written around 1933. Ibid., 341. "Sacrifices" directly addressed the question of profound existence.

57 In "Notice autobiographique," Bataille wrote, "Once *Contre-Attaque* dissolved, Bataille immediately decided to form with some of the friends who had been participating in Contre-Attaque, such as Georges Ambrosino, Pierre Klossowski, Patrick Waldberg, a 'secret society' that would turn its back to politics and would envision nothing less than a *religious* goal (but anti-Christian, essentially Nietzschean)." *OC*, 7: 461 (italicized in the original). Bataille dated his interest in forming such an order back to 1925, but he also stated that most participants in Contre-Attaque were in the end driven more by religious than political aspirations. See "Constitution du 'journal intérieur,'" in *L'Apprenti Sorcier*, 339.

58 Bataille, *Visions of Excess*, 179 and 178. Also *OC*, 1: 443, 442.

passive retreat into individualized mysticism but instead constituted, in the manner Bataille was delineating at the secret society, an experiential search for the heart of existence, a community of total beings.

Religion, *Acéphale* was implicitly and explicitly suggesting, needed to replace politics because political movements could only botch the existential search. As Kierkegaard's quote in "The Sacred Conspiracy" warned, one should not confuse one's motivations to pursue existential values with politics' ultimately mundane direction and goals. Within this context, and in spite of its apolitical position, *Acéphale* generated a flow of articles that unmasked the illusory character of politics. The journal tried to expose the danger of fake communities' diminished existence – the loss of human aggressivity. Fascism, in particular, became the target of Bataille's violent critique against attempts to cloak politics in the mantle of religion. One could not risk identifying fascism with existential movements, he maintained. Acéphale's quest for existence required coming to terms with fascism's regressive course. Paradoxically, this quest forced Bataille to engage with politics even though he wished to escape it. Fascism's deceptive actions presented an interpretive challenge that could not be ignored.

Almost all the articles Bataille wrote for the four issues of *Acéphale* that saw the light of print revolved around fascism via a detour through Nietzsche. Or rather one should reverse the formulation, since Nietzsche was the main subject of the journal's discussions and issue 2 of *Acéphale* was entirely dedicated to the theme of "Nietzsche and the Fascists." *Acéphale* intended to clear Nietzsche's name from its association with Nazism. In the process of pursuing this task, the journal engaged in a pointed comparative analysis of fascism's main traits and Nietzsche's philosophy – an analysis which inevitably concluded with a resounding denunciation of the former and an exaltation of the latter.[59] In his own contributions to the journal, Bataille made the point that while fascism meant servitude, brutal force, moral repression, and vile patriotism, Nietzsche advocated freedom, tragic violence, rejection of traditions and morality, extreme love and sacrifice.[60] Fascism never seriously embraced Nietzsche, Bataille argued, and was rather Hegelian. Then turning to the specific case of National Socialism, Bataille proclaimed as remarkable its differences from Nietzsche. National Socialism's racism, love for the past, and attachment to the idea of a community of blood could not be further

59 Bataille had actually begun its article "Nietzsche et les fascistes" with a critique of the anti-Semitic and, more generally, political use of Nietzsche. *oc*, vol. I. See "Nietzsche and the Fascists," in *Visions of Excess.*

60 Ibid.

from Nietzsche's myth of the future and his ideal of the *"sans patrie,"* the ones with no fatherland. Nietzsche hailed the unknown that was yet to come, prided himself on being a "child of the future" and, in Zarathustra's words, looked ahead to the "land of his children."[61] There was no yearning toward former times on Nietzsche's part. On the contrary, for him life needed to be liberated from the chains of the past in order to be truly free. Nietzsche wanted communities rooted in tradition, blood, or race to be overcome by communities of heart based on fraternity and open to the tragedy of anguish.[62] He hoped "to generate a movement that awakens the ultimate foundations (the last causes) of man's being."

Bataille shared Nietzsche's existential interests and maintained that profound existence involved life's emotional engagement with death. Existence equalled tragedy and Bataille envisaged Acéphale as a community of heart where life, joy, and death were at stake, disintegration ensured the movement of existence, and tragedy reigned.[63] The figure of Acéphale mythologically expressed a sovereignty vowed to destruction. In its critique of authority, servility, and use value, it closely approached the Nietzschean idea of the death of God.[64] It also fulfilled Nietzsche's faith in the sect, an "order." In this sense, Acéphale stood in stark opposition to monocephalic societies which took up the charge of exciting emotions only to end by reaffirming the past and utilitarian values. As a Caesarian movement controlled by the leader, fascism in particular could not achieve the status of an acephalic community united by the image of tragedy, the acknowledgment of death, and of a "no beyond."[65] Fascism

---

61 See "Nietzschean Chronicle," in *Visions of Excess*, 193, where Bataille wrote, "Against this world covered with the past, covered with fatherlands like a man is covered with wounds, there is no greater, more paradoxical, more passionate expression." See original French text as "Chronique nietzschéenne," in *oc*, vol. I.

62 On this point, Bataille cited Karl Jaspers. See Bataille's review of Jaspers' book, *Nietzsche, Einführung in das Verständnis seines Philosophierens*, in *oc*, 1: 475. On Bataille's selective reading of Nietzsche as filtered through Jaspers' own existentialism, see Pradeau, *"Impossible* politique et anti-philosophie." Also see Sichère, "Le 'Nietzsche' de Georges Bataille."

63 Bataille wrote in capital letters: "LIFE, IN OTHER WORDS, TRAGEDY," in *Visions of Excess*, 205; *oc*, 1: 482. One can remark here that Bataille's articles for *Acéphale* reflected the "Program" he had prepared in April 1936.

64 The headless man coincided with the Superman according to Bataille. See "Propositions," in *Visions of Excess*, 200; "Propositions," in *oc*, 1: 470. In his reminiscences about Acéphale, Pierre Prévost wrote that the Acéphale was "the mythological expression of the death of God." Prévost, *Rencontre Georges Bataille*, 16.

65 "Life demands that men gather together, and men are only gathered together by a leader or by a tragedy. To look for a HEADLESS human community is to look for tragedy." See "Nietzschean Chronicle," in *Visions of Excess*, 210. See also "The Practice of Joy before Death," in ibid., 236 where Bataille talked about a *"beyond,"* (italicized in the original); "La pratique de la joie devant la mort" in *oc*, vol. I.

was not able to escape the strictures of monocephalic systems, which pursued war only to turn death into glory, thus depriving death of any significant meaning. Fascism ultimately paralyzed the disintegrating movement of existence, the unconditional, purposeless expenditure that universal, as opposed to national, existence implies. Fascism pursued only the reconstitution of the social structure and the reinstitution of the head and curtailed all Nietzschean aspirations to escape servitude and seek destiny.[66]

Posited against Nietzsche's existential philosophy as interpreted by Bataille, fascism stood no chance, even if it appeared to be responding to and following life's passionate movement. Fascism, like all politics, was deceptive, and Bataille showed no tolerance for it. And yet, Bataille's vision of an existential movement to be realized in the secret society turned out to be framed by what Bataille evaluated as the negation of such a movement, that is, fascism itself. Fascism constituted the counteraltar to any proposal for realizing a community of heart, and we will see that this predicament continued to be the case at the Collège as well. We might, then, want to pause and consider the paradoxical trajectory that Acéphale travelled in its painstaking search for an existential "order." As we move to examine the Collège, we need to keep in mind that, despite claims to the contrary, Acéphale was fully entrenched in "the political." In part because Bataille did not want to risk being seen as supporting movements that only pretended to supersede traditional politics, fascism was closely scrutinized by *Acéphale* and came to occupy a central place in its pages. Acéphale, however, refused to confront the theoretical and practical implications of having to consider fascism within an analysis of the sacred. Its refusal created a situation of ambiguity that, in the case of the Collège, not only became a serious liability but also hampered the Collège's innovative efforts to reframe and recast the realm of "the political."[67]

Meanwhile, since they opposed both fascism and politics, Bataille and Acéphale believed that the only solution to the search for community and existence was religion, not in the sense of revealed theology or the pretense of political movements that invoked spirituality, but as an atheological church, a community held together by the ritual performance of myths. Inspired by Nietzsche, Bataille called for an "order," a sect, a secret

---

66 "Nietzsche and the Fascists," in Bataille, *Visions of Excess*. According to Bataille, politics was attracted to and appropriated Nietzsche's appeal to aggressive instincts. For Bataille, however, politics is conservative even when it transgresses reason, and always implies a return to the past.

67 On the political difficulties of Acéphale, see Pradeau, "*Impossible* politique et antiphilosophie," and Marmande, *Georges Bataille politique*.

closed group whose dominant will would free human destiny and open the way to an acephalic existence.[68] In issues 3 and 4 of *Acéphale* published in July 1937, Bataille, and Caillois as well, referred to Dionysus to exemplify what they meant by the religious spirit: socializing and binding together via communal ecstasy and intoxication.[69] If the Latin term *religio* meant tying together, then "brotherhoods" – as groups formed through free choice – would guarantee religious unity, "a communal apprehension of the *sacred*," Caillois specifically wrote.[70] No doubt, Caillois and Bataille placed a different emphasis on the elite character of the individuals constituting a sect; however, they both pursued the Nietzschean vision of a new "order" that drew from myths the stimulus for collective exaltation.[71] With Acéphale, Bataille had indeed concretely implemented that vision in the hope of enabling religious spirit and enacting a sacred community. Unfortunately, those goals were not easily attainable, and the Collège, which Bataille and Caillois were about to launch, eventually took up the charge of furthering the knowledge of the sacred in order to facilitate communal exaltation and accede to the "*totality of being*" (*totalité de l'être*).[72]

68 See "Propositions," in *Visions of Excess*, 198–9, where Bataille wrote, "The formation of a new structure, of an 'order' developing and raging across the entire earth, is the only truly liberating act, and the only one possible, since revolutionary destruction is regularly followed by the reconstitution of the social structure and its head."

69 See Bataille, "Nietzschean Chronicle," and Caillois, "Les Vertues dionisyaques" (translated into English as "Dionysian Virtues" in *The Edge of Surrealism*). Acéphale, the secret society, did not apparently enjoy Caillois's support, although it is hard to establish whether he participated in it at its inception. See Caillois, "Préambule pour l' *Esprit des Sectes*," in *Approches de l'imaginaire*, translated into English as "Preamble to the Spirit of Sects," in *The Edge of Surrealism*. Caillois in retrospective interpreted Bataille's move to secrecy as a way to avoid being obliged to "greater prudence." See Frank's introduction to *The Edge of Surrealism*, 30.

70 Caillois, "Dionysian Virtues," in *The Edge of Surrealism*, 158 (italicized in the original). Caillois wrote of brotherhoods, "They are formed by replacing factual determinations (birth, etc.) ... with a free act of choice that is consecrated by a kind of initiation and solemn admission into the group" (159n2). Frank claims that Caillois is here supporting open and universal Dionysianism, not closed cults. We know, however, that in "The Winter Wind," which he wrote for the Collège, Caillois evoked a "closed society." In "Paris, a Modern Myth," he also referred to the idea of an "aristocracy" as inspired by Baudelaire.

71 See Bataille, "Nietzschean Chronicle," in *Visions of Excess*. See also his "Conclusion annuelle" of 24 September 1937, in which he summarized *Acéphale*'s activity and talked about future issues, in *L'Apprenti Sorcier*, 404–5. The secret society Acéphale had its rituals, rules, and special meeting places. Reading Nietzsche was part of the ritual. See *L'Apprenti Sorcier*, 444n9.

72 "Ce que nous avons entrepris il y a peu de mois ... " *L'Apprenti Sorcier*, 374 (italicized in the original).

In spite of their differences, in fact, and even though scientific knowledge seemed irreconcilable with a religious attitude, both Bataille and Caillois believed that science was necessary to build a structural knowledge of the different collective forms of affective life. Within this context, one might note that at its inception Acéphale was thought of as a study group, and more specifically a "sociological group."[73] Admittedly, the appellation was never used, and Acéphale soon retreated into its true mission: the cultivation of inner experience. Yet, *Acéphale*'s subtitle also contained *Sociology* immediately following *Religion*, and in internal documents of the secret society Bataille acknowledged that inspiration alone would not suffice for Acéphale to recover the conditions of life in common.[74] To be sure, Acéphale's members should embrace irrationality, Bataille argued, but without foregoing knowledge of the mechanisms guiding their impulses. Thus, Bataille suggested considering mythology as the key to a "science of society" that would recognize the value of the results newly obtained by the study of primitive societies and apply to the present the insights available from the past. Anticipating the "Note" that would announce the foundation of the Collège, Bataille called for applying the results of ethnographic research to modern forms of human existence. He called for a "mythological sociology" that would eventually include a move from knowledge to action – the unfolding of experience through a new religious movement or church. In sum, Bataille's interest in myth as the catalyst of communal life inclined him to rely on sociology to understand fully the affective structures of modern societies – another similarity with Caillois. Because sociology was able to observe directly new ritualistic-mythical forms (fascism), it promised to be the science that could finally yield the knowledge which had until then eluded many.[75] Thus, once *Acéphale* opted to refrain from pursuing specific goals, the Collège de sociologie became the privileged forum in which sociology could play its illuminating role. As it turns out, in the hands of Bataille and Caillois, sociology also found itself redrawn and reconfigured.

73 See "Constitution du 'journal intérieur,'" *L'Apprenti Sorcier*, 340.

74 See "Ce que nous avons entrepris il y a peu de mois … " *L'Apprenti Sorcier*, 367–78.

75 Bataille credits Freud for making possible this result thanks to his analysis of the affective structure of the army and the church developed in "Group Psychology and the Analysis of the Ego." *L'Apprenti Sorcier*, 373.

5

At the Collège:
The Social in Excess

THE CLOSE LINK BETWEEN ACÉPHALE AND THE COLLÈGE was apparent at the Collège's inception. Not incidentally, the "Note on the Foundation of a College of Sociology," written in March 1937, was published in the July 1937 issue of *Acéphale*.[1] Two months later, at an Acéphale meeting where he lamented the secret society's failure to attract members, Bataille explicitly stated that the group was now going to rely on the Collège to develop a stronger theoretical basis and to locate potential acolytes.[2] In October 1937, when the Collège's fate was still uncertain, Bataille nonetheless presented the new enterprise as a scientific branch of Acéphale.[3] He confirmed that statement in a retrospective autobiographical note written around 1957: "The *College of Sociology*, founded in March 1936, was in some manner the external activity of this 'secret society.'"[4]

The Collège's role was of course quite different from the active ritualism of an experimental secret society that intended to fulfill existence within a headless community. The Collège was, first and foremost, a study group, and was supposed to engage in a serious in-depth exploration of the elements necessary to build the sacred community for which

1 For the "Note," see Hollier, *The College of Sociology*. For the Collège's link to Acéphale, see the letter of 25 February 1937 of Henri Dubief to Jean Dautry, both members of Acéphale, that indicated the Collège's incipient birth: "Bataille met with Caillois and Chevalley at the Ordre Nouveau and their College of Sacred Sociology is on its way," in Bataille, *L'Apprenti sorcier*, 343.

2 "Conclusion annuelle" of 24 September 1937, in Bataille, *L'Apprenti sorcier*, 405.

3 Letter to Jean Rollin of 16 October 1937, in Bataille, *L'Apprenti sorcier*, 419–21. See also Caillois, "Argument," in *Approches de l'imaginaire*, 59, where he described Acéphale as "anti-intellectual" and "visceral" and the Collège as "cerebral" and pointed out that, their contradictory nature notwithstanding, Bataille never renounced pairing them.

4 Bataille, "Notice autobiographique," in *OC*, 7: 461 (italicized in the original). There seems to be confusion here about dates. We know that Acéphale began meeting in March 1936.

Acéphale was striving. From this point of view, in a move that would have made Durkheim proud, the Collège chose to call itself "Collège de sociologie," thus indicating its trust in sociology's scientific potential.[5] But did Bataille and Caillois have any legitimate credentials to play sociologist? And what kind of sociology were they advocating? This chapter and the next examine the work of the Collège and address these questions through a specific focus on Bataille and Caillois. Chapter 5 discusses the Collège's peculiar vision of sociology, its understanding of the social, and the Collège's conceptualization of the sacred and power. Chapter 6 directs attention to the transfigurations of politics pursued by Bataille and Caillois and assesses the theoretical ambiguities that emerged from the Collège's move to bypass both politics and aesthetics. As noted in previous chapters, by the time of the Collège, Bataille and Caillois had defined art as a negative, anti-social institution that undermined humans' orientation toward the sacred and had called for its liquidation. At the Collège, Bataille's and Caillois's hostile relation with aesthetics combined with their pessimistic evaluation of politics to form a movement that proclaimed the primacy of the social and the intention to intervene in it. How did these antinomies play out and affect the Collège's overall assessment of the current political and social crisis? What kind of practical involvement did the Collège envisage for itself? And were Bataille and Caillois, not to mention the other attendees at the Collège, in agreement on the path to take vis-à-vis the reactivation of the sacred? The next two chapters address these central questions. Before we enter the heart of the matter, however, a brief contextualization of the Collège's genesis and its membership structure are in order.

A SACRED EXCESS

The "Note on the Foundation of a College of Sociology" published in *Acéphale* in July 1937 was signed by six people: Georges Ambrosino, Georges Bataille, Roger Caillois, Pierre Klossowski, Pierre Libra, and Jules Monnerot. Notably absent from this list is Michel Leiris, who would later be considered the third leader of the Collège next to Bataille and Caillois. Of the other signatories, we know that Georges Ambrosino was an atomic physicist who also participated in Acéphale (and before that, Contre-Attaque). Like Ambrosino, Klossowski, who had translated Benjamin's essay on the work of art and other German authors, had followed Bataille from Contre-Attaque to Acéphale. Little is known about Pierre Libra nor is any information available about his place at the

5 On the issue of the Collège's name, see note 6.

Collège. Jules Monnerot had been editor-in-chief of the Surrealist review *Inquisitions* with Caillois, Aragon, and Tzara before collaborating with Acéphale and later signing the Collège's brief manifesto. He did not participate in the Collège and later dismissed it altogether, although he was presumably responsible for its name.[6] I should add that Ambrosino never presented a lecture at the Collège. Klossowski was the only one among the first signatories, other than Bataille and Caillois, who delivered talks at the Collège.

The apparent incongruities between the names on the "Note" and the actual participation of the signatories relay the difficulties of categorizing or defining the Collège. Who was part of the Collège? Or, more consequentially, how can we think of the Collège? Which elements identify the enterprise we today call the Collège? And what did the Collège mean to those who attended? These questions do not necessarily find definitive answers, although Hollier's brilliant work has made the task more feasible.[7] One fact that we can assert, however, is the continuity of Bataille's

6 Claiming paternity on the appellation of the Collège, Monnerot in a 1979 publication stated that he only conceived of the idea. See *Sociologie du communisme*, Annexe 4. Highly critical of the Durkheimian school and their state sociology, Monnerot proposed to "privatize" sociology and establish a group that would examine a field of research left unexplored by the official doctrines. Excited by Bataille's pioneering attempt to interpret fascism, Monnerot asked to be introduced to him by mutual friends. Having "seduced" Bataille with his idea of a Collège de sociologie, he also involved Caillois, shortly after finding out that their ideas on the realization of such a group were not in agreement. In his recollections on the Collège's origins, however, Caillois does not mention Monnerot. Memories are not very reliable, and Caillois in particular often seems confused about dates and events. However, Monnerot's tale is also vague, since it leaves the impression that the project on the Collège was decided in 1933, when he first met Bataille. Monnerot supposedly dropped the idea before Caillois and Bataille took over the project. It seems, however, that in November 1935, at the time of Contre-Attaque, Monnerot was disillusioned with Bataille and his analysis of fascism. See his letter to Caillois, in *Roger Caillois. Cahiers pour un temps*, 196. On the exchange he had with Caillois on this issue, see Monnerot, *Sociologie du communisme*, 545. Later, Monnerot wrote a critical portrait of Bataille, "La fièvre de Georges Bataille" in *Confluences* 8 and 9, now in Monnerot, *Inquisitions*. Yet, as we know, Monnerot signed the "Note on the Foundation of a College of Sociology." He also helped Bataille found the new journal *Critique* in 1946. Pierre Prévost and others who have reminisced about the Collège never mention Monnerot. Jean-Michel Heimonet, however, supports the thesis of Monnerot as founder of the Collège. See his "Le Collège et son double," "Le Collège de Sociologie: Un gigantesque malentendu," and *Politique de l'écriture: Négativité et communication*. On what became of Monnerot in more recent times when he ran as a political candidate on Jean-Marie Le Pen's ticket, see Heimonet, "Préambule," in his *Jules Monnerot ou la démission critique*.

7 Hollier was apparently "accused (or perhaps congratulated for) having 'invented' (Florence, January 1985) the College of Sociology." See "Foreword," in Hollier, *The College of Sociology*, xxiii.

and Caillois's leadership. Between them, they delivered eight of the eleven lectures presented during the 1937–38 cycle and about half of the lectures during 1938–39. Their intellectual interests also determined the course of the general conversation as well as the topics to be explored at the meetings, although the voices that emerged from the Collège were far from being in unison.[8] An eclectic group, the participants in the evening meetings, whether audience or speakers, shared a concern with the critical historical juncture in which they were living. The extent to which they approved of the Collège's intellectual premises and goals as set out by Bataille and Caillois, however, remains unclear. Speakers were invited on the basis of their expertise on issues that became relevant at a given time. Their names belong to the history of the Collège and will remain forever associated with it, but we can scarcely define the essence of the Collège by those names. While some of the lecturers were committed to the theoretical presuppositions and agenda of the Collège and assiduously attended the meetings, others may have been present only sporadically. The same goes for the audience: Walter Benjamin, for example, attended the meetings and was even supposed to deliver a lecture in the spring of 1939.[9] It remains doubtful, to say the least, whether he agreed with the Collège's overall orientation.

8 The correspondence between Bataille and Caillois shows the two leaders' main role in the planning and organization of the lectures. Their role also included selecting the speakers. See Bataille, *Lettres à Roger Caillois* and *Choix de lettres*.

9 Benjamin's link to the Collège is one of the elements contributing to the intellectual curiosity about the group. Benjamin attended some of the lectures at the Collège and is mentioned by Bataille as one of the few to consult about the future of the Collège at the end of the Collège's first cycle (see letter of 17 May 1938 to Caillois in Bataille, *Lettres à Roger Caillois*). Little more is known about Benjamin's actual participation at the Collège's meetings. On this issue, see Weingrad, "The College of Sociology and the Institute for Social Research." What is known, however, is that Benjamin asked Bataille to keep several of his manuscripts and in particular those on the Arcades Project before leaving Paris for Spain and later committing suicide at the Spanish border. Eventually, Bataille, who had kept Benjamin's writings at the Bibliothèque nationale, sent the manuscripts to Adorno. However, he unintentionally left some behind. Bataille had by that time retired from the Bibliothèque and asked his colleague Jean Bruno to locate Benjamin's manuscripts. This might be one explanation for the failed delivery of all Benjamin's writings to Adorno in 1945. See Bataille's letter to Jean Bruno of 23 August 1945: "Among the papers I left behind at the library, there were two manuscripts, one in Russian by Kojève … the other in German by Walter Benjamin in two packets the format of this letter ["du format de cette lettre"], as far as I can remember. They are asking me now for Benjamin's manuscripts for a publication of his posthumous works. Are they in my cabinet, perhaps?" See Bataille, *Choix de lettres*, 242. In the Papiers Georges Bataille, Correspondance, NAF 15853–15854, kept at the Bibliothèque nationale, a note is attached to this letter stating that Kojève's and

Granted all the interpretive complexities, I will examine the speakers' interventions at the Collège as threads for the tapestry designed by Bataille and Caillois. But first I begin by appraising what sociology had to do with this eclectic group that named itself a "Collège de sociologie."

Sociology and the Sacred

We know that in 1933–34 Bataille had collaborated in the preparation of a sociology course at the journal *Masses*;[10] from 1930 to 1933, he had read or consulted Durkheim, as well as other members of the Durkheimian school, several times;[11] he had abundantly drawn from French sociology to compose his essays "The Notion of Expenditure" and "The Psychological Structure"; and in general, he was fascinated by Mauss's inspirational lectures, whether from attending them or more likely hearing second-hand reports from his "oldest friend," Alfred Métraux.[12] Caillois, in his turn, had been a student of Mauss between 1933 and 1935 at the École Pratique des Hautes Études, where Mauss was in charge of the Section des sciences religieuses.[13] At the École, Caillois was being trained in the historical and ethnological study of religion, and in 1936 he received a diploma for his work from the Section des sciences religieuses.[14]

Benjamin's papers were sent to the Department of Manuscripts in March 1964. On Benjamin at the Bibliothèque nationale, see Pierre Missac, "Walter Benjamin à la Bibliothèque Nationale."

10 The course was supposed to be led by Bataille, Pierre Kaan, Michel Leiris, and Aimé Patri. For an analysis of *Masses* and Bataille's role in it see Marina Galletti, "'Masses': un 'Collège' mancato?"

11 See Bataille's borrowings from the Bibliothèque nationale, "Emprunts de Georges Bataille à la Bibliothèque Nationale (1922–1950)," *OC*, vol. 12. The other Durkheimians whose books Bataille borrowed from the library were Mauss, Marcel Granet, Henri Hubert, and Georges Davy. In his "Notice autobiographique" of around 1958, Bataille stated, "Durkheim's work and even more Mauss's, exercised an unquestionable influence on me." *OC*, 7: 615.

12 Bataille thus refers to Métraux in his preface to *Eroticism*, 9. Métraux was one of Mauss's early students. See his reminiscences in Métraux, "Rencontre avec les ethnologues." Also see Lecoq, "Métraux, rue de Rennes." According to Lourau, the sociological work with the most influence on avant-garde culture in France, beginning with Bataille's "The Notion of Expenditure," is Mauss's *The Gift*. See his *Le gai savoir des sociologues*, 242.

13 Mauss's teaching repertoire included a vast array of religions of "non civilized people," as the Annuary of the École reports, and particularly focused on the relationship between religion and magic.

14 Caillois also followed, even more assiduously than Mauss's, the lectures of the scholar of comparative religions Georges Dumézil. Dumézil was at the time working on the

Thus, Bataille's and Caillois's reliance on sociology at the Collège was not the result of a newly discovered interest but rather the fruit of years of reflection, if not training. If we consider the question of the orientation their sociological interests took, it is not surprising, in view of their background, that Bataille and Caillois embraced Durkheim. Contrary to the general contempt in France's intellectual milieus for Durkheim's positivism and institutional status, the Collège indeed appropriated the French master's intellectual project, though not without a critical stance, and on that basis built its own program of study.[15] Even more remarkable, the Collège considered the Durkheimian school as a whole and did not isolate Durkheim from his collaborators. Despite the fact that 1930s critics rarely associated Durkheim with Mauss and clearly underestimated Durkheim's later endeavour – *The Elementary Forms of Religious Life* – the Collège focused on the Durkheimians' ethnological work, their analysis of myths, religion, and sacrifice. The Collège encapsulated this realm under the term "sacred sociology" defined as "the study of all manifestations of social existence where the active presence of the sacred is clear."[16]

---

comparative study of the myths of the gods Ouranos and Varuna, among other mythological topics.. Caillois often acknowledged his intellectual debt to Dumézil. See in particular Caillois, *Rencontres*, and preface to *L'Homme et le* sacré, 13, where he wrote, "I find it impossible to measure exactly my debt to M. Georges Dumézil." He also dutifully recognized Mauss's teaching, especially in *L'Homme et le sacré* and in his eulogy for Mauss, "Le Grand Pontonnier," published in *Cases d'un échiquier*. See English translation, "The Great Bridgemaker," in Caillois, *The Edge of Surrealism*. Felgine cites a formula of Jorge Luis Borges as possibly applying to Caillois's idea of religion at the time: "Theology is a branch of the history of the fantastic." See Felgine, *Roger Caillois*, 86 where she also discusses Caillois's relationship with Dumézil.

15 According to Clark, because Durkheim had been central to the reform of French education, he had become the target of criticism from many intellectuals on both the right and the left. Durkheim's influence on the development of a secular morality, and the impact of his pedagogical vision on public education, attracted the ire of such Catholics as Charles Péguy who accused sociology professors of regimenting young people, establishing a tyrannical system, and founding sects. See Clark, *Prophets and Patrons*. The identification of sociology with socialism generated another strand of attacks on the Durkheimians, while accusations of conservatism both at the political and philosophical levels were hurled at them. See for instance Sorel, "Les théories de M. Durkheim." Pierre Bourdieu and Jean-Claude Passeron claim that during the 1930s Durkheim bore the weight of an anti-materialist stance that in the traditional discourse of philosophers indicted the reductive nature of scientific explanation. Durkheimian sociology was declared guilty of scientism, lack of creativity and meaning, and of obliterating the value of the subject. See Bourdieu and Passeron, "Sociology and Philosophy in France since 1945."

16 Hollier, *The College of Sociology*, 5. In the course of writing "The Psychological Structure" Bataille first introduced the formula "sacred sociology." In addition, some people referred to the Collège as the "Collège de sociologie sacrée" (the College of sacred sociology). See Dubief's letter to Dautry, cited above, and Prévost's reminiscences: "The

Inspired by Durkheimian sociology, the Collège used it as a tool to redirect the study of social structures toward society's "vital elements" – those virulent aspects of human sociality that had emerged in the study of the primitives and that science tended to ignore or avoid. The Collège held that sociology needed to excavate the "deep strata" of modern collective life in order to identify human activities that are "*creators* of unity" and that have the power to transform the individual's nature.[17] Thus, as Bataille made immediately clear in his first lecture of 20 November 1937, sacred sociology at the Collège was not the same as religious sociology, nor was it simply a part of sociology. Sacred sociology was concerned with the "communifying" movement of society; it explored what Bataille thought of as the "burning" issue, that is, human existence in its fundamental expression as communal living.[18]

Bataille had already voiced the need for a science of society's affective movements in an Acéphale document of spring 1937; in it, he had also cautioned against knowledge exclusive of action.[19] What he then named "mythological sociology," which was about to metamorphose into "sacred sociology," ought to be deeply involved with determining existence, and he opposed the idea of science for science's sake. Science could only be upheld if it provided the knowledge necessary to act on the world, and he found it difficult to reconcile science's principles of autonomy and neutrality with his concern for human destiny. Although he felt compelled to endorse the value of scientific objectivity, Bataille maintained science's lesser importance in the face of the human issues it was mobilized to resolve.[20] Science was a means to an end and needed to take up

---

time before the war was marked by the College of sacred sociology," in Prévost, *Rencontre Georges Bataille*, 9. It is not clear if "sacred" was ever part of the Collège's name, and if so why it was dropped. Benjamin in a letter to Max Horkheimer of 28 May 1938 also referred to the Collège as the "college of sacred sociology." Cited in Weingrad, "The College of Sociology and the Institute of Social Research," 146.

17 See Hollier, *The College of Sociology*, 5, 10, 74.

18 Bataille, "Sacred Sociology and the Relationships between 'Society,' 'Organism,' and 'Being,'" in Hollier, *The College of Sociology*, 74. Bataille talked about a "taste for burning" in "The Sorcerer's Apprentice," in Hollier, *The College of Sociology*. Hollier also notes that Monnerot spoke of "burning issues." See *Le Collège de Sociologie*, 21. On the Collège's interest in sacred sociology, see Jamin, "Un sacré Collège ou les apprentis sorciers de la sociologie."

19 The document "Ce que nous avons entrepris ..." anticipated the "Note" and already indicated the presence of the osmosis between Bataille and Caillois. See Bataille, *L'Apprenti sorcier*, 367–78.

20 On the topic of objectivity, see Bataille, "Sacred Sociology," in *The College of Sociology*, 82. On science, see Bataille's long note to "The Sorcerer's Apprentice," in *The College of Sociology*, 12.

the risk of being consumed by "burning" questions.[21] If a line was supposed to be drawn between knowledge and action, its contours remained blurred for Bataille, and he accepted the division as an operating tool rather than a factual reality. Eventually one needed to move "from the will for knowledge to a will for power," as Caillois osmotically wrote in his 1938 augmented reprint of the "Note."[22]

The Collège, in sum, despite reclaiming French sociology, did not subscribe to all its principles. Most notably, the Collège was not inspired by Durkheim's intent to found a sociological science: the Collège was instead taken by Durkheim's conception of society as a collective being.[23] In Bataille's assessment, the prevailing interest in primitive people at the turn of the century had drawn attention to ethnology and sociology as disciplines that revealed the predominance of society over the individual. At a time when individualist culture was coming to terms with itself, even as it was damning social constraints, a different vision of collective life spurred by the "discovery of the primitives" began to come to the fore. For Bataille, Durkheim's importance resided there, in the attention he dedicated to demonstrating the supremacy of the social.[24] More specifically, the essence that Bataille distilled from Durkheim's doctrine revolved around two points: 1) society is a whole different from the sum of its parts; 2) the sacred is the constitutive element of society.[25] Taken together the two points implied one general conclusion: if the social is superior to the individual, something that ethnographic evocations of primitive societies suggested, then one needed to understand how the sacred worked in maintaining the social link. At the Collège "sacred sociology" pursued this understanding: sociology's purpose was to locate and resurrect the sacred in a society that seemed to have lost its sense of community. Sociology had a transformative role that far surpassed its aspirations to methodological exactness. At the Collège, science was used, not adored; pure knowledge was supposed to be rejected as sterile.

21 The "Note" talked about the "contagious and *activist* character" of the findings such research might bring to the fore as the one reason that kept researchers from looking into it. Hollier, *The College of Sociology*, 10 (italicized in the original).

22 Bataille had originally written about the move "from knowledge to action" in "Ce que nous avons entrepris ...," *L'Apprenti sorcier*, 373.

23 See Bataille's recounting of the Collège's experience in "Le sens moral de la sociologie," a review essay of Monnerot's book *Les faits sociaux ne sont pas des choses*. The review was first published in *Critique* in 1946 and is now in *oc*, vol. 11.

24 Bataille had already started debunking the methodological component of Durkheim's œuvre in his 1933 study "The Psychological Structure" where he vowed to combine French sociology with German phenomenology and psychoanalysis.

25 See Bataille, "Le sens morale de la sociologie," *oc*, vol. 11.

Bataille sought to use sociology to critique structural explanations of society and to delve into the realm of affectivity and heterogeneity, the movement of attraction and repulsion generated by non-homogeneous objects. As Bataille had already argued in 1933, one needed to reinscribe the psychological in the sociological domain. Therefore, although inspired by him, Bataille mounted an assault on Durkheim's timid sociological analysis which, he feared, risked establishing the homogeneity of phenomena while avoiding social life's crucial dimensions. Instead, as Bataille wrote in a note on the margins of the original manuscript for "The Psychological Structure," one needed to define sacred sociology as heterology, that is, the science of what is other, that heterogeneous reality which is by definition irreducible and non-assimilable.[26] Within this context, the Collège's approach raised a major question about the status of sociology. If sociology deals with phenomena that are lived by us and that furthermore "constitute the essential of what is lived by us ... this heart of our existence," could sociology be equated with the other sciences?[27] And, more importantly, could it conform to the other sciences' approach to knowledge? Bataille's answer to both questions was negative, and he had no quandaries about resolving the dilemma by eschewing science's traditional role. Since sociology contained a "sensible" element, and since science normally avoids sensibility or reduces it to a minimum, sociology needed to complement its scientific method by promoting humans' recognition of what lies at the heart of existence. For Bataille there could be no alternative and no half-measures when this act of recognition was at stake. "[M]an's recognition of himself" was "the basic object of my endeavor," he wrote. It stood as the Collège's essential task.[28]

Sociology's scientific approach was supposed to bring to the surface and reveal to the individual what was unconscious and unknown. In this sense, the Collège's recourse to sociology hinged on sociology's ability to offer the scientific tools for achieving existential awareness. Failure to achieve this ultimate goal led Bataille to criticize even Hegel in favour of Mauss and Freud. Despite positing "negativity" (with the meaning of "destructive action") at the basis of human life, Hegel had been incapable

---

26 Bataille, *OC*, vol. 1, notes, 636. Bataille sometimes called heterology "base materialism," matter that is an object of disgust, or "scatology." See Hollier's introduction to *The Collège of Sociology*, xix and Bataille "La valeur d'usage de D.A.F. Sade," in *OC*, vol. 2 especially 61, 62 (English translation as "The Use-Value of Sade" in Bataille, *Visions of Excess*). In a fragment entitled "Zusatz," Bataille also briefly raised the issue of the relationship between heterology and French sociology. See *OC*, 2: 171.

27 Bataille, "Attraction and Repulsion II: Social Structure," delivered on 5 February 1938, in Hollier, *The Collège of Sociology*, 114.

28 Ibid., 115.

of adopting methods of investigation such as sociology and psychoanalysis that would help penetrate the heart of existence. Hegelian phenomenology, Bataille claimed, represented "the mind as essentially homogeneous." And he continued, "It seems to me that the marked heterogeneity established between the sacred and the profane by French sociology, or between the unconscious and the conscious by psychoanalysis, is a notion that is entirely foreign to Hegel."[29] Although Bataille admired the violent connotations and anti-utilitarian tone of Hegel's "negativity," he sought to go beyond a mere recognition of negativity's presence. One needed to comprehend negativity and scientifically locate it in relation to the sense of loss and the idea of the horrid, i.e., those phenomena at the heart of existence.[30] By relying on the duality of sacred and profane, Durkheimian sociology had been able to highlight the centrality of movements of repulsion in the creation of human communities. French sociology thus had an advantage over Hegelian phenomenology.

Bataille evidently refused to abide by the rules of conventional sociology. He never ceased repeating until the abrupt ending of the Collège that he deemed sociology "the domain, in fact, the only domain, of life's major decisions."[31] Research needed to coexist with life, and the sociology of the Collège was supposed to pursue exactly that goal, no matter the risks.[32] After all, as Caillois had stated in the "Note," one element linked the Collège's participants: the need for "a more precise knowledge of the essential aspects of social existence."[33] That desire alone would weave the individual strands into a knot, a moral community in charge of prospecting a larger existential brotherhood. Armed with the strength of its common, though unusual, interest, the Collège set up a program of lectures that systematically presented the foundational concepts of a sacred sociology. These concepts were supposed to guide members in their investigations and provide them with a solid basis on which to build knowledge of an as yet unexplored field. For while it

29 Ibid., 117.

30 Bataille coined his phrase "unemployed negativity" in a letter to Kojève after Kojève delivered his lecture on "Hegelian Concepts" at the Collège on 4 December 1937. In the letter, Bataille responded to Kojève's discussion of Hegel's notion of negativity. Hollier, *The College of Sociology*. For an analysis of Kojève that deals with themes close to the Collège, see Macherey, "Kojève et les mythes."

31 See the lecture "Brotherhoods, Orders, Secret Societies, Churches," in Hollier, *The College of Sociology*, 156.

32 Bataille especially talked about these risks in "Attraction and Repulsion II," in Hollier, *The College of Sociology*.

33 Bataille, "Note on the Foundation of a College of Sociology," in Hollier, *The College of Sociology*, 5.

resorted to science, the Collège never took it for granted nor did Bataille consider science unproblematic. Ironically, the issue of scientism eventually became an excuse to justify the Collège's break up; Bataille found himself isolated in his call for sociology to play an existential role.

Defining the Social: The Power of Horror

Bataille and Caillois delivered the first lecture at the Collège on 20 November 1937. Entitled "Sacred Sociology and the Relationships between 'Society,' 'Organism,' and 'Being,'" it engaged the critical question of the nature of society. Caillois offered a historical survey of sociological thought that introduced the audience to studies he deemed essential to the Collège's scientific pursuits.[34] Durkheim and his students figured prominently on the list, which Caillois had redacted with a specific focus on the relationship between societies and individuals.[35] Bataille's intervention also evoked Durkheim by way of the latter's definition of society as something other than the sum of the individuals composing it.[36] Staunchly opposed to a contractual theory of the social, Bataille attacked the individualist culture of present-day France and proposed adopting the notion of "compound being" to refer to society.[37] Sacred sociology was based on the acknowledgment that "*in addition* to the individuals who make up society, there exists an overall movement that transforms their nature."[38] That communifying movement was what the Collège intended to investigate; it lay at the heart of the sacred.

34 There are no extant texts of Caillois's intervention on that day. The information provided here is drawn from the notes of Jacques Chavy that have been edited by Claudine Frank in Caillois, *The Edge of Surrealism*, 148–54.

35 Ibid., 152.

36 This definition was central to many of Bataille's sociological studies and Bataille reiterated it at several of the Collège's lectures as a reminder of the group's original premises. See "Le fascisme en France" and "La structure sociale" in *OC*, vol. 2; "Attraction Repulsion I" and "Sacred Sociology of the Contemporary World," in Hollier, *The College of Sociology*. Durkheim stated that his definition of the social was influenced by Charles Renouvier: "[W]e inherited from Renouvier the axiom: a whole is not the same as the sum of its parts." See Durkheim, *Textes*, 1: 405.

37 In the specific lecture of 20 November 1937, Bataille proposed to adopt "being" as a replacement for "organism." Bataille used the term "organism" to refer to groups of cells. See Hollier, *The College of Sociology*, 76–7. On the issue of consciousness that the term "being" raises, see Bataille's discussion, 79. Bataille believed that such discussion was not about terminology but had real life consequences. On the differences between Bataille and Caillois on these questions, see Bataille's letter to Caillois of 21 November 1937, in Bataille, *Lettres à Roger Caillois*, 67–70.

38 "Sacred Sociology" in *The College of Sociology*, 74 (italicized in the original). In this lecture, Bataille made recourse to analogies with atoms and molecules, an indication that

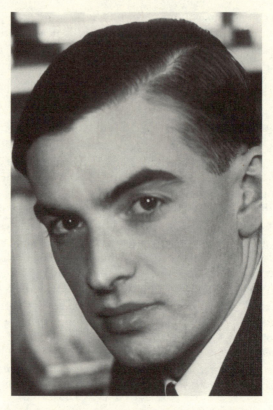

9 Roger Caillois circa 1939. Estate Gisèle Freund/
IMEC Images

But how, Caillois asked, could the social and the individual be reconciled? What were "the mutual relations of man's *being* and society's *being*"? And shouldn't one rethink social existence from the point of view
of its "primordial longings and conflicts"?[39] In a sense, the Collège was
resurrecting the old phantasm of the sociology/psychology dualism with

he might have relied on Ambrosino's expertise in this field. See Hollier, *The College of
Sociology*, 406n3. As several commentators have pointed out, Bataille asked Ambrosino to
write with him *The Accursed Share*. Although his request was not accepted, Bataille thanked
Ambrosino in the introduction to that book.

39 See his "Introduction," in Hollier, *The College of Sociology*, 9, 10. We can see here that
Caillois had subscribed to Bataille's "existentialist" terminology. "Introduction," an expanded version of the "Note," was first published in the *Nouvelle Revue Française* of July 1938
along with essays by Caillois ("The Winter Wind"), Bataille ("The Sorcerer's Apprentice"),
and Leiris ("The Sacred in Everyday Life").

which Durkheim had inconsistently struggled for many years and which Mauss was in the process of redefining. The Collège wanted to understand how individual instincts ascended to and were transformed at the social level. Coincidentally, at the same time that the Collège was being organized, Bataille, along with Pierre Janet and other scholars, founded a short-lived Society of Collective Psychology.[40] The Society, which emerged from a previous group interested in ethnographic psychology, stated as its dual goals to examine the role of psychological factors in social phenomena, especially those at the unconscious level, and to facilitate the convergence of the isolated disciplines of psychology and sociology. Bataille, one can infer, felt the need to deepen his knowledge and understanding of the psychological embeddedness of social relations outside the Collège. It is worth noting that the themes of his intervention of 17 January 1938 at the Society of Collective Psychology on "Attitudes towards Death" constituted the corpus of his 22 January and 5 February 1938 lectures at the Collège on the theme of "Attraction and Repulsion."[41] These two lectures, like the talk at the Society, revolved around the double valence of the dead in their power to assemble a society and they evoked the power of horror in uniting a group.

At a previous intervention on "Animal Societies" of 18 December 1937, Caillois and Bataille, while analyzing Étienne Rabaud's theory of interattraction, had already introduced the question of what spurs a communifying movement. Rabaud, who studied animal societies and was a representative of the branch Cuvillier categorized as *zoosociologie*, had written an anti-Durkheimian book.[42] In it, he had denied society sui generis existence; he had also argued that the group is the result of an individual interattraction which in no way affects the nature of the individuals participating in it. In "Attraction and Repulsion," Bataille offered a counter-theory that not only reiterated a Durkheimian belief in the superiority of the group over the individual but also emphasized the power of horror to assemble a community; in addition, it addressed the issue of the dynamic interaction linking attraction and repulsion.[43] Inspired by

---

40 On this, see *OC*, vol. 2, notes, 444–5. Other members of the Society were Adrien Borel, René Allendy, Paul Schiff, Michel Leiris, and Pierre Janet as president.

41 Bataille's lecture invoked the "collective soul." Bataille suggested that the collectivity amounts to more than the sum of its parts and he proposed to consider the dead in their role within the overall movement of society. See *OC*, 2: 281–7. The document was dated 17 January 1938, although other sources list the lecture as occurring on 18 January. See *OC*, vol. 2, notes, 444.

42 See Cuvillier, *Introduction à la sociologie*, 36.

43 See lecture of 22 January 1938, "Attraction and Repulsion I: Tropisms, Sexuality, Laughter and Tears," in Hollier, *The College of Sociology*.

Robert Hertz's major work "Collective Representation of Death," Bataille conceived the sacred as based on death's original role in the actual creation of communities.[44] Accordingly, the dead unchain a communifying movement that originates in the horror that death provokes in humans. At first, humans react negatively to the dead through a common feeling of repulsion. Gradually, however, their fear transforms into a more positive sentiment: the left pole, identified with the impure, gives way to the right pole, which is connected to the pure, and the sacred then reveals itself in all its ambiguity.[45]

At the Society of Collective Psychology, Bataille had acknowledged the paradoxical character of a theory that situated society's origins in feelings of horror and disgust. Yet, at the Collège he would maintain and further explicate the psychological impulse of disgust at the basis of the social. In addition, he described more precisely the relationship between attraction and repulsion as overlapping and not merely sequential. Bataille insisted that we are attracted by what most disgusts us. The nucleus around which societies develop is formed by "a set of objects, places, beliefs, persons, and practices that have a sacred character" and that are unspeakable and untouchable, that is, taboo.[46] Around that nucleus, to which we tend to concentrate, collective human emotions develop and are unleashed through an intense reaction of repulsion. Such repulsion is at the basis of the social and defines what is specific about human nature as compared to animals. Taking the example of a French village to illustrate the pre-eminence of repulsion in creating the social, Bataille brought attention to the church as a sacred place around which village people gather and within which all profane activity is banned. The church, Bataille continued, inspires awe and a considerable amount of dread with its ossuary, dead bodies buried underneath, and symbolic ceremonies of sacrifice held daily. At the same time, the church exercises a force of attraction for the villagers, who often converge on it during feast days, even as they share the anguish and guilt of the repeated symbolic sacrifice.[47]

44 See Hertz, *Death and the Right Hand.* The original title of Hertz's essay was "Contribution à une étude sur la représentation collective de la mort."

45 The polarity of the sacred was at the centre of several theories of religion at the time, from the one proposed by Robertson Smith to those of Rudolf Otto and Robert Hertz.

46 See lecture of 22 January 1938, "Attraction and Repulsion I," in Hollier, *The College of Sociology,* 106.

47 At this point Bataille discussed how his own lived experience in the form of memories of the situations he was describing allowed him to advance science. Bataille distinguished lived from common experience. He referred to the former as "fabricated," that is, already affected by the knowledge of sciences such as psychoanalysis and French sociology. For Bataille, those sciences made it possible to become aware of sacred things and their

Non-Christian religions similarly provided examples of the dynamic relationship linking attraction to repulsion, Bataille believed. Indeed, they displayed even richer activities than those found in the modern West. Anthropological and sociological works had supplied numerous instances of this richness through an investigation of the institution of the taboo, the differentiation between sacred and profane, and the impure nature of specific sacred objects and activities. For Bataille, these studies amply demonstrated the plausibility of his interpretation. In addition, and very crucially for the Collège's approach to the sacred, the studies indicated that the valence of sacred objects was mutable and that the sacred constituted a force which, like mana, cannot be possessed. Finally, they also proved that the transmutation of sacred objects was only possible in one direction, that is, from left to right. Bataille's theory of the conversion of the central nucleus into a positive pole appeared to confirm this trend, as repulsion gave way to attraction and the left sacred turned into the right sacred.[48]

Equipped with a preliminary theory according to which unity paradoxically emerges out of horror, Bataille retained a firm understanding of the centrality of psychological dynamics in social relationships. He then moved to focus on the structural manifestations of the sacred – those phenomena to which Caillois had called attention in his "Introduction" to the Collège published by the *Nouvelle Revue Française*. There, Caillois encouraged finding "the points of coincidence between the fundamental obsessive tendencies of individual psychology and the principal structures governing social organization."[49] Before we examine these social structures, however, it is worth taking an additional look at the individual psychology to which Caillois was referring. Although neglected by the Collège, specific manifestations of individual psychology were brought to life in Leiris's original lecture of 8 January 1938 delivered in advance of Bataille's talks on "Attraction and Repulsion" and entitled "The Sacred in Everyday Life."[50] What Caillois had defined as

---

repugnant character. "My being able to put forward this idea was due to an abnormal conscious perception subsequent to scientific discoveries assimilated throughout the course of a life devoted in part to systematic knowledge." See "Attraction and Repulsion II: Social Structure," in Hollier, *The College of Sociology*, 121.

48 In his study of double burial, Hertz had effectively illustrated this process of transformation of the dead body from noxious to domesticated. See "Collective Representation of Death," in *Death and the Right Hand*.

49 "Introduction," in Hollier, *The College of Sociology*, 11.

50 On the marginality of Leiris at the Collège, see Hollier, *Le Collège de Sociologie*, 94–5. Hollier explains what led to promoting Leiris to third leader of the Collège, but also makes very clear the elusiveness of the title since none of the participants at the Collège associated

"the fundamental obsessive tendencies of individual psychology" or "the primordial longings and conflicts of the individual condition" became the core of Leiris's discussion of the ambiguity of the sacred.[51]

Leiris began his report by asking "What, for me, is the *sacred?*"[52] With a unique focus on objects and practices of everyday life, he answered by evoking personal experiences of places and activities that were simultaneously attractive and dangerous because forbidden. Leiris addressed "that combination of respect, desire, and terror that we take as the psychological sign of the sacred."[53] And he looked for the "unofficially" sacred among those phenomena that one could describe as the "profane" sacred. Thus, relying on his childhood memories, he classified different rooms in his house according to their right or left sacred polarity (the parents' bedroom as the locus of authority and the bathroom as the source of secrecy, for instance). Outside the domestic sphere, Leiris recalled his fascination with a nearby racetrack, where gamblers thrived and money was squandered, but also with brothels – places far removed from bourgeois respectability and morality. Finally, Leiris found in language a source for the sense of imponderability that separates events and occurrences from the profane realm. The evocative power of words opened a space to revelations and discoveries that helped him attain the sense of the extraordinary, even if at the same time they caused him to lose his footing, the certainty that comes from an internalized and mindless usage of language.[54]

By retracing the origins of the sacred in feelings, that is, in the psychological process that ensues from the filtering of memories and the reaction to immediate experiences, Leiris made tangible a concept that seemed otherwise elusive. His recovery of the sacred in everyday life helped confirm, and for many of the Collège's attendees also clarified, the ambiguous nature of the sacred, its simultaneous power of attraction

---

Leiris with the leadership of the group. For a discussion of Leiris within the context of *Acéphale*, see Greeley, *Surrealism and the Spanish Civil War*. Greely discusses the differences between Leiris's theory of myths and violence in his *Miroir de la tauromachie* (1938) and the views of myths and violence that characterized *Acéphale*.

51 Hollier, *The College of Sociology*, 11, 10. On Leiris's lecture see also Jamin, "Quand le sacré devint gauche."

52 Ibid., 24. On the history of this text see Hollier, *Le Collège de Sociologie*, 95–102.

53 Hollier, *The College of Sociology*, 24.

54 The link between language and the sacred was explored by another presenter at the Collège. On 16 May 1939, Jean Paulhan discussed proverbs in Madagascar and their ambiguous nature in terms of the sacred. He also related those who manipulate proverbs to some types of secret societies. See Hollier, *Le Collège de Sociologie*.

COLLÈGE DE SOCIOLOGIE

ANNÉE 1937-1938 .. LISTE DES EXPOSÉS

Samedi 20 novembre 1937
LA SOCIOLOGIE SACRÉE et les rapports entre "société", "organisme", "être", par Georges Bataille et Roger Caillois.

Samedi 4 décembre 1937
LES CONCEPTIONS HÉGÉLIENNES, par Alexandre Kojève.

Samedi 19 décembre 1937
LES SOCIÉTÉS ANIMALES, par Roger Caillois.

Samedi 8 janvier 1938
LE SACRÉ, dans la vie quotidienne, par Michel Leiris.

Samedi 22 janvier 1938
ATTRACTION ET RÉPULSION, I. Tropismes, sexualité, rire et larmes, par Georges Bataille.

Samedi 5 février 1938
ATTRACTION ET RÉPULSION. II. La structure sociale, par Georges Bataille.

Samedi 19 février 1938
LE POUVOIR, par Roger Caillois.

Samedi 5 mars 1938
STRUCTURE ET FONCTION DE L'ARMÉE, par Georges Bataille.

Samedi 19 mars 1938
CONFRÉRIES, ORDRES, SOCIÉTÉS SECRÈTES, ÉGLISES, par Roger Caillois.

Samedi 2 avril 1938
LA SOCIOLOGIE SACRÉE du monde contemporain, par Georges Bataille et Roger Caillois.

■ Les exposés des mois de mai et juin 1938 seront entièrement consacrés à la MYTHOLOGIE.

■ Le COLLÈGE DE SOCIOLOGIE se réunira dans la Salle des Galeries du Livre, 15, rue Gay-Lussac (5ᵉ). Les exposés commenceront à 21 h. 30 précises ; ils seront suivis d'une discussion. L'entrée de la salle sera réservée aux membres du Collège, aux porteurs d'une invitation nominale et (une seule fois) aux personnes présentées par un membre inscrit. L'inscription est de 5 fr. par mois (8 mois par an) ou de 30 fr. par an (payables en novembre). La correspondance doit être adressée à G. Bataille, 76 bis, rue de Rennes (6ᵉ).

INVITATION NOMINALE valable le _____ ■_____

10 Announcement of lectures at the Collège de sociologie, 1937–38. Georges Bataille, *Œuvres complètes*, vol. 2. © Éditions Gallimard

and repulsion.[55] All the instances of ordinary practices mentioned by Leiris were indeed characterized by contradictory feelings and perceptions that testified to the sacred's ambiguous nature. In addition, Leiris's focus on the combination of fears and desires provoked by daily events and objects helped direct attention to the presence of the sacred outside the recognized "official" areas of religion, fatherland, and morality. Last but not least, his personal approach hinted that the sacred had not disappeared from contemporary Western societies.

Leiris's discussion supported the theoretical scaffolding being erected by the Collège in its attempt to locate and redefine the sacred in the modern world. Ambiguity, in particular, served as an essential category for gaining entrance into the structural manifestations of the sacred – the topic to which Bataille and Caillois attended next.

Tragic Power and the Ambiguity of the Sacred

Caillois and Bataille delivered two lectures immediately following those on "Attraction and Repulsion" that directly engaged with two social structures: power and the army. For Bataille power and the army were created through, and in turn produced, communifying movements, and he had cited them in his first lecture at the Collège as "rightful object[s]" of a sociology concerned with those human activities that create unity.[56] The two lectures indeed sustained the Collège's original mission to assess the presence of the sacred in modern societies. The analysis of power and the army also led the Collège onto the embattled field of politics in which, contrary to its original intentions, the Collège plunged head-on. The fight for resurrecting the sacred, which Bataille and Caillois were demonstrably proud to lead, could not avoid taking contemporary reality into account. Fascism, once again, came to haunt Bataille as the most compelling demonstration of the impact of affective reactions on a seemingly desacralized world.[57]

55 On this point, see Jean Wahl's impressions in Hollier, *The College of Sociology* (originally published as "Au Collège de Sociologie"). Wahl specifically addressed the audience's reactions to the talk. He also wrote, "Bataille and Caillois, who preside over the destinies of this college, had invited Michel Leiris to speak. It was, I believe, the first meeting in which one had the feeling of some intensity from the beginning to the end of the lecture," 102.

56 Bataille, "Sacred Sociology," in Hollier, *The College of Sociology*, 74.

57 We should add that Bataille was planning to publish a book on fascism, probably comprising his writings on the subject, in a series Caillois was going to edit for Gallimard on "Tyrants and Tyrannies." Bataille considered giving it the title "tragic destiny" along with

The lecture on power of 19 February 1938 was supposed to be delivered by Caillois who, being ill, delegated Bataille to convey his thoughts. As it turns out, Bataille injected his own interpretive vein into the text he presented in lieu of Caillois.[58] Despite their different emphases on the topic, however, Bataille and Caillois shared one basic premise: by classifying power as a communifying movement, they hypostatized its sacredness. On the basis of this hypostatization, they then described power's sacred nature and explained its origins in connection with the problem of order. At the heart of both operations lay the notion of the ambiguity of the sacred, they claimed, a notion that further complicated the dynamics of the opposition between sacred and profane. Ambiguity therefore required additional consideration. One could indeed argue that the ambiguity of the sacred was the running theme of the Collège's ruminations. Caillois's lecture of 15 November 1938, which opened the second cycle of the Collège, was entitled "The Ambiguity of the Sacred." It eloquently summarized the main presuppositions on which the Collège built its program. The lecture, whose text has not been found, became a chapter of Caillois's book *L'Homme et le sacré*. Since the chapter illuminates the tenets of Caillois's planned lecture of 19 February 1938, I will examine it as background to the topic of power as elaborated by Caillois and Bataille.

L'Homme et le sacré was written during the Collège's years and, according to its author, marked Caillois's "intellectual osmosis" with Bataille.[59] In the book Caillois sought to elucidate the "*syntax*" of the sacred by systematizing Bataille's theory of the origins of the social – a theory suggesting that the sacred is a fundamentally ambiguous nucleus of attraction and repulsion that commands contradictory emotions.[60] Using the example of the pure/impure binary, Caillois provided persuasive, though scattered, evidence supporting the thesis of the duality of the sacred originally put forward by several scholars of religion and to which Durkheim also subscribed. More specifically, Caillois claimed that the sacred's duality reflected or rather determined the organization and regular rhythm of the world. Although the sacred's pure and impure corresponded to good and evil in the domain of the profane, unlike the profane the

---

the subtitle "Essay of sacred sociology of fascist Europe" (as capitalized in the original). See his letter to Caillois of 3 March 1938 in Bataille, *Lettres à Roger Caillois*, 84.

58 Bataille affirmed in his lecture on "Power," "Frankly, it is difficult for me purely and simply to replace Caillois and limit myself to saying what would have seemed to him essential." Ibid., 126.

59 See Caillois, *L'Homme et le sacré*, Avant-propos, 11.

60 See Claudine Frank's introduction to Caillois, *The Edge of Surrealism*, 26 (italicized in the original).

sacred was not dominated by things but by forces – mana – which, being highly mobile, could easily acquire a different valence depending on place and circumstance. Thus, whether one referred to it as saintly or filthy, right or left, pure or impure, the same force, for lack of a fixed nature, could be either malevolent or benevolent. The Latin meaning of "sacred" perfectly conveyed the sacred's equivocal essence; *sacer*, for the Romans, designated "the person or thing that cannot be touched without being dirtied or making dirty."[61] Because of its indeterminate, fluid character, the sacred then provokes our ambivalent reactions. We can be in awe in front of it but also tremble; we can trust it and at the same time fear it; we can confide in it as well as be terrorized by its magnitude.

For Caillois, Rudolf Otto's characterization of the sacred as simultaneously *fascinans* and *tremendum* encapsulated our contradictory psychological response to the sacred realm.[62] *Fascinans-tremendum* evoked an experience of both ecstasy before God and fear for the sins committed. Caillois concluded that the sacred is a "dangerous energy, incomprehensible, hardly manageable, and eminently efficacious."[63] Because of its unfixed and contagious nature, rituals and prohibitions surround the sacred and regulate its relationship with the profane, lest the cosmic order, which comprises nature and society, be endangered by a sudden imbalance between the two spheres.[64] Although Caillois distinguished between a "sacred of respect" that operates in normal times and a "sacred of transgression" that is linked to exceptional times, in his schema both the right and left sacred were in the end opposed to the profane. They both discharged, and were constituted by, some kind of force and energy that the profane was utterly lacking.

But what makes the individual accept restrictions? Or, more specifically, how is subjective experience transformed into a regulated conduct that is intended to maintain order in the world and avoid the overwhelming equivocal force of the sacred? Also, how is it possible to maintain the

61 Caillois, *L'Homme et le sacré*, 40. In *Man and the Sacred*, 35 the translation reads "the one or that which cannot be touched without defilement." Bataille made a similar point in "The Use Value of D.A.F. Sade" in *Visions of Excess*, 102n2.

62 Otto, *The Idea of the Holy*.

63 Caillois, *L'Homme et le sacré*, 21; *Man and the Sacred*, 22.

64 In the case of the criminal, Caillois reasoned, his impurity makes him sacred; the guilty one then achieves a divine nature in the reversible movement of pure and impure. This process occurs because of the magnitude of the criminal's attack against the sacred. The shock of such crime, the inexpiability of its polluting act, motivates society to break off contact with the dangerous elements in its midst. The criminal is then declared sacred in the fully ambiguous meaning of the term: he is taboo, untouchable, and is therefore separated from the rest of the group. Ibid.

sacred's creative potential? At this theoretical juncture, Caillois addressed the issue of power. For Caillois, power presided over the relationship between sacred and profane; he also believed that power's transformation coincided with the dilution of the sacred's original ambivalence. In his discussion of the pure and impure binary, Caillois had observed that the pure was often identified with harmony and cohesion and the impure with irregularity and dissolution. The pure corresponded to order and the norm and the impure referred to disorder and effervescence; together they were critical in ensuring the vitality of the sacred. However, Caillois perspicaciously noted that eventually the categories of pure and impure came to be conceived as separate. Furthermore, an examination of the relationship between the realms of the sacred and the profane showed that the profane had taken over the field of meanings previously inhabited by the pure. The desire for order being dominant, there resulted an ossification of the relationship between the pure and impure and also of the sacred/profane split with the consequence that the sacred's vital, creative energy risked being abated, if not evacuated. Caillois concluded that the genesis of modern power resided in the undoing of the original equilibrium between the sacred and the profane.[65] On the level of social organizations, this process is evident when groups cease to co-operate and instead strive for predominance, thus losing their internal balance. They move from a diffused form of power to a concentrated one; a hierarchy then ensues that imposes sovereignty. At this point, the principle of respect presiding over clan groups is replaced by the principle of individuation. Diffused power then gives way to a concentrated power in which personal power and the asymmetrical relations between the sovereign and its subjects that power produces develop and become prevalent.[66]

Of course, Caillois still saw power as almost identical with the sacred: it was a force, mana, something that attracts us into obeying and following. In a 1937 review essay on the French prime minister, Léon Blum, he

65 On this issue, Caillois was especially influenced by Dumézil.

66 Caillois presented two ideal-typical case scenarios. In the instance of societies with diffused power, the relationship between two phratries regulates the distribution of sacred and profane. Members of one phratry are free to access what is forbidden to the other phratry, and vice versa. The two phratries complement each other through their opposite definition of what the sacred and profane are. In the cases of concentrated power, it is the dyad prince-masses that operates and maintains, though hierarchically, the division between sacred and profane and guarantees its equilibrium. The prince is allowed what the masses are forbidden, and vice versa. The difference between this case scenario and the other is that, in the concentration of power, relationships are not reversible. *L'Homme et le sacré*, 115–16.

stated this point very clearly. Power, "whether exercised or submitted to, is a kind of immediate conscious data in the face of which a being has an elementary reaction of attraction or repulsion … power necessarily belongs to the domain of the sacred … appears as impregnated with the sacred, or rather as its very source."[67] The individual sovereign was merely a vessel for power because, being sacred, power is enacted by people's emotions.[68] Once power is recognized as such, however, the sovereign comes to occupy a special place. Prescriptions and rituals, whereby power displays its difference from those who submit to it, surround the king and maintain order. Even if sacred and profane appear to be complementary in these power relations, in reality their balance is now off. Order occurs at the expense of the sacred and implies that the equilibrium between sacred and profane has been broken. In other words, the individuality of power designates the disappearance of the ambiguity of the sacred, the closing, that is, of the oscillation between right and left, good and evil, pure and impure, prohibition and transgression. In the end, if the polarity of the sacred suggested that cohesion and dissolution alternate, the elimination of one necessarily caused the desacralization of the world, Caillois believed. Precisely this occurrence constituted the critical issue for the Collège and the one that had motivated its birth in the first place. It is no wonder that Bataille wrote an entire new text for the meeting of 19 February 1938, when he was instead supposed to be speaking for Caillois and conveying his thoughts.

Bataille's intervention loosely followed the argument Caillois had developed in *L'Homme et le sacré*. Bataille presented the inherently sacred nature of power in order to record the process of its eventual deterioration and decline. And he claimed that power partakes of the sacred, of its fascinating and at the same time tremendous mana; power makes us tremble because it is seductive and also fearful. Alluding to a previous lecture, Bataille stressed that power is an emotional relationship that mediates human interattraction and cannot, as Caillois had warned, be considered a mere imposition enforced by the police.[69] Rather, the

---

67 See Caillois's review of Léon Blum's works in the *Nouvelle Revue Française*.

68 This formula sounds quasi-Weberian in its stress on relationships and its dismissal of violence in the charismatic kind of power. Caillois's notion is, however, very different from Weber's general emphasis on legitimacy, and seems to anticipate Michel Foucault's theory of power as creating and not negating. In a letter to Caillois of 25 May 1966, Foucault cites their common "Dumézilian 'ascendance,'" although not with specific reference to the issue of power. See Caillois, *Roger Caillois*, 228. Also see Frank Pearce, "'Off with their heads.'"

69 In "Attraction and Repulsion I," Bataille wrote of the difference between animal and human societies: "Human interattraction is not immediate, it is *mediated*, in the precise

opposite dynamic unfolds in which power creates the institutions that accompany it. Therein resides the paradox of power; it depends on those it subjects and requires their participation, assent, and emotional involvement, be it in terms of attraction and/or repulsion.

Having established the affective nature of power, Bataille proceeded to focus on the decaying effects of prohibitive power. In the last part of the second lecture on "Attraction and Repulsion," when talking about primitive agglomerations, he had raised the issue of interdictions, especially in relation to the original crime that generates communifying movement and leads to the establishment of prohibitive power. Now, he took into consideration Caillois's analysis of individualized power – the instance in which the person of the king appears to be eliciting the reactions of awe, fear, and respect normally unchained by the numinous. Bataille agreed with Caillois that the ambiguity at the heart of the sacred threatens to undermine the privileged position of the king. In particular, when a disruption occurs in the order of things, the sovereign can be held responsible; his sacredness then takes the negative valence of the left sacred and the king becomes liable to be sacrificed and put to death. For Bataille, however, the possibility of killing the sovereign led to theorizing about the link between the king's sacrifice and the historical transmutations of power. More specifically, the originality of Bataille's analysis, and where he moved away from Caillois, lay in his assessment that any attempt to eliminate the potentially tragic fate of the king inevitably led to an emasculation of power. The end of sacrifice meant the end of true existence as well as the dissolution of the tragic community formed by reactions of repulsion to crime; the possibility of murdering the king, in contrast, ensured the tragic essence of power.[70]

Historically, according to Bataille, the royal institution's creation of an armed force at the king's command exemplified the attempt to eliminate the tragic status of the sovereign.[71] When sacred force is merged with military strength, power is transformed from being a source that promotes community into an institutionalized authority in charge of

---

sense of the word; that is, the relations between two men are profoundly changed as a result of their both being situated within the orbit of the central nucleus." See Hollier, *The College of Sociology*, 107 (italicized in the original).

70 It is important to reiterate here that for Bataille crime constitutes the tragic act. Bataille, however, made a distinction between the answers to this fundamental postulate: "Tragedy offers human beings the identification with the criminal who kills the king: Christianity offers identification with the victim, the slain king." Ibid., 135.

71 See "La royauté de l'Europe classique" in *OC*, vol. 2. In the lecture of 2 April 1938, Bataille took the example of the czar's disappearance as a case that demonstrated the elimination of power's sacred potential. See Bataille, *La sociologie sacrée du monde contemporain*.

regulating, administering, and policing. Such power ends up escaping tragedy and diverting its energy toward the pursuit of personal interests. It denies or hides the original crime and tries to reroute to its own benefit the overall movement animating the human community. In this situation, power emerges as a conservative force that alienates the sacred's original energy. It fatally alters the community's overall affective movement with the result that one does not merely witness the transformation of the left sacred into a right sacred but also, and more significantly, the loss of a sacred centre *tout court.* At this point, Bataille claimed, the void left by an emptied sacred unchains another dynamic in which the propertied classes resent their inability to acquire profit within a weakened form of power. They therefore appeal to the remnants of sacred forces, violence, and the military. Fascism, as Bataille had already concluded in "The Psychological Structure," would be one end-result of this process, marking the fallen fate of the sacred in modern societies and the ascendance of a fake community at the helm of the political.

With the lecture on power Bataille began an analytical operation vis-à-vis the contemporary world that simultaneously unveiled the absence of the sacred and surveyed its deceptive reappearance in the guise of militarized fascist movements. The examination of power and the sacred led Bataille to re-evaluate the double-edged nature of fascism's heterogeneous pretensions in a historical context where affective forces held increasing attraction. Bataille's lecture on "The Structure and Function of the Army" of 5 March 1938 inserted itself within this critical project of identifying the false premises of fascism's appeal to the sacred.[72]

Bataille began his lecture by analysing the army as a communifying movement and he argued that, besides being formed by people trained to fight, the army was especially characterized by a bond that transforms single individuals and turns them into a sui generis formation. This "constituted body" leads a separate existence apart from the larger national body and has distinctive characteristics and independent meaning. The army, Bataille claimed, was a whole within a larger whole, a community within the larger human community but for one notable difference: the bond linking soldiers in an army was founded on sharing destiny. It was therefore stronger than the bond uniting the loosely connected members of a society because the army does not merely pursue utilitarian

---

72 The text of the lecture has not been found, but Bataille's summary of it in his subsequent presentations at the Collège of 19 March and especially the summarizing lecture of 2 April and his other writings on the topic of the army provide hints as to the orientation of his thought at the time. See Hollier's selection on the topic of the army, in Hollier, *The College of Sociology.*

ends in the form of attack and defence, Bataille ultimately asserted. The army also strives for glory in the face of death and, in so doing, closely approaches the sacred realm.

After positively presenting the army as a formation creative of unity, Bataille's analysis turned more negative.[73] In the face of the overgrown development of nationalist militarism in Europe, Bataille denounced the deceitful sacred dimensions of military power. Although he praised armed struggle over work's "functional movement" and emphasized the role of revolution, Bataille pointed to the enormous disparity between the "tragic man" and the "lout man." The latter, he declared in the lecture of 19 March, "violently turns everything that excites him to the *outside* ... never allows for any inner conflict and looks on death as a source of external pleasure."[74] Death is directed toward the enemy and becomes a mere chance that hangs on the vagaries of the battlefield. Conflicts are thus transformed into nationalist militarism. The tragic man, in contrast, is aware of human existence as tragedy and takes death upon him in the form of religious sacrifices. "It is the sacrificial blaze, not the animality of war, that has made men arise, those paradoxical beings, made greater by the terrors that enthrall them and that they overcome," Bataille declared.[75] In the name of tragedy, and equipped with a critique that far exceeded the boundaries of the sociological discipline, Bataille posed existence against function. He thus staged an attack against accepting life as servitude, calculation, and security.[76] Within this context, the army became a target of his critique since it was closely related to functional movements.[77]

---

73 This turn is especially evident in the lectures of 19 March and 2 April.

74 Bataille, "Brotherhoods, Orders, Secret Societies, Churches," in Hollier, *The College of Sociology*, 147.

75 Bataille, "The Structure and Function of the Army," in Hollier, *The College of Sociology*, 143.

76 On this issue, see also "The Sorcerer's Apprentice," in Hollier, *The College of Sociology*. Along with Caillois's "The Winter Wind," some draft of this essay was read at the organizing meeting of the Collège in March 1937 before its actual publication in the *Nouvelle Revue Française* in the summer of 1938.

77 In *The Accursed Share* (*La part maudite*), Bataille also distinguished between military societies and warrior societies. See Métraux's comments in "Rencontre avec les ethnologues." One should also take into account the influence on the Collège of Dumézil's analysis of the Indo-European cultures. Dumézil saw these as structured in a tripartite way: sovereignty, war, and production. Bataille was particularly interested in the warrior function in connection to the issue of sovereignty. In Dumézil's account, sovereignty implied both a political and a religious side represented in the gods Mitra and Varuna and their focus on order and transgression respectively. One implied the other as in the Hegelian *Aufhebung*. However, a third element could intervene in the relationship and threaten it with the warrior god Indra. On Dumézil and Bataille, see Hollier, "January 21st."

Bataille saw the contemporary world as being adjudicated by two equally defeating forces: the platitude of democracy, characterized by the absence of the sacred, and the hypnotism of the military, a simulacrum of the sacred. He believed that neither democracy nor the military could escape the equalizing power of function; they both engendered a diminished, enslaved existence. As in the invisible, but still pernicious, disease of consumption, life was slowly being reduced to a functional status, and tragedy appeared unable to take root.[78] Individuals were developing the illusion of breaking free from the yoke of enslaved existence and believed they could escape the constraints of the social. In reality, functional movements were growing and attracting people by their gravitational pull and, since functional movements are by definition servile, existence was being diminished in their presence and becoming subordinated to utilitarian goals. It follows that individuals achieve what they consider freedom from society's constraints only to end up in a worse servitude. Whenever individuals identify existence with function, society becomes dominated by work and empty human relations, and individuals are anaesthetized against death and tragedy. Within this context, functional work could not but accelerate the rapid decline of society's overall movement – a development that was occurring in the Soviet Union. There, the militarization of society and the sponsoring of patriotic values did not provide a viable answer to the loss of community. Nor was Bataille convinced that fighting could resolve the problem of a moribund existence. To the contrary, he denounced fascism's militarization of Europe: the idea of a community based on the concepts of race, fatherland, and blood was just false, a bad imitation, nothing short of an insult.

As discussed in the previous chapter, the theme of tragedy was at the heart of Bataille's preoccupation. Tragedy qualified human existence in its pursuit of destiny and in opposition to functionality and interest, and Bataille was wary of movements that posited usefulness as an a priori value. When function is confused with existence, human life becomes subservience, he believed, and only the awareness and knowledge of the tragic spirit, that is, only the acceptance of tragedy, makes it possible for human beings to constitute a sacred community. In view of the tight link he saw between tragedy and community, it is not surprising that tragedy loomed large in Bataille's presentations at the Collège. It was central to the lectures on the army, on brotherhoods, and the summarizing lecture of 2 April that revisited the role of the army and the functional nature of work. Furthermore, one should add, tragedy was also the topic of

---

78 See "The Sorcerer's Apprentice" in Hollier, *The College of Sociology.*

Klossowski's unplanned intervention of 19 May 1938, one of the three lectures not delivered by either Bataille or Caillois in the first year of the Collège.[79]

In reality, Klossowski merely read his recent translation of Søren Kierkegaard's *Antigone*. The philosopher's perspective on the Greek tragic figure, however, fit the Collège's concern with the existential role of tragedy. Kierkegaard addressed the difference between the tragic conflict of antiquity, which transcends the individual, and the tragic conflict of modernity, which revolves around the hero's subjectivity. And he argued that in modernity fate is turned into a subjective outcome: one's life is considered the result of actions for which the individual, isolated from past, family, and community, is solely responsible. In light of the dilution of the tragic following the advent of Christianity, Kierkegaard argued for the need to incorporate the tragic of antiquity into the modern tragic in order to recoup tragedy's true essence. Although Bataille was never an adept of Kierkegaard, the philosopher's interpretation of Antigone supported Bataille's quest for tragic modes of existence. In addition, Kierkegaard anticipated Bataille's and Caillois's critiques of aesthetics as particularly directed to the individualized genre of the novel.

Although neither Bataille nor Caillois delivered a lecture on the novel at the Collège, we know that Caillois deemed the novel the epitome of myth's lesser strength and diluted nature and on this basis denounced it. Bataille, in turn, contrasted the novel to myth and wrote that the latter "is perhaps fable, but this fable is made the opposite of fiction if one looks at the people who dance it, who act it, and whose living *truth* it is."[80] A critique of the novel was part and parcel of the Collège's understanding of the social, although it was left to another speaker to present the issue to the Collège's audience. Using a line of interpretation similar to Caillois, the Hellenist René Guastalla discussed the origins of literature on 10 January 1939.[81] "The Birth of Literature" distinguished ancient,

79 Apparently, Bataille, Jean Wahl, and Denis de Rougemont also participated in this session on tragedy, probably as respondents to Klossowski's presentation. See Hollier, *Le Collège de Sociologie* for details on the lecture. Klossowski collaborated with the left-wing Catholic review *Esprit* and was part of the current of "personalism" led by Emmanuel Mounier. Personalism negatively evaluated materialism and individualism in favour of spiritual values. It upheld the need for a "third way" between capitalism and communism while also rejecting fascism. On the revues that gathered young intellectuals in the 1930s see Touchard, "L'Esprit des années trente."

80 See "The Sorcerer's Apprentice," in Hollier, *The College of Sociology*, 22.

81 The text of the lecture has not been found but Hollier draws from a chapter with the same title that was part of the book Guastalla was writing at the time, *Le Mythe et le livre* (The Myth and the Book), published in 1940.

collective myths from modern myths and characterized the latter as literary and based on the single author. Guastalla focused in particular on the
birth of literature as it took place in Greece and identified the origin of
individual myths in the separation of the citizens from the city. While in
the distant past a person was naturally bonded with the city and belonged
to it, today we have abandoned this organic relationship of dependence
and rather "choose" a group. As a consequence of the emancipation of
Ionian philosophy from the original social bond and the Sophists' orientation toward individualism, Euripides emerged, the first real writer of
literature. With him, conflicts became internalized and Euripides fore-
cast the modern writer "confronting the world, outside the world."[82]
Guastalla concluded his lecture by reaffirming the link between failure of
sociality and art's individualism, the exact situation Bataille had denounced as the loss of tragic sense and for which art as well as politics
were guilty. For Bataille, indeed, Guastalla's narrative ultimately revealed
"the miseries of literature."[83] Against individualism and its aesthetic incarnations, Bataille, but also Caillois, invoked community.

Bataille was, however, cautious about the chances of reinstating true
social existence through communifying movements. Caught between a
fake sacred and a sacred void, he appeared deeply skeptical about society's future and warned about illusory forms of the sacred. Even the
"rightful objects" of sacred sociology – power and the army – seemed unable to remedy the contemporary social crisis. The particular, ambivalent
nature of the sacred, nevertheless, left the door open for an equally ambivalent solution. Surprisingly, in spite of all his negativism, Bataille retained a flicker of hope that the sacred could be rekindled by way of the
same movements that had replaced tragedy. After reaching their lowest
point in the wake of the First World War, Western societies, Bataille noted, were witnessing new powerful movements that were creators of intense centres. "[T]hree new monarchies, much more than dictatorships,
rather true divine powers" had reversed the process of social disaggrega-
tion and paved the way for a true resurgence of the overall movement.[84]
Bolshevism, fascism, and Nazism had shown the power of communifying
forces. The Collège's task was now to devise ways in which to revive an
existentially based sacred while bringing down its simulacrum. One

82 Hollier, *The College of Sociology*, 214. Comments about the lecture reveal that Guastalla,
according to some of the Collège's attendees, was not saying anything new. See Hollier, *Le
Collège de Sociologie*, 472–3.

83 See his letter to Caillois of 17 December 1938, in which Bataille proposed to have
Guastalla lecture at the Collège, in Bataille, *Lettres à Roger Caillois*, 94.

84 Bataille, *La sociologie sacrée du monde contemporain*, 31.

needed, in Bataille's words, an analysis of "the secondary dynamic forms that have always introduced the possibility of reactivating the social tragedy."[85] Those forms were secret societies and elective communities, and they constituted the topic of the 19 March 1938 lecture Bataille delivered at the Collège in place of Caillois .

Reactivating the Sacred

As Denis Hollier observes, the lecture "Brotherhoods, Orders, Secret Societies, Churches" is at the heart of the Collège's project.[86] It reveals the Collège's deepest intentions. It also discloses the profound differences dividing the two leaders. Because Bataille had to stand in for Caillois and originally interpreted the notes Caillois prepared on the topic, some of the dissonances between their points of view emerge from Bataille's presentation. One needs to keep in mind, however, that in spite of their disagreements, both Bataille and Caillois envisioned elective communities as the answer to a diminished world. They regarded brotherhoods as the privileged place for starting a community that would eventually become, in Caillois's words, "the nucleus of a wider conspiracy" and be able to exert power [87] Bataille had already argued in a previous lecture that once society has exhausted its energy and can no longer fulfill its role as unifier, one needed to resort to secondary organizations. Now, with military-fascist domination spreading in Europe and with nationalism reaching intolerable levels, Bataille lamented the end of the religious world and held out one last hope: "If there existed a virulent religious organization, new and uncouth from head to toe, one sustained by a spirit incapable of a servile structure, a man might yet learn – and retain – that there is something else to love other than this barely concealed image of financial necessity that one's country is when up in arms. There is something else worth living for, something else worth dying for!"[88] As he witnessed the domination of the military over "hypnotized human masses," Bataille pessimistically assessed the diminished role of community and tragedy in contemporary social life. He then took the occasion of the lecture on brotherhood to reiterate his own "existential" understanding of community.[89]

---

85 Lecture on "Power," in Hollier, *The College of Sociology*, 136.
86 See Hollier's comments, in Hollier, *The College of Sociology*, 145.
87 See Caillois's "Introduction," in Hollier, *The College of Sociology*, 11.
88 "Brotherhoods," in Hollier, *The College of Sociology*, 149.
89 Ibid., 147.

Bataille held that to exist meant to act without an end, to waste, not conserve, and to accept death as one's own tragic dimension. Within this interpretive framework, the power of secret societies resided in their radical negation of the principle of necessity. As he declared at the conclusion of the lecture, "[T]he innermost power of the very principle of the 'secret society' is precisely that it constitutes the sole radical and working negation, the sole negation that does not simply consist in words, of that principle of necessity in the name of which all contemporary mankind collaborates to waste existence."[90] Bataille placed no trust in democratic solutions; tragedy could only be enacted by means of elective communities. However, he distinguished between secret and conspiratorial societies. While the latter pursued specific goals and were oriented toward action, existential secret societies were characterized by "the pure and simple will to be ... regardless of any particular goal."[91] In them, people gathered together in order to exist, not fulfill a task, and refused to be subjugated by the demands of a servile world that was concerned only with function. Bataille revealingly confessed his distance from a practical-strategic approach to social intervention. The tragic spirit pervading the Acéphale's experiment, it would seem, had willy-nilly spread its contagious energy to the Collège.

Although he shared Bataille's analysis of the modern decline of the sacred, Caillois had a more pragmatic and elitist view of secret societies and did not shy away from the idea of conspiracy. "The Winter Wind," published in July 1938 in the *Nouvelle Revue Française* as the programmatic manifesto of the Collège, along with Bataille's "The Sorcerer's Apprentice" and Leiris's "The Sacred in Everyday Life," expressed Caillois's distinctive position on these questions.[92] Caillois sketched out a plan for converting individualist rebellion into a constructive form of power in charge of overturning the presently static society.[93] At first,

90 Ibid., 155.

91 Ibid. Also see the conclusion to "The Sorcerer's Apprentice," in Hollier, *The College of Sociology*, 23: "'Secret society'... must not be understood, as it ordinarily is, in the vulgar sense of 'conspiratorial society.' For the secret has to do with the constitutive reality of existence that is seductive, not with some act that is contrary to the security of the State."

92 An expanded version of Caillois's original "Note on the Foundation of a College of Sociology" was also published in the same issue. Ibid.

93 See "The Winter Wind," in Hollier, *The College of Sociology*. In the article he co-wrote with Henri Beuchat for *L'Année sociologique* of 1904–1905, Mauss talked of winter as a time of gathering, at least in the social life of the Eskimo. See "Essai sur les variations saisonnières des sociétés Eskimos." They wrote, "Winter is a season when society, highly concentrated, is in a chronic phase of effervescence and overactivity," (470) (for the English translation see Mauss, in collaboration with Henri Beuchat, *Seasonal Variations of the Eskimo*). Marcel Granet's voluminous work on China also focused on winters. A Durkheimian and a

Caillois accused "great individualists" of a nihilistic attitude that led them to criticize everything social and thus accelerated the destruction of the sacred in a relentless process of profanation. These individualists had not realized that their activity provided only an illusion of freedom based on words in the absence of action. Caillois then recommended that they reverse their priorities by sacralizing rather than profaning. Caillois envisioned the transformation of the individualists' sense of rebellion into an "imperialist attitude" characterized by discipline and calculation. Since Lucifer was the demon of lucidity who "accepted that force was the law of the world," Caillois called for shifting from Satanic rebellion to a Luciferian will for power – a will that would aim at making sacred, rather than profaning, at building and not destroying.[94] "It is healthy to desire power, whether over souls or bodies, whether prestige or tyranny," Caillois wrote.[95] A common will to combat society would unite individuals and give them strength as a group. One would then witness a "*sursocialization*," an overtight and overpowering bond cemented by the sacred in its capacity as unifier.[96]

Caillois advocated the formation of a "new aristocracy" whose special qualities fulfilled the innovative task of taking on power and rescuing the social from extreme profanation. He went as far as describing some of the main ethical aspects of this closed community: he listed, among others, honesty, contempt, love of power, and courtesy. Fully embracing the hierarchical and divisive implications embedded in the notion of aristocracy, even as he rejected race, territory, and tradition as the bases for an affective link, Caillois argued that the weak could not be part of this

---

close friend of Mauss, Granet was supposed to be lecturing at the Collège in 1939. See Bataille, *Lettres à Roger Caillois*, letters 21 and 24.

94 See also "The Birth of Lucifer" in *The Edge of Surrealism*, 171. "La Naissance de Lucifer" was first published in *Verve* (December 1937). Caillois connects the birth of Lucifer to the rise of the intellectual in the wake of the Romantic separation of the artist from government subsidies.

95 See "The Winter Wind," in Hollier, *The College of Sociology*, 41. Caillois's Luciferian tendencies also led him to be interested in shamanism. He sponsored two lectures on the topic by a student of Mauss, Anatole Lewitzky. The lectures were delivered at the Collège on 7 and 21 March 1939. On Lewitzky, who worked at the Musée de l'Homme, see Hollier, *Le Collège de Sociologie*. Lewitzky later became a member of the French resistance and was executed by the Germans in 1942 along with six other members of the Musée's resistance network. See Patrick Ghrenassia, "Anatole Lewitzky: De l'ethnologie à la Résistance." On the Musée's resistance network, see Blumenson, *The Vildé Affair*.

96 Frank translates *sursocialisation* as "supersocialization," in Caillois, *The Edge of Surrealism*, 156. See Hollier, *The College of Sociology*, 401n7 for a history of this neologism. Caillois first used it in an April 1937 book review of Philippe De Félice, *Poisons sacrés, ivresses divines*. The book explored the connection between drugs and religious experience.

association. Closed communities counted on morally strong individuals whose aggressiveness Caillois exalted as a "virtue" that bound the group together and was to be exercised in a lucid way.[97] Aggressiveness was not the attribute "of triumph but of legitimate conquest," Caillois claimed; it had an objective and could not be employed for violence's sake. [98] Harsh and severe, and aggressively virtuous, the Luciferian spirit would supposedly guide the formation of the elective community. The Luciferian spirit would ultimately lead the new aristocracy to victory and reverse the lamentable contemporary process of desacralization.

Unlike Bataille, who refused to give any firm contours to his idea of an existentially based community, Caillois presented the traits he believed were crucial to an "activist" brotherhood endowed with transformative power.[99] Expressing no existential anguish, unlike Bataille, Caillois added a strategic, tactical element to his vision of a restricted group, a secret society in charge of overturning through a collective effort the desacralized status of the present world. And yet, despite their differences, Bataille and Caillois ultimately concurred that secret societies were closely connected to a sacred that expends, gives way to collective ecstasy, and promotes paroxysmal death. They thought of an incandescent, turbulent sacred, an explosive force undeterred by death.[100] In the notes Caillois handed over to Bataille for the lecture on "Brotherhoods," he proposed a range of secret societies – from more restricted to closed to activist. He suggested that all secret societies were unified by ferment, some kind of intoxication that opposed the static cohesion of the administrative world. By revisiting the right and left poles of the sacred, Caillois wrote that on the right stood the sacred bound by rules and taboos; on

97 In "Dionysian Virtues," first published in *Acéphale* 3–4 (July 1937), Caillois wrote that "virtue" means "*what binds together.*" See Caillois, *The Edge of Surrealism*, 159 (italicized in the original). Caillois also used "value" to mean "virtue" as in "Aggressiveness as a Value," in *The Edge of Surrealism*, first published in *L'Ordre nouveau* in June 1937 as "L'Aggressivité comme valeur."

98 Caillois, "Aggressiveness as a Value," in *The Edge of Surrealism*, 165.

99 Even the notion of power evoked by Caillois seems quite at odds with Bataille's non-committal critique of institutional power and its degenerating trend. According to Marie-Christine Lala, in Bataille's schema sovereignty is postulated on the evacuation of power. "In order to reign one needs to resign from power." See "Da 'La structure psychologique du fascisme' ai fondamenti di 'La Souveraineté," 65. Bataille particularly developed his notion of sovereignty in *The Accursed Share*. For Bataille, sovereignty depends on the loss of self and cannot be seized or possessed. It can only be sought.

100 See "Brotherhoods," in *The College of Sociology*, 156: "Only *existence* in its integrity, implying turbulence, incandescence, and a will for explosion undeterred by the threat of death, can be regarded as the one thing that, itself impossible to subjugate, must necessarily subjugate anything consenting to work for others" (italicized in the original).

the left, an orgiastic sacred spread its energy through expenditure, waste, and the violation of interdictions. Ferment allowed secret societies to play the crucial function of rejuvenating society and lifting it from a static void; ferment made it possible for societies to overcome routinized order and create a world anew. This vision of a sacred that violates was central to Caillois's prescriptive approach to the impending social crisis. This was clear even in his eulogy of Marcel Mauss written in 1950 but published several years later in *Cases d'un échiquier*.

In the eulogy, entitled "Le Grand Pontonnier" ("The Great Bridge-maker"), Caillois recounted one of his many meetings with Marcel Mauss in the courtyard of the Sorbonne.[101] It was 1937, and Caillois had just decided on the topic of his future thesis (which he never completed): the religious vocabulary of the Romans. As they walked together toward the bus stop, Mauss expressed his approval of the project proposed by Caillois. At the same time, he began to warn the young scholar about the many traps he might find on his way to elucidating the subject, including as a start the very word *religio*.[102] Mauss encouraged Caillois to explore the meaning of *religio* beyond its common understanding of "link." He directed him to a lexicographer who defined *religio* as a straw knot: "*religiones tramenta erant.*" These knots could be interpreted as those used to build bridges. Indeed, Mauss suggested, the master of religion in Rome is called *pontifex*, literally the builder of bridges. Do people realize when they talk about the pontiff that his name means the great builder of bridges? Caillois confessed to being struck by this revelation but remaining still unclear about its logic and significance, until, that is, Mauss, climbing on the bus that had just arrived, told him to think of the *ordo rerum*, the order of things, the internal arrangement of the elements in the universe as conceived by the gods. Religion is supposed to prevent any attempt at disrupting this arrangement, although the equilibrium is hard to maintain. Any violation of the rules could upset the order, including building a bridge, because in the natural arrangement of things a stream of water is not supposed to be crossed: one can either swim or float in it. Building a bridge is thus a "sacrilegious subterfuge that … jeopardized the world's order" and only brought misfortune to its authors.[103] It ruined the equilibrium of the universe by trespassing limits and disrupting nature. Of course, bridges are ultimately built, causing

101 See "Le Grand Pontonnier," in Caillois, *Cases d'un échiquier*.
102 On Mauss's habit of teaching while walking, see Dumont, "Une science en devenir."
103 "The Great Bridgemaker," in Caillois, *The Edge of Surrealism*, 340; "Le Grand Pontonnier," in *Cases d'un échiquier*, 25.

who knows how much anguish to those in charge of administering the sacred. But the fear of building bridges remains, Caillois realized, if we take bridges as the not too ethereal metaphor for constructing where reverence still prohibits it and where tradition reigns. In actuality, we remain afraid of breaking the order of things and we do not seem to be aware of the value held by the transgressive act. The sacred, however, Caillois concluded, needs to be violated in order to flourish; we ought to profane in order to make history. That is, after all, how the Pope became the Pontiff, the *Grand Pontonnier*.

In *L'Homme et le sacré*, Caillois explicitly emphasized the role of violations. He ended the chapter on the sacred of respect by evoking the inevitable ruin the world would face if the order sustained by prohibitions could not be exceeded, that is, if the system could not be rejuvenated, nature renewed, and society recreated. Caillois augured a "positive act," a "simulacrum of creation" that would fence off such a danger, and he located in festivals one potential instance of revitalization.[104] Not by chance, he ended his tale of the *Grand Pontonnier* by stating that "[f]estivals are bridges as well, though of a different kind."[105] If the transgressive act consisted in disrupting the order of things, festivals were the social manifestation of the transgressive act par excellence, the necessary moment that ensured the sacred's creative ability to revamp the social. Along similar lines, one should note, Bataille's second lecture on "Attraction and Repulsion" linked the expending of energy to existence, in particular collective existence, and suggested that there is no life without expenditure. Bataille also discussed the phenomenon of prohibition as the mechanism that opposes licence, and he concluded that "as human beings we cannot live without breaking the barriers we must give to our need to expend."[106] Expenditure implies prohibitions, and transgression guarantees free loss. Or as he wrote a few years later, transgression simply "suspends a taboo without suppressing it"; it manages to keep their mutual relationship in place through a dialectical movement that sustains the human propensity to excess.[107]

For Caillois, the excess evoked by Bataille was particularly epitomized in festivals, the topic of his lecture at the Collège of 2 May 1939. Chapter

---

104 Caillois, *L'Homme et le sacré*, 119.

105 "The Great Bridgemaker," in Caillois, *The Edge of Surrealism*, 342; "Le Grand Pontonnier," in *Cases d'un échiquier*, 27.

106 Bataille, "Attraction and Repulsion II," in *The College of Sociology*, 123.

107 *Eroticism*, 36. Bataille defined this operation as Hegelian or as an "*Aufhebung*." Bataille developed the theme of transgression in *L'Érotisme* (*Eroticism*) several years after the Collège. The work borrowed heavily from Caillois, as Bataille openly acknowledged. See in particular the chapter "Transgression."

four of *L'Homme et le sacré* was also dedicated to festivals, one should add, and was probably the basis of the 2 May 1939 lecture.[108] Entitled "The Sacred as Transgression: Theory of the Festivals," it immediately followed the chapter on "The Sacred as Respect: Theory of Taboo," which, as mentioned earlier, had ended with the warning that the world could not be preserved by order and risked implosion without a "simulacrum of creation." Festivals corresponded to such simulacrum; because of its excess, sacrileges, expenditure, and paroxysms, the festival reintroduced the sacred and undermined the routinization of order. Festival broke the barrier of prohibition and revealed that not the rule, but what the rule isolates, is sacred. Since the sacred could only be attained by transgressing the rule, Caillois began to explore concrete ways to bring people together through a communal ecstasy that would approximate the sacred. He thus resorted to Dionysianism as a way to accomplish the task.

Dionysianism, according to Caillois, showed that forms of turbulence, which are extremely asocial if lived individually, can turn into "sursocializing" forces. Following this logic, he believed that festivals could reignite the Dionysian spirit necessary to transform the individualized, isolated existence of declining democratic societies; that spirit would make possible a revived and renewed social experience.[109] Although Caillois held ascetic virtues and intellectual rigour in high regard, he saw no contradiction in the fact that he was invoking "ivresse" with reference to festivals.[110] He identified celebrations with excess, licence, collective effervescence. And he interpreted the festival's violence as not merely an emotional discharge but as holding a ritual meaning whose magical efficacy was dependent on excess.[111] Bataille had raised a similar point in "The Sorcerer's Apprentice," where he postulated the link between myth and ritual in their capacity to express and convey communal experience. Once enacted ritually, the myth comes to be possessed by the collectivity and turns into a living experience, Bataille argued.[112] Myth is thus

108 Caillois published a version of this chapter as "Théorie de la fête" in the *Nouvelle Revue Française* of December 1939. Benjamin seemed interested in this piece, as he wrote to Gretel Adorno on 17 January 1940: "Caillois actually published a theory of the pageant in the *Nouvelle revue française*, which I plan to discuss in my first report on French books for Max." See Scholem and Adorno, *The Correspondence of Walter Benjamin*, 626.

109 See Caillois, "Dionysian Virtues" in *The Edge of Surrealism*.

110 Frank, however, believes that Caillois was all about self-restraint. *The Edge of Surrealism*, introduction to "Aggressiveness as a Value," 161.

111 See "Fêtes ou la vertu de la licence," in Lambert, *Les Cahiers de Chronos*, originally published in *Verve* no. 4 (Winter 1938). Caillois had already linked myth to ritual in "Le mythe et l'homme," in *Recherches philosophiques*.

112 Bataille introduced a prescriptive element in his analysis by recommending that a sorcerer's apprentice play the role of inventing mythology, although he did not specify how

inspired by ritual and, at the same time, inspires the ritual action undertaken by a group during a process of self-recognition, a process often violently and excessively staged in sacrileges and sacrifices at the time of
festivals.[113]

For both Bataille and Caillois, excess was foundational to festivals, and
they linked excess to the critical phase of social renewal. While order,
measure, and rule lose their force over time because they only conserve,
disorder is necessary for achieving a new order. "The destiny of licen-
tiousness thus appears as the fecundation of the world," a return to the
primordial chaos, Caillois wrote.[114] Excess being a sine qua non of festivals in Caillois's model, and festivals being the sine qua non of society's
existence, waste, paroxysms, and destruction provided periodic infu-
sions of energy to healthy historical formations. "Everything that is not
consumed rots away," Caillois dramatically asserted.[115] Or, in Bataille's
lexicon, only violence can reactivate the social tragedy. How this mechanism would work concretely in advanced societies remained a central
problem for Caillois and, more generally, for the Collège in their search
for the sacred's reincarnations. Caillois's intuition of the socio-political
dimensions of ecstasy, however, even if underdeveloped, demonstrated
his attunement to the historical moment dominated by dictatorships
that relied on emotional participation. The crucial issue for the Collège
then became whether it would be able to move from an anthropological-
theoretical level to the practical question of re-enacting the sacred and
promoting festivals in 1930s Western societies. Within this context, after
a first year of general theoretical assessments on sacred sociology, the
second cycle of the Collège's lectures focused on specific historical phenomena and general manifestations of the sacred that could speak to the
issues facing contemporary reality. Against this background the Collège
was truly challenged to confront the political dilemmas implicit in its
sacred sociology.

such invention would escape the traps of fiction. Bataille recognized that "such projects are
vague," in Hollier, *The College of Sociology*, 23. See Kojève's critique of this position and
Hollier's comments, in Hollier, *The College of Sociology*, 85–93. Bataille developed his notion
of "unemployed negativity" in response to Kojève's critique.

113 See note 1 at the beginning of chapter 4 of *L'Homme et le sacré*, 123.

114 Caillois, "Fêtes ou la virtue de la licence," in Lambert, *Les Cahiers de Chronos*, 103.

115 Caillois, *L'Homme et le sacré*, 178; *Man and the Sacred*, 138.

6

Politics at the Collège

WITH THE LECTURES ON SACRED SOCIOLOGY, animal societies, and the relation between attraction and repulsion, Bataille and Caillois had laid the foundations of the Collège's theoretical framework. Bataille discussed the scientific approach of sacred sociology and endorsed Durkheim's notion of society as a sui generis construct.[1] Caillois, in his analysis of animal societies, illuminated the dynamics of social interattraction, easing the way to Bataille's presentation of the ambiguity of the sacred and the social consequentiality of horror.[2] In addition to these themes, the lectures of the Collège's first cycle considered the overall communifying movement of society and estimated that its intensity had substantially decreased in the contemporary world due to the decline of such sacred centres as the church, the monarchy, and the nobility. Bataille warned in his summarizing lecture of 2 April 1938 that the three political formations corresponding to Bolshevism, fascism, and Nazism had reawakened passions and agitation only to reabsorb them into functional movements. Secret societies and the brotherly bonds that facilitated the renewal of turbulence through transgressive acts, particularly on the occasion of festivals, were the only apparent solution to degenerated existence, Bataille and Caillois concluded.

1 In the 2 April 1938 lecture, and in the wake of Durkheim, Bataille restated the importance of considering society as more than the sum of its individual components. He proposed his own view of society as a "field of forces" traversing individuals in spite of their will. In the first part of the lecture, he spent a considerable amount of time on this issue, which would suggest that he perceived a strong resistance among the Collège's audience. Bataille indeed signaled the prevailing obstinacy in considering social existence from the individual point of view. At the same time, he rejected a social analysis based on "the man among thousands" (*l'homme entre mille*). See Bataille, *La sociologie sacrée du monde contemporain*, 18, 23.

2 The revolving valence of the sacred was also affirmed by Leiris in his lecture on "The Sacred in Everyday Life." At the time, the philosopher Jean Wahl characterized this lecture as momentous in its influence on the audience wishing to support the Collège's project.

Fundamentally in agreement on the role of secret societies, Bataille and Caillois nevertheless differed significantly on the issue of their potential. Bataille acknowledged that the topic was not his competency, and his comments on the "Brotherhoods" lecture simply pushed forward his existential notion of community. He appeared unable or even unwilling to propose concrete models or plans for action. Even though he had originally conceived the Collège as a corrective and an addendum to the more existentially based Acéphale, he seemed to have distanced himself from practical concerns. Caillois's adherence to activism, in contrast, emerged as much more engaged and lasting. One then wonders if the virulence and will to power invoked in the "Introduction" to the Collège were more in line with Caillois's intentions than Bataille's, since we know that the latter's existential drifting was the cause of the Collège's final split.[3]

Caillois's active pursuit of a model of social regeneration has generally attracted little discussion compared to that paid to Bataille. My examination of the Collège's relationship to politics in this chapter, in contrast, draws heavily on Caillois's works. Through the prism of his writing activities at the end of the 1930s and into the 1940s, I believe we are better able to fathom how the Collège attempted to reawaken the sacred. We are also able to sharpen the distinction between Caillois and Bataille and reconsider the multivocality of the Collège de sociologie, becoming more aware of the Collège's difficult, tortuous path.

The chapter begins by contextualizing the Collège's second cycle of lectures within contemporary events in Europe and revisits the themes explored by the Collège's speakers from the end of 1938 to July 1939, the date when the Collège came to an end. I focus on the issue of democracy as it was addressed in particular by Bataille. I then probe the question of enacting the sacred that had motivated the foundation of the study group in the first place and that continued to linger even when not explicitly tackled. The chapter discusses the problem of "spiritual power" and highlights the Collège's political liabilities; it also sows the seeds for an interpretation of the Collège that takes ambiguity as the inevitable price to be paid when rethinking the political in a non-functionalist way.

ESCHEWING THE POLITICAL

In late September 1938, France, Great Britain, and Italy signed a pact with Hitler that allowed Nazi Germany to annex Czechoslovakia's Sudetenland. The Munich Agreement, reached in the aftermath of an

---

3 See Bataille's last lecture "The College of Sociology" and his correspondence with Caillois and Leiris, in Hollier, *Le Collège de sociologie.*

uncertain and tense period of international crisis, marked Germany's return as equal partner to the negotiating table after the end of the First World War and the Treaty of Versailles. As peace appeared to be restored in Europe and the danger of war faded, the accords seemed to assuage mounting fears of conflict, especially in France and Great Britain. In the general climate of hope and relief that settled in the West, a few days after the Munich Agreement, and in the name of the Collège, Caillois wrote a document condemning the pact. The "Declaration of the College of Sociology on the International Crisis" was published in the November 1938 issue of the *Nouvelle Revue Française* and later in *Esprit, Volontés,* and *La Flèche.* Having upheld and defended, along with fellow Surrealists, the plea for peace against colonial excursions in the early 1930s, Caillois was now evaluating the Munich Agreement as a symptom of a great crisis lying at the centre of human existence. For Caillois, this crisis went beyond the current political situation, even though his analysis focused on the critical circumstances that posited non-fascist Europe against the expansionist will of Hitler. The "Declaration" was less interested in examining the development of the crisis and its final resolution than in accounting for the "collective psychological reactions" the events had provoked.[4] More specifically, Caillois was disheartened by democracies' "fear" of war. Such timidity demonstrated democracies' inability to evaluate realistically the trajectory of a nation, such as Germany, that grounded its politics in aggression. To the Collège, it was clear that one could not escape war by negating it. The general exhalation at the apparently diverted danger was merely "a sign of man's *devirilization*," Caillois wrote, the signal of a lost strength.[5] It presaged the deadly Arctic air evoked by "The Winter Wind" – a cold current that swept away men who, as Bataille echoed in "The Sorcerer's Apprentice," were "deprived by fear of the need to be a man" and were thus unable to confront human destiny.[6]

For both Bataille and Caillois, "devirilization" had become a code word for the loss of power in contemporary societies – what they perceived as the fear and avoidance of risk. In "The Sorcerer's Apprentice," Bataille had argued against the modern emergence of the "functional man" and its role as replacement for the whole person. As existence appeared to have "ceased to be *existence*," Bataille advocated the need to be seduced by the image of destiny – anything that sparked hope and fear

4 See "Declaration," in Hollier, *The College of Sociology,* 44. See also Caillois's letter to Jean Paulhan of 16 September and 7 and 21 October 1939, in Cahiers Jean Paulhan 6, *Correspondance Jean Paulhan-Roger Caillois.*
5 Caillois, "Declaration," in *The College of Sociology,* 45 (italicized in the original).
6 Bataille, "The Sorcerer's Apprentice," in *The College of Sociology,* 14.

and that could not be measured in terms of usefulness.[7] Virility meant abandonment, gamble, and chance, a readiness to be consumed. If virility declined, so did the unfolding of human destiny.[8] In a similar vein, Caillois's post-Munich analysis of devirilization defined as "*deprived of destiny*" those who could not face the possibility of death and who refused the thought of battles and war.[9] These modern characters were the result of a society that had lost any bond and that rested, instead, on individualism and the relaxation of ties.[10] Caillois thus took the historical events of the time as opportunities to reaffirm the Collège's analysis of an emptied social. And he confirmed the Collège's will to be more than a research group: the Collège constituted "a center of energy" whose goal included recomposing modes of collective existence.[11] On this point Bataille and Caillois agreed. The Collège was not interested in pursuing pure political action; it considered politics within a more comprehensive attempt at reconstructing existence through the cultivation of total bonds. Politics was the side effect of the Collège's search for community, not its motivating factor.

In spite of this programmatic position, the Collège's will to reconfigure the modern sacred necessarily implied an analysis of the political forms that best suited the development and establishment of communal bonds. Such an analysis became central to the preparatory work underlying the activist portion of the Collège's program; it represented a basic building block for sketching the contours of the moral community the Collège intended to achieve.[12] Not surprisingly, among the topics covered by the Collège's second cycle of lectures one finds democracy, Hitlerism, revolution, political associations, and monarchy. Delivered by invited guests for the most part, the talks addressed the Collège's thematic concerns with

7 Ibid., 17 (italicized in the original).

8 Bataille cited the example of a man seduced by a naked body – a reference that begs for an analysis of the Collège's masculinist point of view. On virility and its link to tragic destiny, see also the seventeen-point program Bataille redacted for Acéphale at the meeting of 29 September 1938, in Bataille, *L'Apprenti sorcier*, 463–70.

9 Caillois, "Declaration," in Hollier, *The College of Sociology*, 45 (italicized in the original).

10 As mentioned, such diagnosis had also emerged at Acéphale in September 1938. Acéphale's program of 29 September proclaimed the value of elective communities against communities of blood, territory, or interest; stated the religious power of the tragic gift of oneself against the power of the military; exalted "chance" and also "limitless laughter" as elements that explained an absurd universe; and reiterated the "love of destiny" and of "joy facing death." See Bataille, *L'Apprenti sorcier*, 463–70.

11 "Declaration," in Bataille, *The College of Sociology*, 46.

12 See "Notes de Michel Leiris," in Hollier, *Le Collège de Sociologie*, especially 814.

particular emphasis on the subject of myths.[13] By weaving these themes into historically rooted events and characters, the discussions offered different perspectives from which to evaluate the sacred's incarnations and its simulacra within the context of contemporary Europe.

On 29 November 1938, Denis de Rougemont, who was very close to the Collège's positions, lectured on the logic of myth by recounting the parallel evolution of war and love.[14] According to de Rougemont, a link united the fighting and sexual instincts in the West, and he located the origins of this link in the Middle Ages' code of chivalry. The code of courtesy implemented by medieval society in order to ritualize love and tame passion reached out to affect the rules of battle too, as the art of love gave birth to the art of war. Thus tournaments contained the bloody and brute reality of conflicts within the symbolic framework of regulated ceremonial. More generally, battles followed a quasi sacred protocol and military life was conceived in ascetic terms.

Eventually, de Rougemont claimed, the passion that characterized both love and war diminished, and the ardent knights of the Middle Ages turned into disciplined troops. Technological innovations in the military and the introduction of firearms eliminated passion and turned death into a detached, unemotional outcome, while love also became an affair of interest, a convention. Formalized and regulated, the sacredness of knighthood gave way to the "profane" classic modes of war guided by diplomacy and economic interests. At that point, societies tried to resurrect the myth of passion and to give military power new means of ritual expression. By the end of the nineteenth century, however, at the apex of bourgeois culture, love became sentimental and war commercial. In 1914, the disregard for myth proved to have disastrous consequences as war turned into a "total" act of destruction and annihilation. Disconnected from humanity and instinct and deprived of rules, war "turns against the passion from which it originated" – a new phenomenon in the history of the world.[15] Now become total, war can no longer be compared to love; it is instead a sadistic crime that does not express

13   The notice that announced the first lectures of the 1937–38 year at the Collège listed mythology as the topic to be covered over the months of May and June. From what is known, these lectures did not take place, but one can surmise that the topic was moved to 1938–39. Several of the lectures in the second cycle addressed the question of myths.

14   See "Arts d'aimer et arts militaires," in Hollier, *Le Collège de Sociologie*. The lecture is not in the English edition of *The College of Sociology*. De Rougemont was a personalist and, like Klossowski, was part of the group gathered around the personalist journal *Esprit*. For information on de Rougemont, see Hollier, *Le Collège de Sociologie*.

15   Ibid., 439.

normal sexual instinct and rather represents a perversion of passion, a castration complex. In its turn, sex is no longer the major locus of passion. Consequently, passion needs a new place in which to unleash, which it finds in politics. Mass politics in particular, described by de Rougemont as "the continuation of total war by other means," is able to transpose individual enthusiasm to the collective level and leads to the unconscious pursuit of war and death.[16] De Rougenont, however, warned that although death is the ultimate end of the total war, it has lost all meaning.[17] De Rougement exposed the false sovereignty of fascist regimes and accused Hitler's totalitarian state of replacing the myth of passion with its simulacrum. Hitler, in Bataille's lexicon, deprived death of its tragic dimensions and rationally exploited, through an abuse of power, the masses' starvation for passionate participation.

In a later lecture of 18 April 1939, and from a different standpoint, Hans Mayer also tackled the role of myth in Hitlerism by zeroing in on the issue of Hitler's popularity among the "masses," and particularly the middle classes.[18] Mayer considered it absolutely crucial to unpack this political phenomenon, and he criticized the failure of historical schools to do so when analyzing the origins of Hitler's power. Once we recognize that a political myth has been successful, he claimed, we need to decipher the attraction that its symbols and words exercise over those who subscribe to them. Convinced that National Socialism did not invent anything new in terms of myths, Mayer's historical analysis pointed to nationalism, anti-bourgeois sects, and secret orders as elements on which Hitler built his political agenda. Those sentiments and associations were present in early German nationalism and postwar Germany, and according to Mayer Hitler was able to reawaken and channel them to fit his political agenda.[19] Although Mayer focused his intervention on defining the conditions that led to an anti-bourgeois movement and the founding of National Socialism in the interwar years, his goal was to understand

16 Ibid., 442. Here de Rougemont followed Clausewitz's famous formula.

17 In "La menace de guerre," first published in *Acéphale* 5 (June 1939), Bataille wrote, "A man 'who lives' represents death as that which accomplishes life: he does not consider it a misfortune. In contrast, a man who does not have the strength to give his death a tonic value is like something 'dead.'" Bataille, *oc*, 1: 550.

18 Like Benjamin, Mayer, described by Weingrad as an "eclectic thinker," was affiliated with the Institute for Social Research (see Weingrad, "The College of Sociology and the Institute of Social Research," 154). His lecture supposedly took place instead of Benjamin's talk on fashion (but these facts remain uncertain). For his memories of Benjamin and the links between the Institute and the Collège, see Mayer, *Walter Benjamin*.

19 Mayer criticized the thesis of the eternal German as well as that of the centrality in National Socialism of Nordic, neo-pagan myths.

why people followed Hitler and believed in his words. Mayer's lecture thus furthered the Collège's program; through the identification of the fundamentals that made possible Hitler's success, National Socialism could be exhibited as a fake sovereignty. That knowledge would then assist in building a truly heterogeneous, sacred countermovement.[20]

Klossowski's lecture of 7 February 1939 on "The Marquis de Sade and the Revolution" evoked one instance of heterodoxy that emerged out of the 1789 revolutionary spirit. With an analysis reminiscent of Bataille's lecture of 2 April 1938, Klossowski focused on the processes of social decomposition and recomposition epitomized by the revolution and looked at de Sade as a tragic figure who took upon himself the crime of which the collectivity was guilty. More specifically, Klossowski claimed that the regicide from which the French republican regime originated assigned the republic a degree of criminality without which it could not live and that it could not expiate. By killing the king, God's representative, the republican government was destined to live in a state of permanent immorality. De Sade suggested that the republic should become aware of its evil foundations in order to avoid falling into the instinct of conservation. In Klossowski's reading, as Carolyn Dean astutely argues, de Sade's "willingness to 'pay all alone,' to act as the repository of human guilt, was the only viable means of asserting the claims of human existence in a world that turned human beings into things."[21]

The tragic existential perspective promoted by Klossowski confirmed the Collège's interest in enhancing the heterogeneous at a time that not only witnessed its demise but also its corruption. In the wake of the Munich Agreement and its manifest lack of "virility," all the speakers at the Collège engaged with the fate of myths in order to build the knowledge necessary to confront the crisis of democracy.[22] Only Bataille,

20 Bataille also gave a lecture that presumably addressed similar themes, but its text has not been found. Entitled "Hitler and the Teutonic Order," the lecture took place on 24 January 1939. See Hollier, *The College of Sociology* and *Le Collège de Sociologie* for comments on this unpublished lecture.

21 Dean, *The Self and Its Pleasures*, 174. Dean examines Klossowski's interpretation of de Sade through the reading of a number of essays written by him on the marquis. See also Klossowski, *Sade My Neighbor*.

22 Georges Duthuit also gave a lecture on "The Myth of the English Monarchy" on 20 June 1939. The text of the lecture has not been found, but presumably Duthuit, who was an art historian, drew from a recent visit to Paris by the British royals to build an analysis of the myth surrounding them, especially as documented in the popular press. On Duthuit and this lecture, see Hollier, *Le Collège de Sociologie*. Hollier notes that several lectures of the second cycle focused on myths as created by the press. He also indicates that Duthuit participated in the Society of Collective Psychology with a talk on art's representation of death

however, directly addressed the structure of democracy in relation to the crisis of September 1938.

The question of democracy was evidently central to the political debates of the 1930s. Vilified by most of the avant-garde, including the groups with whom Bataille and Caillois had been involved before the Collège, democracy nonetheless appeared as a benign evil when compared to the widespread postwar fascism cum militarism. And yet, democracies had failed to understand or face up to fascism and Nazism. Could democracy be salvaged? And did democracies have any redeeming features? These questions loomed in the background of the Collège's ruminations but resurfaced with particular urgency in the aftermath of the Munich Agreement. For the Collège, that pact and the events leading to it had exposed democracy's lack of a spiritual backbone, its lack of soul. The rejoicing of French citizens when peace was proclaimed, even as soldiers were ready to reach the border, indicated their total identification with the government, whether it was on the left or right. People could switch their support from one extreme to the other, from war to peace, without thinking twice. In Bataille's mind, there was something extremely disturbing in this picture of passivity, as he evaluated it in the evening lecture of 13 December 1938 on "The Structure of Democracies."[23] Such passivity confirmed his belief that the integrity of national territory was democracies' only sacred domain. Once France was not threatened geographically, it could make deals with Hitler with no hesitation, no scruples, and no regrets.[24] Was this all democracies would do and could do?

According to Bertrand d'Astorg's report on the lecture, Bataille was pessimistic and deemed democracy's crisis deadly. After all, Bataille had always opposed elective communities to de facto communities based on the notion of fatherland. Julien Benda, in the audience that evening, conceded to Bataille that what one needed was an act of faith. For Benda, however, reason constituted the object of democracy's act of faith. Unpersuaded by Benda's argument, Bataille claimed that there are moments "in which man, even when he no longer knows if there are essential values involved in the struggle, must accept being on intimate terms with suffering and death, without wishing to know in advance what reality

---

and wrote about the Collège for some American publications that introduced the Collège to the American public in the early 1940s.

23 See Hollier, *The College of Sociology*. In the announcement that was published by the *Nouvelle Revue Française*, the title of the lecture appeared as "La Structure des démocraties et septembre 1938." See Hollier, *Le Collège de Sociologie*, 354.

24 See also Caillois's critique of the United States in the "Declaration," in Hollier, *The College of Sociology*.

will spring from it."[25] D'Astorg reported that when communicating these thoughts Bataille seemed to become "lyrical."[26] Other testimonials spoke of a sense of solemnity in Bataille's intervention. As Pierre Prévost described it, Bataille "alone, sitting behind a small table, had the face of the important days … the face of drama, even of tragedy."[27] Bataille suggested that the rational cost-gain argument (avoid the deaths caused by war) in favour of the pact with Hitler did not foresee the eventuality of a bigger loss, of falling, that is, under the grip of Nazism. France's and Great Britain's short-sighted decision to appease Hitler on the basis of a rational calculation would instead cost democracy its soul. This was another reason to indict democracy and its degenerative evolution.[28] Democracy's opportunism was indefensible. From this point of view, the Collège could not and did not wish to support democracy.

Bataille's lecture and Caillois's "Declaration" were not strictly speaking political. They did not propose an alternative form of government or regime, at least not in conventional terms. At the end of the "Declaration," Caillois advocated "the awareness of the *absolute lie* of current political forms and the necessity for reconstructing on this assumption a collective mode of existence that takes no geographical or social limitation into account and that allows one to behave oneself when death threatens."[29] The Collège mistrusted politics as fundamentally "deceptive";[30] power always came at the expense of the overall communifying movement. Both Bataille and Caillois wished to distance themselves from politics.[31]

---

25 See d'Astorg's report in Hollier, *The College of Sociology*, 195. The report was published in *Les Nouvelles Lettres*, no. 4 (December 1938).

26 "The sociologist gave way to the lyric, a human sound arose." Hollier, *The College of Sociology*, 194–5.

27 Prévost, *Rencontre Georges Bataille*, 54. Prévost also wrote that it was difficult to describe what that face looked like to those who did not know Bataille.

28 Several intellectual groups in the 1930s critiqued democracy's failure to fulfill its promise. Prévost presents the argument elaborated by L'Ordre Nouveau movement. Ibid. See also Loubet del Bayle, *Les non-conformistes des années trente*.

29 "Declaration," in Hollier, *The College of Sociology*, 46.

30 See especially the lecture on "Power," in Hollier, *The College of Sociology*, 133.

31 We know that, following the first "Declaration," Bataille was planning to present a brief personal exposé at the Collège's meeting of 19 March 1939 entitled "The new defenestration of Prague." The lecture would present the Collège as "an introduction to a new practice" whose task was first of all to "make people understand that what they are now amounts to no more than nothing." Bataille would then speak about two political principles of sacred sociology that emphasized the need for an organization around which integral existence could be recomposed. He planned to conclude his lecture by invoking the critical importance of making space for the sacred as the only element endowed with "the power to order life" (*ce qui seul possède la puissance d'ordonner la vie*). See Bataille, *Lettres à Roger Caillois*, 100.

In so doing, however, I claim, they drew an artificial line between their researches on the social, on the one hand, and their investigations into the political, on the other, even as they were engaged by the tragic course of world events. Bataille and Caillois manifested a curious tendency to deny the interconnectedness of fields within the social structure. Thus, besides implicitly countering Mauss's definition of total social fact – his innovative theory of sociology's comprehensive task – they also undermined the Collège's own implicit intuition of the wider net that the political casts through its contagious spreading.[32] This outcome occurred despite the fact that the Maussian concept of totality was at the core of the Collège's sociological identity.[33]

The notion of total social fact pointed to the interpenetration of physical, social, and psychological factors, as well as political and aesthetic ones, and had allowed Mauss to overcome a mechanical conception of the duality between the social and the individual. To be sure, Mauss had not fully adopted the notion, and like the Collège seemed blind to the expansive role of the political. Thus, he did not go beyond the conventional understanding of politics as electoral maneuvering and party politicking even though contemporary examples provided ample evidence to the contrary. Fascism, and in many ways Bolshevism, had revolutionized the approach to governing by pushing the limits of political intervention deep into the social through the institution of totalitarian forms of government. But even the Durkheimians' study of primitive societies had brought to the fore the overlapping of "political" and "religious" elements in societies characterized by "mechanical solidarity"; they had indeed disclosed the porous nature of institutional divisions when dealing with simple forms of social organizations. And yet it took an escalation of attacks on Durkheim's doctrine in the 1930s before Mauss finally recognized his own shortsightedness.[34] In a 1932 article on "Scholarly

32 In an Acéphale document of October 1938, for example, Bataille listed among the domains of knowledge of interest to Acéphale "sacred sociology or sacred politics," which he defined as "the study of the sacred considered as determining the social structure." See Bataille, *L'Apprenti sorcier*, 507.

33 In the letter he sent to Bataille to announce his departure from the Collège in July 1939, for example, Leiris reproached the organization for contradicting Mauss's notion of total phenomenon. See Hollier, *The College of Sociology*, 355. Bataille replied that for him the total phenomenon was an "essential notion." See "Georges Bataille à Michel Leiris," letter of 5 July 1939, in Hollier, *Le Collège de sociologie*, 829. On Bataille and Mauss see also Jean-Christophe Marcel, "Bataille et Mauss: un dialogue de sourds?"

34 In 1931, Marion Mitchell wrote an article claiming that Durkheim, with his identification between group and society, foreshadowed the nationalism of the Action française and even of Italian fascism. See "Emile Durkheim and the Philosophy of Nationalism." In 1936, the French philosopher Alexandre Koyré accused Durkheimian sociology of

Forerunners of Fascism," in which he took Durkheim to task for having "served to prepare the soil for fascism," the Dutch scholar Svend Ranulf published extracts from his correspondence with Mauss on the merits of Durkheim's work.[35] Ranulf accused Durkheim, as well as Comte and Tönnies, of glorifying *Gemeinschaft* and deprecating *Gesellschaft*, an indulgence he considered equivalent to a piece of fascist propaganda unsupported by genuine science. In particular, Ranulf indicted Durkheim's critique of individualism and his idealization of the past. In a first letter of 6 November 1936, Mauss conceded to Ranulf, "That great modern societies, and ones that had anyway emerged from the Middle Ages, could be subject to suggestion as Australians are by their dances, and made to turn around like children in a ring, is something we had not really foreseen. We did not put our minds to this return to primitivism." In a second letter of 8 May 1939, he added, "I think all this is a real tragedy for us, an unwelcome verification of the things we had been suggesting and the proof that we should perhaps have expected this verification in the bad rather than the good."[36] Mauss insisted that this second passage be added to the publication of the first, since he probably realized that his characterization of the present historical events as a "return to primitivism" sounded inadequate, if not simplistic. His second statement more directly addressed the link between collective effervescence and the solidification of group ties. It also alluded to the potential risk of a totalitarian turn, at least within modern societies.

One could argue that questions of authority and influence among archaic societies should have alerted Mauss to the intermingling of power and culture. That this link remained instead invisible to Mauss, or undertheorized, seems less surprising, though not more justified, when one considers the general trend, especially in 1930s France, to evaluate Durkheim's sociology as detached from contemporary political reality. Raymond Aron, who in the 1930s introduced German social theory in

totalitarian tendencies for having emphasized the value of social cohesion. See his book review "La sociologie française contemporaine" published in the *Zeitschrift*, the journal of the Frankfurt school's critical theorists (at the time, the *Zeitschrift* was published in Paris by the Librairie Félix Alcan). In a 1941 book, William McGovern enlisted Durkheim among those he considered irrationalists and etatists because of Durkheim's emphasis on collective conscience. See *From Luther to Hitler*.

35 See Ranulf, "Scholarly Forerunners of Fascism," 33.

36 Ibid., 32 (originally cited in French, my translation). For the texts of the letters in English, see Mike Gane, *The Radical Sociology of Durkheim and Mauss*. Mayer wrote to Horkheimer that the Collège in particular had "persuaded me that a dialogue with Durkheimism is far from being something peripheral," and he referred to the "totalitarian tendencies" inherent in Durkheim's "new political and social religiosity." Cited in Weingrad, "The College of Sociology and the Institute of Social Research," 154.

France, remembers his enthusiasm and admiration for Weber's work, which, in contrast to Durkheim, he saw as applicable to the analysis of current social forms.[37] For Aron, French sociology lacked the theoretical tools needed to interpret the present historical time. Weber's approach to political sociology satisfied Aron's sociological hunger with notions such as charisma, power, state, and legitimacy.[38]

As discussed in chapter 1, the urge to build legitimacy for the new discipline had convinced Durkheim that immediate political concerns needed to be kept out of the nascent social science of sociology. Uncle and nephew put aside concrete analyses of present-day reality; they were discouraged from more fully considering the contemporary implications of their findings on primitive societies.[39] In his correspondence with Ranulf, Mauss acknowledged Durkheimian sociology's failure to address the relations between the sacred and politics and he testified to his and Durkheim's excessive reliance on the concept of the social for explaining reality. Despite Durkheim's attempts at overcoming dualisms and Mauss's own work on totality, the Durkheimians indeed created a monster-social, a looming, all-encompassing notion-force that functioned as the main engine of sociological explanation and the production of reality. In a circular manner, the social accounted for the social, at least as long as one dealt with the past as opposed to the present, the "there" as opposed to the "here," the "primitives" as opposed to the "civilized" – which was exactly what Durkheim and Mauss had done.[40]

Curiously, Mauss's apparent surprise at the consequences of the modern sacred was echoed by Caillois's later recollections of the Collège's activities. In a 1970 interview with Gilles Lapouge, Caillois declared, "The war had shown us just how inane the College of Sociology's endeavor had been. The dark forces we had dreamed of setting off had unleashed themselves entirely of their own accord, with results quite

37 See Aron, *Memoirs*, especially 43–7. Aron wrote, "Why was it that, in my contact with the Germans and particularly Max Weber, I was drawn to sociology, while Emile Durkheim had repelled me?" 43.

38 On this absence in Durkheim, see my discussion in chapter 1.

39 In his *Memoirs*, Aron wrote, "What a tragic irony – as Marcel Mauss himself recognized – that Durkheim's idea of the birth of religious faith in collective trance, in torchlight, was incarnated in Nuremberg, with thousands and thousands of young Germans adoring their own community and their Führer," 46.

40 This critique might sound unfair in view of Mauss's important contribution to the revitalization of sociology. My intention is, however, to indicate the theoretical assumptions and constraints that put limits on some of Mauss's claims.

different from what we had expected."[41] In 1945, talking about the pre-Nazi movements who relied on myths to change society, Caillois also ruminated that "the original dreams could hardly let one foresee the terrible historical irruption that such effervescence would ultimately bring about."[42] Mauss's and Caillois's disclosure, their recognition of being caught off-guard by the effects of different manifestations of the sacred, reveals the depth of their undertheorization of the political. This undertheorization led them to conceive of a social in excess, a notion captured by Caillois's neologism of *sursocialization*. In the specific case of Caillois, and also Bataille, the focus on community was tied to a denigration of democracy and a rejection of politics conceived in its more restricted meaning of administration, interests, governing, and maneuvering, and also to a dehistoricized anthropological notion of power.[43] That kind of politics, as Bataille put it, bored him "as much as the memory of bills when I fall asleep."[44] This was a "little" politics with no soul, profane through and through. It stood in opposition to a politics that, based on a tragic understanding of existence, led to a "community of heart" founded on mythology.

Bataille had been inspired by Nietzsche's idea of a grand politics. But in his interpretation of the philosopher's writings, he isolated the phenomenological experience of the political from the larger field of social relations in which the political is embedded. Similarly, the Collège rejected becoming a political organization, yet it vowed to pursue the study of mythology in view of founding a new sacred community. In this way, I would argue, the Collège unwittingly expanded the horizons of the political as it simultaneously precluded itself from trespassing on politics proper. This never-resolved conflict left its mark on the Collège's legacy and actually determined its end – Caillois accused Bataille of taking a "mystical" path. Bataille was now interested in the *liens du coeur* that unite groups, those "deep emotional bonds" of which he wrote to Caillois in a letter of 6 June 1939. In that letter, Bataille described the lecture he was going to deliver at the Collège that evening: "My exposé will begin from this principle: that society gravitates around some nuclei formed by deep emotional bonds – what I will represent as the principle itself of the

41 See "Interview with Gilles Lapouge," in Caillois, *The Edge of Surrealism*, 145.
42 See "Preamble to the Spirit of Sects," in *The Edge of Surrealism*, 210, or "Préambule pour l'esprit des sectes," in Caillois, *Approches de l'imaginaire*.
43 The same could be said for Durkheim and Mauss.
44 Letter to André Masson of 3 February 1942, in Bataille, *Choix de lettres*, 179.

Collège's activity."[45] By the time of this lecture, Bataille was ready to dis-claim any intention of seeking power, of swinging, that is, "from a will for knowledge to a will for power." As he went against Caillois's stated inten-tion in his "Introduction" to the Collège, the collaborative efforts be-tween Bataille and Caillois ended; the sacred pact that had linked them was ultimately broken.

Power Recanted

If one engages in a parallel reading of Acéphale and the Collège, Bataille's supposedly mystical turn is not hard to fathom, especially since the unscholarly status of Acéphale allowed him to express more personal reflections.[46] In the summer of 1938, Bataille identified Acéphale's es-sence, "against all politicians," in "the principle that *to exist, to be* only counts for us, that the primordial preoccupation with *action, doing* is for us the sign of an abdication."[47] Relying more and more on Nietzsche, Bataille sought a total renunciation of any teleological existence in fa-vour of impermanence. His opposition to Caillois's final call that the Collège take up the task of being a "spiritual power" was consistent with this line of thinking. Bataille's polemical exchange with Caillois on the question of "spiritual powers" indeed shows the growing distance be-tween them with regard to the Collège's role. During the last frantic days of the Collège's activities, Bataille wrote to Caillois and Leiris insisting on defining the Collège as an organization "posing" the question of spiri-tual power, a power that would provoke sacrifice and therefore the sa-cred. Bataille clearly communicated his resentment of Caillois's criticisms on this matter; for him, the Collège should not and could not pretend to be one such spiritual power.[48] Bataille was firmly opposed to a more authoritative role for the Collège.[49] Caillois, in contrast, had become

---

45   Ibid., 159. The lecture Bataille delivered that evening was entitled "Joy in the Face of Death," in Hollier, *The College of Sociology.*

46   For one interpretation of Bataille's thought in terms of continuity, see Suleiman, "Bataille in the Street."

47   Bataille, "Déclaration," in *L'Apprenti sorcier,* 446.

48   See the letters in Hollier, *Le Collège de Sociologie,* 819–39.

49   See his letter to Caillois of 13 November 1939, in Bataille, *Choix de letters,* 173–4, and Prévost's testimonial, in Prévost, *Rencontre Georges Bataille,* 70. See also Bataille, "La menace de guerre" in *OC,* vol. 1, where Bataille wrote, "If one intends to go to the limits of human destiny, it is impossible to remain alone. One needs to form a true Church, one needs to claim a 'spiritual power' and constitute a force capable of development and influence. In the present circumstances, such a Church should accept and even desire fighting as an af-firmation of its existence. But it should essentially relate fighting to its own interests, that is, to the condition for the 'fulfillment' of human possibilities" (550). In "La menace de

impatient with the Collège's principle of non-action, that is, with what he considered the group's frailty and caution.[50] A supporter of rigour, strength, and imperviousness, as opposed to Bataille's focus on wounds, openings, and bleeding, Caillois advocated mastery.[51] His idea of spiritual power emphasized orders and their leadership role, especially in a society characterized by the split between the temporal and the spiritual. To this end, Caillois strongly denounced the intellectuals' pretensions to absolute values. In place of a loose social formation of intellectuals, one needed a hierarchical organization whose members renounced enjoyment and personal freedom and formed a strong, close community.[52] These exceptional figures would work to promote values that were not abstract and eternal but rather historical and subject to change according to the needs of the times. Genuine clerics, Caillois concluded, "do not defend values; they create and supply them" in the manner of a Society of Jesus.[53] Caillois foresaw a church that relied on the unity of thought and action and spread its faith like a contagion, so as to extend its order to the outer world. The elective communities he had been theorizing all along at the Collège found their ultimate embodiment in

---

guerre," Bataille again provided a critical evaluation of fascism: "Fascism subordinates all values to struggle and work in a servile manner. The fate of the Church that we define would have to be linked to values that are neither military nor economic" (551).,

50 See Caillois's a posteriori lament in "Êtres de crépuscule" in *Le rocher de Sisyphe*, 160–1, where he wrote, "We were too delicate, too scholarly, too difficult … Then we had come too late, we were too few, our hearts were too weak." The essay is filled with terms that evoke weakness, sensitivity, and frailty as opposed to those Arctic qualities Caillois favoured. However, Caillois also reproached the crepuscular being for lacking passion and love, that is, "warm" sentiments. One might add that weakness was the problem Caillois identified with individualists in "The Winter Wind." It is believed that "Êtres de crépuscule" corresponded to the document "Examen de conscience" that Caillois sent to Bataille to be read at the last meeting of the Collège and which Bataille cited in his correspondence of July 1939 with Caillois and Leiris. See Bataille, *Choix de lettres* and *Lettres à Roger Caillois*.

51 See for example "The Winter Wind," in Hollier, *The College of Sociology*. In his last lecture at the Collège, Bataille proposed that "human beings are never united with each other except through tears or wounds," *The College of Sociology*, 338. On the difference between Bataille and Caillois in terms of the antinomy between heart and rigour, see Jean Wahl's 1936 comments about the journals *Acéphale* and *Inquisitions*, cited in Felgine, *Roger Caillois*, 134: "Caillois looks for rigor, Bataille appeals to the heart, enthusiasm, ecstasy, the earth, fire, bowels."

52 See "Sociologie du clerc," published in August 1939 by the *Nouvelle Revue Française*, translated into English as "Sociology of the Intellectual," in Caillois, *The Edge of Surrealism*.

53 Ibid., 199. One might add that the issue of activism had been a constant of Caillois's thought since the mid-thirties. In retrospect Caillois talked about "Pour une orthodoxie militante," published in *Inquisitions*, in the following way: "I was envisioning a form of revolutionary thought that would not be restricted to the intellectual sphere, but would open out onto real life." See "Interview with Gilles Lapouge," in Caillois, *The Edge of Surrealism*, 142.

Caillois's vision of a new intellectual order formed by church militants, a vision that he thought the Collège should enact.

In his 1970 interview with Lapouge, Caillois explicitly described the Collège as wanting "to develop a mode of thought that would strive to impose itself in the temporal world, as it was obvious that the spiritual dominated the temporal."[54] He also recognized, however, that he and Bataille differed on the use of the Collège's research. Bataille's preoccupations remained caught within the confines of the group's essence and dynamics, a self-reflective meditation of sorts.[55] Caillois was more pragmatic and prescriptive. The idea that a tightly knit community could ignite a spiritual power and supersede a society devoid of it remained a constant motif in Caillois's work years after the Collège's end. In 1943, his invocation of order took the shape of a "communion of the strong." Indifferent to earthly goods, this elite group would cultivate self-mastery and discipline with the goal of eventually placing itself outside the ruling society while ushering in a new order.[56] A spiritual power could only be generated by a spiritual group devoted to ideals, Caillois insisted.[57]

It is, then, all the more surprising that in 1945 Caillois recanted his faith in a closed order of exceptional individuals and denounced the Collège's enterprise along with Acéphale's rituals. Curiously, Caillois also obliterated his past differences with Bataille on the wisdom of assuming spiritual power. In "L'ésprit des sectes," he brought to light the dangerous path sects can entertain once they move away from their isolated, restricted role in order to conquer power.[58] In very bleak tones, Caillois depicted the degeneration of the sect's spirit and denounced the sect's abuses, repressive behaviour, and persecution of universal values. He concluded that it is impossible for a sect to ascend to power and lead a large number of people without betraying its central virtues. The tragic result of such transformation would be war, Caillois dismally proclaimed; the expansion of the sect to national levels would only bring about armed conflict.

Caillois's new position on the sect unquestionably entailed a reversal. This turnaround appears even odder considering that in the section of

54 Ibid., 143.

55 On Bataille's mystical path, see Jean Bruno, "Les techniques d'illumination chez Georges Bataille."

56 See Caillois, *La Communion des Forts*, which also contained "Sociology of the Intellectual." The book was first published in Mexico and re-edited in France with several chapters omitted out of fear of censorship.

57 Ibid., introduction.

58 "L'esprit des sectes" was published in Spanish in Argentina in 1945. It was later reprinted in French in *Instincts et société*. Caillois also published one initial section of the essay "La secte au pouvoir" in *France libre* 8, no. 43 (15 May 1944): 26–31.

the essay where he negatively described the sect Caillois discussed the same qualities and characteristics that were at the basis of his earlier support for the sect: morality, severity, asceticism. And whereas he had earlier asserted the need for the sect to assume power, now Caillois pessimistically discounted the sect's ability to avoid the trajectory of war. The living example of Nazism's rise to power obviously exerted a strong influence on Caillois's bleak analysis of the sect at this time.[59] Yet, the target of his sharp attack in the preamble to the essay turned out to be the Collège de sociologie and its supposed alter ego, Acéphale. Caillois had become adamantly critical and denied any redeeming feature to what he considered the Collège's "delusional" will to establish an order through Acéphale's ritual of a human sacrifice. Bataille's extremism was not congenial to Caillois, and yet it was Bataille who, contrary to Caillois, had opposed the Collège's ascent to spiritual power.[60]

Caillois's wish to distance himself from the Collège's experience may have distorted his memories, a distortion also due to his different understanding of social phenomena elaborated in the early 1940s after his break from Bataille. At that point, Caillois's rethinking seemed to undermine the theoretical foundations of the Collège. In his lectures on totalitarianism delivered in 1940, he eerily affirmed, "Totalitarian doctrines are based on instinct and the release of obscure forces that are rebelling against the intellect; we must praise lucidity and self-mastery."[61] To be sure, lucidity and self-mastery were qualities Caillois had always privileged in his 1930s writings. Nevertheless, the Collège's raison d'être had

59 Caillois had already elaborated a critique of Hitler and Nazism in some lectures he delivered in 1940 on "The Nature and Structure of Totalitarian Regimes" (see Caillois, *The Edge of Surrealism*) and "The Nature of Hitlerism," the latter published in *Sur* in October 1939 as *Naturaleza del hitlerismo*. At that time, however, he had not given up his idea of order. Benjamin evaluated Caillois's analysis of Hitlerism in quite critical terms. In a letter to Gretel Adorno of 17 January 1940, he wrote, "There is, by the way, a rather funny piece of work that just appeared in Argentina. It is a booklet published by [Roger] Caillois that is an indictment of nazism (sic) containing arguments gleaned from the world press, printed without the slightest changes or modifications. It was not necessary to travel to the farthest regions of the intelligible and terrestrial world to write this booklet." See Scholem and Adorno eds., *The Correspondence of Walter Benjamin*, 626. In 1938 Benjamin had also written a critical review of Caillois's essay "L'Aridité" in *Zeitschrift für Sozialforschung* under the pseudonym of J.E. Mabinn.

60 It might be hard to evaluate in a definite manner the consequences of Bataille's and Caillois's different ideas on spiritual power. Wahl, for example, considered Bataille's position more dangerous than Caillois's and Leiris's, at least "for the mind," (cited by Frank in her introduction to *The Edge of Surrealism*, 39). Wahl offered his reflections in response to a questionnaire Caillois sent him in 1944 on the topic of spiritual power.

61 See the lecture of 28 September 1940 on "The Future Order," in Caillois, *The Edge of Surrealism*, 231.

been its re-evaluation of instincts and emotions, those "deep strata" of modern collective life whose interplay with myths Caillois had singled out in his "Introduction" to the Collège. The Collège had highlighted the fundamentally psychological nature of the phenomena of attraction and repulsion at the heart of the sacred and had indicated the need to reconfigure political analysis on the basis of those new categories. In his review of Robert Lowie's work in December 1937, for instance, Caillois suggested drawing a link between the primitives' life and "the violence of contemporary political effervescence."[62] He also revealed that he had adhered to these principles when, the Collège ended, he acknowledged that "[t]he dark forces we had dreamed of setting off had unleashed themselves entirely of their own accord" or when he lamented the contemporary historical consequences of "effervescence."[63] One then wonders why Caillois recanted his past.

In the end, in Caillois's vision of social and political change the model of the lucid, self-mastered elite that would replace a weakened society far surpassed the sacred of excess and paroxysm. Sketched out in several writings, this order of disciplined individuals, who were aggressive and productive, strong and firm, found its apotheosis in "La Hiérarchie des êtres" published in *Les Volontaires* in April 1939. There, in a discussion of the similarities and differences between fascism and communism, Caillois again proposed his conception of an aristocracy of exceptional individuals whose superiority was based on their lucidity rather than any kind of predetermination, be it class, race, or fortune. This hierarchy of beings was destined to form an order, an elective community willing to "subjugate," by virtue of its superior qualities of command, fellow creatures who were unable to conduct themselves or lead. Unusually gifted, these special individuals were also characterized by a total disdain for earthly goods – a sort of asceticism, a chastity that actually proved their virility, not in the existential sense privileged by Bataille, however, nor as a sexual virility based on the temptation of the flesh. Their virility evoked a manly, sense-deprived will to power, the not uncommon fantasy at the time of a man unseduced by the woman-mass.[64] Indeed, in "La Hiérarchie des êtres," Caillois made strongly negative comments about the masses. In his schema, they constituted the opposite of the aristocratic group he

62 See his review of *Traité de sociologie primitive* and *Manuel d'anthropologie culturelle*, first published in *Les Cahiers du Sud* (December 1937), now in Lambert, *Les Cahiers de Chronos*, 65.

63 "Interview with Lapouge," and "Preamble," in Caillois, *The Edge of Surrealism*, 145, 210.

64 As in the case of Mussolini, one could add (see Falasca-Zamponi, *Fascist Spectacle*). See Caillois, "La Hiérarchie des Êtres."

deemed necessary to face modernity's crisis and democracy's inability to confront fascism.[65] Caillois contended that the "blinded" crowds were in the hands of the fascist dictatorship, a system of rule that, contrary to common interpretations, was not based on aristocratic conceptions but rather appealed to the idea of equality at the basis of democracy.[66] The similarity Caillois detected between democracy and fascism then helped him reaffirm his belief in aristocracy as the only real opposition to fascism, the only opposition to any idea of superiority based on biology or predestination.[67] Caillois also contrasted those who wanted to satisfy their senses with those who had the taste for domination. He believed that pursuing the pleasure of the flesh was a sign of the inferiority of the "masses," a mark of their nature as slaves.[68] Power, in contrast, was gendered but sexless.[69] It was deaestheticized, and by default suggestive, as will be discussed later, of an aestheticized politics that, having lost substance, became mere ornament.[70] What role could the sacred then play within this framework? Did the new order need the sacred to emerge and impose itself?

In "La Hiérarchie des êtres," Caillois did not even mention the sacred, although he expressed a certain disregard for legality. Caillois' conception of power as "severe" implicated a critique of law as the foundation of power. As he wrote in 1937, "it is almost like destroying [power] and certainly consuming it if one does not abuse it when necessary."[71] Power equated tragedy for it was irreducible and never innocent, and ought to be used implacably and with no guilt.[72] In *L'Homme et le sacré*, Caillois had

---

65 Caillois thought that fascism had been able to appropriate and surpass some of democracy's fundamental principles, but he lamented the inadequacy of analyses that examined this issue.

66 "La Hiérarchie des êtres." See also *La Communion des Forts*, introduction, 15–16, where Caillois wrote, "[I]f only interest guided these masses! The collective being, however, lacks both the will and the intelligence that some times allow the individual to control himself. The masses are elementary, blind, anonymous ... They don't even resemble beasts whose instinct at least guides them, they rather resemble inert matter."

67 "La Hiérarchie des êtres." Fascism, as Caillois rightly noted, shifts his conception of inequality onto the outside, on an "us versus them" mentality that finds its ultimate application in war.

68 Ibid., 324.

69 See Hollier's discussion of this issue in "Mimesis and Castration 1937," where he refers to the political as "non-sexual."

70 As discussed in the introduction, Benjamin seemed particularly aware of the Collège's risk of aestheticizing politics. See Klossowski, "Between Marx and Fourier" and "Lettre sur Walter Benjamin" and Agamben, "Bataille e il paradosso della sovranità."

71 See his book review of Léon Blum, in *Nouvelle Revue Française*, 675.

72 For his difference from Bataille on this point, see Hollier's comments, in Hollier, *The College of Sociology*, 126.

also argued that power belonged to the sacred with its absolute singularity, irreducible character, and ability to command obedience.[73] He never explained, however, what made power sacred or what guaranteed its longevity. *L'Homme et le sacré* suggested that, in the long run, order suffers from usury and needs to be regenerated through festivals, paroxysms, and excess. If, on the one hand, the sacred acts as the guarantor of taboos and rules, on the other hand, it ensures innovation and improvisation through expenditure and the violation of rules. Caillois's focus on "paroxysmal death" and "collective ecstasy" in his theory of festivals, however, did not inform his view of the aristocratic order. Granted, effervescence is not for the strong who rather rely on "severity." But what happens to the wild side of the sacred in the face of the aristocratic hierarchy Caillois envisaged? [74] How does the aristocratic order connect with the ordinary individual? And, more generally, can the world be regenerated without excess?

Caillois never resolved these dilemmas, and it is impossible to find any substantive discussion in his writings of the relationship between the sacred of respect and the sacred of expenditure within the aristocratic order. Even his most pointed analyses of closed communities (such as "The Winter Wind") do not confront the issue. He also left unexplored the problem of how the left and right sacred were reconciled in the modern constitution of a hierarchical group in charge of spiritual power. In the end, Caillois's ideal of Luciferian strength proved longer lasting than his reliance on an effervescent sacred.[75] Stripped of all "rêveries," dreams, and fantasies, the image of power that resulted from Caillois's discussions

---

73 Caillois, *L'Homme et le sacré*, 111.

74 See for example the essay "La sévérité," in Caillois, *La Communion des Forts*. In 1939, Caillois's accusations against Bataille's paroxystic tendencies began to escalate. See his correspondence with Paulhan of 16 September and 21 October 1939. On 16 September Caillois wrote with regard to the declaration that he was preparing on Hitler, "I will write to Bataille about this. When ready, I will send him as well as you the declaration. I hope he will understand that if he wants it to have an immediate effect, we will have to keep silent any paroxystic claim." On 21 October, Caillois again wrote to Paulhan about his doubts that Bataille will adhere to his declaration because "it does not contain ... the minimal paroxystic aspect." See Cahiers Jean Paulhan 6, *Correspondance Jean Paulhan-Roger Caillois*, 120, 122. It is not clear what Caillois meant by paroxystic. His late lamentation against the Collège and its paroxysm, as seen above, seemed to focus on Acéphale's proposal of a human sacrifice. On this question see "Preamble," in Caillois, *The Edge of Surrealism* and "Intervention surréaliste (Divergences et connivences)," in *Cases d'un échiquier*, first published in the *Nouvelle Nouvelle Revue Française* of April 1967 with the title "Divergences et complicités."

75 Caillois, however, also resurrected paroxysm in later years. See his 1964 preface to *Instincts et société*. Then in 1981 he wrote, "I nevertheless perceived the frailty of instincts and deliriums, in spite of their charm which made of me their fanatical partisan. I could

emerges in all its rigidity and coldness, like the heroes of "The Winter Wind" who survive the chilly Arctic climate.[76] These men emerge un-scathed by the natural "cleansing" that eliminates "the fragile, the sickly, and the birds," and they are instead "intoxicated with the glacial, tonic violence that beats their stiff and frozen hair against their faces."[77]

As unsettling as these lines appear, what is more disturbing about Caillois's vision of a disciplined secret community is his apparent un-awareness of the politically charged implications of such an ideal. Caillois did not realize that his vision of secret community could support both the rejection of democracy and a value-free appreciation of elective commu-nities like the Ku Klux Klan.[78] Unwilling to embrace an expanded notion of the political, Caillois failed to detect the consequences of his idealiza-tions. He also ignored the calculating, rational side of Nazism and its mass appeal, a failing of the Collège and others as well. Coeval political analyses tended to focus on the ecstatic relationship between masses and dictator while neglecting the Nazi movement's organizational strength.

Fascism, or the Return of the Aesthetic Repressed

Before we discuss the Collège's shortcomings, it is significant that an enterprise that so avowedly renounced politics provoked politically ori-ented reactions. After the *Nouvelle Revue Française* published Bataille's, Caillois's, and Leiris's signature pieces in 1938, one of the first commen-taries singled out Caillois's idea of superior men who conquered the world through self-mastery and aggressivity. For René Bertelé, this aristo-cratic revolution amounted to a "fascist revolution," and he warned about the danger of such seductive ideas. Bertelé concluded: "It should be reasonably brought to Roger Caillois's attention that he is running this risk."[79] Georges Sadoul offered a similar critique of Caillois's vision of the intellectual – a vision which, he deemed, closely resembled fascist ideas.[80] In 1939 even Jean Paulhan, whose *Nouvelle Revue Française*

---

see their fault." He defined his old aspirations as "whims, boredom and disgust ... of a privileged of culture." See "Notes pour un itinéraire de Roger Caillois," 166, 168.

76 See "Preamble," in *The Edge of Surrealism*, 209, where Caillois wrote that "it is in the nature of myth to seek realization and try to mold reality to its own image."

77 Caillois, "The Winter Wind," in *The College of Sociology*, 42.

78 See "Aggressiveness as a Value," in *The Edge of Surrealism*, 164, where Caillois cited the example of the Ku Klux Klan ("L'Aggressivité comme valeur," 58).

79 Hollier, *The College of Sociology*, 368.

80 Sadoul found Caillois's position "remarkably similar to the basic premises of the fas-cist adventurers, those Führers whose ambitions, by means of secret and paramilitary organizations, have been able to establish the domination of a brotherhood over the masses

published the writings of the Collège, suggested a congeniality of the Collège's ideas with Hitlerism, in particular the notion that exceptional individuals deserve power.[81] Previously, in a letter to Caillois of 5 August 1938 that reported on the reactions to the foundational writings of the Collège, Paulhan had described the reactions as questioning, "But why is the *nrf* becoming fascist?" In parenthesis he wrote as an explanation, "I think it's the tone of the *Winter Wind.*"[82]

The emphasis on heroes, the violent, and the strong was prominent in the early negative reception of the Collège. In contrast, one finds scarcely any reference to Bataille's idea of the sorcerer's apprentice.[83] Even in recent years when Bataille has become the main target of accusations of fascism, the critiques focus on the general political implications of the Collège. The Collège's illusion of renouncing politics by giving up revolution is particularly targeted. An excess of the social, a *sursocialization*, cannot sustain that illusion, the argument goes; even taking into account historical uncertainties, a new community cannot be born in a vacuum. This point, more than any other, makes Bataille and Caillois susceptible to the critique of historical abstraction: their anthropological approach leaves them vulnerable to attack (one need only think of Caillois's categories of analysis: severity, aridity, aggressivity, or his subscription to biologism).[84] Most often, critics indict the Collège because of the lack of a direct and consistent opposition to fascism. Equivocation, as Hollier convincingly argues, was at the heart of the Collège.[85] Whether this means that the Collège was fascist, however, is highly debatable.[86]

---

of the people, to the benefit of a great capital whose existence seems not even to be suspected by the professors of the College of Sociology." Ibid., 372.

81 See Cahiers Jean Paulhan 6, *Correspondance Jean Paulhan Roger Caillois,* letter to Caillois of 7 October 1939, 121. Paulhan was responding to a letter from Caillois, now in Argentina, who intended to write a declaration condemning Hitler as an "abscess" from which Europe needed to be "healed" (119). See footnote 74 above. Paulhan could not see how Caillois was going to justify this conclusion in view of the aforementioned congeniality between the Collège and Hitlerism.

82 Ibid., 87 (italicized in the original).

83 See "The Sorcerer's Apprentice," in Hollier, *The College of Sociology.* I am referring to outside reception of the essay. As for the Collège's inner circle, we know that Kojève did not appreciate Bataille's idea of reinstituting the sacred. For a more recent discussion of this topic, see Fourny, "Roger Caillois au Collège de Sociologie."

84 Adorno, for example, considered Caillois's essay on the praying mantis as displaying an anti-historical position. See Weingrad, "The College of Sociology and the Institute of Social Research."

85 See his "On Equivocation between Literature and Politics," in Hollier, *Absent without Leave.*

86 Carlo Ginzburg is the most prominent supporter of this thesis. See "Mythologie germanique et Nazisme: Sur un ancien livre de Georges Dumézil." For Dumézil's response, see

In the controversy over the Collège's fascist connotations, the Italian philosophers Giampiero Moretti and Rocco Ronchi resort to the aesthetic category of the sublime to describe the Collège's risky enterprise of attacking fascism from within, of assailing it, that is, with its own weapons as Bataille had advocated.[87] According to Moretti and Ronchi, ambiguity stems from the Collège's willingness to confront fascism on its own ground, to pursue, that is, the transformation of the sublime into a rule of conduct, a living myth for the elective community.[88] Because the sublime can be confused with the "institutionalized sublime" of fascism and, more generally, of totalitarian regimes, invoking the sublime and subordinating reason to it is always ambiguous [89] For Moretti and Ronchi, however, the Collège was responding to fascism's inadequate version of the sublime, its mystified use of it: fascism was a fake that needed to be unmasked in order to meet "authentically" the demand for sublimity. This position had after all been the trademark of Bataille's interpretation of fascism's nature and essence, albeit not of its historical causes. "The Psychological Structure" had indicated the failings of fascism's form of heterogeneity, its structural inability to achieve full-blown sovereignty. Following this lead, the Collège had conceived itself as an organism that combined knowledge of heterogeneity with "a will to power" so that, as Moretti and Ronchi put it, one would be able to "subtract the sublime from the hands of the fascists who reclaimed it and to offer it another real 'chance.'"[90] In Acéphale, this chance was made to depend on the Nietzschean figure of Dionysus, who supposedly offered an alternative model to the human power over the terrible (the sublime). In a reversal of roles, the terrible, through Dionysus, ruled over humans; paroxysms and excess provided an external measure of the inverted relationship, a sign of sovereign existence, tragedy.

One can readily foresee the risks that such an enterprise would involve. For the Collège, however, the counterpart to avoiding risk would be the absence of destiny, the devirilization Caillois had denounced in the "Declaration" on the Munich Agreement. Bataille in turn had repeatedly stated in his interventions at the Collège that he deemed sociology

---

"Science et politique: Réponse à Carlo Ginzburg." On different takes on the issue of fascism and the Collège, see Sichère, "Bataille et les fascistes"; and Richard Wolin, "Left Fascism: Georges Bataille and the German Ideology," in *The Seduction of Unreason*. See also Mayer's recollections of the Collège in "Georges Bataille et le fascisme: souvenirs et analyse."

87 Moretti and Ronchi, "L'ermeneutica del mito negli anni Trenta."

88 In this way, the Collège would surpass both the scientist, who sees only the ruins of myth, and the poet for whom myth is a private fantasy. Ibid., 86.

89 Ibid., 90.

90 Ibid., 92.

worthy of confronting "life's major decisions."[91] "CONFRONTATION WITH DESTINY is still, in my view, the essence of knowledge," he told the audience at the last lecture of the Collège on 4 July 1939. Once we accept "to be questioned by the sociological sphinx," we inevitably open up an "inexhaustible interrogation."[92] The Collège was aware of the risks involved in its enterprise, but for Bataille this only proved "how disconcertingly new is the direction necessary at the paradoxical moment of despair."[93] In an almost sacrificial mode, one could hazard, Bataille took upon himself the challenge of the historical times. And yet, in keeping with Moretti and Ronchi's discussion, it is evident that Bataille and Caillois revealed a complete lack of understanding of the sublime's aesthetic roots, its transformations, and reconfigurations.

Once the Collège was terminated, Bataille avoided these issues *tout court.* Although he was still hoping to resume meetings in the fall of 1939, the Collège was never resurrected in Paris and lived a kind of afterlife in Argentina, where Caillois had moved in the summer of 1939.[94] Bataille, who planned to write on the war, eventually gave up.[95] From the distant lands of South America, Caillois continued to "trust the path traced" by the Collège and actively engaged with the political events that were shattering Europe in the early 1940s.[96] At this time, Caillois published a chapter from *L'Homme et le sacré* in the *Nouvelle Revue Française* with the title "Théorie de la fête" (Theory of Festival). But this time, the chapter ended differently. In the book version, Caillois had concluded the section on "Expenditure and Paroxysm" with the reflection that the old opposition between festivals and work had been replaced by vacation and

91　Lecture on "Brotherhoods," in Hollier, *The College of Sociology,* 156.

92　Ibid., 334, 340.

93　Bataille, "The Sorcerer's Apprentice," in Hollier, *The College of Sociology,* 23.

94　There was an attempt by Marcel Moré to resume the Collège's activities, but it failed. See Bataille's letter to Caillois of 13 November 1939, in Bataille, *Lettres à Roger Caillois,* and Paulhan's letter of 13 April 1940 to Caillois, in Cahiers Jean Paulhan 6, *Correspondance Jean Paulhan-Roger Caillois,* 137. "But the Collège is far away," Paulhan also wrote to Caillois on Christmas Day 1941 (147). Writing to Paulhan from Argentina on 11 November 1939, Caillois talked about "a sort of section of the C[ollège de] S[ociologie] formed by the same people as in Paris: professors of philosophy, writers and disciples of Maritain" (125). See also Queneau's letter of 21 February 1940 to Moré and Moré's response of 8 March 1940 in Queneau, "Correspondance inédite (1934–1967)."

95　See Paulhan's letter to Caillois of 25 May 1940, in Cahiers Jean Paulhan 6, *Correspondance Jean Paulhan-Roger Caillois,* 139.

96　"Overall I feel inclined, and also in my thinking ... to trust the path traced by the C[ollège de] S[ociologie]." Letter to Paulhan of 16 December 1939, 129. Acéphale also ended in 1939. On 20 October 1939, Bataille sent a note to Acéphale's members stating, "I ask you to consider yourselves relieved of all bonds toward me. I will remain alone." Bataille, *L'Apprenti sorcier,* 563.

working days. Vacations had become the individualized response to the human need for breaking out of the ordinary. In the version published in the *Nouvelle Revue Française*, Caillois instead pronounced the end of festivals. If at first prosaic vacations looked like the moment that would suspend the fixed timetable of regulated work, they now corresponded to a truly empty space. They constituted an isolating experience rather than a communal and communifying activity. Vacations, one could add, did not display any element of the sacred; rather they were a profanation of sacred time. Relaxation had taken over paroxysm, and Caillois lamented, "Is a society with no festivals not a society condemned to death?"[97]

Caillois, as previously discussed, seemed to be caught in an internal struggle between dreaming of paroxysm and lucidly recognizing the modern disappearance of the sacred. In 1950, in yet another reversal, a new edition of *L'Homme et le sacré* claimed that, although dispersed and disguised, the sacred had not vacated the modern world. Even if festivals had ceased to constitute the mythical locus of society's rebirth, something else was taking their place. Festivals were being replaced by an activity that equally expressed the need to overcome profane limits, counteract the rules and obligations of everyday productivity, and make space for waste and expenditure. Wars came to represent for Caillois the substitute for festivals. A time of collective effervescence, wars brought social paroxysm to its extreme through a dialectical process of fascination and terror that opposed the destruction and violence of armed conflict to the peaceful time of prosperity. Caillois's analysis of war as the counterpart to festivals pursued a strict analogical comparison that shed light on the principal characteristics shared by the two paroxystic phenomena, including the intensity of their exuberance, fury, violence, and excess. Later expanded in "Le Vertige de la guerre," the analysis made the point that one should not consider festivals and wars as equivalents because their content resulted in joy and horror respectively.[98] Caillois nevertheless argued that both were total phenomena: they completely crushed the rule of economic rationality and unified the group in a common experience that marked the renewal of the social. War created a

97 See Hollier, *The College of Sociology*, 302 (Hollier presents the different versions of the book's ending). Here Caillois seems to rejoin his teacher Mauss who, in "Essai sur les variations saisonnières des sociétés Eskimos," in *Sociologie et anthropologie*, identified vacations with the summer months and the languishing of urban life. Mauss posited summer as a full time of festivals in rural environments.

98 "Le Vertige de la guerre," 153, in *Quatre essais de sociologie contemporaine*. In the Avant-propos to the book, Caillois claimed that the essays were studies of the sacred in modern societies. Caillois insisted on the symmetry between festivals and war. See also "De la fête à la guerre," which would become the conclusion to "Le vertige de la guerre."

religious state of mind; a sense of the sacred affected the warriors on the battlefields, the male community longing for renewal.[99]

But hadn't Bataille warned about the non-tragic phenomenology of death, which characterized the military, as opposed to the religious sacrifice of life?[100] And in any case, could the fraternity of the front extend to the society at large without reaffirming a community of soil, blood, and nationalism? In Caillois's version, the sacred risked becoming a personal epiphany within a social context, the temporary release of individual instincts and emotions with the goal of overcoming the "fatigue of life" (*fatigue de vivre*).[101] To be fair, Caillois eventually concluded that war is divisive in the modern realities characterized by the formation of national entities and centralized states.[102] But what implications did this conclusion involve? Was Caillois suggesting that the sacred as communion and communication, as access to the social, is no longer possible in modernity? And did he think that the Collège's intent was outrageous or merely useless?

By referring to war as a sign of the presence of the sacred Caillois seemed to fulfill the Collège's aims. At the same time, he appeared uninterested in converting that presence into a rekindling of the social. In addition, according to his reading, in order to be sacred a war needed to be total, all powerful, and steering toward a potlatch-like and possibly irreversible destruction. But hadn't Caillois criticized Bataille's extreme emphasis on excess? The contradictory answers to the questions that emerge from Caillois's work indicate that he never settled his relationship with the sacred. His understanding of and approach to the issue oscillated, at times turning the sacred into a generic notion, at other times making the sacred into something one simply needed to desire. In the end, the sacred remained an unresolved question for Caillois, a tragic conviction for Bataille. What can one then make of these inconclusive theories? The next chapter discusses the legacy of the Collège and assesses its central role in raising critical questions about the notion of the sacred within the context of a renewed attention to the issue of "community."

---

99 See "Guerre et sacré," in Caillois, *L'Homme et le sacré*, Appendix 2, 228.

100 It is true that Bataille in a letter to Caillois of 1 October 1945 also supported the "thesis" that festivals and wars are analogues. However, he depicted war as a "*subordinate* operation," at least in its modern economic version in which war "lost the *sovereign* character it had shared with festivals." See Bataille, *Lettres à Roger Caillois*, 133. Bataille's letter reported on his reading of a version of "Guerre et sacré," published by Caillois in Argentina in 1946. See note 31–1, 134, in *Lettres à Roger Caillois*.

101 Caillois, "Guerre et sacré," in *L'Homme et le sacré*, 233.

102 In "Guerre et démocratie," Caillois argued that the army had taken over the nation and the nation recouped its energy only in war.

7

Rethinking the Political

The Collège's search for modern configurations of the sacred took Bataille and Caillois along several exploratory paths in pursuit of the foundational elements that bind a community. Whether their critical reflections involved the dynamic movement of attraction and repulsion from which the social nucleus supposedly originates, or addressed the ambiguous nature of secret orders and brotherhoods, their goal was to define a yet-to-be-constituted sacred sociology. As they boldly confronted the unfinished nature of their disconcerting enterprise, however, Caillois and Bataille never lacked direction. On the contrary, their sociological activity relied on a firm point of reference: it operated within a specific historical framework at whose analytical centre stood the fascist phenomenon. The novel political formations instituted by Mussolini and Hitler were the catalysts for the Collège's reflections on modern societies and their dysfunctions. Indeed, the Collège studied the heterogeneous world of myths and rituals – the sacred – in order to counter fascism with its own weapons. As Bataille had argued, beginning with the 1933 "The Psychological Structure" and following with the programmatic papers issued by Contre-Attaque, fascism necessitated a response on both the theoretical and the practical-political levels. Thus, fascism occupied a central space in the Collège's discussions; it constituted a phantasmatic presence in the debates that engaged the attendees of the evening lectures.

The Collège's understanding of democracy unfolded within the parameters laid out by its approach to fascism. In this scenario, democracy came to play the Cinderella role. It constituted an inadequate, unfulfilling system of "empty structures," a weakened and lifeless social form – in

sum, a losing bet.[1] Evaluated against the requirements of the effervescent sacred unleashed by fascism, democracy appeared anemic at best, if
not sick to the bone. Furthermore, democracy did not seem able to overcome fascism's appeal. Bataille's lecture on 21 February 1939, "The
Commemoration of Carnival," which examined the democratic corpse,
advocated a parallel rebirth of carnivalesque effervescence to counteract
the deadly homogenization of time. This quasi-Bakhtinian vision of world
renewal was founded on a belief in the egalitarian impulse of masquerad-
ing and was conceived as helping to resuscitate a famished democratic
structure.[2] The text of the lecture on carnivalization, however, has never
been found. Nor do we have the text of the only lecture expressly on the
topic of democracy delivered by Bataille on 13 December 1938. By and
large, very little material was produced by the Collège on the question of
democracy itself. We know, however, that the general discussion following Bataille's talk of December 1938, and especially the exchange between Bataille and Benda, left the audience baffled and confused.[3]

Democracy remained seriously undertheorized by the Collège, although one must admit that navigating this notion in the 1930s made
for rough sailing, especially given the attraction that revolution and
communism still exercised over intellectuals on the Left. Benda, for example, embraced both communism (at least the Communist party) and
democracy and conceived them under the same umbrella of defence
against fascism. In an article of April 1939 published in *Les Volontaires*,
Benda declared that in spite of the fundamental differences separating
the two political formations, at least in terms of principles, "because
democrat, I give my support, in the present circumstances, to the

1 That is how Pierre Prévost defined democracies in "Le Collège de Sociologie" published in *La Flèche* of 26 May 1939, now in Hollier, *The College of Sociology*, 375; *Le Collège de
Sociologie*, 863. Prévost talked about "cadres vides."

2 On the lecture and the difficulty of evaluating its exact content, see Hollier's discussion in Hollier, *Le Collège de Sociologie*, 533–43. Hollier's reconstruction of the lecture is
based on Bataille's correspondence with Caillois and Paulhan and indicates that Bataille's
reference to Carnival picked up again the Collège's argument about the crucial role of
festivals and Dionysianism. Hollier also directs attention to a lecture that Caillois seems to
have presented at the Collège on that same night of 21 February 1939 (although doubts
remain whether the lecture took place). According to Caillois, the talk dealt with the "sociology of the executioner." In May 1939, Caillois published an essay on the same topic in
Sur. It addressed the death of France's official executioner and emphasized the ambiguous
nature of the sacred particularly as embodied by the official state killer.

3 See my discussion of "The Structure of Democracies" in chapter 5. See also Hollier,
Le Collège de Sociologie, 455–9; *The College of Sociology*, 194–5.

Communist party."[4] His reason for taking this position was fairly straightforward: only the French Communists were defending democratic values at the time; only they were upholding human rights (*droits de l'homme*). Confronted with a bourgeois class that he felt had betrayed those values for fifty years, Benda expressed no regret for supporting, as an intellectual and a democrat, the Communists. According to him, realism and idealism needed to be revisited and eventually conjoined; the analysis of principles should not be divorced from an examination of actual behaviour. Within this context, Benda recognized the limitations of the existing French democracy but did not wish to throw out the baby with the bath water and liquidate democracy *tout court.* Yet democracy's status emerged as ambiguous from his account, which makes the Collège's own ambiguities toward the democratic model less surprising, if not more palatable.

Outside the context of the Collège, Caillois's contribution to the question of how to overcome fascism – published along with Benda's article in the same 1939 issue of *Les Volontaires* – also generated a contradictory evaluation of democracy. For Caillois, the present situation could not be saved by democracy, and democracy had only two equally bleak options: it could choose to be eliminated by fascism through force or to imitate fascism to the point of becoming one with it.[5] The latter solution was not as outrageous as one might imagine, he claimed. The notion of equality of rights (a central tenet of democracy) was not extraneous to fascism's doctrine of individuals' equal subordination to the national community. The one true difference between democracy and fascism was that the former extended equality to all citizens of the world, while the latter reserved it to its nationals. Was that a small difference, one might ask. Caillois steered clear of the question. In so doing he failed to address the fundamental principles that define fascism and democracy.[6] Or,

---

4 See "Démocratie et communisme," 295. Benda apparently discarded the idea that democracy should have any other mystique than the mystique of free discussion. See Hollier's comments on Benda in Hollier, *Le Collège de Sociologie.*

5 "La Hiérarchie des Êtres." Caillois wondered "if democracy is not vis-à-vis fascism in a state of constitutional weakness, such that it can't effectively resist fascism without becoming like it." Hollier, *Le Collège de Sociologie,* 318.

6 Several attempts were made during the 1930s to single out democracy's similarities with other political formations in order to render the concept of democracy more flexible and less unique. Paulhan, for example, thought that the main vehicle for affirming democracy's egalitarianism was the idea of a democratic leader selected by chance and not on the basis of elections – an individual who was not distinguishable from others. Such a characteristic would also draw democracy closer to monarchism. See Paulhan, "La démocratie fait appel au premier venu," and Hollier's discussion of Paulhan in Hollier, *Le Collège de sociologie,* 538–41 in particular.

alternatively, those principles were meaningless to him since neither fascism nor democracy contemplated the necessity of an elective community, the naturally emerging hierarchical "order" Caillois cherished. Having to dispense with both fascism and democracy, Caillois held out one last hope: that communism would appropriate the anti-egalitarian ideal necessary to emerge as a victorious "order" over the incapacity of other governmental forms.[7]

Years later, Caillois regretted several of the positions he had taken during the time of the Collège, but in his post-1940 studies there are very few critical reflections addressing the inadequacies of his assessment of democracy as laid out in "La Hiérarchie des Êtres."[8] In fact, Caillois's evaluation of democracy in the early 1940s followed a no less ambiguous course and was characterized by vague invocations of "universal values" and "the Republic."[9] Caillois's distinction between classic democracies and the "kind of democracy that generates totalitarian regimes" added to the confusion by reinstating the ideal of an aristocratic order, albeit one based on "merits and rights" – a religious order deprived of "coercive power."[10] Posited against the model of totalitarian regimes, the prototype of democracy advocated by Caillois rejected illusions in the name of rational transparency.[11] Embedded within this utopian ideal of a moral authority

---

7 See the conclusions to Caillois, "La Hiérarchie des Êtres."

8 See also the first version of Caillois, "Athènes devant Philippe" published in *Sur* in May 1940. For a different version, see Caillois, *Le rocher de Sisyphe*.

9 See "The Nature and Structure of Totalitarian Regimes," in Caillois, *The Edge of Surrealism*, 220; "Défense de la République" originally published in *Sur*, now in Caillois, *Circostancielles*; and "Discussions of Sociological Topics: On 'Defense of the Republic,'" in *The Edge of Surrealism*. In these essays, Caillois still held onto the aristocratic values he had expressed in "La Hiérarchie des Êtres." In "Défense de la République," for example, he wrote that in democracy "there ordinarily reigns such a maniacal aversion for any superiority outside the establishment that mediocrity ends up being the master." He then went on to invoke "a regime destined to form and protect elites." See Caillois, *Circostancielles*, 19, 22. In "The Nature and Structure of Totalitarian Regimes," lecture 10, "The Future Order," Caillois stated that "democracy can fight totalitarian regimes only by imitating them." See Caillois, *The Edge of Surrealism*, 231, although in this instance Caillois invoked imitation in order to overcome fascism.

10 See "Défense de la République," in Caillois, *Circostancielles*, 21, and "Discussions of Sociological Topics," in Caillois, *The Edge of Surrealism*, 214. Caillois also stated, "I do not much like the word 'aristocracy.' It too readily evokes a social class, and one that is, moreover, defined by birth and fortune. I would rather speak of a hierarchy of merits and rights … It involves a kind of *Order*, in the religious sense of the word." "Discussions of Sociological Topics," in Caillois, *The Edge of Surrealism*, 214 (italicized in the original).

11 See "The Nature and Structure of Totalitarian Regimes," lecture 2, "The Concept of Leader," delivered on 30 August 1940, in which Caillois also proclaimed, "The modern

separated from actual power, democracy, in Caillois's impervious definition, came to replace communism and played the role of an undefined last hope, the only hope.[12]

The Collège did not emerge unscathed from its generally impoverished analysis of democracy. Although it had the brilliant intuition of placing democracy and totalitarianism in an analytical face to face, it always evaluated the former in terms of "lack" with reference to the fascist regimes. That assessment then resulted in the production of fuzzy notions such as "community," "identity," and "heterogeneity," which were supposed to remedy democracy's lack but were in truth divorced from a political syntax and pragmatics that could account for the fascist reality. How, for example, was one to reconcile the issues of unity and identity when considered in relation to totalitarianism's similar claims? What affinity did the heterogeneous have with the communal? Was the communal only a function of effervescence, or was effervescence the foremost condition of a community's existence? And if the sacred conjoins what is contradictory, if it seeks a non-identical unity, is its subscription to equivocation always value-free? The Collège left these questions unanswered, making it easier for its critics to direct against the group equally equivocal accusations of subscribing to fascism.

Beyond the Collège's lack of response, however, the question remains of its legacy on these issues. Has historical experience redefined the cruxes at the core of the Collège's ambiguity? In other words, is it possible to conceive of community in non-ambiguous terms and avoid political ambivalence? Jean-Luc Nancy, who has contextualized his work on community within Bataille's framework, has resorted to the term "inoperative" (or "unworkable") (*desoeuvrée*) to describe community.[13] He does so in order to remove any potential totalitarian implication from the notion of community since "community" runs the risk of evoking fusion – the communion of the identical – especially when taken as an essence.[14] Nancy has travelled a great distance in his efforts to formulate a philosophical language that avoids the pitfalls of using "community" when referring to an already structured whole, a totalized, self-contained body. His newly coined term "compearance," or "being in common," is intended to

---

nation is not a religious community that must obey the revelations of a visionary. Politics is not a matter of mystical ecstasies or of blind faith" (221).

12 "Even if it only had this advantage, democracy, at least, allows one to hope." See "Défense de la République," in Caillois, *Circostancielles*, 24.

13 Nancy, *The Inoperative Community*.

14 See Christopher Fynsk, "Foreword: Experiences of Finitude," in Nancy, *The Inoperative Community*, vii–xxxv.

counteract the notion of a common being and to indicate, in contrast, that community is "*what happens to us*"; it is a condition of society.[15] *Gesellschaft* – the illusion we hold of a community gone awry – was not built on the ruins of *Gemeinschaft,* Nancy claims. What we sense we might have lost is actually "constitutive of 'community' itself." [16] By distancing ourselves from the idea of communal fusion we can prevent the suicide of the community: immanence would only destroy a community.

The difficulty of articulating the complex nature of our "being in common" reveals and confirms the ambiguity inherent in enacting a communion that does not turn into a project, does not defeat its own work, and does not create a substance, be it nation, blood, or homeland.[17] When invoking community, a collective hypostasis seems almost inevitable, Nancy observes. And he concludes: "Perhaps we should not seek a word or a concept for it, but rather recognize in the thought of community a theoretical excess (or more precisely, an excess in relation to the theoretical) that would oblige us to adopt another *praxis* of discourse and community."[18]

The inability of language, and even of models, to think about and talk of community in ways that avoid creating the monster of an organic totality sheds light on the Collège's difficulty in overcoming the contradictions deriving from any reference to community. At the same time, the failure of language raises the question of how to rethink the political within a vision of the non-consensual nature of communities. Can one still invoke unity without falling prey to totalitarian temptations? Desperately looking for solutions to the supposed absence of community, the Collège hurried to embrace alternatives to democracy, deeming the latter unfit to fulfill our need for the sacred. Although its choices proved hasty at best, in the process of reimagining life in common the Collège put its finger on the wound that had been vexing modern political life in the West since the French Revolution, pointing to the conflicting elements at work in the creation of a social community. The Collège ultimately exposed the contradictory nature of the very notion of community.

15 Ibid., 11 (italicized in the original).
16 Ibid., 12.
17 For Nancy, who draws from Bataille, community is revealed through death. The death of others, more specifically, exposes me to my finitude. Finitude is what we ultimately share in a community. See especially *The Inoperative Community*, 26–8. The idea of community that Bataille particularly developed after the Collège in *L'Expérience intérieure* (*oc*, vol. 5) already appeared in his lectures at the Collège, especially "Joy in the Face of Death" and "The College of Sociology." See Hollier, *The College of Sociology. L'Expérience intérieure* is published in English as *Inner Experience.*
18 Nancy, *The Inoperative Community,* 25–6.

Twenty years after Bataille's and Caillois's experiment, the ambivalence the Collège revealed through its hailing of the sacred re-emerged as a topic of analysis in the work of Claude Lefort, who, in an original twist, posited ambiguity as a central feature and essence of democracy. Within Lefort's model, ambiguity does not toll democracy's death knell; rather it becomes the basis of a unity that is founded on division. Without directly referring to the Collège, yet addressing its main concern, Lefort has drawn to an end the intellectual parabola of the group via a recentring of the democratic project. Because Lefort's political philosophy articulates and analytically dissects the intricate question of the relation between democracy and totalitarianism, because that question was at the basis of the Collège's own theorizing on the sacred, and because the Collège found a very weak resolution to the question, an examination of Lefort's work constitutes an ideal place from which to re-evaluate the significance of the Collège's sociological intuitions and the implications of its interpretive failures. Reading Lefort against the Collège allows us to better estimate the value of the Collège's sociological vision. It also helps to assess the role that the Collège's research on the sacred and its ambiguity can play when reconsidering the question of democracy and rethinking the political in a post-totalitarian era.[19]

TOWARD A THEORY OF DEMOCRACY: CLAUDE LEFORT

In 1951, Lefort published an important essay critiquing Lévi-Strauss's interpretation of Mauss's *The Gift*.[20] A testimonial to Mauss's influence on generations of French intellectuals, Lefort's article praised Mauss's effort to explain a social phenomenon by linking it·to other different

---

19 Although my turn to Lefort is guided by theoretical arguments, it is important to mention that Lefort knew Bataille. According to Surya, Lefort was among the few friends who visited Bataille at Carpentras where Bataille had moved in 1949 during some of the most difficult years of his life. See Surya, *Georges Bataille*, 491. Among Bataille's papers at the Bibliothèque nationale, I was able to find only one postcard Lefort sent to Bataille but no major epistolary exchange. I am not aware of any of Lefort's writings in which he discussed Bataille. Lefort died in October 2010 and it is now left to his interpreters to locate unpublished references to Bataille, if any.

20 "L'échange et la lutte des hommes," first published in *Les Temps modernes*, now in *Les Formes de l'histoire*. Lefort's earlier writings revolved around Marxism and the experience of the Soviet Union (a topic that remained an essential point of reference for him). For a short history of Lefort's intellectual and political development up to 1975, see "An Interview with Claude Lefort," originally published in French in 1975. For a more recent and comprehensive discussion of Lefort see Flynn, *The Philosophy of Claude Lefort*.

phenomena in the same society.[21] In particular, Lefort applauded Mauss's idea of "total man" and his focus on the whole as a means through which to reach an understanding of lived experience.[22] When interpreted phenomenologically, Mauss's consideration of the whole contributed to the sociological knowledge of society's self-understanding; it constituted a valuable tool in the analysis of social relationships and, more precisely, of exchange. Mauss revealed to Lefort the advantages of examining social phenomena in their concrete unfolding rather than abstractly. In contrast, Lévi-Strauss's "mathematization" of the gift-giving cycles of reciprocity uncovered only a partial view of reality and left aside a more comprehensive evaluation of the gift's meaning and social role.[23]

Against Lévi-Strauss's interpretation, Lefort drew his own conclusions about the significance of the gift and the potlatch ceremony. Both are mechanisms through which people establish difference and identify similarity in a process of mutual recognition that allows a collectivity to form itself as an "I" out of a plurality of subjectivities ("We"), and in opposition to nature.[24] The gift, Lefort stated, is "the act par excellence through which man conquers his subjectivity."[25] It also reveals the nature of the social bond – the conditions that make a society possible.[26] Lefort's interpretation of *The Gift* highlighted the critical issue of society's institution and foundations and led him to sketch out his original theory of society's

21 Lefort confessed his surprise at the fact that scholars still identify sociology with Durkheim's "reductionist" tendencies in the face of Mauss's innovative approach. See "L'échange et la lutte des hommes," 15.

22 A student of Maurice Merleau-Ponty, Lefort had a phenomenological as well as an existentialist orientation.

23 In his critique of Lévi-Strauss, Lefort indicated the importance of signification over the symbolic. See "L'échange et la lutte des hommes," 16.

24 Lefort wrote that "the idea that the gift needs to be returned presupposes that the other is another me who *has* to act like me; and this gesture in its turn has to confirm to me the truth of my own gesture, that is, my subjectivity." Ibid., 27. In the préface to *Les Formes de l'histoire*, Lefort stated that *The Gift* "puts in question the identity of the Subject" (10). Karsenti detects here the influence of Hegel's *Phenomenology of the Spirit* through Kojève's reading. See Karsenti, *L'homme total*, 282n2.

25 "L'échange et la lutte des hommes," 25. On the limits of Lefort's psychological-existential approach to the social, see Poltier, *Claude Lefort*, especially chapter 1, "Une phénoménologie du social." According to Karsenti, *L'Homme total*, 97n3, Merleau-Ponty was the first to indicate the import of Mauss's work to phenomenologists.

26 For an excellent discussion of Lefort's interpretation of *The Gift*, see Dick Howard, "Introduction to Lefort." Lefort admired Kardiner's concept of base personality. See "L'idée de 'personnalité de base'" (first published in 1951) in Lefort, *Les Formes de l'histoire*. Lefort praised Kardiner as an interpreter of Mauss's legacy: "Mauss's call, which was also Marx's, to identify total man with total society was never better understood." *Les Formes de l'histoire*, 69.

essential characteristics. Because the gift exchange and the potlatch were particularly prominent in social nuclei where change is rare, however, Lefort did not merely address the question of how a society institutes itself and holds together. He also began to ask how a society enters the realm of history. The specific case of "primitive" social formations, those Hegel had deemed outside History because lacking a state, offered Lefort a chance to build his active conception of society's making. It also provided him with an opportunity to address his long-standing concern with the idea of a universal history.[27]

According to Lefort, a constant operation oversees the way a society relates to itself. There are, that is, particular ways in which a society "is" in time and these ways are revealed in the process through which members of a group appropriate the culture of the whole while affirming and confirming its teleology.[28] Even when stagnating, societies reveal human intention and work through culture: they show their singular "manner of being in time."[29] In this sense, societies are never static because social coexistence requires negotiating rules that express the kind of relations members of the group envisage as befitting them. It thus follows that lack of change (history) does not imply lack of "historicity" – the relations people have with their past and future. "Primitive" societies are "societies without history" because they purposefully fight against the threat of the new and struggle to maintain their form of organization, their unity. The "primitives'" historicity is revealed by the way they dynamically set up and perform relationships that articulate the rules of social coexistence. Those rules express the community's general experience of the world and its will to impede change and remain the same. "Primitive" societies' historicity, in sum, displays their becoming. Therefore, we should think of two types of historicity: one for stagnant societies and one for historical societies.[30] This division does not imply that there are differences of essence between the two: both express human intention and both are the result of a collective cultural elaboration that looks

27 I do not mean to imply that Hegel had no influence on Lefort's thought, especially if we consider Lefort's Marxist formation.

28 See "Société 'sans histoire' et historicité," in *Les Formes de l'histoire*, first published in 1952. Lefort calls this process "*self-creating culture*" (*culture culturante*) (35) (italicized in the original).

29 Ibid., 33. Lefort also wrote, "Stagnation is not a fact of nature, but a fact of coexistence; it is implicated in the way in which humans perceive themselves and relate to each other, that is, in collective praxis" (45).

30 Lefort was aware of the problems inherent in his choice of the term "stagnant." See Lefort, *Writing*, 212.

back at the past and ahead into the future.[31] For Lefort, the crucial issue
when studying different societies was not how to account for humanity's
stasis within a model of progress as linear. It was recognizing how and
when coexistence in stagnant societies turns into history.[32] What unchains a new formulation of human relations that ushers in the change?
And how is transformation generally possible?

Twenty years after Lefort's first essay on societies' historicity, Pierre
Clastres's *La Société contre l'État* (*Society against the State*) supported Lefort's
argument by specifically claiming that the refusal of social division and
of the state, not the refusal of history, lay at the basis of "primitive" communities.[33] The critical matter when assessing the "primitives" is then
not their inability to achieve state formation, but the fact that they will-
ingly oppose it. "Primitive" society needs to be considered a political society, Clastres concluded: its intention is political and clearly emerges
from the kind of practices and institutions it adopts with the goal of stop-
ping any attempt to build power above the community.[34] Clastres confirmed Lefort's theory that "primitive" societies voluntarily shut out
history for fear of the dangers associated with change. In addition,
Clastres theorized that "primitive" communities' rejection of history, as
well as of social conflict, division, power, and the state expressed their
political nature. Clastres, as Lefort put it, discovered that "at the heart
of primitive society was the question of the political," a question that

31 For Lefort, there is not merely one History, in the way Hegel and rationalist philosophers conceived of it as linked to the establishment of the state. There are societies that
refuse history and at the same time participate in the course of historical development.
Lefort was critical of the notion of One History. As he wrote in the preface to *Les Formes de
l'histoire*, 8, "we have never adored the divinity History ... When we started writing, it was to
question the idea of a universal History, of a becoming of Humanity, ruled by laws."

32 Lefort wrote, "[I]f one admits that history, conceived as the engendering of the new,
is not given with coexistence, one would need to understand how coexistence becomes
history." See "Société 'sans histoire' et historicité," in Lefort, *Les Formes de l'histoire*, 47. The
answer Lefort sketched out was: labour. Labour marks the historical society's distancing
from the struggle for recognition typical of the intersubjective relations among the "primitives" (46–7).

33 *La Société contre l'État*; English translation as *Society Against the State*. Clastres wrote that
"the history of peoples without history is the history of their struggle against the State"
(186).

34 In "Dialogue with Pierre Clastres," first published in 1987, now in *Writing*, Lefort
wrote, "Clastres was not affirming that there existed societies without power, ones therefore
that were unaware of division ... It was his judgment ... that primitive society had been
built up as a *society against the State*, that it had mounted a system of defenses in order to
make it impossible to form a power that, detached from the community, would have the
freedom to turn around against it and enslave its members to a chief" (215–16).

became central to Lefort's own intellectual endeavours as he began to elaborate a theory of society as essentially political.[35]

Lefort developed this new line of thought at the end of the 1950s, after leaving the group Socialisme ou Barbarie, which he had co-founded with Cornelius Castoriadis in 1948.[36] Influenced in particular by the experience of the Soviet Union's regime and by the work of Machiavelli, Lefort elaborated an original approach to historicity and built a theory of society based on the figuration of power as a symbolic instance. Opposed to the project of positive knowledge carried out by political science and political sociology, Lefort advocated examining "the political" in an expansive way in order to overcome the traditional partition of the social sphere into different domains. Lefort, in sum, refused to investigate politics as a particular and isolated sector of social life. He looked instead for the political in "various facts, acts, representations and relations," and "in areas where its existence usually goes unnoticed or is denied."[37] Through this quest, Lefort ultimately pursued "the symbolic dimension of the social."[38] According to him, political science was mistaken in its refusal to recognize that the delimited sphere it calls politics is the result of a fiction that has been possible only in modern societies. The construct derives from the moderns' experience of social life and is shaped by the historical and political circumstances of modernity.[39] Rethinking politics for Lefort implied a reconstruction of the dominant

35 Ibid., 214.

36 On Socialisme ou Barbarie, see "An Interview with Claude Lefort."

37 See introduction, in Lefort, *Democracy and Political Theory*, 6, 1.

38 Ibid., 6.

39 In "The Question of Democracy," *Democracy and Political Theory*, 12, Lefort wrote that "any system of thought that is bound up with any form of social life is grappling with a subject-matter which contains within it its own interpretation." For Lefort, there are no independent "facts" one can refer to, but only those that make sense to us. We can think only through the categories that are available to us – the system of representations within which we interpret facts. See Poltier's discussion, "La pensée du politique de Claude Lefort." Just as Nancy resisted defining the notion of community, Lefort resisted defining the political. He wished to overcome the conceptual limits that a predetermined meaning would entail. His theory thus "happens" *in medias res*, at the heart of things, and reflects the indeterminacy of that which it is deemed to explain. Some of Lefort's commentators identify this factor as one of the reasons for Lefort's lack of popularity compared to other contemporary public intellectuals. See Alain Caillé, "Claude Lefort, the Social Sciences and Political Philosophy." Caillé writes, "[F]or him, content and form have a close relationship which, moreover, tends to become paradoxical, and thus to make his work difficult to approach and its exposition and commentary even more so" (48). Conversely, Lefort's limitless search for the political makes possible a highly original approach to the question of what constitutes social unity.

approach to the study of politics. It involved a new "sensitivity to the *historical*" as well as renewed skepticism toward the idea of an immutable principle at the basis of the social.[40]

Lefort took as his starting point the thesis that thought does not pre-exist the society that institutes it; there is no pure thought independent of the socio-historical world, or the "social space," in which it operates. Conversely, a social space can exist only by virtue of a system of significations: one cannot separate society from the representations that give it shape. Lefort held that social space should be thought of as a space of intelligibility: society contains its own interpretation.[41] Understanding a society means tapping into the universe of significations produced by that society – a universe that regulates its internal life, social divisions, and the kinds of relations individuals entertain with each other. Like Durkheim's less thought out version of instituted cultural representations, Lefort's account of signification showed that the different principles presiding over diverse forms of society make it possible for individuals who inhabit the same social space to share behaviour and orientations.[42] It is because they are part of the same universe of significations that individuals enter into relations with each other, and because they have a common understanding, they can interact. The questions Lefort faced next were: how do we come to conceive of the social space to which we belong as one and as united and how do we recognize each other (especially in view of our differences) as part of the same space of intelligibility? The answer he provided entailed a symbolic dimension: in order for a society to conceive of itself as one, there needs to be a separate place that individuals feel is above them and in which unity can be imagined as such. The place in which that image of unity can be projected turned out to be, for Lefort, the place of power. Through its relationship to such a place, taken as that which reflects society's self-definition, a society constitutes itself: by seeing itself represented, society develops its sense of unity, the

40 See "Introduction," in Lefort, *Democracy and Political Theory*, 5 (italicized in the original). Lefort also wrote, "My purpose here is to encourage and to contribute to a revival of political philosophy." See "The Question of Democracy," *Democracy and Political Theory*, 9.

41 Ibid., 12.

42 A similar attention to the cultural nature of human societies links Lefort and Castoriadis to Durkheim. On the affinity between Durkheim and Lefort and Durkheim and Castoriadis, in particular the latter's notion of "social imaginary" as shared significations that bind societies together, see Doyle, "The Sacred, Social Creativity and the State," and Rundell, "Durkheim and the Reflexive Condition of Modernity."

sense of its "being." In other words, the symbolic representation of a society's unity in the place of power actualizes society as a whole.[43]

Lefort's discussion of the political carried several implications. First, the political is held to be constitutive of the social, which also means that within Lefort's model there is no society without power. Second, a society cannot pre-exist its political definition; the social and the political are imbricated with each other. Third, power does not merely reflect social unity: it also provides the image of the principles that order society and that inform its internal divisions. This means that by looking at a society's place of power we can identify the principles governing that specific society, the image of social unity to which a particular society subscribes. Finally, and overall, Lefort's theory suggested that unity emerges as the main problem facing a society. In a paradoxical move, however, Lefort also argued that the unity ensured by the place of power depends on a primal division: the separation of society from its representation, that is, from the place of power.[44] This point served as potent ammunition for Lefort's claim that unity can only be guaranteed by division rather than by denying difference. The analysis of monarchy, democracy, and totalitarianism as imaginary orders that reflect and represent different models of social space provided Lefort with concrete cases with which to demonstrate the significance of recognizing division as the basis for unity.[45]

Power and the Symbolic Dimension of the Social

By following Machiavelli, Lefort interpreted social division as constitutive of the social and not a merely contingent, and therefore eliminable, factor in political relations.[46] In Lefort's reading, Machiavelli posited the

43 On Lefort and representation, see Nässtrôm, "Representative Democracy as Tautology."

44 On this point, see Poltier, "Qu'est-ce que la pensée du politique?"

45 Faithful to a phenomenological mode of inquiry that interrogates its own presuppositions, Lefort opposed political philosophy's normative ideal of a good society, that is, its subscription to the belief that a right and rational society would exclude opposition by deeming it irrational.

46 This is one of the reasons why Lefort took his distance from Marx. Marx's mechanical understanding of historical development proved too restrictive when gauging the role of the political. Indeed, the model of absolute knowledge proposed by Marxism had proved inconsistent when faced with "ahistorical" primitive societies, according to Lefort. It had also showed itself unable to explain the degeneration of the Soviet phenomenon. See Lefort's article on Marx and Machiavelli, "Réflexions sociologiques sur Machiavel et Marx: la politique et le 'réel,'" first published in 1960, now in Lefort, *Les Formes de l'histoire*;

opposition between people and those who command them as inevitable and irreducible.[47] In addition, Machiavelli saw division as creative of the social space that makes possible both a human and a political society. Power regulates the division, but without denying it; it is supposed to control class struggle, not resolve it. Within this context, Machiavelli invited Lefort to reject any appeal toward constituting a harmonious society, as well as any attempt to envisage the end of social division in the pursuit of a totalizing harmonic collectivity – the kind of aesthetic state that eliminates difference. He also encouraged Lefort to recognize conflict as the mechanism that puts society in place. When social conflict is denied through the crushing of the weak, the result is a corrupted society. Conflict, in contrast, guarantees that power cannot be appropriated by any one person or group and will remain at stake in the confrontation between opposing sides.

In the wake of Machiavelli, and despite what might appear as an oxymoronic juxtaposition, Lefort became particularly interested in examining the problem of conflict within democracy.[48] Unlike the Collège, he believed that democracy is the antidote to the desacralization of the modern era – the place where diversity and unity coexist and division is recognized.[49] Lefort indeed warned that obsession with unity only degrades the social. How, then, did Lefort come to this conclusion? In his analysis of the unity of social space, as mentioned earlier, Lefort posited that a symbolic pole allows the social to perceive itself as the same. This pole functions as the place that holds the image of a united society and displays the principles underlying social relations in that specific social space. By naming this pole the place of power, Lefort implied that power is constitutive of society and that the two implicate each other: they are

---

"Outline of the Genesis of Ideology in Modern Societies," first published in 1974, now in *The Political Forms of Modern Society*; and Lefort's description of Merleau-Ponty's critique of Marxism, "La politique et la pensée de la politique," first published in 1963, now in *Sur une colonne absente*. Lefort claimed that a reflection on politics cannot be disconnected from a reflection on the theory of politics (70).

47 This position helped Lefort reject political philosophy's abstract rationalism. Lefort's book on Machiavelli, the result of long years of work, was published in 1972 as *Le travail de l'œuvre Machiavel*. For an instructive discussion of this "cumbersome" work see Flynn, *The Philosophy of Claude Lefort*, especially part one, "Lefort as Reader of Machiavelli."

48 In "Pour une sociologie de la démocratie," first published in 1966, now in *Éléments d'une critique de la bureaucratie*, Lefort wrote, "Every totalitarian system pretends to ignore conflict ... Couldn't one say that democracy is characterized in contrast by its intention to face the heterogeneity of values, behaviors and desires, and to make of conflicts an engine of growth?" (345).

49 To be fair, one must again recognize that the Collège's position toward democracy was not settled or unilinear.

instituted at the same time. In other words, the symbolic dimensions of the social are inseparable from the coming to be of the social itself. Power provides the scene for society's self-representation, as well as for exposing society's generating principles.[50]

But what differentiates societies' symbolic orders? And how do these symbolic orders represent difference and division? For Lefort, all societies are internally divided; the element that differentiates them is the mode in which they deal with their divisions. These divisions are dependent on the fundamental separation of the real from the symbolic – a separation that is constitutive of society.[51] Changes in the status of power indicate a mutation of the symbolic order and they ultimately unsettle the way a society thinks of itself. If we examine the monarchical system of the *ancien régime*, for example, we see that power was embodied in the person of the king, who mediated between humans and God. The king represented divine justice at the same time that he was subject to it (due to the dual nature of the sacred, one could add), and through the double nature of his body, both mortal and immortal, he expressed "the principle that generated the order of the kingdom."[52] The king reminded the people of the divine nature of their society, whose unity he guaranteed through his own bodily presence. Because they recognized themselves in him, the people formed a social unity and at the same time conceptualized the limits of the sovereign to intervene in society.[53]

The element that makes democracy intriguing and difficult to theorize, in comparison to monarchy, is the fact that in it "[t]he locus of power becomes *an empty place*."[54] In democracy, no particular person holds power because the exercise of power is subject to redistribution and is periodically reallocated on the basis of a contest that is dependent on specific rules. This contest indicates that conflict becomes institutionalized in democracy: conflict is at the heart of the democratic exercise of power. And this power is by definition open to change: it does not rest in anybody's hands. Because of these peculiar characteristics, power in democracy becomes disincorporated, or disembodied. It loses its control

50 See "Outline of the Genesis of Ideology in Modern Societies," in Lefort, *The Political Forms of Modern Societies*, especially 194.

51 The dynamic relation between representation and reality was already being thought out by Lefort in the 1960s. See "Pour une sociologie de la démocratie," in *Éléments d'une critique de la bureaucratie*, where he also advanced a critique of scientism.

52 See "The Question of Democracy," in Lefort, *Democracy and Political Theory*, 17.

53 It is important to remember that, according to Lefort, the monarchical system was not despotic since the prince did not hold unlimited power. This is a crucial point in Lefort's argument that power cannot be appropriated. Ibid.

54 Ibid., 17.

over law and knowledge, and these in turn constitute themselves into separate spheres independent from, and irreducible to, power. As Lefort put it, "democratic society is instituted as a society without a body, as a society which undermines the representation of an organic totality."[55] Conflict becomes legitimized along with the experience of uncertainty and the loss of a substantial identification with a body, a person, a unitary entity. The opposite desire for an embodied power, for the certainty of unity and homogeneity, works instead as the catalyst for the emergence of totalitarianism. The fantasy of the People-as-One then replaces the anonymity of the empty place.

Lefort did not argue that totalitarianism is the culmination of democracy, as many tend to believe, since the rule of law in democracy never coincides with the rule of power. Totalitarianism is rather the inversion of democracy's meaning; it implies its collapse.[56] This conclusion led Lefort to hold that the principles on which democracy is founded, in particular its recognition of division as constitutive and essential, make democracy the best form of society.[57] A comparison of democracy with the totalitarian political form allowed Lefort to sustain his argument.[58]

By the late 1970s, Lefort was advocating totalitarianism as a new sociohistorical category for understanding the logic and appeal of fascism and Bolshevism. He denounced the inability of political and cultural commentators to use this category, an inability which he took as a sign of their incapacity to conceive of society in political terms and to reflect on the nature of the division between state and civil society.[59] The Left, in particular, had approached political power as secondary to the economy and had generally ignored power's symbolic dimensions, thus failing to understand the system of representations that in Lefort's schema drive the institution of society, be it democratic or totalitarian. Lefort's analysis, in contrast, revolved around power's symbolic role, and in the case of modern democracy Lefort specifically argued that power occupies a symbolically empty place. Democracy had become the social form in which anybody can exercise power, although nobody can appropriate it. Therefore, "on the one hand, power emanates from the people; on the

---

55 Ibid., 18.
56 See "Human Rights and the Welfare State," first published in French in 1984, now in Lefort, *Democracy and Political Theory*.
57 See Poltier, "Qu'est-ce que la pensée du politique?"
58 On this comparison as driving Lefort's work, see Molina, *Le défi du politique*.
59 See "The Logic of Totalitarianism," first published in French in 1980, now in Lefort, *The Political Forms of Modern Society*, for the reasons why the communist Left refused to associate fascism with communism. Lefort also criticized intellectuals for failing to consider Hannah Arendt's study of totalitarianism.

other, it is the power of nobody."[60] This contradiction does not diminish democracy's value, according to Lefort. On the contrary, it makes democracy thrive: its overcoming would bring the end of democracy.

No doubt, a problem arises when the place of power is no longer perceived as merely "symbolically" empty but as "really" empty, when the people do not see themselves as guiding power or as the source of power's legitimacy any longer. At that point, a single party can claim to be representing people and on the basis of that identification appropriate power. Reversing the principles of democracy, the party abolishes the separation between state and civil society and seeks to eliminate any sign of internal social division. The image of the Party-as-One takes hold and becomes the centre of a new system of representations that displays the model of a society without divisions.[61] For Lefort, totalitarianism indicates the presence of this new symbolic order; and one needs to understand the modern dictatorships of Italy, Germany, and Russia by taking such order into account.[62] In these dictatorships, power becomes self-referential and does not need to respond to any external limit (such as God in the case of the monarchy). The image of Power-as-One that Lefort, following Solzhenitsyn, identified with the *Egocrat* is then accompanied by the image of the People-as-One, that is, the rejection of any difference within society and the pursuit of a project of uniformization that reaches deep into daily life and strives for a harmonious whole.[63] The enemy then becomes the counter altar to people's unity, the element that threatens the health of the whole and undermines the integrity of the body. At the same time, reference to the enemy indicates that there is an "us" as opposed to "them" and also confirms the absence of internal divisions: the People-as-One constitute themselves into one integral body.[64]

---

60 Ibid., 279.

61 Lefort developed this point in *La complication*. See English translation, *Complications*.

62 See "The Logic of Totalitarianism," in Lefort, *The Political Forms of Modern Societies*, especially 284.

63 See *Un homme en trop*, 68, where Lefort wrote that the word *Egocrat* suggests "not a master who governs alone, freed from laws, but the one who concentrates social power in his persona and in this sense appears (and appears to himself) as if he didn't have anything outside himself, as if he had absorbed society's substance, as if, absolute *Ego*, he could indefinitely expand without meeting any resistance from things."

64 As already remarked by Peter Murphy, Lefort seems to hint here at the sublime aspect of totalitarian politics. See Murphy, "Between Romanticism and Republicanism." I discuss this issue in *Fascist Spectacle*, introduction.

In several of his writings, Lefort analysed the attraction people feel for the name of One, their desire to feel united within one body.[65] He found the best anticipation of the dynamics characterizing this attraction in Étienne de la Boétie's formula of "servitude volontaire" – a formula which was based on the popular appeal of the tyrant's body taken as representing the fiction of the social body.[66] For Lefort, this image of the self-sustaining, homogeneous body best conveys totalitarianism's main difference from democracy; for in democracy the body is no longer there. The democratic revolution assaulted the corporeality of the social by destroying the body of the king and literally cutting off the head of the body politic. The result was what Lefort called a "disincorporation" of individuals and the prevalence of numbers through the idea of universal suffrage – a very different configuration than in totalitarianism.[67] Furthermore, with the body gone, with no "body" occupying the space of power, (democratic) power inevitably appears empty and up for grabs. Democracy inaugurates a time of uncertainty, indeterminacy, and doubt, which is exactly what totalitarianism then attempts to overcome through the reaffirmation of the body in the figure of the People-as-One led by the "invulnerable" dictator.[68] This latter move would seem to indicate a return to pre-democratic times, to the body politic of monarchical society that had been dissolved by the democratic revolution. Lefort, however, warned that there is no going back to the figure of the absolutist monarch. In the case of the totalitarian model, and this is what makes it unique, there is no ultimate power to which one needs to respond as the king did to God. The Egocrat only "coincides with himself, as society is supposed to coincide with itself."[69]

65 According to Lefort, the name *Un* (One) "delivers Subjects from the fear of division, from the ordeal of the plural, and, finally, from the enigma of the human institution of society." See "Philosopher?" first published in 1983, now in Lefort, *Writing*, 241.

66 Lefort wrote the following about the idea of voluntary servitude: "In discovering La Boétie, I had been struck to see this idea associated with that of an attraction for the *body* of the tyrant, or more generally of the king, of the master in whom is found to be incarnated the fiction of the social body." Lefort, *Writing*. Lefort's commentary on Étienne de la Boétie's *Le discours de la servitude volontaire*, published in *Writing*, is entitled "Le nom d'Un" (The name of One). It draws out the implications of the desire for One. On Lefort and de la Boétie, see also Habib, "*De la servitude volontaire*."

67 "The Image of the Body and Totalitarianism," first published in French in 1979, now in Lefort, *The Political Forms of Modern Society*.

68 Lefort described the dictator's body as a "mortal body which is perceived as invulnerable, which condenses in itself all strengths, all talents, and defies the laws of nature by his super-male energy." Ibid., 300.

69 Ibid., 306.

Ambiguity and the Empty Space of Power

Lefort recognized the difficulty of dealing with democracy's indeterminacy, a predicament that could result in a totalitarian turn and the recurrence of the religious in the form of new beliefs and representations.[70] He was also very aware of people's tendency to "surrender to the attractions of a renewed certainty."[71] Within his theoretical framework, however, surrender would signify the death of democracy as a social form, for the *mise en forme* of democracy coincides with a symbolic mutation that ultimately dispenses with the image of the body.[72] Therefore, lest democracy end, there can be no return to an organic image, "the fantasy of an organic society."[73] The indeterminacy of democracy can never be resolved because only the vacating of the locus of power makes democracy possible: "Power becomes and remains democratic when it proves to belong to no one," Lefort affirmed.[74] A gap between administrative power and political authority is the condition for democracy's existence; and this gap can be ensured only if the representational nature of democracy is maintained along with the separate articulation of power, knowledge, and law and the ultimate granting of political freedom (substantive versus formal).[75] Human rights are built on the separation between right and power, on a regime founded "upon *the legitimacy of a debate as to what is legitimate and what is illegitimate.*"[76] Such a regime presupposes the existence of a public space that no one owns but where everyone can speak and listen while recognizing one another as part of that space. The presence of the debate then guarantees that the people's right to an opinion

70 See "The Permanence of the Theologico-Poltical?" in Lefort, *Democracy and Political Theory.*

71 Ibid., 234. Lefort developed a critique of immortality as a discourse that resists democracy. See "The Death of Immortality?" first published in French in 1982, now in *Democracy and Political Theory.*

72 In "The Permanence of the Theologico-Political?" Lefort wrote that "the notion of shaping (*mise en forme*) ... implies both the notion of giving meaning (*mise en sense*) to social relations ... and that of staging them (*mise en scène*)," 218–19.

73 See Lefort, "Hannah Arendt and the Question of the Political," first published in French in 1985, now in *Democracy and Political Theory*, 55.

74 See Lefort, "Human Rights and the Welfare State," first published in French in 1984, now in *Democracy and Political Theory*, 27.

75 Her lack of appreciation for the representational side of democracy led Lefort to criticize Arendt. See "Hannah Arendt and the Question of the Political," in *Democracy and Political Theory.*

76 See "Human Rights and the Welfare State," in *Democracy and Political Theory*, 39 (italicized in the original). See also "Politics and Human Rights," first published in French in 1980, now in *The Political Forms of Modern Society.*

will be exercised, and suggests that people's rights can be violated only by the erosion of the public space, not by the mistakes of the majority's opinion. As Lefort put it, "in the event, the majority may prove to be wrong, but not the public space."[77] The affirmation of particularity, in combination with the idea of legitimacy, upholds the symbolic efficacy of the notion of rights and makes sure that even when the power of the state seems to be increasing in democratic societies, new demands will challenge and question that power on a continuous basis.[78] An eventual fatal attack on democracy, in sum, will not ensue from an excess of private individual interests, but from the perception of power as "really" empty, that is, from the diminished effectiveness of the symbolic system.

Regrettably, the indeterminacy of democracy creates a genuine possibility of such a vacuum, whereupon those who exercise power are seen as hungry for domination, "concerned solely to satisfy their desires," and consequently deserving of contempt.[79] Since it dissolves the separation between state and civil society, the phantasmatic solution of totalitarianism appears to deliver a much sought after sense of certitude and unity: totalitarianism reassures people and soothes their fears even as it hides fundamental divisions.[80] Lefort, however, warned that the totalitarian remedy to the empty space of power in democracy – totalitarianism's attempt to resolve the indeterminacy of the democratic symbolic order – installs an inversion of the principles that guide the *mise en scène* of democracy. And it fundamentally undermines democracy's unfolding. At that point, the representation of popular sovereignty undergoes a mutation that posits the people's unity as real, rather than symbolic,

77 See "Human Rights and the Welfare State," in Lefort, *Democracy and Political Theory*, 41.

78 In "Politics and Human Rights," in *The Political Forms of Modern Societies*, Lefort had already made the case that human rights are political. When examining the dissidents' request for rights in the Soviet Union, Lefort situated the political nature of their request in the incompatibility between rights and the totalitarian system. For Lefort, those rights are only possible in a society that totalitarianism denies. Therefore, "rights are constitutive of politics" (243–4). To consider them as individual rights in the case of totalitarianism means to deny their political essence, Lefort argued, making it impossible to call into question the nature of the state. Indeed, when there is a violation of human rights, one should look at it as part of the logic of the system that does not accept the separation between power and social life. See 251–2.

79 See Lefort, "The Image of the Body and Totalitarianism," in *The Political Forms of Modern Societies*, 305.

80 For Lefort, what characterizes totalitarianism is not so much the state's absolute power as the attempt to eliminate the separation of state and civil society. Lefort focused on lived experience when examining totalitarianism. See Lefort, *L'Invention démocratique*, ii. On totalitarianism, see Lefort, *Complications*.

eliminating the possibility of conflict and division and thus creating the totalitarian fantasy of the People-as-One. For Lefort, this return to an identitarian claim ultimately signals the death of democracy.

Against its many detractors, Lefort rehabilitated democracy as the true expression of collective sovereignty.[81] He analytically dismantled the theory of totalitarianism as democracy's extreme outgrowth and also challenged the Collège's and others' vision of democracy as flat and homogenizing. He showed that conflict is the central element of democracy's self-representation and functioning. One could even hazard that the contestation to which democracy is open endows it with that "effervescence" the Collège thought was missing in modern societies: conflict is the guarantee against homogenization and incorporation, as well as against identitarian unity.[82] Within this context, any invoking of the sacred should be distrusted because it would only indicate a weak point of the social – a misunderstanding of the historical nature of democracy and a misrecognition of the principle that generates it.[83] In the monarchical system the religious entered into the political – when the king mediated between the transcendental and the mundane. This is no longer the case in a democratic *mise en scène*. The nostalgic search for the sacred can only signal the "vertigo in face of the void created by an indeterminate society" and can thus lead to totalitarianism.[84] Invocations of the sacred exude the same emotional need that motivates people to exit the democratic empty place to be incorporated into a bodily unity.[85]

How does Lefort compare to the Collège? And where does the Collège stand within Lefort's theoretical framework? We know that Lefort's analysis of society's political forms did not accommodate the need for emotional outburst, an existential, disinterested "being together" – a central issues for the Collège. For Lefort, unity can only be symbolic, and one has to reject any reference to an embodied representation or risk falling into the totalitarian logic. To be fair to Lefort, he recognized that totalitarianism, as well as monarchy, has an emotional foundation and attracts people's affective support. He wrote striking passages about the captivating

---

81 Lefort, *Writing*, 264.

82 See Poltier, *Claude Lefort*, 81.

83 "The Permanence of the Theologico-Political?" in Lefort, *Democracy and Political Theory*.

84 "The Image of the Body and Totalitarianism," in Lefort, *The Political Forms of Modern Society*, 304.

85 Following Lefort, Stefan Dudnik argues that today's images of open bodies replace past representations of bodies as organic totalities and testify to democracy's indeterminacy. See his "Cuts and Bruises and Democratic Contestation."

image of the body of the king as a precipitator of identification.[86] The sovereign's natural, physical, sexed body, Lefort argued following Jules Michelet, allowed for a "carnal union" between the people and the monarch.[87] Lefort recognized that the attraction of unity draws people away from the uncertainty and indeterminacy of democratic society. He identified the "logic of love" in the monarchical political form as resurfacing in the totalitarian imagination of the body as One. For him, the mechanisms of incarnation through which power is embodied reveal and ensure the imbrications of politics and religion typical of Western societies before the advent of modernity.[88] Lefort, however, believed that the disincorporation of power in democracy ultimately puts an end to these imbrications. And to the question whether the theologico-political is permanent, he firmly answered in the negative. The break from that model was for him radical; what looks like a return to the religious is a phenomenon that appears only in times of social crises, when the division on which democracy bases its unity comes to be represented as intolerable. The return of the sacred signals the death of democracy, not because of the latter's inadequacies (as the Collège seemed to think) but because of a lack of understanding of democracy's generative principle.

For Lefort, division is constitutive of the democratic space. Political competition and conflict guarantee that power will not be appropriated by anyone; the empty place of democracy allows for a form of human coexistence that makes possible the exercise of freedom. The abolition of division in the fantasy of the organic community at one with itself, in contrast, rules out the possibility of freedom because civil liberties are

---

86 "The Permanence of the Theologico-Political?" in Lefort, *Democracy and Political Theory*, 242.

87 Lefort cited the discovery of an "erotico-political register" in the dynamics that conjoin people and king. He wrote, "It is the image of the natural body, the image of a God made flesh, the image of his marriage, his paternity, his liaisons, his festivals, his amusements and his feasts, but also the image of his weaknesses or even his cruelties, in short all the images of his humanity, that people their imaginary, that assure them that the king and the people are conjoined." Ibid., 245. Michelet's analysis of the monarchical incarnation inspired Lefort's thinking about the power of the body to attract people's love for the king. Michelet emphasized that the king's might did not merely descend from his power's divine origins, but rather from the people's love for him and the fallibility and charm of his natural body.

88 Lefort argued that "a theologico-political *formation* is, logically and historically, a primary datum." "The Permanence of the Theologico-Political?" in *The Political Forms of Modern Societies*, 249 (italicized in the original). There is no sense in distinguishing between the two until the new form of the social (democracy) begins to take shape. "[A]ny move towards immanence is also a move towards transcendence," Lefort continued, and this dynamic sustains the imbrications of politics and religion (254).

dependent on the principle that makes competition a condition for power.[89] According to Lefort, the fact that in democracy all have the right to denounce a particular expression testifies to the vibrancy of that right. There can be no universal basis on which to evaluate what is legitimate because "right cannot be immanent within the social order without the very idea of right being debased."[90] What counts is the existence of a public space where everyone exercises "*the right to have rights.*"[91]

Lefort's rejection of universalism and his refusal to grant priority to any principle defined as sacred underwrote his belief in the indeterminacy of meaning.[92] Interrogation was the key to Lefort's enterprise – the openness to the impossibility of knowledge's closure.[93] Bataille's final words at the Collège, when he invoked an "inexhaustible interrogation," resound here.[94] Indeed, despite their differences, both Bataille and Lefort deemed "questioning" central to human existence and on this basis challenged sociology's positivist temptations.[95] Unlike Lefort, however, the Collège only implicitly expanded its notion of the political and did not theorize the historical overlap of the political and the religious, whether or not this overlap can be considered as terminated in modernity. Entrenched within the social-scientific tradition of Durkheim, the Collège embraced the modern point of view of the separation of the value-spheres and evacuated the political from its analysis of the social.[96]

89 Poltier argues that the question of freedom is at the centre of Lefort's thought. See his *Claude Lefort*. Lefort examined the question of freedom in connection with the issue of human rights, which, as already mentioned, he refused to consider within the perspective of "individual" rights, that is, outside of the political. See his "Politics and Human Rights," in Lefort, *The Political Forms of Modern Societies*, 244.

90 "Human Rights and the Welfare State," in Lefort, *Democracy and Political Theory*, 41.

91 Ibid., 40 (italicized in the original).

92 According to Caillé, however, this is not a sign of Lefort's deconstructionism. On the contrary, although Lefort attacked both realism and positivism, he was equally critical of deconstructionism's teleological tendencies. See Caillé, "Claude Lefort, the Social Sciences and Political Philosophy."

93 "What is to interrogate, then? In a sense, it is to grieve for knowledge. In a sense, it is to learn, despite this grief, or better still, to renounce the idea that there is in the things themselves ... an all positive meaning." See preface, in Lefort, *Les formes de l'histoire*, 9.

94 See Hollier, *The College of Sociology*, 340.

95 For Lefort, thinking the political "submits to the exigency that one take on the questions that are at the heart of every human establishment." See preface, in Lefort, *Les formes de l'histoire*, xlii. Lefort was then led to abandon the social sciences in favour of political philosophy. On this issue, see Caillé, "Claude Lefort, the Social Sciences and Political Philosophy."

96 Based on Lefort's analysis, one could also argue that the Collège lacked awareness of its own positionality within a form of society that was marked by the distinction of the value spheres.

In addition, and like Durkheim, it de-historicized social formations by working within the framework of a two-way dichotomy: "primitive" versus modern societies. The Collège slid over historical transformations and reified the social as a self-contained, invariable system. It then charged the social with the task of building a community but had difficulty defining community in a way that avoided the straight-jacketed model provided by Nazism and Stalinism. To be sure, the Collège was well aware and suspicious of de facto communities, but was also adamantly skeptical of democracy, which it considered the epitome of the absence of community. The Collège could not stand "empty structures":[97] as Lefort rightly recognized, it is not easy to renounce an embodied relationship with power.[98] Unwilling to face the conundrum of the political, the Collège was left struggling in a theoretical quagmire.

Lefort's approach in turn is not devoid of problems.[99] Yet, by radically altering the terms of the debate on democracy – a debate that often revolves around the questions of reason and discussion and their role in displacing conflict through its staging – Lefort hit at the heart of the issue of community. In an even more consequential move, Lefort emphasized the ambiguity of democracy and its anti-totalitarian essence, its potential as antidote to the closure of power, popular rights, and sovereignty.[100] He exposed the danger and consequences of the appeal of the One when people refuse to accept the symbolic and empty character of unity in democracy. The Collège, in comparison, proved vulnerable to accusations of courting the One even as it fought against such an outcome. The Collège's ideal of building an order that would guide a renewed community seemed to clash with its aspirations to the egalitarianism of the carnivalesque, leading one to wonder whether the Collège was seeking the community or effervescence – a continuous state of instability – and whether it could reconcile unity with heterogeneity. Was Bataille's vision of a sovereign community able to function as an antidote

---

97 See Prévost as cited in Hollier, *The College of Sociology*, 375.

98 From this point of view, one should probably reconsider the role of Acéphale for Bataille – a headless figure that nonetheless was still made up of a body.

99 See Caillé, "Claude Lefort, the Social Sciences and Political Philosophy," and Poltier, "Qu'est-ce que le politique?" for an analysis of the problems. In particular, Caillé cites Lefort's difficulty in neatly demarcating the boundaries between the political, the theological, and the symbolic.

100 Doyle argues that Lefort's work reasserts the centrality of sovereignty in the question of democracy. See "Democracy as Socio-Cultural Project of Individual and Collective Sovereignty."

to the sovereign?[101] Could a sense of unity be formed without reference to the other, the fictional construction of an enemy?[102] Although it is difficult to provide definitive answers to these questions, Lefort's political philosophy, in my estimation, helps illuminate the dilemmas the Collège faced in its struggle to theorize the modern sacred. In particular, Lefort pointed to the risks of ignoring the theologico-political origins of modern social forms: within his theoretical framework, the political and the theological reveal and govern the symbolic dimensions through which we establish our relation with the world.[103] For Lefort, the representation of power and social division preside over the constitution of the social; human coexistence is thus shaped by the imagination. His analysis alerts us to the misguided nature of a dehistoricized comparison with the archaic world that does not take into account the specificity of modern social forms, a path followed by the Collège. Bataille's and Caillois's reliance on Durkheim's vision of effervescent "primitive" communities drove them along the blinded path of historical oblivion and grossly generalized case comparison. Granted, one cannot separate the elaboration of a political form from that of a religious form in that both govern human access to the world through their symbolic dimensions.[104] For Lefort, though, the entanglement of the two came to an end once power was transformed and disincorporated in democracy's "empty place."[105] For the same reason, according to him, modern social science views politics as a separate realm from the religious. Power is no longer represented with reference to an outside, a divine origin, or as depending on a community. It does not conjure society as one.

The Collège was far from elaborating a theory of historical social forms in the manner of Lefort, and one can certainly not blame it for this lack. My comparison of the Collège with Lefort, however, brings out the

101 For a discussion of this issue see Jay, "The Reassertion of Sovereignty in a Time of Crisis."

102 Carl Schmitt's famous distinction of friend and foe is pertinent here.

103 See for example his "Nation et Souveraineté." Lefort also criticized the thesis of politics as religion in "La Révolution comme religion nouvelle." As is well known, the question of the theologico-political was at the centre of Leo Strauss's philosophy. Lefort wrote about Strauss in several of his works, although not with specific reference to the question of the theologico-political.

104 "The Permanence of the Theologico-Political?" in Lefort, *Democracy and Political Theory*, 221–2.

105 According to Poltier, the critique of the desire for One is inseparable from the defence of freedom in Lefort's schema. See his "La pensée du politique de Claude Lefort." Caillé questions the wisdom of considering democracy as peculiar to modern societies, and wonders whether it is possible to think of democracy as transhistorical within Lefort's perspective. See Caillé, "Claude Lefort, the Social Sciences and Political Philosophy."

potential of the Collège's endeavour. Although the Collège missed its
chance to problematize the historical nature of politics, it critically indicated the importance of addressing the question of the sacred's attraction in modern totalitarian regimes. Like Lefort, the Collège emphasized
the strongly affective human component that grants life to the fantasy of
an organic society. Both pointed to the popular appeal of unity as a key
factor in gauging totalitarianism's logic and its successful unfolding.
That the Collège was "equivocal" about its analysis doesn't make its interpretation less cogent. Reading Lefort against the Collège allows one to
see the power of the Collège's theorizing, as well as the difficulties inherent in the nurturing of democracy. Indeed, one may argue that Lefort
failed to adequately explain how to counter people's attraction for the
One, and that his project risks falling back into a rationalist model.[106]
Lefort exposed totalitarianism's aestheticization of politics, so effectively
denounced by Benjamin, but left aside considering a potential democratic response to affective needs. The Collège, in contrast, dared to confront the dilemma knowing the risks it ran when searching for the sacred.
In the end, whether democracy can fully unfold once internal divisions
are recognized and accepted remains an open issue. Would people ever
renounce the erotic impulse to venerate themselves in the One and as
One? Unresolved, these dilemmas continue to require reflection. The
flame of the Collège's "burning" question has yet to be extinguished.

---

106 Other criticisms include the issue of democratic legitimacy and problems of norma-
tivity. See, among others, Gould's review essay, "Claude Lefort on Modern Democracy."

Conclusions

IN 1946, BATAILLE WROTE TO HIS OLD FRIEND and one-time collaborator Raymond Queneau, inquiring about potential competent reviewers for a book by Georges Dumézil to be featured in his new journal *Critique*. Bataille went on to lament that "Sociology has decidedly rejected me to the point that I don't know any sociologist any longer."[1] Although the Collège de sociologie had played its last act seven years earlier with a dramatic solo appearance by Bataille on 4 July 1939, and although Bataille's personal intellectual journey had taken a quite different turn after the Collège's dissolution, Bataille was still expressing nostalgia and fondness for sociology in the mid-1940s. In reality, the Collège had never reached closure. When its planned resumption in the fall of 1939 was abruptly halted by Hitler's invasion of Poland on 1 September and France's subsequent declaration of war against Germany, however, the proposal for a brainstorming and soul-searching conference was crushed. With no group with which to associate, Bataille, in an isolating move, found himself pursuing "inner experience," an intimate but not necessarily individualized or self-absorbed search for the subject's relationship to the world.[2] In the flux of historical events, the ideal of an activist intervention into the social as originally conceived by the Collège faded from Bataille's horizon. His profound reliance on sociology, however, did not evaporate in light of his solitary reflections, nor did his belief in sociology's value, though qualified, flounder. Reading Bataille post-Collège leaves the impression that not only did he not renounce sociology after the fact but he integrated it in his developing work on inner experience. Sociology had not been a misstep or a youthful sin, at least not as long as one was open to rethinking sociology's status.

---

1 Cited in Lecoq, "L'œil de l'ethnologue sous la dent de l'écrivain," 116.
2 See *L'expérience intérieure*, in Bataille, *OC*, vol. 5, and Bataille, *Inner Experience*.

Bataille's 1946 review of Jules Monnerot's *Les faits sociaux ne sont pas des choses*, a book that he found disappointing, reiterated the Collège's faith in sociology.[3] In his analysis of the text, Bataille stated that the recognized need for a rigorous science had allowed Durkheim's doctrine to expand beyond academic circles in the 1930s. The doctrine had thus attracted young intellectuals hungry for tools that would help them counter the growing disintegration of the social fabric. Bataille cited two critical points in Durkheim's theory, points the Collège had eagerly embraced and that Monnerot had failed to note: first, society is a whole that is different from the sum of its parts; second, the sacred is the constitutive element of society.[4] Sociology's overall validity resided in its potential for "*disinterested knowledge,*" Bataille continued.[5] Sociology was, therefore, able to go beyond practical, mundane issues in order to meet the harder challenges of revealing us to ourselves and overcoming the strictures of an existence governed by petty interests.

Years after the closure of the Collège, and with a sleek argument that valorized Durkheim's teaching more highly than in the past, Bataille defined social activities that set out to pursue specific goals as *nothing but* the sum of all individuals participating in them.[6] He considered these activities a very poor rendition of society's ideal. If one wanted to gauge the excess of the social, that is, the momentous operation when society becomes "more" than the sum of its parts and we are transfigured in this whole, he argued, one ought instead to confront the sacred. The sacred constitutes the "more" that differentiates the whole society from the sum of its individuals and helps illuminate the component of ourselves that is not confined by interest. For Bataille, "we personally started from this whole that exceeds us. We exceed ourselves in it and through it we are *more* than this limited existence," even though we are scarcely conscious of this process.[7] Bataille was well aware of Durkheim's intention to develop a methodological approach for the scientific study of social facts. He pointed out, however, that even the feature of "constraint," which

3 Bataille, "Le sens moral de la sociologie," first published in *Critique* now in *OC*, vol. 11.

4 Ibid.

5 See Bataille's 1950 book review "Sociologie. Henri Calet – Beatrix Beck," first published in *Critique*, now in *OC*, 12: 30 (italicized in the original).

6 My emphasis. Bataille wrote, "Every time that a social activity pursues a given goal that is within reach, there is nothing *more* in the *whole* than the sum of the activity of the individuals participating in it." *OC*, 12: 29 (italicized in the original).

7 Ibid. The original reads, "[N]ous sommes personnellement parti de ce tout qui nous dépasse, nous nous dépassons en lui, par lui nous sommes *plus* que cette existence limitée" (italicized in the original).

Durkheim deemed central to a definition of social fact, had not deterred Durkheim from pursuing the social through the analysis of those phenomena that simultaneously attract and repel us. Durkheim, as well as Mauss, had been able to bring to the surface and situate within science the study of the sacred in modernity. In this operation, they had demoted theology's exclusive claims to the holy; furthermore, their research on primitive religions had demonstrated that sociology (science) was to theology what chemistry was to alchemy.[8]

Bataille continued to frame sociology in scientific terms throughout the 1940s, even as he simultaneously criticized science's general principle of abstracting objects from the totality. This criticism emerged in particular in his 1951 review of Caillois's augmented edition of *L'Homme et le sacré*.[9] Here, without renouncing Durkheim's scientific vision or his original identification of sacred and social, Bataille redefined the status of the sacred in sociology and disputed established assumptions. More specifically, Bataille advocated that the sacred, although an object of science, should not, like other objects, be taken in isolation. The sacred constituted a concrete totality and was based on communication and contagion. It followed that the accepted division of sacred and profane, the idea, that is, that the sacred depends on the profane for its definition, was ill-posed.[10] For Bataille, the profane derived from the sacred. The attempt to abstract objects from the totality ultimately resulted in a mutilation – quite a different conclusion from Durkheim's primal position.

By recasting the relationship between sacred and profane, Bataille reconfigured the sociological realm and at the same time challenged sociology's scientific penchant. For if in the sacred subject and object are interdependent, if the sacred "always intimately affects the subject" and deeply penetrates our experience, how can we take the sacred as a mere object to be apprehended from the outside?[11] For Bataille, this question emerged with all its consequentiality in the specific instance of our confrontation with death. In this situation, cold knowledge approaches the corpse as a scientific object that needs to be dissected in order to establish death's physical causes and consequences. We realize, however, that science is unable to account for the anguish we feel in the tragic moment

8 Ibid., 32.

9 Bataille, "La guerre et la philosophie du sacré," first published in *Critique*, now in OC, vol. 12.

10 Bataille has been variously criticized for his acceptance of the division sacred/ profane. See for example Agamben, *Homo Sacer*. It is, however, evident that Bataille came to a different understanding of this issue over time.

11 Bataille, "La guerre et la philosophie du sacré," in OC, 12: 49, where the original reads "toujours importe au sujet intimement."

when we face death. The scientific approach leaves the critical existential dimension aside and alters the meaning of what it reveals. In so doing, it "abandon(s) the prey for the shadow" and gives up meaning.[12] But is it possible to access the sacred without acknowledging its horror, Bataille asked. Is it possible or even wise to ignore the implications of the tragic? By articulating these dilemmas, Bataille exposed the difficulty of dealing with an "object," such as the sacred, that continuously undoes its limits. He believed that although sociology had taken up the challenge of studying the sacred, the tensions generated by the strictures of objectivity, to which sociology was bound, risked hollowing its efforts. Sociology at the minimum had to be aware of this risk.[13] The understanding of the "totality of being" was at stake.

The notion of the totality of being evoked by Bataille in his review of Caillois resurfaced in several of his writings in the 1940s and 1950s. Here Bataille brought to the fore various questions that had emerged at the Collège vis-à-vis Mauss's concept of total phenomenon. In the late 1930s, Bataille was wary of sociology's tendency to eschew lived experience and saw a disjunction between his approach and Mauss's. In the 1950s, however, Bataille's reflections on the sacred moved him closer to Mauss's suggestive idea of total phenomenon, even though Bataille held onto a notion of totality as "being which exceeds the limits of the possible and until death."[14] Bataille's rapprochement with Mauss occurred, in a surprising development, through aesthetics, which Bataille had begun to re-evaluate after the Collège. With a sleight of hand, Bataille rescued art from its profane status of deceptive trick and turned aesthetics into a bridge that linked the natural to the human world. Unexpectedly, aesthetics became another means for Bataille to reiterate his anti-idealistic beliefs, the non-utilitarian essence of true existence. Art was reinserted into the sacred in a move that no doubt constituted the most striking innovation in Bataille's post-Collège intellectual stance.

Inspired in part by recent discoveries of primitive drawings at the Lascaux caves of southern France, Bataille revisited the question of art's potential by focusing on art's historical transformations. More specifically,

12 Ibid., 50.

13 In the "Appendice" for *Théorie de la religion* (probably redacted in 1948), Bataille wrote, "It seems to me that Émile Durkheim is being unjustly slandered these days. I take my distance from his doctrine but not without holding onto its essential core." See *OC*, 7: 58.

14 See Bataille's book review "René Char et la force de la poésie," first published in *Critique*, now in *OC*, 12: 129, where Bataille wrote of totality as "l'être excédant des limites du possible et jusque dans la mort."

by describing modernity as a time when artists had achieved autonomy and were no longer serving a master or pursuing functional goals, Bataille envisaged in art the ability to interpret humans' aspirations toward non-useful ends.[15] As he stated in 1944 with a rehabilitating gesture toward literature, the authentic writer refuses servility.[16] Even the much-maligned Surrealism could be redeemed within this new perspective, and Bataille wrote about Surrealist poetry's sacred character.[17] In the face of art's withdrawal from the world of objects, that is, from thinking in terms of function, Bataille interpreted art as an instance of sacrifice – the ultimate expression of the sacred. Art refused to be reduced to useful value or submit to beauty and, thus, constituted a movement against subordination.[18] Bataille defended his view of art on the basis of art's origins. He held that art's birth coincided with the awareness of a lost savagery, the poetic rendition of animality at the precise time when humans were beginning to distinguish themselves from beasts in the act of drawing. The Lascaux caves' representations showed that humans resisted the world of durable things which they were in the process of creating. They tried to efface their ascent to humanness. In fact, the Lascaux drawings portrayed only poetic images of animals, Bataille argued, and humans, when present, were depicted with animal heads. Hidden from this art was our incipient humanity, our growing difference from the animal world as we began to embrace reason and pursue practical ends.[19]

With this original reading of art's origins, Bataille's new assessment of the sacred combined with his early critique of spiritual elevation and

15 Among Bataille's several discussions of art at the time, see *Lascaux ou La Naissance de l'art*, in *OC*, vol. 9 (published in English as *Lascaux; or, The Birth of Art: Prehistoric Painting*), and "L'utilité de l'art," "L'impressionnisme," and "L'équivoque de la culture," in *OC*, vol. 12. On *Lascaux*, see Ungar, "Phantom Lascaux."

16 See Bataille, "La littérature est-elle utile?" first published in *Combat*, now in *OC*, vol. 11.

17 See "Lettre à M. Merleau-Ponty," first published in *Combat*, now in *OC*, vol. 11. See also notes to "De l'existentialisme au primat de l'économie," where Bataille showed that he sided with Surrealism against Sartre and existentialism, and where we learn that he was preparing a critique of Heidegger's "philosophy of fascism" (573). For a draft of this critique, see Bataille, "Critique of Heidegger." For a commentary on this writing, see Geroulanos, "An Anthropology of Exit: Bataille on Heidegger and Fascism." For an interpretation of the Collège as Surrealist, see Richardson, "Sociology on a Razor's Edge."

18 See Bataille, "La laideur belle ou la beauté laide dans l'art et la littérature," first published in *Critique*, now in *OC*, vol. 11. In "The Notion of Expenditure," Bataille had already linked the sacred and poetry. See Bataille, *Visions of Excess*.

19 See Bataille, "Le passage de l'animal à l'homme et la naissance de l'art," first published in *Critique*; and "Au rendez-vous de Lascaux, l'homme civilisé se retrouve homme de désir," first published in *Arts*, both in *OC*, vol. 12.

11 Georges Bataille at Lascaux, circa 1955. Photo by Éditions
d'Art Albert Skira

resulted in a reconsideration of art. But if art was rehabilitated, one
should add, this move did not engender a reappraisal of politics, art's
Cinderella sister at the Collège. On the contrary, in the early 1940s
Bataille remained curiously distant from politics. He instead became increasingly entrenched in deciphering the inner workings of experience
and, in the wake of Maurice Blanchot, concluded that community was
impossible.[20] In his last lecture at the Collège of 4 July 1939, Bataille had
already manifested his propensity to think of unity in terms of loss.
Taking erotic activity as a supreme instance of this form of experience,
Bataille had argued that only by losing a part of themselves did individuals in a couple form a new being. Only by giving up their unity did lovers
form a bond. As he more precisely stated, "Love expresses a need for
sacrifice: Each unity must lose itself in some other that exceeds it."[21] A
community could be thought of only as loss, he continued: "When elements arrange themselves to create the whole, this is easily produced
when each of them loses, through a tear in its integrity, a portion of its

20 On Blanchot's influence on Bataille, see, among others, Surya, *Georges Bataille*, especially the chapter "La communauté des amis."
21 Bataille, "The College of Sociology," in Hollier, *The College of* Sociology, 337.

particular being for the benefit of the communal being."[22] Loss and wounds were conditions for communication, and in its turn communication identified and established the sacred. This approach to the sacred became Bataille's priority, and his work on inner experience unfolded along these lines. How can experience be communicated? - the question presided over much of Bataille's post-Collège activity.[23] To be sure, community was not a new interest for Bataille since it had been a central concept at the Collège. The focus, however, had now shifted away from the intent to activate a sacred social and moved toward a general vision that sought modes of "being in common" based on sharing experience. A community could not be enacted out of will by unleashing violent energy and turbulence, Bataille seemed to conclude. Communication, he wrote, "is something that in no way adds on to human reality but rather constitutes it."[24] The appeal of an excess of the social needed to be mediated by this awareness.

Meanwhile, in the faraway land of Argentina, Caillois's post-Collège activities moved in quite a different direction. Caillois had left France in June 1939, missing the last lecture at the Collège. He was supposed to return in the fall, at which point the Collège would hold a small conference. History, however, took the upper hand. After France, along with Great Britain, declared war against Germany, Caillois remained in Buenos Aires, where he attempted to establish a subsidiary of the Collège. While back in Paris the group had dispersed, in South America Caillois kept alive themes and issues that had been paramount at the Collège. His discussions of politics and democracy, published by the journal *Sur* in the section on sociological themes, mirrored and developed concerns voiced in the evening lectures at the Galeries du Livre.[25] Caillois's critical

22 Ibid., 338. Bataille's reference to lovers has striking resonance with Max Weber's discussion of the erotic sphere in the context of the rationalization of everyday life. Weber wrote of the erotic relation, "This boundless giving of oneself is as radical as possible in its opposition to all functionality, rationality, and generality." He continued by affirming that the meaning of the relation "rests upon the possibility of a communion which is felt as a complete unification, as a fading of the 'thou.'" See Weber, "Religious Rejections of the World and Their Directions," 347.

23 In 1943, Bataille participated in a Collège d'études socratiques, which was in charge of "elaborating an ensemble of scholastic presuppositions regarding inner experience." See *OC*, 6: 476, "Note." See also Annexes 2, Collège socratique, *OC*, vol. 6.

24 See *L'expérience intérieure*, *OC*, 5: 37, where Bataille critiqued Heidegger. See English translation, *Inner Experience*, 24. The translation reads, "[C]ommunication is a phenomenon which is in no way added on to Dasein, but constitutes it."

25 On Caillois's Argentinian stay and his relationship with Victoria Ocampo, see, among others, Felgine, *Roger Caillois*, and Marina Galletti, "Du Collège de sociologie aux 'Debates sobre temas sociologicos.'"

approach to aesthetics also remained unchanged in the early 1940s and
continued to drive his assessment of the social. *Puissances du roman,* which
Caillois published in 1942, examined the sociological link between the
novel and society and not surprisingly concluded with a condemnation of
the novel.[26] A typical product of modern times, the novel, Caillois proclaimed, would seem to have a pedagogical mission that aims at instruct-
ing the reader about phenomena that escape our consciousness. However,
the characters in the novel most often reflect the "personal," and therefore profane, world of the novelist. Writers examine only their own passions, experiences, and memories whereas ancient literature espoused
"collective" deeds, that is, the sacred in the guise of national legends and
myths. In addition, in the case of novels, readers identify with the heroes,
who are in their turn reflections of the authors. In the past, instead, art
represented and epitomized the social world in which it was embedded.
Finally, the novel does not elicit one's sensitivity or intelligence and merely focuses on the problems of a decomposing society, thus accelerating
social disintegration: the novel distracts people from facing reality in a
"virile" way.[27] Using the example of architecture, Caillois compared
sumptuous constructions, as expression of the collectivity, to the solitary
activity of the reader immersed in the imaginary world of the novel. The
disappearance of monumental architecture marked the end of an era
when constructions symbolized collective greatness.[28] Incidentally, we
know that architecture embodied the opposite meaning for Bataille, who
condemned it as complicit with authority.[29]

Caillois viewed the novel as compromising society's solidity or, in
Durkheim's language, social solidarity. The novel's focus on psychological interiority tended to enervate and exhaust the readers' vigour. Its increasing attention to physical love isolated the couple in the bedroom,
whose walls literally separated the two individuals from the rest of the
world. In another instance that clearly showed Bataille's and Caillois's
opposing views, Caillois proclaimed that bed "is truly the place where
society counts the least for man."[30] The physical act of copulating cuts
the individual off from the group as no other act can: in the secrecy
of the bedroom, the social dissolves. By portraying lovers' embraces, the
novel manifests and precipitates the collapse of collective links: the

26 *Puissances du roman,* now included in Caillois, *Approches de l'imaginaire.*
27 Ibid., 167.
28 Ibid., 211.
29 See Hollier, *Against Architecture.*
30 Ibid., 225. See Hollier's discussion of the differences between Bataille and Caillois in
"Foreword," in Hollier, *The College of Sociology.*

individual retires to his/her personal universe, the world of imagination and dreams. The novel, in sum, represented for Caillois the relentless victorious march of the private, the defeat of the collective, the profanation of the social.[31]

Although Caillois eventually acknowledged that the novel could critique the condition of asociality, the recomposed whole that he envisioned entailed the disappearance of the novel, along with the end of profane myths. Following the Collège's originary vision, Caillois saw no role for art in rekindling the soul of modernity, and he maintained his negative evaluation. To be fair, Caillois's examination of the novel in principle excluded aesthetic considerations. As he wrote, "This work is, and is nothing but, a sociological study ... since it limited itself to examine the role of the novel in society, it had to avoid all aesthetic or moral considerations."[32] Caillois thought of the novel as a bastardized product of literature of minimal aesthetic value: the novel eluded the parameters of an art form. Yet the novel still belonged to the realm of literature, and Caillois's operation of evacuating art from the novel only amplified his strong contempt for an individualizing practice that he considered the lowest of any artistic endeavour. For Caillois, art's road either led to a precipice or meandered in a distracting and pointless way. In reaching his goal of intervening in the social, Caillois did not contemplate any crossing of paths with art.

Caillois and Bataille went separate ways after the Collège, physically and intellectually. Although Caillois appeared to be more faithful to positions and interests he had held at the Collège, Bataille, too, never abandoned the impulses that had originally driven him to sponsor the study of the sacred. In a letter to Caillois of 24 November 1957 in which he announced his new publishing project, the journal *Genèse*, Bataille wrote, "We are still dealing after all with the continuation of this Collège, which appears to have a really hard time dying out."[33] In spite of the twists and turns in his intellectual production, Bataille never saw himself as suppressing his sociological quest. Rather, his pushing the question of community to the extreme had taken the sociological discussion to a new level, one that was more lucid and better able to distance the notion of

31 As is well known, these issues were also central to Lukàcs's and Benjamin's theories of the novel.

32 Caillois, *Approches de l'imaginaire*, 153.

33 Bataille, *Lettres à Roger Caillois*, 140. The subtitle of *Genèse* was *Sexologie, Psychoanalyse, Philosophie de la Sexualité* (*Sexology, Psychoanalysis, Philosophy of Sexuality*). One wonders what to make of Klossowski's statement to Henri-Lévy that "Caillois and he (Bataille) hated each other. One has not said it enough, but they hated each other." See Henri-Lévy, *Les aventures de la liberté*, 169.

togetherness from political equivocation. The most valuable legacy of
the Collège is indeed to be found in Bataille's serious and responsible
rethinking the parameters of "being together." Although the Collège
misrecognized aesthetics' radical, sensual dimension in spite of promoting affectivity, and although it underestimated the profoundly political
nature of its theorizing, by attending to the sacred the Collège emphasized the emotional and symbolic-imaginary underpinning of society
and warned about the sacred's ambiguous incarnations. The Collège
thus encourages us to reflect on such notions as that of a community that
seeks to undermine unity, a political that intends to escape politics, or a
sovereign power that gives up authority.[34]

Bataille had always cautioned against and opposed communities of
fact. His simultaneous refusal of transcendence and invoking of the sacred, however, rendered his analysis of community obscure and ambiguous, if not dangerously equivocal. Yet, in the wake of Bataille, Roberto
Esposito has demonstrated the sociological potential of challenging generally accepted notions. Esposito's newly coined category of "impolitical"
defines a reaction that does not merely oppose the political but specifically indicts the political that is made into a value or a theology.[35] The
latter phenomenon, according to Esposito, is not so much the result of a
lack of religion in modernity, as many believe, as it is a consequence of
the lack of politics – a depoliticization. In light of the autonomy of the
separate value spheres, and because economic interests have risen to play
a central role in modern life, politics has become decentralized and dis-
empowered.[36] Within this context, political theology is an attempt to reinstate the political as a power that, founded on decision, is also guided
by the idea of the Good. The question then is: How can one attack politics or refuse it, when this move ends by re-establishing theology's unitar-
ian urge? Esposito's alternative is the "impolitical," an approach that rests
on Bataille's notion of community intended as that which puts people in
relation while differentiating – a whole united by what makes different.

Not unlike Nancy, Esposito makes the case that the conceptual language of philosophical-political discourse thwarts community at the same
time that it names it.[37] This happens because the concepts of individual
and totality, or particularity and identity, take community as a property

34 Derrida's idea of "living in common" seems to originate from a similar line of
thinking.
35 Esposito, *Categorie dell' impolitico.*
36 This is also in part Habermas's position.
37 Along similar lines, "experience" suffers from linguistic strictures. See Jay, "The
Limits of Limit-Experience."

– a predicate that indicates subjects belonging to the same whole. Such a predicate "adds to" the subjects' original nature and makes them "more" subjects, even if it is generated from them. In romance languages, however, community means the exact opposite of property: it indicates what is not of one's own. If we take the term *munus*, from which community originates, one of its meanings is duty along with its different connotations of obligation, office, and gift (*onus, officium, donum*). Community could thus be defined as an ensemble of people united by a duty or lack: I owe you. Property within this context is emptied out into its negative.[38]

This politico-philosophical reading of community does not, to be sure, appear to be conducive to a concrete political program; nor does it absolve Bataille and the Collège from an unresolved relationship with the political in general and fascism in particular. Although Bataille eventually redeemed aesthetics and reframed it within his conception of the sacred, his and Caillois's dismissal of the category "art," their impatience with politics, and their focus on the social led to theoretical and practical impasses that marred the Collège's reception as well as its survival. Despite all limitations, however, as Lefort's and Esposito's arguments help to show, the Collège demonstrated, albeit contradictorily, that community can be translated into a politico-philosophical vocabulary only at the cost of a distortion or perversion. If community is at the heart of our contemporary hopes and fears, the Collège de sociologie demonstrates the importance of interrogating our vision of togetherness. Rethinking the political should require nothing less.

38 See Esposito, *Communitas*. According to Esposito, Hobbes's theory of contract is a response to the realization that what humans have in common is the potential of being killed by any other human. "Communitas" for Hobbes implied the gift of death; one could stop the threat to individual integrity only by instituting its opposite: the contract. With the contract, communal social relations are sacrificed in favour of exchange – the modern paradigm that Bataille criticized as "restricted economy." The latter entails the conservation of all that is functional against the excessive drive that motivates the individual to reach the limit at the risk of death itself.

Bibliography

Abrams, M.H. "Art-as-Such: The Sociology of Modern Aesthetics." *Bulletin of the American Academy of Arts and Sciences* 38, no. 6 (1985): 8–33

Acéphale: Religion, sociologie, philosophie, 1936–1939. Edited by Michel Camus. Paris: Jean-Michel Place 1980

Adamson, Walter. *Embattled Avant-Gardes: Modernism's Resistance to Commodity Culture in Europe.* Berkeley: University of California Press 2007

Ades, Dawn, and Simon Baker, eds. *Undercover Surrealism: Georges Bataille and Documents.* Cambridge: MIT Press 2006

Agamben, Giorgio. "Bataille e il paradosso della sovranità." In Risset, *Georges Bataille: Il politico e il sacro,* 115–19

– *Homo Sacer: Sovereign Power and Bare Life.* Translated by Daniel Heller-Roazen. Stanford: Stanford University Press 1998

Alexander, Jeffrey C., ed. *Durkheimian Sociology: Cultural Studies.* Cambridge: Cambridge University Press 1990

– and Philip Smith, eds. *The Cambridge Companion to Durkheim.* Cambridge: Cambridge University Press 2005

Allen, N.J., W.S.F. Pickering, and W. Watts Miller, eds. *On Durkheim's* Elementary Forms of Religious Life. New York: Routledge 1998

Aron, Raymond. *Memoirs: Fifty Years of Political Reflections.* Translated by George Holoch. Foreword by Henry A. Kissinger. New York: Holmes and Meier Publishers 1990

Auffret, Dominique. *Alexandre Kojève. La philosophie, l'État, la fin de l'histoire.* Paris: Grasset 1990

Balakian, Anna. *André Breton: Magus of Surrealism.* New York: Oxford University Press 1971

– *Surrealism: The Road to the Absolute.* New York: The Noonday Press 1959

Barnes, H.E. "Durkheim's Contribution to the Reconstruction of Political Theory." *Political Science Quarterly* 35, no. 2 (1920): 236–54

Bataille, Georges. *The Accursed Share.* Vol. 1. Translated by Robert Hurley. New York: Zone Books 1991

– *L'Apprenti Sorcier: Du Cercle Communiste Démocratique à Acéphale.* Edited and annotated by Marina Galletti. Paris: Éditions de la Différence 1999

– "Architecture." *Documents* 2 (1929): 117

– "L' art primitif." *Documents* 7 (1930): 389–97

– "Le bas matérialisme et la gnose." *Documents* 1 (1930): 1–8

– "Le cheval académique." *Documents* 1 (1929): 27–31

– *Choix de lettres 1917–1962.* Edited and annotated by Michel Surya. Paris: Gallimard 1997

– "Critique of Heidegger." Translated by Stefanos Geroulanos. *October* 117 (Summer 2006): 25–34

– "Les écarts de la nature." *Documents* 2 (1930): 79–83

– *Eroticism.* Translated by Mary Dalwood. London: J. Calder 1962

– "L'esprit moderne et le jeu des transpositions." *Documents* 8 (1930): 489–92

– "Figure humaine." *Documents* 4 (1929): 194–201

– "Le gros orteil." *Documents* 6 (1929): 297–302

– "Informe." *Documents* 6 (1929): 382

– *Inner Experience.* Translated by Leslie Anne Boldt. Albany: State University of New York Press 1988

– "Le 'Jeu lugubre.'" *Documents* 7 (1929): 369–72

– "Joan Miró: peintures récentes." *Documents* 7 (1930): 399–403

– "Le langage des fleurs." *Documents* 3 (1929): 160–8

– *Lascaux; or, The Birth of Art: Prehistoric Painting.* Translated by Austryn Wainhouse. Geneva: Skira 1955

– *Lettres à Roger Caillois, 4 août 1935–4 février 1959.* Edited by Jean-Pierre Le Bouler with an introduction by Francis Marmande. Paris: Éditions Folle Avoine 1987

– "Matérialisme." *Documents* 3 (1929): 170

– "Métamorphose." *Documents* 6 (1929): 333–4

– "Œil." *Documents* 4 (1929): 216

– *Œuvres Complètes.* 12 vols. Paris: Gallimard 1970–88

– Papiers Georges Bataille, Correspondance, NAF 15853–15854. Bibliothèque nationale

– *La sociologie sacrée du monde contemporain.* Edited, annotated, and with an introduction by Simonetta Falasca-Zamponi. Paris: Lignes-Manifestes 2004

– "Soleil pourri." *Documents* 3 (1930): 173–4

– *Visions of Excess: Selected Writings, 1927–1939.* Edited with an introduction by Allan Stoekl. Translated by Allan Stoekl with Carl R. Lowitt and Donald M. Leslie Jr. Minneapolis: University of Minnesota Press 1985

– and Raymond Queneau. "La critique des fondements de la dialectique hégélienne." In Bataille, *Œuvres Complètes*, Vol. 1. 12 vols. Paris: Gallimard 1970–88

Becq, Annie. "Creation, Aesthetics, Market: Origins of the Modern Concept of Art." In Mattick, *Eighteenth-Century Aesthetics*, 120–54

Benda, Julien. "Démocratie et communisme." *Les Volontaires* no. 5 (April 1939): 295–302

Benjamin, Walter. *Illuminations*. Edited by Hannah Arendt. Translated by Harry Zohn. New York: Schoken Books 1973

– *Reflections: Essays, Aphorisms, Autobiographical Writings*. Edited with an introduction by Peter Demetz. Translated by Edmund Jephcott. New York: Harcourt Brace Jovanovich 1978

Berthoud, Gérald. "Pourquoi Marcel Mauss?" *Revue européenne des sciences sociales* 34, no. 105 (1996): 7–20

Besnard, Philippe. "Présentation." *Revue française de sociologie* 20, no. 1 (January–March 1979): 3–6

– ed. *The Sociological Domain: The Durkheimians and the Founding of French Sociology*. Cambridge: Cambridge University Press 1983

Besnier, Jean-Michel. "Georges Bataille in the 1930s: A Politics of the Impossible." *Yale French Studies* 78 (1990): 169–80

Biles, Jeremy. *Ecce Monstrum: Georges Bataille and the Sacrifice of Form*. New York: Fordham University Press 2007

Blachère, Jean-Claude. *Le modèle nègre: Aspects littéraires du mythe primitiviste au XXᵉ siècle chez Apollinaire, Cendrars, Tzara*. Dakar: Nouvelles Éditions Africaines 1981

Blanchot, Maurice. *The Unavowable Community*. Translated by Pierre Joris. Barrytown: Station Hill Press 2006

Blumenson, Martin. *The Vildé Affair: Beginnings of the French Resistance*. Boston: Houghton Mifflin 1977

Bois, Yve-Alain, and Rosalind Krauss. *Formless: A User's Guide*. New York: Zone Books 1997

Boldt-Irons, Leslie Anne, ed. *On Bataille: Critical Essays*. Albany: State University of New York Press 1995

Bonnet, Marguerite. "Á partir de ces 'mécaniques' à la fois naïves et véhémentes…" *Pleine Marge* no. 1 (May 1985): 18–28

Bouglé, Célestin. *Bilan de la sociologie française contemporaine*. Paris: Alcan 1935

Bourdieu, Pierre. *The Rules of Art: Genesis and Structure of the Literary Field*. Translated by Susan Emanuel. Stanford: Stanford University Press 1999

– and Jean-Claude Passeron. "Sociology and Philosophy in France since 1945: Death and Resurrection of a Philosophy without Subject." *Social Research* 34, no. 1 (1967): 162–212

Breckman, Warren. "Democracy between Disenchantment and Political Theology: French Post-Marxism and the Return of Religion." *New German Critique* 94 (Winter 2005): 72–105

Breton, André. *Communicating Vessels*. Translated by Mary Ann Caws and Geoffrey T. Harris. Lincoln: University of Nebraska Press 1990

– *The Lost Steps.* Translated by Mark Polizzotti. Lincoln: University of Nebraska Press 1996
– *Manifestes du Surréalisme.* Paris: Pauvert 1977
– *Manifestoes of Surrealism.* Translated by Richard Seaver and Helen R. Lane. Ann Arbor: University of Michigan Press 1969
– "Les mots sans rides." *Littérature* nouvelle série 7 (December 1922): 12–14
– *Œuvres complètes,* Vol. 2. 3 vols. Edited by Marguerite Bonnet. Paris: Gallimard 1992
– *Les pas perdus.* Paris: Gallimard 1924
– *Les vases communicants.* Paris: Gallimard 1932 [1955]
– *What is Surrealism? Selected Writings.* Plymouth: Monad Press 1978
– and Philippe Soupault. *Les champs magnétiques.* Paris: Éditions du Sans Pareil 1920
Bruno, Jean. "Les techniques d'illumination chez Georges Bataille." *Critique* (August-September 1963): 706–20
Buck-Morss, Susan. "Aesthetics and Anaesthetics: Walter Benjamin's Artwork Reconsidered." *New Formations* no. 20 (Summer 1993): 123–43
Bürger, Peter, *Theory of the Avant-Garde.* Translated by Michael Shaw. Foreword by Jochen Schulte-Sasse. Minneapolis: University of Minnesota Press 1984
Bürger, Peter, and Christa Bürger. *The Institutions of Art.* Lincoln: University of Nebraska Press 1992
Burke, Edmund. *A Philosophical Enquiry into the Origin of Our Ideas of the Sublime and Beautiful.* 1756. Edited with an introduction and notes by Adam Phillips. Oxford: Oxford University Press 1990
Busino, Giovanni. "Marcel Mauss, interprète d'un phénomène social total: le bolchevisme." *Revue européenne des sciences sociales* 34, no. 105 (1996): 75–91
Cahiers, Jean Paulhan 6, *Corréspondance Jean Paulhan-Roger Caillois 1934–1967.* Edited by Odile Felgine and Claude-Pierre Perez. Introduction by Laurent Jenny. Paris: Gallimard 1991
Caillé, Alain. "Claude Lefort, the Social Sciences and Political Philosophy." *Thesis Eleven* 43 (1995): 48–65
Caillois, Roger. *Approches de l'imaginaire.* Paris: Gallimard 1974
– *Cases d'un échiquier.* Paris: Gallimard 1970
– *Circostancielles, 1940–1945.* Paris: Gallimard 1946
– *La Communion des Forts. Études sociologiques.* Marseille: Éditions du Sagittaire 1944
– "De la fête à la guerre." *Liberté de l'esprit* 21 (May 1951): 129–32
– *The Edge of Surrealism: A Roger Caillois Reader.* Edited by Claudine Frank. Translated by Claudine Frank and Camille Naish. Durham: Duke University Press 2003
– Review of *L'Exercice du pouvoir,* by Léon Blum. *Nouvelle Revue Française* (October 1937): 6736

- "Guerre et démocratie." *La Nouvelle Nouvelle Revue Française* 1, no. 2
  (February 1953): 235–54
- "La Hiérarchie des Êtres: Relations et Oppositions de la Démocratie, du
  Fascisme et de la Notion d'Ordre." *Les Volontaires* no. 5 (April 1939): 317–26
- *L'Homme et le sacré.* Paris: Gallimard 1939
- *Instincts et société. Essais de sociologie contemporaine.* Paris: Gonthier 1964
- "The Logic of Imagination (Avatars of the Octopus)." *Diogenes* no. 69 (1970):
  75–98
- *Man and the Sacred.* Translated by Meyer Barash. Glencoe: The Free Press
  1959
- "Le mythe et l'art: nature de leur opposition." *Deuxième Congrès International
  d'Esthétique et de Science de l'Art.* 1: 280–2. Paris: Alcan 1937
- *Le Mythe et l'homme.* Paris: Gallimard 1938
- *La Nécéssité d'esprit.* Paris: Gallimard 1981
- *The Necessity of the Mind.* Venice: The Lapis Press 1990
- "Notes pour un itinéraire de Roger Caillois." In *Roger Caillois. "Cahiers pour un
  temps."* Paris: Pandora Éditions 1981
- *Puissances du roman.* Marseille: Éditions du Sagittaire 1942
- *Quatre essais de sociologie contemporaine.* Paris: Olivier Perrin 1951
- *Rencontres.* Paris: Presses Universitaires de France 1978
- *Le rocher de Sisyphe.* Paris: Gallimard 1946
- "La secte au pouvoir." *France libre* 8, no. 43 (15 May 1944): 26–31
Caruso, Paolo, ed. *Conversazioni con Claude Lévi-Strauss, Michel Foucault, Jacques
  Lacan.* Milan: Mursia 1969
Chytry, Joseph. *The Aesthetic State: A Quest in Modern German Thought.* Berkeley:
  University of California Press 1989
Clark, Terry N. *Prophets and Patrons: The French University and the Emergence of the
  Social Sciences.* Cambridge: Harvard University Press 1973
Clastres, Pierre. *La Société contre l'État. Recherches d'anthropologie politique.* Paris:
  Éditions de Minuit 1974
- *Society Against the State: Essays in Political Anthropology.* Translated by Robert
  Hurley with Abe Stein. New York: Zone Books 1987
Clifford, James. *The Predicament of Culture: Twentieth-Century Ethnography,
  Literature, and Art.* Cambridge: Harvard University Press 1988 [1981]
Cohen, Margaret. *Profane Illumination: Walter Benjamin and the Paris of Surrealist
  Revolution.* Berkeley: University of California Press 1993
Coleman, Francis X.J. *The Aesthetic Thought of the French Enlightenment.*
  Pittsburgh: University of Pittsburgh Press 1971
Colleyn, Jean-Paul. "Le sacrifice selon Hubert et Mauss." *Systèmes de penséee en
  Afrique noire* 2 (1976): 23–42
Condominas, Georges. "Marcel Mauss, père de l'ethnographie française." Part 1.
  Critique 28, no. 301 (June 1972): 118–39

Conklin, Alice . "Civil Society, Science, and Empire in Late Republican France: The Foundation of Paris's Museum of Man." *Osiris* 17 (2002): 255–90

Conley, Katharine. "Modernist Primitivism in 1933: Brassaï's 'Involuntary Sculptures' in *Minotaure*." *Modernism/Modernity* 10, no. 1 (2003): 127–40

Connor, Peter. *Georges Bataille and the Mysticism of Sin*. Baltimore: Johns Hopkins University Press 2000

Couteneau, Georges. "L'art sumérien: les conventions de la statuaire." *Documents* 1 (1929): 1–8

Cuvillier, Armand. *Introduction à la sociologie*. Paris: Colin 1939 [1936]

Damisch, Hubert. "Du mot à l'aspect. Paraphrase." In Hollier, *Georges Bataille après tout*, 81–99

Dean, Carolyn. *The Frail Social Body: Pornography, Homosexuality, and Other Fantasies in Interwar France*. Berkeley: University of California Press 2000

– *The Self and Its Pleasures: Bataille, Lacan, and the History of the Decentered Subject*. Ithaca: Cornell University Press 1992

Décultot, Elisabeth. "Aesthetik/esthétique: Étapes d'une naturalisation (1750–1840)." *Revue de méthaphysique et de morale* 2, no. 34 (2002): 7–28

Derrida, Jacques. "From Restricted to General Economy: A Hegelianism without Reserves." *Semiotext(e)* 2, no. 2 (1976): 25–55

Dias, Nélia. *Le Musée d'ethnographie du Trocadéro (1878–1908): Anthropologie et muséologie en France*. Paris: Éditions du CNRS 1991

Didi-Huberman, Georges. "Comment déchire-t-on la ressemblance?" In Hollier, *Georges Bataille après tout*, 101–24

– *La ressemblance informe ou le gai savoir visuel selon Georges Bataille*. Paris: Macula 1995

Di Donato, Riccardo. "Marcel Mauss et la 'Völkerpsychologie.'" *Revue européenne des sciences sociales* 34, no. 105 (1996): 67–74

Documents: Doctrines, Archéologie, Beaux-Arts, Ethnographie. Reprint. Preface by Denis Hollier. 2 vols. Paris: Jean-Michel Place 1991

Doyle, Natalie. "Democracy as Socio-Cultural Project of Individual and Collective Sovereignty: Claude Lefort, Marcel Gauchet and the French Debate on Modern Autonomy." *Thesis Eleven* 75 (November 2003): 69–95

– "The Sacred, Social Creativity and the State." In *Recognition, Work, Politics*, edited by Jean-Philippe Deranty, Danielle Petherbridge, and John Rundell, 231–62. Leiden: Brill 2007

Drury, Shadia. *Alexandre Kojève: The Roots of Postmodern Politics*. New York: St. Martin's Press 1994

Dubief, Henri. "Témoignage sur Contre-Attaque (1935–1936)." *Textures* 6 (1970): 52–9

Dudnik, Stefan. "Cuts and Bruises and Democratic Contestation: Male Bodies, History and Politics." *European Journal of Cultural Studies* 4, no. 2 (2001): 153–70

Dumézil, Georges. "Science et politique: Réponse à Carlo Ginzburg." *Annales ESC* no. 5 (September-October 1985): 985–9

Dumont, Louis. "Une science en devenir." *L'Arc* 48 (1972): 8–21

Durkheim, Émile. *The Division of Labor in Society.* Introduction by Lewis Coser. New York: Free Press 1997

– *The Elementary Forms of Religious Life.* Translated with an introduction by Karen E. Fields. New York: Free Press 1995

– *Les Formes élémentaires de la vie religieuse. Le système totémique en Australie.* Paris: Presses Universitaires de France 1998

– *Journal sociologique.* Edited with an introduction by Jean Duvignaud. Paris: Presses Universitaires de France 1969

– *Lettres à Marcel Mauss.* Edited by Philippe Besnard and Marcel Fournier. Paris: Presses Universitaires de France 1998

– *Moral Education: A Study in the Theory and Applications of the Sociology of Education.* Edited with an introduction by Everett K. Wilson. Foreword by Paul Fauconnet. New York: Free Press 1961

– *On Morality and Society.* Edited with an introduction by Robert Bellah. Chicago: University of Chicago Press 1973

– *The Rules of Sociological Method.* Edited by George E.G. Caitlin. Translated by Sarah A. Solovay and John H. Mueller. New York: Free Press 1964

– *Socialism and Saint-Simon.* Edited with introduction by Alvin W. Gouldner. Translated by Charlotte Sattler. Yellow Springs: The Antioch Press 1958

– *Sociology and Philosophy.* Translated by D.F. Pocock. Introduction by J.G. Peristiany. London: Cohen and West Ltd. 1953

– *Suicide: A Study in Sociology.* Edited by George Simpson. Translated by John A. Spaulding. New York: Free Press 1997

– *Textes.* Edited by Victor Karady. 3 vols. Paris: Éditions de Minuit 1975

– and Marcel Mauss. *Primitive Classification.* Translated, edited, and with an introduction by Rodney Needham. Chicago: University of Chicago Press 1963

Eagleton, Terry. *The Ideology of the Aesthetic.* Oxford: Blackwell 1990

Einstein, Carl. "Aphorismes méthodiques." *Documents* 1 (1929): 32–4

– "L'exposition de l'art abstrait à Zurich." *Documents* 6 (1929): 342

– "Gravures d'Hercules Seghers." *Documents* 4 (1929): 202–8

– "Negerplastik ('La sculpture nègre')." In Margit Rowell, ed., *Qu'est-ce que la sculpture moderne?* edited by Margit Rowell, 344–53. Paris: Centre Georges Pompidou 1986

– "Pablo Picasso. Quelques tableaux de 1928." *Documents* 1 (1929): 35–47

– "Rossignol." *Documents* 2 (1929): 117–18

Esposito, Roberto. *Categorie dell' impolitico.* Bologna: Il Mulino 1988

– *Communitas. Origine e destino della comunità.* Turin: Einaudi 1998

Falasca-Zamponi, Simonetta. *Fascist Spectacle: The Aesthetics of Power in Mussolini's Italy.* Berkeley: University of California Press 1997

Faublée, Jacques. "L'École sociologique française et l'étude des religions dites 'primitives.'" *L'Année sociologique* 28 (1977): 19–40

Fauconnet, Paul, and Marcel Mauss. "Sociologie." In Mauss, *Œuvres*, 3: 139–77

Favre, Pierre. "The Absence of Political Sociology in the Durkheimian Classification of the Social Sciences." In Besnard, *The Sociological Domain*, 199–216

Felgine, Odile. *Roger Caillois, biographie.* Paris: Stock 1994

ffrench, Patrick. *After Bataille: Sacrifice, Exposure, Community.* London: Legenda 2007

Filloux, Jean-Claude. *Durkheim et le socialisme.* Geneva: Droz 1977

Flynn, Bernard. *The Philosophy of Claude Lefort: Interpreting the Political.* Evanston: Northwestern University Press 2005

Fournier, Marcel. "Durkheim, *L'Année sociologique* et l'art." *Études durkheimiennes*, Bulletin d'information no. 12 (January 1987): 1–10

– *Marcel Mauss.* Paris: Fayard 1994

– *Marcel Mauss: A Biography.* Princeton: Princeton University Press 2006

– " Si je devais réécrire la biographie de Marcel Mauss ..." *Revue européenne des sciences sociales* 34, no. 105 (1996): 27–37

– and Christine DeLangle, eds. "Autour du Sacrifice: Lettres d'Émile Durkheim, J.G. Frazer, M. Mauss, et E.B. Tylor." *Études Durkheimiennes* (Fall 1991): 2–12

Fourny, Jean-François. "Roger Caillois au Collège de Sociologie: la politique et ses masques." *The French Review* 58, no. 4 (March 1985): 533–9

Friedland, Roger. "Drag Kings at the Totem Ball." In Alexander and Smith, *The Cambridge Companion to Durkheim*, 239–73

Galletti, Marina. "Du Collège de sociologie aux 'Debates sobre temas sociologicos:' Roger Caillois en Argentine." In *Roger Caillois, la pensée aventurée*, edited by Laurent Jenny, 139–74. Paris: Belin 1992

– "'Masses': un 'Collège' mancato?" In Risset, *Georges Bataille: Il politico e il sacro*, 77–94

Gane, Mike, ed. *The Radical Sociology of Durkheim and Mauss.* London: Routledge 1992

Gemerchak, Christopher. *The Sunday of the Negative: Reading Bataille Reading Hegel.* Albany: State University of New York Press 2003

Geroulanos, Stefanos. "An Anthropology of Exit: Bataille on Heidegger and Fascism." *October* 117 (Summer 2006): 3–24

Gerth, Hans, and C. Wright Mills, eds. *From Max Weber: Essays in Sociology.* Translated with an introduction by Hans Gerth and C. Wright Mills. New York: Oxford University Press 1946

Ghrenassia, Patrick. "Anatole Lewitzky: De l'ethnologie à la Résistance." *La Liberté de l'esprit* no. 16 (1987): 237–53

Giddens, Anthony. "Durkheim's Political Sociology." *Sociological Review Monograph* 19 (1971): 477–519

Ginzburg, Carlo. "Mythologie germanique et nazisme: Sur un ancien livre de Georges Dumézil." *Annales ESC* no. 4 (July–August 1985): 695–715

Goldwater, Robert. *Primitivism in Modern Art.* Cambridge: Belknap Press 1938 (enlarged edition 1986)

Gould, Carol C. "Claude Lefort on Modern Democracy." *Praxis International* 10, nos. 3–4 (October–January 1990–91): 337–45

Greeley, Robin Adèle. *Surrealism and the Spanish Civil War.* New Haven: Yale University Press 2006

Griaule, Marcel. "Légende illustrée de la Reine de Saba." *Documents* 1 (1930): 9–16

– *Masques Dogons.* Paris: Institut d'Ethnologie 1938

– "Poterie." *Documents* 4 (1930): 236

– "Un coup de fusil." *Documents* 1 (1930): 46

Guastalla, René. *Le Mythe et le livre.* Paris: Gallimard 1940

Haar, Michel. *Par delà du nihilisme. Nouveaux essais sur Nietzsche.* Paris: Presses Universitaires de France 1998

Habermas, Jürgen. *The Structural Transformation of the Public Sphere. An Inquiry into a Category of Bourgeois Society.* Translated by Thomas Burger with Frederick Lawrence. Boston: MIT Press 1991

Habib, Claude. "*De la servitude volontaire.* Une lecture politique." In Habib and Mouchard, *La démocratie à l'œuvre,* 191–211

– and Claude Mouchard, eds. *La démocratie à l'œuvre. Autour de Claude Lefort.* Paris: Éditions Seuil 1993

Hawkins, M.J. "Émile Durkheim on Democracy and Absolutism." *History of Political Thought* 2, no. 2 (Summer 1981): 369–90

Heimonet, Jean-Michel. "Le Collège de Sociologie: Un gigantesque malentendu." *Esprit* 89 (May 1984): 40–56

– "Le Collège et son double: Jules Monnerot et le Collège de Sociologie Interrompu." *The French Review* 60, no. 2 (December 1986): 231–40

– *Jules Monnerot ou la démission critique, 1932–1990 – Trajet d'un intellectuel vers le fascisme.* Paris: Éditions Kime 1993

– *Négativité et communication. La part maudite du Collège de sociologie, l'Hégélianisme et ses monstres, Habermas et Bataille.* Paris: Jean-Michel Place 1990

– *Politique de l'écriture: Bataille/Derrida: Le sens du sacré dans la pensée française du surréalisme à nos jours.* Chapel Hill: University of North Carolina Press 1987

Henri-Lévy, Bernard. *Les aventures de la liberté. Une histoire subjective des intellectuels.* Paris: Bernard Grasset 1991

Hertz, Robert. *Death and the Right Hand.* Translated by Rodney and Claudia Needham. Introduction by Edward Evans-Pritchard. Aberdeen: Cohen and West 1960

Hess, Jonathan. *Reconstituting the Body Politic: Enlightenment, Public Culture, and the Invention of Aesthetic Autonomy.* Detroit: Wayne State University Press 1999

Hollier, Denis. *Absent without Leave: French Literature under the Threat of War.* Translated by Catherine Porter. Cambridge: Harvard University Press 1997

– *Against Architecture: The Writings of Georges Bataille.* Translated by Betsy Wing. Cambridge: MIT Press 1989

– ed. *Le Collège de Sociologie 1937–1939.* Paris: Gallimard 1995

– ed. *The College of Sociology 1937–39.* Translated by Betsy Wing. Minneapolis: University of Minnesota Press 1988

– ed. *Georges Bataille après tout.* Paris: Éditions Belin 1995

– "January 21st." *Stanford French Review* 12 (Spring 1988): 31–47

– "Malaise dans la sociologie." *L'Arc* 48 (1972): 55–61

– "Mimesis and Castration 1937." *October* 31 (Winter 1984): 3–15

– "La valeur d'usage de l'impossible." *Documents.* Reprint. Paris: Jean-Michel Place 1991

Howard, Dick. "Introduction to Lefort." *Telos* no. 22 (Winter 1974–75): 2–30

Hubert, Henri, and Marcel Mauss. "Introduction à l'analyse de quelques phénomènes religieux." In Mauss, *Œuvres*, 1: 3–65

– *Sacrifice: Its Nature and Function.* Translated by W.D. Halls. Foreword by E.E. Evans Pritchard. Chicago: University of Chicago Press 1964

Isambert, François. "L'élaboration de la notion de sacré dans l'école durkheimienne." *Archives de sciences sociales des religions* 42 (1976): 35–56

Jacknis, Ira. "Franz Boas and Exhibits: On the Limitations of the Museum Method in Anthropology." In Stocking, *Objects and Others*, 75–111

Jackson, Julian. *The Popular Front in France: Defending Democracy, 1934–38.* Cambridge: Cambridge University Press 1988

James, Wendy, and N.J. Allen, eds. *Marcel Mauss: A Centenary Tribute.* New York: Berghahn Books 1998

Jamin, Jean. "Aux origines du Musée de l'Homme: La Mission ethnographique et linguistique Dakar-Djibouti." In *La Mission Ethnographique Dakar-Djibouti 1931–1933*, 7–86. Bordeaux: Université de Bordeaux II 1984

– "De l'humaine condition de 'Minotaure.'" In *Regards sur Minotaure. La revue à tête de bête*, 7–86. Geneva: Musée d'art et d'histoire 1987

– "L'ethnographie mode d'inemploi: De quelques rapports de l'ethnologie avec la malaise dans la civilisation." In *Le mal et la douleur*, edited by Jacques Hainard and Roland Kaehr, 45–79. Neuchâtel: Musée d'ethnographie 1986

– "Objets trouvés des paradis perdus: À propos de la Mission Dakar-Djibouti." In *Collections passion*, edited by Jacques Hainard and Roland Kaehr, 69–100. Neuchâtel: Musée d'ethnographie 1982

– "Quand le sacré devint gauche." *L'Ire des Vents* 3, no. 4 (1981): 98–118

– "Un sacré Collège ou les apprentis sorciers de la sociologie." *Cahiers Internationaux de Sociologie* 68 (January–June 1980): 5–30

Jay, Martin. *Downcast Eyes: The Denigration of Vision in Twentieth-Century French Thought.* Berkeley: University of California Press 1994

- *Force Fields: Between Intellectual History and Cultural Critique.* London: Routledge 1992
- "The Limits of Limit-Experience: Bataille and Foucault." *Constellations* 2, no. 2 (October 1995): 155–74
- *Songs of Experience: Modern American and European Variations on a Universal Theme.* Berkeley: University of California Press 2005

Jones, Robert Alun. "Robertson Smith, Durkheim and Sacrifice: An Historical Context for *The Elementary Forms of the Religious Life.*" *Journal of the History of the Behavioral Sciences* 17, no. 2 (April 1981): 184–205

Joyce, Conor. *Carl Einstein in* Documents *and His Collaboration with Georges Bataille.* Philadelphia: Xlibris Corporation 2003

Karady, Victor. "Durkheim et les débuts de l'ethnologie universitaire." In *Émile Durkheim: Critical Assessments,* edited by Peter Hamilton, 7:139–55. 8 vols. London and New York: Routledge 1993

Karsenti, Bruno. *L'homme total: sociologie, anthropologie et philosophie chez Marcel Mauss.* Paris: Presses Universitaires de France 1997

Kleinberg, Ethan. *Generation Existential: Heidegger's Philosophy in France.* Ithaca: Cornell University Press 2005

Klossowski, Pierre. "Between Marx and Fourier." In *On Walter Benjamin: Critical Essays and Recollections,* edited by Gary Smith. Cambridge: MIT Press 1988
- "Entre Marx et Fourier." *Le Monde,* 31 May 1969: 4
- "Lettre sur Walter Benjamin." *Mercure de France* 1067 (July 1952): 456–7
- *Sade My Neighbor.* Translated by Alphonso Lingis. Evanston: Northwestern University Press 1991

Koyré, Alexandre. "La sociologie française contemporaine." *Zeitschrift für Sozialforschung* 5 (1936): 263–4

Krauss, Rosalind. *The Originality of the Avant-Garde and Other Modernist Myths.* Cambridge: MIT Press 1985

Kristeller, Paul. *Renaissance Thought and the Arts: Collected Essays.* Princeton: Princeton University Press 1990

La Critique sociale. Reprint. Paris: Éditions de la Différence 1983

Lacroix, Bernard. *Durkheim et le politique.* Paris: Presses de la fondation nationale des sciences politiques 1981

Lala, Marie-Christine. "Da 'La structure psychologique du fascisme' ai fondamenti de 'La Souveraineté." In Risset, *Georges Bataille: Il politico e il sacro,* 60–6

Lambert, Jean-Clarence, ed. *Les Cahiers de Chronos: Roger Caillois.* Paris: Éditions de la Différence 1991

Lapouge, Gilles. "Entretien avec Roger Caillois." *Quinzaine litteraire* (15–30 June 1970): 6–8

Larmore, Charles. "Bataille's Heterology." *Semiotext(e)* 2, no. 2 (1976): 87–104

Laserra, Annamaria. "Bataille e Caillois: osmosi e dissenso." In Risset, *Georges Bataille: Il politico e il sacro,* 20–36

Laude, Jean. *La peinture française (1905–1914) et l'art nègre. (Contribution à l'étude des sources du fauvisme et du cubisme).* Paris: Klincksieck 1968

Lawton-Lévy, Catherine. *Du colportage à l'édition. Bifur et les Éditions du Carrefour. Pierre Lévy, un éditeur au temps des avant-gardes.* Geneva: Éditions Metropolis 2004

Lecoq, Dominique. "Métraux, rue de Rennes." In *Présence d'Alfred Métraux*, edited by Les Amis de Georges Bataille. Paris: Acéphale-Les Amis de Georges Bataille 1992, 141–50

– "L'œil de l'ethnologue sous la dent de l'écrivain." In *Écrits d'ailleurs: Georges Bataille et les ethnologues*, edited by Dominique Lecoq and Jean-Luc Lory, 109–18. Paris: Éditions de la Maison des Sciences de l'Homme 1987

Lefort, Claude. *La complication. Retour sur le communisme.* Paris: Fayard 1999

– *Complications: Communism and the Dilemmas of Democracy.* Translated with an introduction by Julian Bourg. New York: Columbia University Press 2007

– *Democracy and Political Theory.* Translated by David Macey. Minneapolis: University of Minnesota Press 1988

– *Éléments d'une critique de la bureaucratie.* Genèva: Droz 1971

– *Essais sur le politique. XIXᵉ–XXᵉ siècles.* Paris: Éditions Seuil 1986

– *Les Formes de l'histoire. Essais d'anthropologie politique.* Paris: Gallimard 1978

– "An Interview with Claude Lefort." *Telos* no. 30 (Winter 1976–77): 173–92

– *L'Invention démocratique. Les limites de la domination totalitaire.* Paris: Fayard 1994

– "Nation et Souveraineté." *Les Temps Modernes* no. 610 (2000): 25–46

– "Le nom d'Un." In *Le discours de la servitude volontaire*, edited by Étienne de la Boétie, 247–307. Paris: Payot 1976

– *The Political Forms of Modern Society: Bureaucracy, Democracy, Totalitarianism.* Edited with an introduction by John Thompson. Cambridge: MIT Press 1986

– "La Révolution comme religion nouvelle." In *The French Revolution and the Creation of Modern Political Culture.* Vol. 3, *The Transformation of Political Culture 1789–1848*, edited by François Furet and Mona Ozouf, 391–9. Oxford: Pergamon Press 1989

– *Sur une colonne absente. Écrits autour de Merleau-Ponty.* Paris: Gallimard 1978

– *Le travail de l'œuvre Machiavel.* Paris: Gallimard 1972

– *Un homme en trop. Réflexions sur "L'Archipel du Goulag."* Paris: Gallimard 1976

– *Writing: The Political Test.* Translated and edited by David Ames Curtis. Durham: Duke University Press 2000

Leiris, Michel. *L'Afrique fantôme (De Dakar à Djibouti, 1931–1933).* Paris: Gallimard 1934

– "Alberto Giacometti." *Documents* 4 (1929): 209–14

– "Le 'caput mortuum' ou la femme de l'alchimiste." *Documents* 8 (1930): 461–6

– "Civilisation." *Documents* 4 (1929), 221–2

– "Crachat" (section 2: L'eau à la bouche). *Documents* 6 (1929): 381–2

– "De Bataille l'impossible à l'impossible 'Documents.'" *Critique* nos. 195–196 (August–September 1963): 685–93
– "The Discovery of African Art in the West." In *African Art*, edited by Michel Leiris and Jacqueline Delange, 1–55. Translated by Michael Ross. New York: Golden Press 1968
– "Du Musée d'ethnographie au Musée de l'Homme." *Nouvelle Revue Francaise* 299 (August 1938): 344–5
– *Glossaire j'y serre mes gloses.* Paris: Éditions de la Galerie Simon 1939
– "L'homme et son intérieur." *Documents* 5 (1930): 261–6
– "Jean Brunhes, *Races.*" *Documents* 6 (1930): 375–6
– *Miroir de la tauromachie.* Paris: Acéphale 1938
– "Notes sur deux figures microcosmiques des XIVe et XVe siècles." *Documents* 1 (1929): 48–52
– "L'œil de l'ethnographe (Á propos de la Mission Dakar-Djibouti)." *Documents* 7 (1930): 405–14
– "Toiles récentes de Picasso." *Documents* 2 (1930): 57–71

Lemert, Charles. *Durkheim's Ghosts: Cultural Logics and Social Things.* Cambridge: Cambridge University Press 2006

Leroux-Dhuys, Jean-François. "Georges Henri Rivière, un homme dans le siè-cle." In *La Muséologie selon Georges Henri Rivière: cours de muséologie, textes et témoignages.* Paris: Dunod 1989, 11–31

Lévi-Strauss, Claude. "La sociologie française." In *La sociologie au XXe siècle.* Vol. 2, *Les études sociologiques dans les différents pays,* edited by Georges Gurvitch with Wilbert Moore, 513–45. Paris: Presses Universitaires de France 1947

Lewis, Helena. *The Politics of Surrealism.* New York: Paragon House 1988

Lindenberg, Daniel. *Les Années souterraines (1937–1947).* Paris: La Découverte 1990

Loubet del Bayle, Jean-Louis. *Les non-conformistes des années trente: une tentative de renouvellement de la pensée politique française.* Paris: Éditions Seuil 1969

Lourau, René. *Le gai savoir des sociologues.* Paris: Union Générale d'Éditions 1977

Lukes, Steven. *Émile Durkheim: His Life and Work: A Historical and Critical Study.* Stanford: Stanford University Press 1973

Lunn, Eugene. *Marxism and Modernism: An Historical Study of Lukàcs, Brecht, Benjamin and Adorno.* Berkeley: University of California Press 1982

Macherey, Pierre. "Kojève et les mythes." *Les Lettres françaises* 1 (1990): 18–19

Marcel, Jean-Christophe. "Bataille et Mauss: un dialogue de sourds?" *Les Temps Modernes* 54, no. 602 (December 1998–January/February 1999): 92–108

Marmande, Francis. *Georges Bataille politique.* Lyon: Presses Universitaires de Lyon 1985

Martelli, Stephano. "Mana ou sacré? La contribution de Marcel Mauss à la fon-dation de la sociologie religieuse." *Revue européenne des sciences sociales* 34, no. 105 (1996): 51–66

Mattick, Paul Jr, ed. *Eighteenth-Century Aesthetics and the Reconstruction of Art.* Cambridge: Cambridge University Press 1993

Maubon, Catherine. "'Documents:' una esperienza eretica." In Risset, *Georges Bataille: Il politico e il sacro*, 47–59

Mauss, Marcel. *Écrits politiques.* Edited by Marcel Fournier. Paris: Fayard 1997

– *The Gift: The Form and Reason for Exchange in Archaic Societies.* Foreword by Mary Douglas. Translated by W.D. Halls. New York: W.W. Norton 1990

– "M. Marcel Mauss … " *Documents* 3 (1930): 177

– *The Nature of Sociology.* Translated by William Jeffrey. Introduction by Mike Gane. New York: Berghahn Books 2005

– "L'œuvre de Mauss par lui même." *Revue française de sociologie* 20, no. 1 (January–March 1979): 209–20

– *Œuvres.* Edited by Victor Karady. 3 vols. Paris: Les Éditions de Minuit 1968–1969

– *On Prayer.* Translated by Susan Leslie. Edited with an introduction by W.S.F. Pickering. Concluding Remarks by Howard Morphy. New York: Berghahn Books 2003

– *Sociologie et anthropologie.* Introduction by Claude Lévi-Strauss. Paris: Presses Universitaires de France 1950

– *Sociology and Psychology: Essays.* Translated by Ben Brewster. London: Routledge and Kegan Paul 1979

– *Techniques, Technology and Civilisation.* Edited and translated by Nathan Schlanger. New York: Berghahn Books 2006

– "Un Inédit de Marcel Mauss. Politique." *Archives européennes de sociologie* 44, no. 1 (2003): 6–26

– in collaboration with Henri Beuchat. *Seasonal Variations of the Eskimo: A Study in Social Morphology.* Translated with an introduction by James J. Fox. London: Routledge and Kegan Paul 1979

Mayer, Hans. "Georges Bataille et le fascisme: souvenirs et analyse." In *Georges Bataille et la pensée allemande.* Paris: L'Association des Amis de Georges Bataille 1986, 79–93

– *Walter Benjamin. Réflexions sur un contemporain.* Paris: Gallimard 1995

McGovern, William. *From Luther to Hitler: The History of Fascist-Nazi Political Philosophy.* Boston: Houghton Mifflin 1941

Merleau-Ponty, Maurice. "De Mauss à Claude Lévi-Strauss." In Merleau-Ponty, *Éloge de la philosophie et autres essays*, 145–69. Paris: Gallimard 1953

Métraux, Alfred. "Rencontre avec les ethnologues." *Critique* 195–196 (August–September 1963): 677–84

Miami Theory Collective, ed. *Community at Loose Ends.* Minneapolis: University of Minnesota Press 1991

Missac, Pierre. "Walter Benjamin à la Bibliothèque Nationale." *Revue de la Bibliothèque Nationale* no. 10 (Winter 1983): 30–43

Mitchell, Andrew J., and Jason Kemp Winfree, eds. *The Obsessions of Georges Bataille: Community and Communication.* Albany: State University of New York Press 2009

Mitchell, Marion. "Émile Durkheim and the Philosophy of Nationalism." *Political Science Quarterly* 46 (1931): 87–106

Moebius, Stephan. *Die Zauberlehrlinge: Soziologiegeschichte des Collège de Sociologie (1937–1939).* Konstanz: UVK 2006

Molina, Esteban. *Le défi du politique: Totalitarisme et démocratie chez Claude Lefort.* Paris: L'Harmattan 2005

Monnerot, Jules. "La fièvre de Georges Bataille." *Confluences* 8 (October 1945): 874–82, and *Confluences* 9 (February 1946): 1009–18.

– *Inquisitions.* Paris: José Corti 1974

– *Sociologie du communisme: Échec d'une tentative religieuse au XXᵉ siècle.* Paris: Éditions Libres-Hallier, 1979 [1949]

Moretti, Giampiero, and Rocco Ronchi. "L'ermeneutica del mito negli anni Trenta. Un dialogo." *Nuovi argomenti* no. 21 (January–March 1987): 80–106

Mortensen, Preben. *Art in the Social Order: The Making of the Modern Conception of Art.* New York: State University of New York Press 1997

Murphy, Peter. "Between Romanticism and Republicanism: The Political Theory of Claude Lefort." *Thesis Eleven* no. 23 (1989): 131–42

Murray, Stephen. "A 1934 Interview with Marcel Mauss." *American Ethnologist* 16, no. 1 (February 1989): 163–8

Nadeau, Maurice. *Histoire du Surréalisme.* Paris: Éditions Seuil 1944

– *The History of Surrealism.* Translated by Richard Howard. Introduction by Roger Shattuck. Cambridge: Belknap 1989

Nancy, Jean-Luc. *The Inoperative Community.* Edited by Peter Connor. Translated by Peter Connor, Lisa Garbus, Michael Holland, and Simona Sawhney. Foreword by Christopher Fynsk. Minneapolis: University of Minnesota Press 1991

Näsström, Sofia. "Representative Democracy as Tautology: Ankersmit and Lefort on Representation." *European Journal of Political Theory* 5, no. 3 (2006): 321–42

Otto, Rudolf. *The Idea of the Holy: An Inquiry into the Non-Rational Factor in the Idea of the Divine and Its Relation to the Rational.* Translated by John W. Harvey. London: Oxford University Press 1958

Paudrat, Jean-Louis. "From Africa." In Rubin, *"Primitivism" in 20th Century Art,* 1: 125–75

Paulhan, Jean. "La démocratie fait appel au premier venu." *Nouvelle Revue Française* 306 (March 1939): 478–83

Pearce, Frank. "'Off with their heads': Public executions with Klossowski, Caillois and Foucault." *Economy and Society* 32, no. 1 (February 2003): 48–73

Pelliot, Paul. "Quelques réflexions sur l'art sibérien et l'art chinois, à propos de bronzes de la collection David-Weill." *Documents* 1 (1929): 9–21

Piel, Jean. "Quand un vieil homme trempe sa plume dans le fiel." *Critique* 444 (May 1984): 424–30

Pierre, José, ed. *Tracts surréalistes et déclarations collectives.* 2 vols. Paris: Éric Losfeld 1980

Pinto, Louis. *Les neveux de Zarathoustra. La réception de Nietzsche en France.* Paris: Éditions Seuil 1995

Poggi, Gianfranco. "The Place of Political Concerns in the Early Social Sciences." *Archives européens de sociologie* 21 (1980): 362–71

Poltier, Hugues. *Claude Lefort: La découverte du politique.* Paris: Michalon 1997

– "La pensée du politique de Claude Lefort, une pensée de liberté." In Habib and Mouchard, *La démocratie à l'œuvre*, 19-49

– "Qu'est-ce que la pensée du politique? Une introduction au projet philosophique de Claude Lefort." *Revue de théologie et de philosophie* no. 126 (1993): 119–41

– *Passion du politique: La pensée de Claude Lefort.* Geneva: Labor et Fides 1998

Pradeau, Jean-François. "*Impossible* politique et anti-philosophie: sur les articles 'nietzschéens' d' *Acéphale.*" *Les Temps Modernes* no. 602 (December 1998–January/February 1999): 132–46

Prévost, Pierre. *Rencontre Georges Bataille.* Paris: Jean-Michel Place 1987

Queneau, Raymond. "Correspondance inédite (1934–1967)." Edited by Claude Rameil. *Cahiers Raymond Queneau.* Levallois-Perret: Les amis de Valentin Bru 1987

– "Premières confrontations avec Hegel." *Critique* 19, nos. 195–6 (August–September 1963): 694–700

Ramp, William. "Effervescence, Differentiation and Representation in *The Elementary Forms.*" In Allen, Pickering, and Watts, *On Durkheim's* Elementary Forms of Religious Life, 136–48

Ranulf, Svend. "Scholarly Forerunners of Fascism." *Ethics* no. 50 (1939): 16–34

Richardson, Michael. "Sociology on a Razor's Edge: Configurations of the Sacred at the College of Sociology." *Theory, Culture & Society* 9, no. 3 (August 1992): 27–44

Richman, Michèle. *Sacred Revolutions: Durkheim and the Collège de Sociologie.* Minneapolis: University of Minnesota Press 2002

Riley, Alexander. "Durkheim contra Bergson? The Hidden Roots of Postmodern Theory and the Postmodern 'Return' of the Sacred." *Sociological Perspectives* 45, no. 3 (Fall 2002): 243–65

– "Renegade Durkheimians and the Transgressive Left Sacred." In Alexander and Smith, *The Cambridge Companion to Durkheim*, 274–300

Risset, Jacqueline. *Georges Bataille: Il politico e il sacro.* Naples: Liguori 1987

Rivet, Paul. "L'étude des civilisations matérielles; ethnographie, archéologie, préhistoire." *Documents* 3 (1929): 130–4

– and Georges Henri-Rivière. "La Mission ethnographique et linguistique Dakar-Djibouti." *Minotaure* 2 (1933): 3–5

Rivière, Georges-Henri. "Le Musée d'ethnographie du Trocadéro." *Documents* 1 (1929): 54–8

– "My Experience at the Musée d'Ethnologie." The Huxley Memorial Lecture 1968. In *Proceedings of the Royal Anthropological Institute of Great Britain and Ireland,* no.1968 (1968): 17–21

– Introduction. "L'œil de l'ethnographe (À propos de la Mission Dakar-Djibouti)." *Documents* 7 (1930): 405–6

Robertson Smith, William. *Lectures on the Religion of the Semites.* Edinburgh: Adam and Charles Black 1889

Roger Caillois. Cahiers pour un temps. Paris: Centre Georges Pompidou 1981

Roth, Michael. *Knowing and History: Appropriations of Hegel in Twentieth-Century France.* Ithaca: Cornell University Press 1988

Roudinesco, Elisabeth. *Jacques Lacan and Co.: A History of Psychoanalysis in France, 1925–1985.* Translated, with a foreword, by Jeffrey Mehlman. Chicago: University of Chicago Press 1990

Rubin, William. "Modernist Primitivism: An Introduction." In Rubin, *"Primitivism" in 20th Century Art,* l: 1-79

– ed. *"Primitivism" in 20th Century Art: Affinity of the Tribal and the Modern.* 2 vols. New York: The Museum of Modern Art 1984

Rundell, John. "Durkheim and the Reflexive Condition of Modernity." In *Recognition, Work, Politics,* edited by Jean-Philippe Deranty, Danielle Petherbridge, and John Rundell, 203–30. Leiden: Brill 2007

Schaeffner, André. "Igor Strawinsky, musicien vivant." *Documents* 1 (1929): 62–4

– "Des instruments de musique dans un musée d'ethnographie." *Documents* 5 (1929): 248–54

– "Les 'Lew Leslie's Black Birds' au Moulin Rouge." *Documents* 4 (1929): 223

Schiller, Friedrich. *On the Aesthetic Education of Man in a Series of Letters.* 1793. Translated by Elizabeth M. Wilkinson and L.A. Willoughby. Oxford: Clarendon Press 1967

Scholem, Gershom, and Theodor W. Adorno, eds. *The Correspondence of Walter Benjamin 1910–1940.* Translated by Manfred R. Jacobson and Evelyin M. Jacobson. Chicago: University of Chicago Press 1994

Scott, Joan. *Only Paradoxes to Offer: French Feminists and the Rights of Man.* Boston: Harvard University Press 1996

Senghor, Léopold Sédar. "Foreword." In *Leo Frobenius 1873–1973: An Anthology,* edited by Eike Haberland. Translated by Patricia Crampton. Wiesbaden: Franz Steiner 1973

Shattuck, Roger. *The Innocent Eye: On Modern Literature and the Arts.* New York: Farrar, Straus, and Giroux 1984

Short, Robert. "The Politics of Surrealism, 1920–1936." *Journal of Contemporary History* 1, no. 2 (September 1966): 3–25

- "Sur 'Contre-Attaque.'" In *Entretiens sur le surréalisme*, edited by Ferdinand Alquié, 144–76. Paris: Mouton 1968

Sichère, Bernard. "Bataille et les fascistes." *La Règle du Jeu* nos. 8 and 9 (1992, 1993): 152–78 and 80–94.

- "Le 'Nietzsche' de Georges Bataille." *Stanford French Review* 12 (Spring 1988): 13–30

Sorel, Georges. "Les théories de M. Durkheim." *Le devenir social* 1, no. 1 (April 1895): 1–26 and 148–80.

Souvarine, Georges. "Prologue." In *La Critique sociale*. Reprint. Paris: Éditions de La Différence 1983, 7–26

Stedman Jones, Susan. *Durkheim Reconsidered.* Cambridge: Polity 2001

Stocking, George W. Jr., ed. *Objects and Others: Essays on Museums and Material Culture.* Madison: University of Wisconsin Press 1985

- "Qu'est-ce qui est en jeu dans un nom? La Société d'Ethnographie et l'historiographie de l'anthropologie en France." In *Histoires de l'anthropologie (XVIᵉ-XIXᵉ siècles)*, edited by Britta Rupp-Eisenreich, 421–31. Paris: Klincksieck 1984

Stoekl, Allan. *Bataille's Peak: Energy, Religion, and Postsustainability.* Minneapolis: University of Minnesota Press 2007

Stolnitz, Jerome. "On the Origins of 'Aesthetic Disinterestedness.'" *The Journal of Aesthetics and Art Criticism* 20, no. 2 (Winter 1961): 131–43

Strzygowski, Josef. "'Recherches sur les arts plastiques' et 'Histoire de l'art.'" *Documents* 1 (1929): 22–6

Sturtevant, William. "Does Anthropology Need Museums?" In *Proceedings of the Biological Society* 82 (1969): 619–50.

Suleiman, Susan Rubin. "Bataille in the Street: The Search for Virility in the 1930s." In *Bataille: Writing the Sacred*, edited by Carolyn Bailey Gill, 26–45. London: Routledge 1995

Summers, David. "Why Did Kant Call Taste a 'Common Sense'?" In Mattick, *Eighteenth-Century Aesthetics*, 120–51

Sumpf, Joseph. "Durkheim et le problème de l'étude sociologique de la religion." *Archives de sociologie des religions* 20 (1965): 63–73

Surkis, Judith. *Sexing the Citizen: Morality and Masculinity in France, 1870–1920.* Ithaca: Cornell University Press 2006

Surya, Michel. *Georges Bataille: An Intellectual Biography.* Translated by Krzysztof Fijalkowski and Michael Richardson. London: Verso 2002

- *Georges Bataille, la mort à l'œuvre.* Paris: Gallimard 1992

Sweedler, Milo. *The Dismembered Community: Bataille, Blanchot, Leiris, and the Remains of Laure.* Newark: University of Delaware Press 2009

Tarot, Camille. *De Durkheim à Mauss, l'invention du symbolique: sociologie et sciences des religions.* Paris: La Découverte 2003

Teixeira, Vincent. *Georges Bataille, la part de l'art: la peinture du non-savoir.* Paris: L'Harmattan 1997

Terrail, Jean-Pierre. "Entre l'ethnocentrisme et le marxisme." *L'Arc* (1972): 48–54

Thirion, André. *Révolutionnaires sans révolutions.* Paris: Robert Laffont 1972

Tiryakian, Edward. *For Durkheim: Essays in Historical and Cultural Sociology.* Aldershot: Ashgate 2009

– "L'École durkheimienne à la recherché de la société perdue: la sociologie naissante et son milieu culturel." *Cahiers Internationaux de Sociologie* 66 (1979): 97–114

Touchard, Jean. "L'Esprit des années trente: une tentative de renouvellement de la pensée politique française." In *Tendances politiques dans la vie française depuis 1789*, 89–118. Paris: Hachette 1960

Tronchon, Henri. *Romantisme et préromantisme.* Paris: Belles-Lettres 1930

Tzara, Tristan. "Essai sur la situation de la poésie." *Le Surréalisme au service de la Révolution* no. 4 (December 1931): 15–23

Ungar, Steven. "Phantom Lascaux: Origin of the Work of Art." *Yale French Studies* 78 (1990): 246–62

Véron, Eugène. "Esthétique." In *Dictionnaire des sciences anthropologiques.* Paris: Octave Doin s.d., 451–3

Vitart-Fardoulis, Anne. "L'objet interrogé ou comment faire parler une collection d'ethnographie." *Gradhiva*, no.1 (Fall 1986): 9–12

Vogel, Susan, and Francine N'Diaye. *African Masterpieces from the Musée de l'Homme.* Introduction by Jean Guiart. New York: The Center for African Art and Harry N. Abrams Inc. 1985

Wahl, Jean. "Au Collège de Sociologie." *Nouvelle Revue Française* 293 (February 1938): 345–6

Weber, Eugen. *The Hollow Years: France in the 1930s.* New York: W.W. Norton and Company 1994

Weber, Max. "Religious Rejections of the World and Their Directions." In Gerth and Wright, *From Max Weber: Essays in Sociology*, 323–59

Weingrad, Michael. "The College of Sociology and the Institute for Social Research." *New German Critique* no. 84 (Autumn 2001): 129–61

Wilcox, John. "The Beginnings of l'Art pour l'Art." *The Journal of Aesthetics and Art Criticism* 11, no. 4 (June 1953): 360–77

Williams, Elizabeth. "Anthropological Institutions in Nineteenth-Century France." *Isis* 76, no. 3 (September 1985): 331–48

– "Art and Artifact at the Trocadéro: *Ars Americana* and the Primitivist Revolution." In Stocking, *Objects and Others*, 146–66

Winnubst, Shannon, ed. *Reading Bataille Now.* Bloomington: Indiana University Press 2007

Wolff, Kurt H., ed. *Émile Durkheim 1858–1917: A Collection of Essays, with Translations and a Bibliography.* Columbus: Ohio State University Press 1970

Wolin, Richard. *The Seduction of Unreason: The Intellectual Romance with Fascism from Nietzsche to Postmodernism.* Princeton: Princeton University Press 2004

Woodmansee, Martha. *The Author, Art, and the Market: Rereading the History of Aesthetics.* New York: Columbia University Press 1994

– "The Interests of Disinterestedness: Karl Philipp Moritz and the Emergence of the Theory of Aesthetic Autonomy in Eighteenth-Century Germany." *Modern Language Quarterly* 45 (1984): 22–47

Index

Moré, Marcel, 224n94

Moretti, Giampiero, and Rocco
Ronchi: on the Collège's ambiguity,
223–4

Moritz, Karl Philipp, 12n27

Mounier, Emmanuel, 191n79

Munich Agreement, 202–3, 207–8

Musée d'ethnographie du Trocadéro:
and ethnographic objects collection, 72–80; and manual instructions for collecting ethnographic
objects, 80–1, 80n61, 81n62

Musée de l' Homme, 80, 81; and the
colonies, 81

Mussolini, Benito, 130, 227

Nancy, Jean-Luc: and community,
231–2, 232n17, 237, 262; on the
political, 21, 23

Négritude, 78, 78n51

Nietzsche, Friedrich, 18, 19; at
Acéphale, 160–3, 160n59, 162n66,
163n71; Bataille and, 124, 156,
156n47, 159, 161n62, 213, 214

Otto, Rudolph, 178n45, 184

Pastoureau, Henri, 143n155

Paulhan, Jean, 229n6; and Caillois,
132, 133, 134, 146, 150n23,
220n74, 221–2, 222n81, 224n94,
229n6; at the Collège, 180n54

Pelliot, Paul, 88, 88n87

Picasso, Pablo, 73n28, 76, 77, 78, 94,
97n123

political, the: definition, 20–1; Lefort
and, 21, 22–3, 237–9, 237n39, 239,
249n95; Nancy on, 21; and politics,
difference from, 20

Prévost, Georges: on Acéphale,
161n64; and the Collège, 167n6,
170–1n16, 209, 209n27, 228n1

"primitives": the Collège de sociologie
and, 171–2; Durkheim and, 33–4,
39–44; the Durkheimians and, 78–
9; interest in, 65–9, 75–8; Lefort
and, 235–6; Mauss and, 33–4, 60–
2, 212. *See also* African art, anthropology, ethnographic object

Primitivism. *See* African art

Queneau, Raymond, 224n94, 253

Rabaud, Étienne, 177

Ranulf, Svend, 211–12

Renouvier, Charles, 175n36

Reverdy, Pierre, 107n14

Richman, Michèle, 23n55

Rivet, Paul, 79, 79n57; on art and ethnography, 81–3, 85n78, 89–90; and
Documents, 89; and the Musée de
l'Homme, 80, 80n58, 80n59, 81–3,
81n64, 82n67, 82n68

Rivière, Georges Henri, 81n65; on art
and ethnography, 82n66, 82n67,
90, 90–1n93; and *Documents*, 85–6,
89–90; and Mauss, 82n69; and the
Musée de l'Homme, 81–3

Robertson Smith, William, 178n45;
Bataille and, 142; Breton and, 142;
Durkheim and, 36, 36n42, 36n44,
41n66; Hubert and Mauss and, 53,
54n122; and sacrifice, 53n118

Rosny, Léon de, 70

Roudinesco, Elisabeth, 32

Rougemont, Denis de, 191n79, 205–
6, 205n14, 206n16

Sade, Marquis de, 99n128, 207

Sadoul, Georges, 113n37, 221,
221–2n80

Saussure, Ferdinand de, 108

Schaeffner, André, 83n72; at
Documents, 89, 91, 91n94, 91n96

Schmitt, Carl, 251n102
Senghor, Léopold, 78
Shaftesbury, Earl of: and disinterestedness, 10–11
Société d'anthropologie, 34n37, 70,
70n21, 71n24
Société d'ethnographie, 70, 71,
71n24
Society of Collective Psychology,
141n148, 177, 178, 207n22
Souvarine, Boris, 125
Strauss, Leo, 251n103
Strzygowski, Josef, 88, 88n88, 88n89
sublime, 11; and the Collège, 223–4
surfascisme, 141–3, 141–2n150,
143n155, 165
Surrealism: and art, 105–6, 109–10,
113; and Bataille, 122–5, 141–3,
257, 257n17; Benjamin on, 104,
108, 110; and Bureau of Surrealist
Research, 109; Caillois and, 118–
21, 133–4, 144; and communism,
111–15, 117; and the Congress of
Writers, 114, 117; and Contre-
Attaque, 117–18, 141–3, 142n152;
and critique of Western civilization,
105; definition of, 106n10; and
dream, 107, 107n14; and the
Franco-Soviet Treaty, 114–15; and
Freud, 107, 107n13; and Hegel,
111, 112; and idealism, 111–13;
and language, 108, 108n16,
108n18, 108n19; and literature,

109, 109n22; Manifesto of
Surrealism, 107, 109n22; and
Marx, 111, 116; and materialism,
111–13; Nadeau on, 106–18; and
pacifism, 110; and poetry, 107–8,
109; and politics and art, 105–6,
111–14, 115–17; and revolution,
111–12; and Rimbaud, 116; and
science, 108, 109; Second
Surrealist Manifesto, 112–13, 123,
124; and *surfascisme*, 141–2, 141–
2n150, 143n155; surreality, 107,
107n11, 113; and Trotsky, 113n37;
and the unconscious, 107, 109,
112–13, 124. *See also* Breton

Topinard, Paul, 70
tribal art. *See* African art
Trotsky, Leon, 134
Tzara, Tristan, 149n17, 167

Verneau, René, 78
Vlaminck, Maurice de, 75, 76, 77n45

Wahl, Jean, 201n2; on the difference
between Bataille and Caillois,
215n51, 217n60; on Leiris's lecture, 182n155, 191n79;
Weber, Eugen, 110, 110n26, 114n40
Weber, Max: Aron on, 212, 212n37;
Bataille and, 259n22; Caillois and,
186n68; and the value spheres, 20
Wildenstein, Georges, 87